Beloved African

Beloved African

Jill Baker

RoperPenberthy Publishing Ltd

Published by RoperPenberthy Publishing Ltd, PO Box 656,
Weybridge, Surrey KT13 3EU

ISBN 978 1 903905 35 7

Cover Design: Angie Moyler

Typeset by Avocet Typeset, Chilton, Aylesbury, Bucks

Printed and bound in the UK by
CPI Mackays, Chatham ME5 8TD

Author's Note

Beloved African was started as a memoir for the family, a year or so after my father's death. We always knew he had played a remarkable role in Rhodesia but I often wondered at the depth of love and respect which was shown to him by leading Africans all over the country. Children, however, seldom really know or understand what their parents have achieved.

I had a reserve of four tapes which I had recorded a couple of years earlier, when on impulse, I urged Dad to respond to some questions. I also knew of 'some letters' which my mother had kept – and we then found all Dad's annual reports. I had no idea it was such an extraordinary resource.

It was only once I started writing, that I found that it was not only a wonderful story of a truly remarkable relationship between two people, but it grew through that to be a stirring, evocative and important story of Africa.

Their letters written every week between 1935 and 1937 reflect Rhodesia and Britain of the time, the politics, the social behaviour and the attitudes. They are the letters of two people falling more and more deeply in love, yet who were separated by what was then a huge distance, with a six-week turnaround in letters. The growth of their relationship, their fears and apprehensions about losing each other, to their final joy of being together, is a tender and gentle opening to the story.

The move to Africa brings quite a different pace – with fascinating observations from a young English lass about all the things she found different, compelling or terrifying. It starts to tell the story of my father's early struggles with 'the Department' … who were at best unable, or at worst, disinclined, to help.

AUTHOR'S NOTE

The story moves on to a heartbreaking ending for a man who was only too aware that time was against him in his attempts to educate sufficient young Africans for the important roles they would be playing in the future of their country. It is a story of the destruction of ideals and the breaking of someone with so much to contribute – yet it also tells of recovery and of hope for the future.

I must thank my wonderful mother, Nancy, for her patience ... for coping with the confusion I caused when facing her day after day, with a barrage of questions, yet never giving up on the task ... for her support and constant encouragement.

I must thank my office for understanding that I had to take time off to get the story finished, when they urgently needed me back at work. I would also like to thank the dozens of ex schoolboys, staff and friends who all responded to my requests for anecdotes and in adding their insight, helped me to shape this into a great story.

Finally, I must thank my brother, Richard, and my friends in Adelaide, South Australia, in Zimbabwe and elsewhere who have read sections of it, helped me research it, advised and supported and encouraged – and made me feel it was worth persevering. Special thanks to Barb and to James.

Why did I do it, having never had even the slightest inclination to write before this ?

I think because I believed that my father never had the recognition his own remarkable father had won. Whilst never diminishing Bob Hammond's great contribution to Plumtree, I felt Dad achieved as much or more, under considerably more troubled circumstances ... but the politics of the time did not allow for this to be acknowledged.

Dedication

This book is, of course, dedicated to my parents, John and Nancy – for a man who battled to achieve his ideals in increasingly difficult circumstances, and a woman who displayed such character and strength in supporting him through thick and thin.

It is also dedicated to everyone in Rhodesia at that time, black and white, who worked so desperately hard to try and find some sort of peaceful and relevant answers to the colony's many problems ... and whose efforts have gone largely unrecognised since.

Contents

CONTENTS

Prologue

This is my father's story, told through my mother's eyes. It is a fascinating and now historically important story.

It has been enhanced by my mother's perceptive and detailed memories from her first impressions to her ongoing role and partnership with my father, with all the emotions, the hilarity and the agonies. It is her heart and soul that moves the story forward through all its adventures.

The important facts and occurrences trace the part one person played in the growth of the last of Britain's Colonies. It is the story of Rhodesia from 1910 to shortly before the Unilateral Declaration of Independence in 1965. It is the story of a race against time – supported by an almost complete record of annual reports written by my father to his Head Office, the African Education Department, from his first three-page overview at Tjolotjo to the twelve or fourteen pages from Goromonzi. Each of them, carbon copies on now wafer thin paper, tightly typed and single spaced.

The wealth of information they contain could alone, fill three volumes this size. I have spent many, many days deciding which portions to use and agonising over whether I have included too much – or too little. This is why sections from his reports and letters are in italics. For some it will be sufficient to scan them in order to move on with the story – for others they contain the detail of an era passed and an all absorbing interest in what was happening at which time and why.

In all cases I have used the terminology, sentiments and phrases current at the time. Where in one chapter the words 'Native' and 'African' appear muddled it is to reflect that period where the word 'Native' no longer held the esteem it once did and was being slowly replaced by the then more acceptable word 'African'. In some cases, the sentiments used might appear harsh in the light of modern thinking, but they reflect the moral tone and disciplines of the period and give greater insight into the overriding concern to provide leadership and guidance. The use of surnames without a prefix was also the manner of address at the time – the exception being the early use of the word 'Teacher' before an African name, denoting a mark of respect and acknowledgement of their role at a time when there were few qualified to earn that term.

In most cases the names used are the original names of the players in the story. In some however, where this might present any sensitivity, names have been changed to protect the people concerned.

I hope that my own understanding and love of Africa shines through in the descriptions and flavour, which underpin the story. I will be forever grateful that I was brought up in such intriguing circumstances with the invaluable chance it gave me to understand the country and its people better than most other "murungu".

My father was an idealist – but he was also intensely practical and absolutely focussed on discipline and the early taking of responsibility as two dominant factors in the making of a leader. Because he himself always found book learning difficult as he was a slow reader, he had extraordinary patience and would spend a great deal of time with those he felt had qualities masked by the fact that they might not be as academically bright. He had little time for hidden agendas or 'do-gooders' with their impractical theories and ideologies and felt they did far more harm than good in Africa.

I remember him as a man of infinite wisdom, of gentleness and courtesy…a man who would command almost instant respect through to his last weeks on this earth…a man with a twinkle in his eye, a sense of humour and infinite patience. Yet, a man who always worried and wondered if he could have done more and whether what he had achieved was good enough.

I also remember with great sadness two comments made to me as a child. When I was 16 he told me that Rhodesia's greatest problem was that half the population at that time was younger than I was. When I asked at the age of 9 or 10 what would happen if one day, the country woke up to find all the white people had left, after some thought he responded:

'… if it happens too soon, I fear the country will go back to what

PROLOGUE

it was when we first came here – and then it is likely to be re-colonised in some way, but by a less benevolent power'

Zambezi River

Chirundu

Kariba

Lake Kariba

MASHONALAND

Sinoia

Umvukwes

Domboshawa

Salisbury

Goromonzi

Marandellas

MIDLANDS

Victoria Falls

Gwaai River

Enkeldoorn

Umtali

Wankie Game
Reserve

Gwaai

MATEBELELAND

Gwelo

Tjolotjo

Nyamandhlovu

Zimbabwe
Ruins

MANICALAND

Bulawayo

Essexvale

Matopos

Plumtree

Mzingwane

Shabani

Fort Victoria

Gwanda

Limpopo River

Beit Bridge

N

Madagascar

Indicates
area enlarged

Southern Rhodesia

Chapter 1

The burglar and the girl

'Nancy, you'll be perfect – there's a *very* nice young man in it – and we start rehearsals tomorrow.'

Oh dear – three weeks into my first real job as a music teacher in Eastbourne, with my life already complicated by the attentions of two other young men. I wasn't at all keen.

'I've got two young men already Mrs. Gladstone. I don't want any more!'

My life in fact, was just great. I had a new job and two attentive admirers who lived very conveniently in different parts of England, so I could balance my time between them remarkably well – keeping each of them oblivious to the existence of the other. Until the time I decided which might be more suitable.

I had grown up with Dick Castle – he was almost part of the family – and his sister Jill was my closest confidante. We partnered each other in countless summer tennis matches and with my country upbringing there was an expectation that I might settle down contentedly as a farmer's wife in Essex.

Jackie Lindsay, on the other hand, was the son of a well-to-do family who shared a bathing hut next to ours on holidays in Kent. I used to sail with the family at Whitstable and stay with them in London. Jackie was at Cambridge University and frequently asked me up for May Balls and other delights. My parents did not approve. He was talented and clever, but didn't know what he wanted to do with himself. 'I think being a doctor is one of the most admirable things anyone can do,' I told him solemnly. He and his sister both ended up practising medicine.

Despite my best intentions not to become involved, I found myself tripping along in high-heeled shoes to Mrs. Gladstone's house on St.

1

Valentine's Day 1935. It was a bitterly cold evening and I was wearing a fashionable dark brown "stockinette" dress under my very sensible, warm coat.

It was dark, it was bleak and it was snowing.

The cosy warmth of a roaring log fire drew me in to the well-furnished drawing room of the quaint old stone cottage in Milnthorpe Road. I hung up my coat and the door shut behind me. Lying on the floor was a tall young man wearing a tweed jacket and plus fours, his black hair falling in a loose curl over his forehead as he pursed his lips and made a high squealing sound to an intrigued fox terrier.

The dog cocked its head to one side, pounced at him then fled to a corner. Bouncing, barking and twisting, it tried to escape as he caught it up in his hands and rolled over, tickling the excited animal and roaring with laughter.

It was not only the dog that was intrigued – for I found myself looking at the most attractive man I had ever seen. Perhaps my freezing walk had been worthwhile after all.

The Burglar and the Girl was a one-act play in which we had been asked to take part and I found that John Hammond had been equally disinterested. He was already committed to acting in another play, *Badger's Green,* and didn't have the time or inclination to do both. A combination of orders from his headmaster and loyalty to Mrs. Gladstone had dragged him along just as unwillingly to this snug hearth, to be whistling at this dog – on this particularly bleak winter's night.

The evening took on a distinct glow. The alacrity with which John leaped up and introduced himself led me to sneak a hope that he might just have been affected in the same way. I found myself looking into kind, delicately blue eyes, framed by long black eyelashes and brows in a lean and tanned face. Eyes looking at me so directly that they seemed to see into my very soul. My diary records:

> *…went to Mrs. Gladstone's for rehearsal – coffee and cigarettes. Mr. Hammond came and we read the play through – quite amusing. He v. good-looking indeed – heavenly eyelashes! Just my ideal but too nice for me I'm afraid…*

In the three short weeks I had been at my new job in Eastbourne I discovered my life was to be ruled by two indomitable headmistresses

– both ex-suffragettes – tough, "no-nonsense" and down to earth.

The schoolhouse door was locked if I did not return by 10 p.m.

So we couldn't waste time on undue pleasantries. By the end of a correctly polite, yet enticing evening, we agreed to a schedule of three rehearsals, a dress rehearsal and one performance. John walked me home. He was certainly unlike anyone else I had ever met before – hardly surprising perhaps, as my sheltered life had been cushioned by its gentle English upbringing.

Born as the elder daughter of an Essex country vet, we lived in a rambling old house in Southminster with a grass tennis court, a wandering nut walk and rose garden, horses and stables, maids and gardeners. My life revolved around lazy days cheering on the local cricket team on the village green, hotly contested tennis and golf matches and in the last three years, working hard for my LRAM (Licentiate of the Royal Academy of Music) in piano at the Royal Academy in London.

As we walked back to my new school, Rippingale, John told me he came from Southern Rhodesia, a country not unfamiliar to me as I had two cousins, brought up as part of our immediate family, now living in Northern Rhodesia.

Rehearsals began. It was a delight to work with someone who was not only a good actor, but obviously just as used to the vagaries of amateur dramatics as I was.

After the dress rehearsal, I went home with a lump in the pit of my stomach – there had been no more offers of a walk home and now we were almost at the final performance. After that I would have no excuse to see him again. As my diary records:

Dress rehearsal in eve – went with Ailwyne (Ailwyne Gwynne, a close friend and fellow teacher) *– JH there – he would have come home with me; only I was with Ailwyne! V. fed up as hardly spoke to him at all. Have last hopes for tomorrow.*

I also wrote to my brother Dick that evening describing my new life at Rippingale, talking about the play and almost inevitably, discussing this man who had so taken my fancy. *'I haven't a hope'* was my miserable comment.

I had discovered during the evening of the dress rehearsal, that John was due to return to Rhodesia only three weeks later. This news left me devastated. I had just had a tantalising glimpse of a type of man I had only dreamed of meeting … I felt an immediate and quite compulsive attraction – and he was now going… within a very few days.

The night of the first performance was somewhat complicated for me by the fact that I had another role in the same concert – playing the piano as part of a quartet. So I had to wear my very smart, duck-egg blue, backless (with feathers) 21st birthday dress – complete with a short white fur jacket – to both the concert and the play.

Fortunately the part I was playing called for me to have been out for the evening and to come home to disturb my handsome Rhodesian burglar at work.

The sting in the tail was that I turned out to be the burglar and the role called for me to knock him out with a candlestick. It was not easy while I was trying hard to make a good impression, to whack John over the head, pocket the jewels, switch out the lights and leave him bleeding and defenceless on the floor.

'Goodbye my not so clever burglar friend…' was my parting shot.

The play went very well – it seemed as though the whole of my old school, Hillcote, had come to watch. But I just dreaded it coming to an end. Every second dragged me towards the point when we would say goodbye.

By the end of the play Dick and Jack, had faded well into the back-ground. I was completely enthralled by this prep-school master and talented actor with film-star looks. I could think of no one and nothing else. I could not eat. My fertile imagination was well and truly nour-ished when John told me he had been born in a mud and pole hut, miles from civilisation and that he had first worn shoes at the age of 14.

With no indication of any reciprocal interest from him, I shook his hand and was going through the motions of saying how much I had enjoyed the rehearsal … but my diary records it more poignantly.

Play went off better still… was about to bid JH goodbye for ever, when he announced he would see me home – then asked me to go to a film on Monday – thrilled to death!

Trying to keep my mind on piano pupils the next day was not easy. My exciting new job now felt routine, dull and restricted. As we went for our mid-morning tea break my apprehension increased. How would we get on when we weren't acting a part?

We met on the bus – shy and rather apprehensive, both recognising that for the first time we were face to face with the person, the character and the personality behind the actors. We knew how little time there was left before John set sail for Africa and how unsure we were of where the next few days might lead.

We were glad to reach the comforting warmth and dim lighting of the "Oak Cabin". I didn't want to cost him too much money, so I chose the cheapest thing on the menu, an egg mayonnaise, for 7d. I confess I remember absolutely nothing about the "flick". We walked home, to find the old ladies glaring through the door, furious that they had been kept up 15 minutes late. Flustered, I rushed in, with a hastily waved goodbye.

The next day – a letter arrived. It was not writing I recognised – slanted, copper plate, neat ...

Dear Miss Sugden,
I hope your reception last evening wasn't too frosty. I can't help saying that I felt amazingly annoyed with your two dear old Ladies though I hope they didn't show the same annoyance towards you.

This confounded play (Badger's Green) looks like occupying every moment which ordinarily is available so that I can't say definitely when we shall be able to do another flick. What I really want to know though is whether you could so get round your two dear old girls as to get them to allow you to come dancing at the Grand on Friday the 22nd. The occasion is the Rugger club dance, usually rather a good show, and one which goes on till about 2 a.m. if one feels so inclined.

Do try to manage it. The Dance starts at about 9 o'clock but we could go out and have a welsh rarebit somewhere beforehand if you could manage it. Failing this will you tea with me at the Grand on Sunday week?
Yours John Hammond

I found out that the Rugger Dance was to be a farewell and thank-you occasion for John from his headmaster, Crispin Hill. However, what I hadn't realised was that John was writing on behalf of his brother Patrick who was up at Oxford. He was the man who needed a partner – John would be going with a girl called Brenda Hogarth.

5

So it *was* too good to be true – it couldn't possibly have been so perfect. Why was I kidding myself? This sudden interest and the walks and flicks were just being polite.

I really didn't want to go. After a lot of anguished reflection, I thought again. John wanted me to join the party. So that was something – and Patrick might turn out to be just as nice. After all, for me… well, it was sufficient simply to be in his company.

Immediately, a greater problem presented itself. The two old girls and their very strict rules. How could I possibly go and fulfil the requirement to be in by ten, if I was only being collected at nine? I would have to resort to some sort of subterfuge, because it was not going to happen otherwise.

Aldro

Dear Nancy

I am glad there is a chance of your being able to come on the 22nd, though I am sorry that you have to go through so much in order to be able to wangle it.

I'm afraid that I am beginning to dislike your two dear old Ladies intensely; the whole thing is so absurd. Forgive me for having made you late on Monday, but if one can't come to bed at 10'20 without creating a stir, life does seem to take on a somewhat depressing outlook.

Can you let me know as soon as possible whether you will be able to come or not, but please don't wreck your chances of coming by trying to get it out of the old girls too soon.

I do hope you can come,

Yours sincerely,

John

Rippingale
Friday evening

Dear J

Do you prefer to be called John or Jack? I was overjoyed to see that you had omitted the Miss Sugden, which reminds me very forcibly that I am a school-ma'am!

After a good deal of difficulty in choosing the right moment in which to attack the nicer of the two old dears, I have asked, and have got, the necessary permission. I feel quite overcome because she was quite pleasant about

6

it! Unfortunately I had to tell a very complicated story! However it is worth it.
Thank you so much for asking me.
Yours in haste,
Nancy

Wild horses wouldn't have kept me away at this stage so, much against my better nature, I fabricated a sick cousin and asked for the night off to go to Brighton by train to see her – promising to be back in time for the "farthing fines" the next day. These were an old school tradition where the duty teacher had to hand out lost property – which pupils could only claim if they paid a farthing. It was my farthing fines duty the next morning and there was no possibility of avoiding it.

Hillcote, the school I had attended as a girl, was just over the road. My old headmistress, known to us all as "Bert" Brown, was a darling. She had become a great friend when I was head girl in my last year at school. She held the old dears at Rippingale in rather low regard and had been trying to lure me back to teach at Hillcote. Her eyes sparkled at the fun of helping me make my tryst. She even made up my old room, so that I would know how to find my way back without waking everyone up. Dear Bert. I gave her a huge hug and rushed back in time for supper and to let John know.

His response was prompt:

Dear Nancy
I am very glad you have been able to get round the old girls and will be able to come on Friday. What about a flick on Monday? I shall catch the 6'50 or 7'00 bus to town… we may be too late for a flick, but I feel that we shall be able to occupy the time at our disposal fairly satisfactorily.
See you tomorrow
Yours,
John

We didn't have time to make the "flick" on that occasion but were able to take a short promenade before he rushed back to apply grease-paint for *Badger's Green.* I was obviously making progress, as just before the dance he wrote again:

My dear Nancy

I was so glad to hear that the old girls are prepared to accept the fact that you are entitled to have friends outside Rippingale and male friends at that. At least, the ice has been broken and life will probably be more tolerable for you now that they realise you are not going to remain a dear old schoolmarm.

I am beginning to wonder if this must be the boat. I have strong misgivings... I think you will have to follow your cousin's example and go to seek your fortunes in Rhodesia. I am sure that we could find a place quite as pleasant to labour in as Rippingale.

What about a short promenade somewhere at about 12 o'c on Sunday morning?

Continue with your "educating" process and we might be able to manage another evening without having to drag in a departed cousin.

Salaams to the old girls,

John

To complicate the issue, I didn't have time to get to Hillcote to change into my finery. So I disguised my evening dress and shoes and pretended I was off on the mundane task of catching a train.

The timing was critical as it was the last weekend of term. The whole school was packing up and preparing to leave. I had to be collected at a very precise moment between John and the Hills finishing their meal and the rest of us going to the dance.

Walking across the road with my backless blue tucked under my ordinary old coat on another freezing night, my disguise would have fooled absolutely no one, had they cared to look a little more closely. Where there's a will there is, of course, always a way. I was ready, waiting, cool, poised and unflappable when the Hills, John, Patrick – and Brenda Hogarth – came to pick me up.

Albert Sandler and his band were playing – the food was forgettable – I can only remember dancing the whole night through – with John. He must have persuaded Pat to look after Brenda Hogarth... as I have no memory of whether she was angry, sad, or simply indifferent. I was on cloud nine.

V. jolly party – loved it. Home everyone in Hill's car, sat on Pat's lap. B on J's for a bit! J held my hand – v. thrilling! Slept in my old bedroom at Hill-cote – slept rather badly!

Bert had been as good as her word; the key was left in its secret place – together with a little note hoping I had enjoyed a wonderful evening. I often wondered if in subsequent "headmistress talk" the three old girls had discussed and probably laughed about my naive little ruse that night. But then knowing my old girls... I'm not so sure.

I was so terrified in case I didn't wake up in time that I hardly slept. But I need not have worried. I was up with the larks, racing across the road well in time for the farthing fines.

But, I was now in even greater anguish. John was due to leave Eastbourne five days later and we didn't seem to have had enough time to talk, to see each other, to find out more – of anything. I had glimpsed something infinitely precious and bitterly resented having to teach at the school and be away from him with so little time left. I couldn't see him that night because he was performing in Badger's Green.

The next day, we broke for morning tea. The post was in. Oh bliss – another letter – in a now instantly familiar hand. Whatever time of the night had he written it? Amazing! John was asking me to help him pack and listen to his radio on the day before he left.

Nancy Dearest
We have just finished our "first night" and the play went off very well, or seemed to...

I am glad to hear that you are coming on Friday. I do want to see you again; the days are going far too quickly now...

Don't fix up anything for Sunday if you can help it. Would you care to come and test your packing ability on my suitcases? No very glum glances came my way on Monday night, or if they did, I'm afraid I failed to notice them, as quite frankly I didn't care very much.

Stuttgart is singing "Deutschland Uber Alles" to indicate midnight, so I must hop out to the post... Good night dear one.
Tons of love,
John

John had been living in digs with a dear old couple in Meads next to Eastbourne. The village was full of character, cobbled streets and low-browed houses – England at its most charming. He had grown very fond of the old pair, living as part of their family, until they had given him his own completely separate bedroom and sitting room. He had just acquired a half share in a radio and was terribly proud of it. It was a great thing in those days to have your own radio – very new and very avant-garde.

I was introduced all round, as well as to one of John's best friends, Michael Richards, who also shared the digs. But I couldn't really take anything much in except John. Where he stood, how he walked – how he caught my eye every few minutes and how he laughed. He did look stunning in smart casual clothes and a tweed jacket. He seemed very relaxed and warm and, best of all, he was apparently delighted to see me.

Woke early – v. excited. Went to J's digs at 10'30 – 38 Meads St. – lovely – wireless. He looked so nice and was too! He went to chapel at 11 and left me with photos and wireless. Stole one photo – rather a bad one. He back late and very apologetic.

We listened to classical music … we talked … we laughed. We found we shared opinions and a sense of the ridiculous. I loved hearing about his family and he revelled in hearing about mine.

Then as the Chopin Waltz in C# minor started playing softly in the background, John asked me to marry him.

I was completely taken aback, thrilled and yet somehow perfectly calm. It all seemed so right and in order even after such a short time. I said something to the effect that I probably would, but we would need to write and get to know each other a bit better first.

He walked me home to be back by 10 – our minds buzzing with the possibilities that lay ahead. I promised to come out and look at Rhodesia. John said that he would consider returning to England to take a permanent job, once he had been back to spend some time with his family. That night, at midnight, he wrote again:

Nancy Darling
I should pack up and go to bed now, but my mind has been so full today that I have hardly been able to give a moment to any thought that was really congenial to my mood.

Darling you must forgive me if I have upset you a lot. I am in the same state myself and can hardly realise that I shall soon have to say goodbye to you for a rather long time. We must try to live in this next few days, without the thought of the time which will have to elapse before, what is now my foremost hope, is realised.

10

Nancy dear you must say if you feel we are doing the wrong thing. I'm afraid that I may have been utterly selfish in asking you to come out to Rhodesia, but I'm afraid you should not have got hold of me in the way you have done.

I must go to bed now. This is really simply to say goodnight my darling, and to say how very much I love you.
Your John

I found it hard to contain my grin. The sheer wonder of it all – and why me? This gorgeous man could have had any one of a dozen British belles all of them plotting and planning to find some excuse to visit Rhodesia. But his feelings for me were no less than mine for him. On Sunday morning I went round to help him pack.

…went into his bedroom (what a thrill!) looked out of window most of time at pouring rain – most depressing without and within! Thought I'd better go back for tea at Hillcote, but quite unnecessary really! Having a conscience is a b….y nuisance!

On Monday, I happened to be free all day and so was John, but our meeting was not a great success. We had so much to talk about – then suddenly we found we didn't know each other very well. There were no reminiscences to help us over the pain of his going. There was nothing definite on which to build our tentative plans for the future. The long, slightly uncomfortable silences were unnerving.

…thrilled at the thought of meeting J, but it didn't go off frightfully well. Met him on front in morning in howling gale. I felt an awful sight – hair blowing etc. Went to a flick, Greta Garbo in something or other… then bus back to Meads, then thought I'd better return as he was going to Hogarth's (blast it!) Went back to Hillcote and had a good weep.

John had to go and say goodbye to the Hogarth's – he had come to know the family well during the time he had been in Eastbourne. Of course he had to go – I knew that. It didn't mean to say that Brenda would entice him away again. My imagination ran riot as I packed away my own things and sat staring out of the window at the rain and sleet as it streamed down blurring the streetlights outside and a mirror of my weeping inside.

We'd agreed to meet at the train and travel up to London together so that he could meet Mummy and my sister Trish who'd be waiting for me at Victoria station.

...waited ages at train for John then at last he appeared with Brenda Hogarth in riding kit — rather depressed — Hells Bells! I got into the train to be tactful and left them to it.

I knew John had proposed to me, but it was still a bit of a shock seeing Brenda at the station. She was looking particularly attractive in her expensively turned-out riding kit. As we waved goodbye I did see her face, and I knew that she knew... I turned to John and he held me tightly as the train gathered speed, leaving Eastbourne behind us.

Mummy and Trish were at Victoria, as promised. I shyly introduced John and explained that he was on his way back to Rhodesia. Mummy invited him down for lunch at our home in Essex the following Thursday... the day before he sailed.

The days passed in an agony of indecision and questioning about what might lie ahead but of course, I was at our little station promptly, hardly breathing with anticipation, to meet him.

The train pulled in. I watched each window go by. He wasn't there!

I walked home in tears — why hadn't I been more decisive in my response to him? Had he decided I was just not right after all? I thought my heart would break. I crept through the back door, up the stairs and lay on my bed, with my face in the pillow. I hadn't the strength to talk to anyone... but Mummy heard me.

She had a telegram.

He'd missed the train but would be arriving on the next one. This would give us only two hours together, as the last train back to London was at 5 p.m. But still, it was something.

I flew down to the station. He was there, as promised. The anxiety of the last few days disappeared as he folded me into his arms and begged forgiveness. Those two hours were infinitely precious. John met all the family, except Daddy, who was in hospital. They were sensitive enough to give us a little time together.

I played the piano; we talked and occasionally lapsed into long silences. There was so much to talk about... yet where did we start in such a short time? We agreed that although there was promise of a future together, we wouldn't rush it, but would write, frequently, come to know each other through our letters and see how things turned out.

I took him back to the station… and in a hiss of steam and a shriek of whistles and squeaking wheels, this wonderful man went out of my life as abruptly as he had come into it.

We had met on St. Valentine's Day 1935, performed the play on the 5th March after only three rehearsals, and he sailed for Cape Town on the 5th April. We had been out together only seven times and we would not see each other again for 15 months.

Chapter 2

Pump meads, ponies
and lettuce for tea

Naming a child should be carefully done. I have carried the result of my parents' devotion to my two grandmothers as an embarrassment and irritation all my life.

I was born Annie Agnes Sugden in my parents' four poster bed in the Elizabethan manor house of Southminster, a small farming village in Essex. Fortunately, everyone knew me as Nancy. After a lifetime of having to trot out this awful name, only ever to officialdom, I found when my maternal grandmother died, that she was never an "Annie" after all – but one of a long line of Annes. That would have been much more acceptable!

My family were an interesting mix of Yorkshire mill owners, clergymen and doctors. The only political relative was my great-great-grandfather, Sir Thomas Craven, once Lord Mayor of London. His granddaughter married William Sugden – a Wesleyan, brought up in Brontë Country at the same time as the famous author sisters, in their tiny village of Haworth in the West Riding of Yorkshire. William knew the Brontës well and our family still owns eight wheelback chairs from the old Black Bull Inn where Branwell Brontë, the sadly dissolute brother of the three famous sisters, used to while away much of his talented, but sozzled youth.

Grandfather Sugden was an Elder in the Wesleyan church and a strict teetotaller. He started life as a science teacher, then joined a mill near Bradford, using his scientific knowledge in the production of a special soft soap to wash out raw sheep's wool. He then married the mill owner's daughter and they bore ten children - four of whom died. Grandmother Agnes was pretty well-off and in mid-life, they decided to buy a big property called Coldspring House together with a couple of hundred acres near Cullingworth in Yorkshire. As its name suggests, the property had a pure spring of water, vital for the making of this special soft soap. The soap was poured into great barrels and loaded up onto horse drawn wagons for delivery to woollen mills locally and overseas.

But my grandfather's real love was his hackney stud. His high-stepping, beautiful horses with their proudly arched necks, were well known not only as a good sound riding horse, but also for being well tempered, ideally suited to pulling the fashionable traps of the day. In the mid-1800s Grandfather accompanied loads of his prize horses overseas… in the little sail and steam ships of the time to sell them to the United States, particularly to Miami.

The boats were so small and the seas so huge, and grandfather was terribly seasick. I was intrigued by the fact that once the ship had left port and for the duration of the journey, he lived on champagne. It was the only thing that gave him any respite. Being a teetotaller I knew it was, of course, purely medicinal!

On my mother's side of the family, I was told that my great-grandmother, another Anne, was a Bourbon princess who spoke French and Spanish. This added great impact when we told stories of the family at school – but in fact, she did lead an extraordinarily adventurous life. After a romantic and often stormy start to their relationship, she married my great-grandfather, Colonel Wheeler, who was in the Indian Army.

In the middle of the Indian Mutiny and in the final stages of her first pregnancy this elegantly born Frenchwoman was hounded down the streets of Delhi by a screaming mob, baying for blood at this symbol of their frustration and anger. They were of, course, completely oblivious to her condition. A Roman Catholic priest saw her plight and as she struggled past, he pulled her into his house. Richard, my maternal grandfather was born a few hours later. History does not relate whether there were any midwives around, or whether the Catholic priest found himself in the midst of a new experience.

When all had been restored to something like normality and my grandmother and her newborn were back in their home, Colonel Wheeler wanted to call his first child Richard Delhi Wheeler for obvious reasons. She, however, was obviously keen to forget the whole experience! Richard Theodore eventually ended up training to become a doctor and was sent from India to Scotland to study.

Grandmother Annie, born Anne Maskell, had a tough life. Her father died of tuberculosis in his twenties, leaving her mother nearly destitute, with two baby girls. However, Anne proved to be a determined young lass with an indomitable spirit. To help hold the family together, and while she was still a teenager, she ran a boarding house for medical students in Edinburgh. Several years later, her reputation was obviously good enough to entice a young medical student from India, to register with her. After a whirlwind romance, Richard Wheeler and Anne Maskell were married. She was just 19.

History repeated itself a generation later, as their daughter, my mother Kathleen, met my father, John Sugden, in Edinburgh where he was doing his training… not as a doctor this time, but as a veterinary surgeon.

After he qualified, he took up a position as a country vet in Essex and he and Mummy bought the Manor House in Southminster. Daddy was a wonderful, warm giant of a man – genial, easy to get on with and popular with almost everyone who knew him. I don't remember hearing him say a cross or cruel word about anyone. My mother Kathleen, or Kitty, Wheeler would have been reckoned by anyone, to be a good catch. She was elegant, slim, sophisticated – a good golfer and pianist with a wonderful zest for life and a great sense of humour.

Southminster was at that time a little market village perched on the east coast of England and separated from the North Sea by three flat, windswept miles of reclaimed marshland. A little village called Bradwell, eight miles away from us and right on that wild and unprotected coastline, had a tiny little stone church which we loved to visit. Started by Bishop Cedd in 600 A.D., it was completely isolated and built hard against the North Sea wall. The place was filled with early history of Danes and Saxons and I loved being a part of it all. There was an untamed and unspoilt isolation about that part of England, which seeped into my whole being.

But Mummy would really have preferred a larger town. Bigger places were much more exciting to her and she loved going up to London. Her childhood with this rather exotic and clever Indian-born doctor for a father had been full of fascinating society people and places. As a young married woman, the tiny village of Southminster, set on the bleakest edge of Essex, must have been a pretty dull alternative.

Our house was very much the centre of the village with its old Norman church, St. Leonard's, on one side and the cricket field, the site for the annual agricultural and flower shows, on the other. The house was very old. I remember clearly ducking under the low doors, the shiny unevenness of the wooden floors and stone steps worn thin in the middle from four centuries of use. It was a well-ordered sort of house – with the typically symmetrical facade and small, glass-saving windows of its time.

My entry into the world was, I gather, absolutely unremarkable except that inconveniently, it was four days after Christmas and winter had been particularly bitter that year – a not uncommon event, being so close to those desolate Essex marshes.

I was born in the last days of 1913. England went to war a few months later.

World War 1 lasted until just a few weeks before I was five. The horror is still with me. I hated being wakened at dead of night to the sound of planes flying overhead and either Nanny or Mummy coming to wrap me up and take me down to the cellar. It was ice cold, dank, dark and dripping with water. We could take no lights with us except for one dim and miserable candle that we could only set a match to once we climbed down the steps. I was simply terrified of it all.

Our lives changed dramatically with the war when four officers of the British Army were billeted to us. One of the officers had a huge, ugly and panting English bulldog. It was always glowering and salivating at me under the dining room table. The ultimate disgust was one evening during supper, when it was sick all over my foot. With no real understanding of the need for sacrifice during this period of the war, all I felt was that these tough-talking men had invaded us. It just wasn't our home any more.

Daddy was exempted from conscription, as he had to keep all the artillery horses fit and ready for action. So having him at home was at least one constant in our lives and the surgery carried on as nearly normal as possible.

One night Mummy and Daddy woke me up in a terrible panic and we rushed outside to see a silent, hovering menace in the sky. I didn't understand what it was, but I do remember the impact it had and the terror it generated as it glided noiselessly past our house. The Zeppelin was filled with German soldiers and Mummy and Daddy realised only too well the implications of its arrival and obvious

18

descent path towards nearby Colchester, en route for London.

Suddenly – there was a spurt of flame and in seconds a fireball filled the sky. It was the most terrifying and incredible sight. The airship had been shot down. The next day, we took probably the first ride of my life in a car, taking a taxi to Colchester to see the burnt out remains and the German soldiers who had survived, being rounded up and herded off to prison camp.

Being the local vet for much of the county, the increasing size of the practice meant we grew rapidly out of the Manor House and we moved forward a couple of centuries – this time to an enormous old Victorian red brick house.

Oakleigh was a wonderful home. It was in North Street, just down the road from the Manor House and it had lots of room for everything and everyone. There were eight bedrooms, a breakfast room, Daddy's study, a dining room and a drawing room both with huge old bay windows looking out onto the garden. An extra-wide front door with leaded light windows on both sides opened into a graciously large, airy central hall which supported a massive but very elegant rose-carpeted staircase. There were also two large cellars and an attic where the cook and the maid lived in two vast but perishingly cold bedrooms. The maids came down to bath in the one and only bathroom in the house every Friday. We were never allowed to bath on that day!

The kitchen was cosy and full of the bustle and smell of homely cooking – great apple pies and loaves of bread – steak and kidney puddings and a huge roast on Sundays.

The old coal stove dominated the room with a row of eight polished and engraved silver meat dishes hung on the wall above it. These graduated from about 12 to 30 inches in length and they were used every day for enormous great meals. I remember the good-natured banter that accompanied all the polishing and scrubbing which went into keeping them shining and spotless. Ornate wrought-iron bells hung off another of the kitchen walls and jangled in response to calls from the surrounding rooms. The scullery, pantry and store cupboard linked by an uneven flagstone passage were all on the ground floor above two underground cellars.

Outside there was a formal rose garden and a winding hazelnut walk. Behind this a grass tennis court, a huge vegetable garden, rows of fruit trees, two roomy stables and a tack room with a loft where a roaring log fire burned all winter. We also had lots of chicken coops and the "Shay" (chaise) house, which was where we kept the trap.

Leading into the garden off North Street were various utility rooms and Daddy's surgery. Huge old Clydesdales and other horses were tied up to a heavy iron ring in the side of the house with a great clomping about of massive shod feet as they waited for treatment. His practice was mostly a large animal practice and always frantically busy … we became used to Daddy not being at home at mealtimes because of some animal crisis or another.

But the house and its surrounds were sheer heaven for a child. Along one side was the "Pump Mead" – a huge meadow where the horses grazed – and we spent hours feeding them and playing hide and seek among the haystacks.

Beyond our garden wall was a row of four little cottages. In one of these, the village coffin maker, Cliff Stammers, could be seen hard at work most days. We used to watch him making the coffins and fingered and admired the beautiful linings… being allowed to drape off-cuts across us as make-believe ball gowns and other finery. 'Hi Cliff, Oi Ol' was our call across the wall. The significance of the coffins' ultimate use completely escaped us, but we were most interested in the process and all those comfortable and luxurious interiors.

My earliest years, most of the time and certainly in all weathers, were spent down at the stables with Fred French, Daddy's right hand man. Fred held the bulls while Daddy castrated them, he groomed the horses, looked after the trap, oversaw the production and picking of the finest fruit and vegetables… and kept an eye on us.

Fred is my greatest memory of happy, pleasant times and when I went to boarding school he'd lovingly buy me toffees, and post them off in a funny old parcel with barely legible writing. Nothing tasted better than Fred's toffees. We loved him dearly and he was with the family for 26 years.

Daddy and Fred had to undertake some awful assignments – particularly when they had to go across to a racing stud on Foul Ness. These horses would of course, have to go and have their valuable foals in the middle of the night – on the coldest and bleakest nights of winter. As a result, Fred and Daddy set off in a rowing boat to cross a couple of nautical miles of wild seas, in order to help them. It was very worrying and we were always relieved to see them safely back.

I had my own pony called Bobby and Jack and Dutchie were our hackney horses. They'd be groomed and polished up each day, bronzed horse brasses gleaming along their harness to pull the trap. My greatest treat was to go off in the trap on the rounds with Jack and Dutchie, Daddy and Fred.

The surgery was a place of wondering and interest – there was always something going on and we grew up with the birth and death of animals and birds as a familiar part of life. I remember from a very young age "helping" Daddy grind up medicines for his animals with an old wooden pestle and mortar. I spent hours in his surgery, marvelling at the perfect little white foal preserved in a bottle of formaldehyde. It was only about 12 inches high, held up by a string round its neck and frozen in a foetal prance – little hoofs about the size of currants, tiny ears, eyes tight shut, soft little nose and mouth. I was always dying to take it out and play with it.

Bishop was another confirmed old bachelor and our main gardener. He always wore a navy blue cap, which had somehow gone pink with age. The love of his life was playing the violin. He wasn't very good, but how he loved his fiddle! No sweeping bowing for Bishop, but joyful, jolly, controlled little sawing movements and a rather restricted range of popular tunes of the time. A rather staccato *Salut d'amour* was his special favourite. Bishop's greatest delight was when Daddy formed a small string orchestra called the Southminster Orpheans. Bishop was asked to be in it.

Every time they played, Daddy had to ask Bishop to take off his precious cap and urge him to 'Open up your bow Bishop'. He would try and try – but he could never quite achieve the flowing cantabile Daddy was after. We in turn, never recognised Bishop without his cap! But he had achieved greatness in the Orpheans – and his contentment was wonderful to see.

We had a horde of casual helpers to service the huge old property. Mrs. Perry did the washing once a week – bearing it away untidily in a cart and bringing it back neat and ironed and smelling fresh. We had three grandfather and several mantel clocks and Mr. Gilbert, whom we irreverently called "luscious lips", cycled nearly three miles every Wednesday afternoon, arriving precisely at 2 o'clock to wind them all up. Mrs. Mizzen, "Mim" to us, was our charwoman and Miss Turpin came to take away things that needed sewing.

I thought we employed half the village. We probably did in one way or another.

Perhaps memory dims or only highlights the best... but my child-hood was a golden time – to me, as well as to my brother and sister. I don't remember any unpleasantness – we loved our greater household and they loved us children, they cosseted us, looked after us... and probably spoilt us terribly.

Parents somehow didn't mix with their children as much in those days. We were very loved, but firmly disciplined and while they went about their business, we were to be seen and not heard. My nanny, Hilda, was large, comforting and motherly – the panacea for all ills. We were "shown off" on special occasions, the girls in frills and Dick in a sailor suit. We had to be on our best behaviour – but we found them fidgety, stiff occurrences and were always longing to be off on some other adventure.

So like most other children we knew, we spent most of our time with the servants. I loved having afternoon tea with the maids and Fred and Bishop. We would have hunks of bread, butter and jam with lettuce – and cake with lettuce. Why on earth lettuce seemed to feature so much I cannot think.

The old manor house might have been the physical centre of the village, but my parents were its focal point. We were lucky to be a family that was naturally good at sports as well. Daddy was cricket captain most of the time we were there and one of the main instigators of the new Burnham golf club – where he was the inaugural captain, a position he held for ten years. He was also a keen member of the Burnham yacht club, Honorary Secretary and organiser of the agricultural shows – and during his spare time, he played the violin.

Daddy always seemed to be driving his pony and trap in a grand parade round the cricket field-cum-agricultural show with a red rosette in his mouth having just won some great prize or other. One wall of our tack room was filled with rosettes of all colours and sizes.

On winter evenings, as the wind squealed across the flat salt marshes, I'd sit snug in the tack room with the log fire roaring and the horses blowing and stamping in the loose boxes, while Fred buffed up the saddles. I will never forget the warmth and comfort of that tack room or that distinctive smell of leather, saddle soap and tar. The rosettes would glow and shine in the flames and I'd relive their individual moments of glory, remembering the proudly arched necks and winning antics of our high-stepping horses.

While the horses and animals were my first love, music was rapidly becoming my second. All the Sugdens played instruments and we seemed to have endless musical uncles. Uncle Harry was a 'cellist and Uncle Albert a creditable baritone. Another uncle, Herbert, was a sort of sometime tenor – who would absolutely fascinate us children because every time he sang in the upper registers he rose up onto his tippy toes in what seemed to us to be some sort of exquisite agony. There were lots of musical evenings at home throughout my childhood, with contributions from the neighbourhood and Mummy accompanying Daddy on the violin. Village concerts were also terrific events. We were always working towards something or other, playing musical instruments, dancing or acting.

I started ballet with a woman who had moved in to our old Manor House. She was a great teacher and I must have shown some talent as I was on full points at the tender age of five, (something that ruined my feet for all time and I have suffered badly with them since). I remember seeing a hand-drawn poster which set my youthful heart aflutter. It was advertising one of our many village concerts, with the promise "Nancy Sugden will dance"!

It was an idyllic childhood and I was very, very lucky – I certainly never appreciated it at the time – but in my first few years in Africa I was to look back often with longing, to the sweetness and love of Southminster and Oakleigh.

As we grew older, we had weekend after weekend of summer tennis parties with friends, many of whom have remained close all my life. The village people used to get a bit sniffy hearing the Sugdens cavorting around on their tennis courts on Sunday afternoons – particularly when "thirty-forty" would ring through the hushed moments of Evensong. We would always go to church in the mornings – of course! In between tennis there was always the music – lots of music… and lots of acting during winter weekends and evenings.

Mummy managed to create this level of sophistication in her own home, but despite all, she still felt isolated and cut off in Southminster and the trap was a slow means of transport to see her friends. To give her full credit, she tried – and succeeded – in being a good wife to a country vet. She was an exceptional pianist, giving continuous concerts in the Dengie Hundred and playing the organ at our local church. She was also ladies' golf captain at Burnham, and year after year won the annual tennis tournaments at the Flower Show… as well as writing up all the books for the practice.

Lighter moments in these early war years were our trips to Bridlington. Daddy, being a Yorkshireman, would take us all up to see his family for a bit of relaxation and to help us escape from the vulnerability of living in a village on the direct bombing route to London.

Shortly after the war was over my brother Dick was born, followed shortly by my sister Trish. I immediately transferred my affection and time to them instead of the dogs and horses.

Dick was very like me, eager to please and rather shy and gentle – he loved the animals and the simple things of life. Trish was a bombshell by comparison. Dramatic in looks and mercurial by temperament, she took quite a bit of handling. Dick and I were, at that stage, rather mousy. Trish had a mass of golden brown curly hair and bright blue eyes. I dropped into the role of protective elder sister to them both, very happily.

One day, when I was just five, there was a stirring in the village. A newcomer.

And what a newcomer for a tiny country village! The tongues started wagging furiously. Tiny, French and very dramatic – dressed in black from head to toe, with her hair scraped back and a mesmerising wall eye – Madame Clara Angeloff – arrived from nowhere. She had once been married to a Russian and the result was two strapping sons, Cyril and Ivan who would come and see her from time to time, stamping fiercely about, wearing fur hats and acting dramatically foreign.

It must have been very difficult for Madame Angeloff to settle into our staid, conservative little English village of the post-war era, full of its suspicions, rumours and fears of anything or anyone foreign. We wondered why she had chosen somewhere like Southminster. Madame Angeloff was not going to let the rumours sway her – she had work to do. She decided to start a school – much to Mummy's relief as difficult decisions were about to be made about my education, including the possibility of having to find me a governess.

About a dozen children, ranging in age from five to 16, sat in her tiny kitchen on hard wooden benches. Her kitchen table had an oilcloth on top of it, and a large portrait of the former Prime Minister, Mr. Gladstone, dominated the room.

Our slates were cleaned by wet and dry rubbers - the wet ones were made out of her old black woollen stockings and the dry, out of her second-hand dresses. The smell was appalling! The only escape from it was to take a book out to the toilet at the back for as long as you dared.

We learned well through her highly individualistic, but soundly based teaching. Our grounding in the "three Rs" (reading, 'riting, and 'rithmetic), French, history and geography was outstanding. Having lived in Europe she would describe graphic and stirring tales of the war across the channel. Her main claim to fame – which she told anyone and everyone who would listen – was that after singing at a concert in Paris, King Edward VII had winked at her. I secretly felt that Mr. Gladstone must have winked at her as well.

In the morning, we all learned in the "classroom" but in the afternoon, we were individually taught music in the front room. I started my first piano lessons with her and ended up staying at Madame's school for seven years.

When I went to senior school at Hillcote in Eastbourne, I was very bothered because I had never attended what might have been termed a "proper" school – or done such horrors as decimals, algebra or geometry. But Madame Angeloff's grounding was so sound that I jumped up a class after only a few weeks because I was so far ahead in everything else.

At the end of the first term at Hillcote, we had to write an essay on what we had heard in a series of weekly lectures on world history. The head girl won first prize... and to everyone's absolute astonishment (especially mine) I came second. There was a staggered silence from the school. But it did make a great difference to me, as I was then regarded as, and felt, unusual and a bit interesting having had this strange early schooling. My only other triumphs at Hillcote were winning the senior tennis cup and ending up as Head Girl.

Hillcote was a lovely school. It was right on the seafront next to Beachy Head. After my young life on the edge of the Essex marshes, I loved the feeling of a sea breeze through my hair – the wetter and wilder the sea, the more I love it. Eastbourne enhanced that love of the coast and I would linger after the other girls had moved on, just to watch the waves, feel the wind and smell the rich goodness of the air.

We were extremely lucky at Hillcote, as our headmistress, Miss Brown (the Bert of the previous chapter) was conscientious in the extreme in making sure her pupils had the very best of everything. As a result, I learned music with Carl Weber (grandson of composer Carl Maria von Weber) and drama with Guy Pertwee – both of them leaders in their field and extremely well respected. They came all the way from London once a week to teach us.

We did a great deal of acting during the term. I remember being part of a group chosen on one occasion to take part in some fund-raising tableau on the pier, dressed up as Zenana women. These were people of high caste families in India and Iran and the word describes that part of the house in which these women were secluded. We had long robes with scarves round our heads and we sold Indian beads and ornaments to raise money. It was an annual event and a great treat to be chosen, as the woman running it was a lovely, gentle person who had dedicated her life to spreading spiritual reform to these Zenana women, as part of her Christian Mission to the Jews.

Dick stayed at Madame Angeloff's for three years before he went off to a prep school called Rosslyn House, near Felixstowe. After this he went on to Felsted where our upbringing again came to the fore in that he excelled at cricket, playing for Gentlemen of Essex before being called up for the Second World War. Trish left Madame's to go to Southminster Grammar, then came on to Hillcote as well. She was probably the best sport of all of us, playing outstanding golf and tennis – and winning the Essex golf championship at the age of 16. We were all very proud of her, but I used to grumble and be very ungracious about the number of times we had to go up to London to watch her play tennis for junior Wimbledon. But Trish's life – and sporting promise – was to be cut short... when she was called up for the WAAF.

I had decided, while at Hillcote to study music. As soon as I left school, I would travel up to London every day, to do the Teachers' Training Course at the Royal Academy of Music in Baker Street. I was fortunate to learn with a fantastic professor at the time, New Zealander, Victor Booth... and I got my LRAM when I was 19. Jobs were particularly difficult to find at that time so Mr. Booth advised me to get a second string to my bow. As a result, I spent a wonderful year indulging my love of art and painting at the Southend School of Art.

At the end of this year, my old headmistress "Bert" Brown invited me back to Hillcote to teach for a year – for board and lodging. This was great – I was back in an environment I loved and back beside the sea in Eastbourne. It also gave me the experience I needed to be in the right place at the right time for a job in the music department at another girls' school, Rippingale - just across the road.

Our house filled up with family and friends from all over England for Christmas 1934 and I made the first speech of my life at my 21st

birthday dance on 29th December – when I wore my backless duck-egg blue dress to devastating effect. Both Jackie Lindsay and Dick Castle were enraptured and my future looked uncomplicated and set fair.

After only three weeks at Rippingale – on my first salary of £70 a year – I was asked to do a play called the *Burglar and the Girl*.

My life was turned on its head.

Nancy Sugden, gentle, rather spoilt, English country girl was, after only a few more weeks, seriously contemplating life as a pioneering colonial. With the naivete and daring of youth, I could hardly wait!

Chapter 3

...of waiting and wondering

John's letters back to Rhodesia shortly after we met, reflect a growing indecision – he was obviously dying to return and see everyone again, but suddenly, inconveniently and at the very last moment, England and certain things English, had become rather precious!

5th March 1935

I have been wondering recently whether I would not find myself back over here for a short time, rather sooner than I had previously imagined. But I have the strongest feelings that I shall never return to live permanently and that Rhodesia will claim me when once I get back there.

We have just finished the matinee and have the evening performance tonight. Yesterday we had the worst dress rehearsal I have ever known!

There is so much over here now that is very dear to me but I think my heart is really in Rhodesia. I feel though that I shall find it hard to settle down. There is such a strong streak in me that must wander or die.

12th March 1935

What an idiot I have let myself in for a play in the school (Badger's Green) and I am heartily cursing myself. We have only three weeks in which to do it and I have a colossal part to do.

The last performance of our show at the village hall last Tuesday night was very satisfactory and our little play got a very good write-up in the local rag. In all we raised nearly 30 pounds which really makes it feel as though our efforts were worthwhile.

I went last evening to a flick with Nancy Sugden, the girl who was in that wee show. She is in one of those unfortunate places where the headmistresses retire solemnly to bed at ten and see that the staff does so as well. How the mistresses stand that is more than I can understand.

26th March 1935

My last letter but one before I set sail. I am annoyed that I shall not have more evenings during which I shall be able to see people.

Patrick was down here for the weekend looking very fit and rather more anglicised than when I saw him last. His enthusiasm for London is simply wonderful – he will certainly get a great deal out of his time over here. He came down on Friday evening and the Hills kindly put him up here.

That evening we had a delightful dance at the Grand. The occasion was the Rugger Club's annual dance. We dined first of all at the Grand and later I went round to pick up Nancy Sugden and Brenda Hogarth. The show went on till about 2 a.m. and I did enjoy it tremendously though I could not help feeling just a little bit sad that it was probably the final spree in Eastbourne. But I am getting so thrilled now at the thought of getting home and seeing all the old haunts again.

I found his first letter to me, written as he waited for the ship to cast off from Southampton surprisingly open and almost disarmingly frank as he talked of the agonies we experienced in that final meeting – and tentative hopes for our future.

Union Castle Line
12th April

Darling One

We have just got on board and will be away in a fairly short time. The train journey down was rather hellish, I seemed like a drowning man in that all the past five years seemed to come into review in that short space of just under two hours. The final climax, my meeting you, rather overshadowed the rest especially in view of yesterday's visit.

It was lovely to see you for that last time, though the journey back reduced me to a state of depression such as I have seldom experienced before.

I can't think why we both went down into such depths of silence whenever we were together. There always seemed so much I wanted to say and yet with this hanging over, it seemed impossible for it to come out. But darling, I do love you so much and feel that eventually things will turn out all right, in spite of the depressing outlook.

I'm afraid I have been far too apt to consider only my own point of view whereas you are the one who has most to be fed up with, especially so if you do finally call on yourself to take the step of coming out there. Please set your mind at rest about other people. I can't imagine myself being more certain about the person whom I shall want to marry some day.

I shall write again from Madeira at greater length and let you know what I am putting up with in my present company. So far they seem to be largely foreign but one or two of them look as though they might be quite good company. One obvious honeymoon couple was sitting near me in the train. I'm afraid I couldn't help feeling envious.

Must away and see if I can find the Hills. Look after yourself Nancy darling and have a good time; and don't forget that I want to hear everything about you.

I had to keep pinching myself to realise that the object of all this affection and undying love was me – Nancy Sugden! I couldn't see what on earth it was that had attracted this glorious man with all his brains and good looks. It was a storybook case of love at first sight for both of us.

As the voyage went on, John became more depressed and more concerned – I learned later that this had something to do with the fact that he hated the sea, but I found almost everything he said mirrored my own uncertainty and insecurity.

Just off the N. African coast

Darling

I was pleased to have your wire on the boat, it was sweet of you to send it and it gave me just that extra little bit of courage when this boat drew gradually away from the side. I don't think I could have stood it had you been on the quay yourself. Even as it was, it was difficult enough to say goodbye to dear old England.

How I hated the first day or two out from port. Luckily I was so sleepy that on Saturday I slept nearly the whole time... so far the elements have been fairly kind and I have only passed one meal on to the fish... others have been less fortunate...

We are now getting far enough south for the sun to take some effect. Last night was simply gorgeous, beautifully warm and pleasantly calm and with a magnificent half-moon almost overhead. How I wished you were on board then, you would have loved it...

I retired to bed in a very depressed state of mind and got into one of my worst introspection moods where I could see nothing good in myself and felt that as far as I was concerned the world would be no worse off if the boat went down.

31

Today I am more cheery and writing to you has given me renewed hope. I still find myself a long way from finding a solution to this problem of life. Going out to only a temporary job has made things much more difficult…

You can have no idea how I shall look forward to the chance of your coming; or do you think I shall have to come back to England again to fetch you?! Incidentally, I had another dream the other night, in which we were attending a wedding, though whose I couldn't say. The details were somewhat vague, but I remember that I was all done up in wedding kit and that halfway through the proceedings you came along and took my arm.

It seems darling, that the fates are definitely going to decree that we shall get married no matter what we do about it. I only hope they don't make us wait too long.

People on board are a cheery crowd though inclined to be hearty. Tomorrow morning we touch in at Madeira for a few hours. I shall go ashore there to break the monotony of the voyage. After that we have 13 days with nothing to offer any variation to life at all…

Let me know all that happens to you Nancy; no detail is too small. Tons of love darling one, I wish to goodness you were here.

How extraordinary that someone with his looks and talents could see nothing good in himself and feel the world would be no worse off if the boat went down. Yes it would, John Hammond, it would. I was horrified at the thought. I'd always been a happy-go-lucky person and never really thought very deeply about things like that. I obviously had quite a bit to learn about him.

Union Castle Line
About Lat. 23 S

Dearest

By the time you get this you will be back again in Rippingale with all that that entails, while I will have embarked on a new job at home.

This trip has been trying beyond my gloomiest expectations and I am longing for a change from this continual expanse of sea, sea and sea. Hardly a boat has come along to give us anything to notice or look at – only a few whales and flying fish which we seem now to have left behind.

In spite of myself I have been dragged in to the sports and entertainments committee; a thankless and exacting job which you would do well to avoid when you make any expedition of this kind. I am now engrossed in an H. G. Wells which deals prophetically with the history of the next 200 years.

The net result of reading it has been to fill me with something very near despair and to make me wonder what on earth we poor individuals can do to improve our lot in the coming 50-odd years.

I'm sorry darling for unloading all these grouses on you, forgive me if they bore you to distraction, but I'm afraid I find my mind turning to thoughts of you whenever I want to get away from any particularly unpleasant activity.

I have managed to get quite a lot of professional amusement out of trying to improve the English of two Swedish girls on board.

They have a keen sense of humour and it has been very good fun having them on board. Among the others there are one or two who have thoughts beyond the mere bubble and froth of the average – but on the whole I have been rather a recluse ...

Hmmmnn – Swedish girls indeed! John had left dozens of girls in England aching with sorrow that he had left... he seemed to me in the short time I had known him, to be constantly surrounded by a bevy of beauties, all drawn to his side as if by a powerful magnet. But somehow, his mind and his integrity left me comforted despite the fact that beside my frivolous letters John's seemed rather intimidatingly deep and intense.

Rippingale

Darling

I was tremendously pleased to get your letter this morning... many thanks too for the snap, it isn't a dreadful thing at all and I simply love it. I'm dreadfully sorry you had that long gap without any letters from me... you will get a whole string of them in the future. That is the worst of Air Mail as one gets so very much ahead of the others – it will probably be easier when you get back to Rhodesia with no air mail yet so that we know how long each letter will take. Otherwise my news is so dreadfully behind yours.

Please don't call your letters dull, I love them, and its frightfully interesting hearing about everything. It's rather difficult trying to picture you doing all these things, good as your descriptions are. I only wish I could just see you for a little bit – I was really awfully glad to have that photo, because without it I couldn't quite sort of "get" your face, if you know what I mean.

I think I have told you in another letter that I asked for a key to the hostel, and it was refused – too bad! I was dreadfully peeved the other night because I got here at about ten minutes to ten and found myself locked out

– so I rang the bell hard for some time and nothing happened. There was a light in one of the old girl's bedrooms so I prowled round to the back and chucked earth up and whistled and made such a filthy noise that I woke some of the children. All this was of no avail because she was having a bath, where-upon I crashed round past the drawing room window and saw the nastier old girl fast asleep in her chair. So I made a bit more noise and saw her suddenly wake up and come to let me in.

By this time it was 10.15 and she was in a tearing rage, saying I was v. late and that she had had to wait up for me etc. The old devil wouldn't believe me until at lunch the next day one of the children innocently asked "was it you Miss Sugden who woke us up ringing the bell?" I felt v. grateful to her!

My froth and bubble always seemed to cross with his more reflective letters. At first it bothered me that I wasn't responding directly, as there would now be a six week turnaround and in between I'd get another letter full of different topics.

Sunday 28th

I had to cry off on Friday through lack of ideas combined with an unpleasant swell… Tomorrow at six o'clock we land in Cape Town to start our 48-hour train journey up country. Quite a crowd of people are going up to Rhodesia so that I shall not be entirely lonesome through that long stretch.

It is strange to feel the change in atmosphere down here. I am sure that had I been unconscious all through this lengthy trip, I would have known on waking up now, that we were not in European waters. The sun has shifted to the North and the stars at night are entirely different. If you can imagine the evening star shining sufficiently brightly to cast a definite reflection on the water and all the other stars lit up proportionately, you could get some idea of the general effect. I wish you could have been on this trip darling, it would have been a grand chance to get to know each other and I feel sure it would have made me less irritable towards the other people on board.

You simply must come out to see this country Nancy even if you eventually were to decide against living in it permanently. I think its wildness and space would appeal to you. Perhaps I am being wildly optimistic, but I hope that about this time next year will see you making this trip also.

I still find it hard to realise that I shall not be returning to Aldro in a week or so… I want to do something really worthwhile with my life but I feel that you will have to have quite a lot to do with it.

34

...OF WAITING AND WONDERING

I began to imagine what the Southern Hemisphere must look and feel like as well as gain a picture of the man and of the life that would be ahead of me – if this were to be my ultimate decision.

Plumtree School
2nd May 1935

Table Mountain was covered in cloud the whole time we were there and the start of the journey through the outskirts of CT and across the Cape Flats struck me as being very uninteresting. It improved as we went inland and started to climb up onto the Plateau. It was very fine going up through the Hex River Pass – two engines were required to get us up – one in front and the other pushing behind and the track curving in and out round the hills eventually coming out on to the flat expanse of the Karoo.

Fortunately we were still in sight of Mountains when darkness fell and we were consequently spared quite a long stretch of that dull waste. Next morning we woke up near Kimberley... it has never struck me before how wide and how open those spaces were. For a whole night and a day we were going through open nothingness.

An occasional town, which seemed to have nothing to justify its existence, broke the monotony of the rattle of the wheels on the rails – but away from the line as far as you could see was simply a vast open stretch with only occasional gum trees and ant hills to break it. Strangely enough though, the colouring of the whole country was rather pleasant in spite of the unchanging vegetation.

Tuesday night brought us into the bush country. The trees all seemed very much smaller than I had imagined them and after two or three abnormally dry seasons, everything was looking very dry and burnt up. Excitement kept me awake until the small hours and I enjoyed coming through countryside, which grew more and more familiar as we got nearer home.

It was delightful to see the family again; Dad was up in Salisbury at the time, but Jean (John's sister) came down from Bulawayo for the day and it was really exciting to see her and Mother and the wee nephew and niece. (the children of elder brother Ian, or "Skinny").

Everything seemed very strange at first, all the buildings seemed so very much smaller than when I last saw them, but they are gradually resuming their proportions again!! It has seemed awfully strange up to now and in fact I have been longing for old England again, but more particularly because of you Nancy. I have been wondering the whole time what you would think of this place, and I hope that when you come along you will not strike the heat as I did.

I have only managed to recognise one or two of the boys through their resemblance to elder brothers whom I know, but they are a very nice crowd – very well built and all amazingly fit and sunburnt. They all seem such large people after the wee mites at Aldro…

John was obviously painting a picture for me of what I would feel when I came out and I was grateful for this. But I have to admit that I was pleased to see with his next letter that he was actually still missing England a bit.

Plumtree School – 9.5.35

I would give anything to see a good old green field again, or a bluebell wood, or even a rainy day. The first few days here were dreadfully hot and with everything unusually dry, following a bad rainy season it has been almost unbearable. I am finding it hard to get acclimatised again. This sudden jump from sea level to 4.5 thousand ft. is a bit trying and has made any form of exertion rather a trial.

The weekend saw us preparing for Jubilations (the 25 year Jubilee celebrations for King George V) … All Plumtree and wife turned out of course and I was able to greet many old faces some of which I had some difficulty in putting names to. The celebrations took the form of a chapel service in the morning and children's sports with other sports in the afternoon followed by fireworks, a bonfire and *Kaffir dancing, after which we retired to the school hall for a dance.

I'm afraid that, apart from the people in the school, most of the people here with a few exceptions have rather unpleasantly satisfied minds. Pigs and mealies (the local name for maize) are about their only topics of conversation and Rhodesia for them fulfils all the necessary qualifications of a first rate country. Their minds are definitely one track, the ruts in which they sit are too deep for them to be otherwise, and they seem to adopt an amazingly complacent attitude to life in general

But I must not be too critical. Perhaps it is too early to judge, as I find my mind running along entirely different lines to theirs and my sense of values is at the moment very foreign to them.

On Tuesday we had a Native parade and a presentation of medals to local Chiefs after which they held cycle sports on the school cricket field which provided considerable amusement and several headlong crashes.

Our day starts at 6'15 in the morning!You can imagine how that appeals to me... nothing on the job front, but I am supremely hopeful...

We were slowly becoming used to the way we could interact with each other and cope with the delay of so many weeks before we had hope of an answer. It wasn't easy and I wasn't a natural letter writer, so there was an element of commitment, admittedly pleasant, but commitment nonetheless, required on my part.

John had been feeling the heat, but now it seemed that the weather had improved.

I went on my first jaunt up to Bulawayo on Saturday and stayed the night. We went up by car, my pater, a cousin who is staying with us at the moment and myself. The cousin who is about my age is a very charming person but is going home to England to marry some bloke who lives up Manchester way. The roads seem dreadful after those in England and it's a nerve wracking business being driven, but we do the 65 miles in just over two hours and as trains only run about three days a week, it is the most convenient way.

I cannot get over the flatness of Plumtree – something that had never struck me before – as we climbed towards the hilly areas we saw some of those wonderful views which the country is so famous for. The clear atmosphere makes views of 20 to 30 miles commonplace and the kopjes stand out in wonderful shades of blue and purple. Setting these off is a foreground of flame-golden grass with shades of colour varying from light gold to deep bronze.

Bulawayo is an odd place. Attractive in some ways but stuck in the middle of a vast plateau so that you can look out for about 20 miles in each direction. It has some buildings which would be a credit to any town but the wideness of the streets seem to make them less impressive than they would otherwise be. The whole place gives the impression that "after all there is plenty of space, so why not use it!"

The "occasion" was firstly Jean's engagement and secondly my return to the fold. Jean is engaged to a pleasant young chap from Bulawayo, John Swire-Thompson and they're hoping to get married sometime during the year.

We went on to the Grand Hotel to dance. It is a pleasant room but the crowd there was even more prim than at the Grand in Eastbourne! I felt I would have liked to drop a bomb into the middle of the room to wake them up. I have asked Jean to arrange a "sitting" so that I can send you a photo-

graph, which is a little more worthy than the last. Give my love to dear old Eastbourne and don't stand too much from the old dears.

After nearly a month at home during which he had been helping out at Plumtree, John was beginning to feel like settling down again, although to what was still a bit of a question mark.

My real difficulty is to accustom myself to this very different kind of life, where amusements and "a good time" are less easily come by. Perhaps I shall be able to get a grip on myself and settle down to something worthwhile. I feel it will be connected with education in some way. They are now introducing a scheme of free education in this country which may bring about unforeseen developments, possibly even in the direction of the starting of private schools.

It is delightful being at home with the family once again and my young niece and nephew are an absolute joy. They are both packed with character and extremely amusing, though John Jeremy's capacity for playing "elephants" is unlimited. I am rapidly becoming a useful quadruped.

I'm afraid I was in rather a black mood on Monday and it was reflected in my letter to such an extent that I had to abandon it. However, it did serve to cheer me up merely being able to get it off my chest. It is rather unsettling, as I can't find any kindred spirit who seems to see the unhealthy state of the world as it is today. But I must not embark... as you will find it neither interesting nor entertaining.

Our communications here are delightfully vague. A train coming in a couple of hours late doesn't seem to put anyone out unduly. On Friday the stationmaster thought it was a holiday and when a train arrived, it had to wait about an hour before calling him back to life again. The railway has been called "the line of least resistance"...

The Gaumont British people have been bush up here for the past few weeks making the film of Rhodes' life – it should be really good when it comes out and I hope you'll get a chance to see it.

Several people went up to see it being shot. On one occasion when they were filming a Matabele attack on a laager, the whole thing was so awe inspiring that the cameraman forgot to shoot. One of the natives, when being asked to play dead found himself lying uncomfortably and got up to get his coat in the middle of the shoot. The poor blighters had it drummed into them so strongly after that that they could hardly be induced to move and come to life again after the scene had been shot!

38

I am so glad your 'flu is better — you must look after yourself more my darling. Your accounts of the bluebells and green fields — but I mustn't continue or I will work myself up into another frenzy of discontent. I am trying so hard to convince myself that this is really the right place for me to be in, that I mustn't allow my imagination to run away with me too much. I am longing for your photo to arrive; I know so well what you mean when you say you can't "get" my face.

The stars were hanging so low in the sky last night — but the Plough, only just above the horizon, indicated that a wee green Isle lay up in that direction, and on that green Isle you were couped up in that "hell-hole" when you should have been out gathering bluebells or primroses. And oh! Darling I wanted you so much.

I would often enclose a little pressed flower or something to remind John of England, as I really did hope that our lives would be spent in England rather than out in Africa. That his cousin Rose was coming back to marry "some bloke from up Manchester way" gave me hope. But suddenly, there was a new dimension — John's increasing certainty that he wanted to be involved in the education of black youngsters instead of white.

The sprig of lilac was simply delightful. I'm afraid the scent had left it, but I could imagine that quite easily…

I have no doubt you will have seen in some of the "popular" press at home the accounts of the strike on the Copperbelt in Northern Rhodesia. Like fools, the officials up there fired on the Natives and killed several of them. They are now holding an enquiry into the whole affair and by the look of things some of those people up there are going to get it in the neck. White people up here will have to reconcile themselves to the rapid rise of the black and incidents such as that are not going to make things easier. There are still those who would have the Native kept down in his present position fearing that they will be unfairly attacked economically. They fail to realise the consequences if we fail to allow or help him to rise in the proper way.

Being such a new country, few people seem to have much time for the finer points of living and concentrate most of their energies on maintaining their material welfare intact without ever troubling much about what the world outside is doing, saying or thinking. I feel there is no long-term future for the white man in this country unless he learns to live comfortably with the black.

To that end I find myself more and more interested in the education of the black instead of white.

To this end I am going up to a Native Education centre near Salisbury called Domboshawa. They apparently have something rather unformed in mind at this stage… but I am looking forward to seeing it immensely. Duties might include such things as instruction of Drill, football and athletics, catering for the boys and supervision of the boarding house. Finally – now don't laugh – I have to supervise all the sanitary arrangements of the place!! I don't suppose you can ever have imagined yourself being connected in any way with a sanitary inspector! For all this they would pay me about 25 pounds a month with accommodation of a kind.

The interesting thing is that there is a reasonable chance of getting a permanent job on the academic side… At all events it will be an interesting experience. The whole branch of Native Development is still very young and there is a chance that by getting in on the ground floor I may be able to get into a worthwhile job with prospects of rising fairly quickly.

I had not yet intimated to Mummy and Daddy that there was anything more serious in my relationship with John than just passing infatuation. I rather dreaded telling them, as I knew Mummy would be pretty het up at the thought of me going so far away. John had asked me whether I had mentioned anything to them and I had to confess I had not – yet.

I wonder if you could make use of Miss Brown's offer to arrange an exchange job for a year so that you could come out and have a look round before you finally commit yourself to live out here. I can well understand that your mother will get somewhat "het up" when she hears of the possibility of your coming out and perhaps it would be as well to let her have some indication that there is more seriousness in it than she imagines. As a matter of fact I feel that I am due to become very unpopular with your family when they hear what is toward… I wonder whether I ought to play the Victorian son-in-law-elect and write myself so that you won't get all the brunt of family displeasure.

With a spot of luck this new job might prove the "open sesame" to my present financial shortage.

A new airmail service had just been introduced and suddenly John and I found we could get a turnaround in our letters of only 19 days.

This was heaven! But I still had to pluck up courage and tell Mummy and Daddy what was happening. Perhaps next holidays…

Guess what? I have two government departments "clamouring" for my services. This morning the Director of Education rang me up from Salisbury wanting to know whether I intended accepting this Domboshawa job and sounded very peeved when I said it was very likely. Then later in the day, came a letter saying that my temporary job here was to be extended for another four months at the same salary they are offering me at Domboshawa. Now I have just had confirmation of the offer from the Director of Native Education. I feel duly flattered by all this, but hope I have not annoyed the D of E to the extent of his refusing to have anything to do with me in the event of my wanting to return to European Education.

I am to have a house, which is still being built, all to myself – but I have to furnish it myself. This I imagine can be done fairly cheaply at the second-hand markets, but I can see that it will knock a fairly large hole in what money I shall then have. There are apparently two other bachelors out there and tennis seems to be the principal diversion.

Some fate seems to be compelling me into it and I can't help feeling that it will be the right thing for me, and I hope, for both of us. The Salisbury district is finer in many ways than this and doesn't suffer in the same way from lack of water. You must let me know darling if any of it sounds unpleasant to you so that I can start scouting around in other directions. This job is only temporary and I hope that if a permanent job comes my way it won't have anything to do with sanitary arrangements.

My letter back at the end of January 1936 seems a little unsympathetic and I obviously hadn't a clue where anything was! But at least, I'd taken my courage in my hands at last.

I am wondering whether you have gone to ………….. yet. I can't understand the name of this place – ever since you first mentioned it I have been very puzzled as to whether it begins with a D, B, S or an O!! Perhaps none of those – but your hieroglyphic might almost be anything.

I do hope you will like it there and won't find it too lonely and uncivilized. I am sorry John, but I couldn't help laughing at the thought of you as a sanitary inspector – it's absolutely marvellous. My Geography is appalling but I have some idea that Salisbury is in Northern Rhodesia – if

41

so, I suppose you will be a long way from Plumtree. If you are anywhere near Mufulira, do look up my cousins…

I broached the subject to Mummy yesterday. She had been talking about what I should do when I left Rippingale, so I realised that the time had come. I broke the news as gently as I could, that I contemplated coming out one day. I think she has somehow expected this, but is upset at the thought.

She sprang rather a bombshell on me by saying that things are rather bad at the moment and she really didn't think that they could afford to have me at home without a job. Apparently with Daddy's illness, locums and assistants, it has been hard for them to keep going. How I do agree with you and loathe this constant struggle for the filthy lucre… it is abominable that it should be so necessary to one's living. It makes my blood boil — all our relatives are so well off and spend their money on such ridiculous things when there is a family here who could do so much better things with it… they don't appear to realise that.

Mummy has masses of common sense and thinks I ought not to be in a hurry to come out, but should try and get a better job after Christmas. At present I get the colossal sum of £70 a year from Rippingale — then I could save what I can and give you time to get settled. Very definitely I must come out sometime and see all these uncivilized spots, but I'm sure that once I saw you again I should forget about the heat, lack of water, insects and animals and any other drawbacks you may have. This is a great tribute to you because I'm simply terrified of bats, spiders, earwigs and all those horrible things, which I imagine are much more horrible with you.

I am already trying to steel myself to spend a night in the hammock in our garden by way of practice, but am sure I shall never do it!! My goodness John, if I ever marry you, I'll make you the most awful wife (I'm not proud of this — it's an everlasting sorrow to me) but I have no idea how to cook or sew or any of these things because I've been thoroughly spoilt and have always had people to do them for me… however with a certain amount of concentration I feel I could learn to do them so that I didn't make so many ghastly mistakes as I do at present.

John was now on his way to Domboshawa. I was rather appalled at the thought of our having to keep on writing letters to each other for another year, but then, I had never thought I would survive through one month, let alone the four it had already been.

I have rather mixed feelings about going, but I always seem to have those about anything I do. I do have a strong feeling that Native Development will eventually see me permanently established within its ranks. People insist on thinking that I am suddenly turned all religious and that I must be inspired by some great missionary zeal. People out here seem to worry too little about anything but their own welfare that they find it hard to realise that anyone but a missionary could possibly be interested in the welfare of the Natives.

One day I am going to write a book about it all and I have no doubt that many of my views will shock people considerably and will probably land me temporarily with complete social ostracism. When I arrived, the Native boys had just got back that day and I could hear the roar of their conversation as they were consuming their evening meal of porridge. I had a peculiar feeling then that this place would get a hold of me and today has not changed my views a bit.

The school grounds extend some 5,000 acres and the buildings are rather scattered. I am staying with the Principal until my house is ready. His house is really magnificent – perhaps we will inhabit it one day? The one I will have has a rather primitive design, but should be comfortable when I get settled into it. Everyone keeps talking as though this is a permanent job – 'oh you can occupy this place for a year until we can x, y, z...' Now that things do seem to have a more permanent look about them I want you to consider very seriously and cool headedly what you would be undertaking if you came out here to join me. I don't want to say too much in case you decided against it, but will put it in its blackest form so that you will not be dreadfully disappointed.

This place is of course still very largely experimental and as such is all the more interesting. It is an important place of its kind and is well known throughout the continent. Its work is almost equally divided between industrial and academic training and one of its main objectives is to try to build up an educated community among the Natives. Unfortunately we still have to fight hard against prejudice which is rife among the white population. It is slowly breaking down but will make the running of an establishment of this kind a fight for many years to come.

For the last few weeks I seem to have been able to think of nothing else but the fact that this job may make it possible for us to get married. But I want you to know what you are coming to.

I have been trying to imagine how you would like it out here. You'd probably have to take up gardening or keep fowls or something to fill in your spare time. In my imagination you fit here perfectly. We have already been for lots

43

of walks and strolls together, although you might not realise it and I always like to try to imagine you waiting in the house whenever I get back to it. It makes it all seem so much less lonely.

The thought of keeping fowls didn't fill me with enthusiasm. John had found that the cost of a return trip from Southampton to Salisbury would cost around £36 and he offered to go 50-50 on the fares, which would make quite a difference. Then quite an extraordinary thing happened. There was quite a celebrated fortune-teller in the area and although I didn't really believe in them and pooh-poohed the whole idea, I was eventually persuaded to go along with Trish and Jill Castle.

It was positively amazing – she said I was definitely connected with music and very fond of it, also painting and acting. This led to my being very sensitive but I shall get over that evidently.

Then she proceeded to say that I had met someone while acting, who was also fond of it and who had made me an offer to go abroad to some distant continent in the near future. This appeared to be in the nature of a romantic offer and though I was still somewhat doubtful about it I was to go because therein lay my chances of happiness and I mustn't be swayed by other people. The one who made this offer is very good looking (?!!) comes of a good family and has some kind of a government job which apparently on account of me, won't be permanent. I mustn't refuse this offer and I must learn to drive a car!

Driving a car was a problem – the rest I could cope with. In fact, my "sensitivity" had always bothered me, but now I found in John someone who was at least as sensitive.

How well I know your feelings in response to some wonderfully played piece of music. On the whole perhaps, I feel it less acutely than I do when I see some wonderful emotion or expression of moral courage shown on the stage or screen. You may think me peculiar but at times I have found that lump in my throat hard to control when watching some very dramatic act being played or when some similar situation occurs in a book. Convention dictates that the genus "male" should not give expression to his deepest emotions through the medium of tears, but I have often thanked the gloom of the cinema hall for hiding my very near approaches to that state.

Darling, you must never worry about your letters being full of "me" – that's just what I want – and please Miss Sugden, stop this confounded habit of running yourself down, I wouldn't stand it from anyone else and from you least of all.

I feel very strongly now that this is the job in which I shall spend most of the rest of my life. At times it rather terrifies me. The responsibility of a job of this kind is simply tremendous and at times I wonder whether I will really be capable of dealing with it.

So much is at stake if a wrong turn is taken and the foundations of Native Education being laid here will very likely form a model for the education of some one and a quarter million black people in the years to come.

At last the photos had come. I had been looking out for them for weeks. Then one evening walking home from the train I saw Trish standing at the gate waving a parcel. I tore it open in a mad excitement and gloated over the photographs, purring, 'Oh, isn't he good looking?' My blasted brother Dick picked one up and said, 'No I don't think so, he looks nice, but a bit shaggy.' He received a very swift kick for that remark.

It did make a difference to me, having the photo, as it was something tangible that I could look at and write to. I had forgotten what he looked like and it was a relief to see that he was as handsome as I had imagined. At last, encouraged by his photo, I made an appointment to have my own taken. It was something I absolutely hated, but because I realised what a difference it made, it was worth the agony… and I felt spurred on enough to embark on some cooking classes costing me 10/- (ten shillings) for the term!

John was certainly giving me a good impression of what life was like at 'Dombo' as he called it and his descriptions of the Natives playing football with bare feet and their wonderful singing and harmonies made me long to get out there as quickly as I could.

His letters were always full of deep and meaningful philosophy and thoughts and in one he had asked what I felt about religion. He had been very committed to the church and got involved with the Oxford Group while he was at Cambridge. Something or other must have happened to make him start to question everything. I seldom had faith enough in my own ability to comment on all this deep thought, but this time I wrote back:

45

All I can think of is – stick to that "childish and unquestioning faith" in a Deity until you find some very definite and equally unquestionable reason not to. One must have something to hang on to and that seems as good and perhaps a little better than any other. That sounds utter bunk and especially coming from me who knows nothing about it at all and rarely thinks of it without getting tied up in knots and giving it up for something easier.

I was looking forward to meeting his family – John appeared to be devoted and close to them all. He'd tell me where his brothers and sister were and what they were doing. I began, slowly, to understand his background. His father seemed to be a remarkable man as well. He was apparently contemplating retiring at the moment and this meant that John had been able to spend some very precious time with him.

He is a wonderful chap and I always feel duly flattered when people tell me that I am like him. He is the type of person whom one can take as a model on which to base one's own life and know that if you live up to it you can't be very wrong. Mentally he's as young as ever he was and has an extraordinary store of energy. His mental youthfulness will be the saving of him when he comes to retire, as it is never easy for anyone to see another person taking over work on which one has spent 30 years.

My job really was awful – I'd be working 14 hours a day with hostel duties and prep and it all seemed such a grind. I would still have pangs about my own musical career and one night went to a most marvellous concert with Adrian Boult and Myra Hess. She played the 4th Beethoven Concerto and something that I usually played at about quarter the speed. I found myself suddenly wishing that I had spent more time on my music and with that my old longing to be a decent pianist or composer came washing back over me.

I always wish I could have gone on with my dear Victor Booth who held out a few hopes for me. However if I had, I shouldn't have met you and that's the one thing for which I bless Rippingale. If I hadn't taken this lousy job I would have been either at home or miles away and there would have been no "Burglar and the Girl" – at least there might have been, but not for this girl.

As time went on, we seemed suddenly to lose our sureness of each other.

My old boyfriend Jackie Lindsay started paying me some determined attention and I wrote and told John about it... which caused
him great agonies. Then I worried that he would find someone else
and he worried back that I would do the same. I wrote and told him
that if anything caused him to fall in love with anyone else, I would
immediately devote my life to good works and become a nurse. He
replied:

*During the past year your presence out here has become a habit of mind if
you see what I mean and I can't conceive of anyone taking that place from
you. But we must both be sane about the whole thing and try to take the
best course. At any rate, I shall not bring you out here on a wild goose chase.
If my "wicked old heart" does betray us, I shall certainly let you know even
though I shall hate the thought of your becoming a nurse.*

The King was dying. George V had been a wonderful and much
beloved monarch and the nation was glued to the radio as the BBC
told us: "The King's life is drawing peacefully to a close." Little did I
realise that John was doing the same thing and that even in the colonies
there was widespread sorrow. I wrote:

*I should think he will be missed by more people than anyone in the world
before. I feel terribly glad that I was born and have lived during his reign.*
   *I don't want to go back to Rippingale – this is the lousiest and coldest
term of the lot. Wish to goodness I could creep away and hide and not go.*
   *Do hope there'll be a letter from you in the morning saying whether it's
OK for me to come in August as I must make my decision about leaving the
d....d place tomorrow. Daddy has been very nice and said that he would like
me here in the summer and will help me with the "wherewithal" for coming
out. This is terribly sweet of him and I feel that my mind has been made up
for me.*

There was a letter – and it said August would be just perfect! The
die was cast. John was thrilled that I would be coming out at last and
it looked as though I could put the money for the fare together all
right. It was a restless, unsettling and difficult time... but now all I had
to do was to wait it out and try to learn as much about John, his family
and his background as I possibly could.

Chapter 4

Thatch, pookies
and barefoot performers

The mosquito net swung and billowed as strengthening gusts of wind funnelled through the stable door. The candle spluttered, almost went out – then flared again. Suddenly, the net spinnakered out and a sheet of flame shot up towards the thatched roof of the hut. As a two-year-old, John remembered very clearly the fascination of watching this happen. Fortunately, his beloved governess Didi came in just at that moment or he would have been incinerated.

'You'll never rear that child,' was the opinion of the tough little local nurse, as his mother Harriet coped with yet another racking dose of infant dysentery. John had several near fatal brushes with death in his early years, but somehow always pulled through and came up smiling. As I came to know him and he told me of all these escapades, I became more and more certain that he'd received direct divine help during that fragile early childhood, so that he could carry out the important work he had to do.

John was born at Plumtree, a small village near the Southern Rhodesian border with Bechuanaland, now Botswana, about 100 kilometres south-west of Bulawayo. It was not an easy place to bring up any child at the beginning of the 20th century because it was hot, dry, primitive and isolated. Despite this, it was a relatively healthy place to live because its location on the watershed of the Rhodesian highveld, meant that it was considerably higher than most of the surrounding grass and *kopje* (stony outcrop hills) countryside. Being so dry meant there were few mosquitos and therefore less of the most feared killer of the time, malaria.

Plumtree started life as a railway siding in 1897 and the school became a reality a couple of years later. In 1899, the Reverend Nelson Fogarty wrote in the *Mashonaland Quarterly*, "It is a terrible thing to think of all the gangers' cottages along this line – miles from any church – full of children brought up without any religious instruction. There is a great need that a man should be constantly travelling up and down, holding services at every place and visiting every cottage along the line."

The first school lessons at Plumtree took place in a railway coach, which was left at each siding for a few weeks at a time. Lessons were erratic, entirely dependent on whether the coach happened to be in Plumtree or elsewhere along the line.

The earliest known inhabitants of the area were the Bushmen who left a legacy of rock and cave paintings on vast granite surfaces scattered through the countryside. They were small, light-skinned hunter-gatherers, perfectly at home in the veldt of southern Africa and able to read the signs and warnings of nature like a book.

These defenceless little people were hunted and chased into the inhospitable deserts by the larger, cattle-owning Hottentots in the 17th century as they moved down through central to southern Africa, on the look out for new grazing. They were in turn, moved out of the region as recently as 1837, by a strong and warlike invasion of a Zulu breakaway group.

Mzilikazi was a chieftain within the army and royal family of the great Chaka. After a violent argument with the aging warrior chief, Mzilikazi stole many head of cattle and led a splinter group away from the Zulu base in the lush tropical lands of modern Natal. Over a period of many months, they fought, conquered and moved their way north, ultimately settling in an area straddling the border between today's Zimbabwe and South Africa, to become the Matabele or Ama'Ndebele people.

Most of the villages around Plumtree were, at the time of early European settlement in 1886, inhabited by an offshoot of the Matabele, the Makalala tribe. The Makalala were serfs of the Matabele until European settlement when they were given equal footing under the government of the Chartered Company.

When the first white settlers arrived, it was tough, uncertain living and during the Matabele rebellion, a few years later, ten percent of that small settler population of the newly proclaimed Rhodesia were killed.

Farms and mines were left abandoned and rinderpest decimated the cattle. Disease, drought and locusts also took their toll. The small settlement at Plumtree remained relatively intact, but defenceless.

This was the reality of Africa at the turn of the century. It was a heartless land where conquest, rape and murder of one tribe by another had been part of the panoply of life for generations. But there had always been enough very fertile land for all and plenty of game.

The first European pioneers into this area were amongst the earliest into the country – a group containing mainly missionaries and prospectors. They soon came up against these strong, intelligent and warlike Matabele and life for both was full of uncertainties.

By the time the first train came through in 1897, treaties had been signed, concessions granted and a surprisingly amicable peace was in place. The European settlers were beginning to recover from early setbacks and morale was improving.

At that stage, Plumtree consisted of only a few shanties, a rough "eating house" and a general store. A certain Clem Estment started the store, trying to fill the demand for bread. He wrote: "... I dug out an ant heap and turned it into an oven, and the shapes and sizes of the loaves of bread that was turned out of it, would look like a curiosity shop to the modern baker today... from a 2lb empty golden syrup tin to a 4 gallon paraffin tin cut in halves – all sold by weight at 1/- (one shilling) per lb!"

The main pioneer column of 1890 had moved farther north into the better climate of Mashonaland to raise the flag in Fort Salisbury.

They left behind a frontier mix of explorers, miners, missionaries, farmers and hunters – many of whom had been there since well before official settlement and had no intention of moving on. There were some real characters amongst them, black and white, who became the stuff of legend for the youngsters of the future, and local names like Mzilikazi, Lobengula, Speke, Hans Lee and Livingstone are written into the country's history books.

Cecil John Rhodes, the new country's founder, died in 1902 only 12 years after the Pioneer Column reached the borders. Despite what populist history might write today, the recorded scenes of mourning and the extraordinary tributes paid to this man by the Matabele people at that time, clearly showed their respect for him as a great chief. Rhodes was carried on the shoulders of the Chief's Impi (select Matabele warriors) to lie in a grave chiseled from solid granite at his chosen destination, World's View in the Matopos Hills near Bulawayo.

By December 1902, in the depression that followed the end of the Boer War, and with the approval and financial assistance of Cecil Rhodes, Plumtree School was established by the Railway Mission of the Anglican Church to cater for the children of railway workers involved in building Rhodes' dream – the rail link from Cape to Cairo.

The school consisted, at that stage, of five huts built of poles held together with mud or *dagga* and with a roof of thatched mopani poles. They had stable doors and highly polished ant heap floors. The huts were based on a traditional African village design, which was cool and spacious, but they were quite a lot larger and ringed with verandahs.

The five huts were placed in a half circle and cost £40 each to build. One became the chapel, another the dining room, a third the dispensary and kitchen and the other two were used as classrooms.

John's father arrived to take over as headmaster in 1906, four years after Rhodes' death. The school boasted a sizeable administration block, a larger dining room and 44 pupils – boys and girls. There was now sufficient infrastructure for some of the original five huts to be taken over as the new headmaster's house and John was born in one of these huts, on 6th March 1910... the fourth child of Robert and Harriet Hammond.

Bob Hammond, or "Tambo" as he was affectionately known, went on to become a legend in Rhodesia instilling the best of British education and moral rectitude into his pupils in this far flung and remote corner of Empire.

The missionary lad...

Bob's father, and John's grandfather, the Reverend R. H. Hammond was a priest in the Church of England before, according to John, the Anglican Church was even thought of. He was one of a long line of educators and ministers or missionaries of the Christian Church in the family.

He was a largely self-educated but very well informed man who published a book of erudite sermons. He had tremendous concern for the less privileged – particularly for children. 'In those days, schools didn't really touch the lower levels of society,' John told me, 'and grandfather did a tremendous lot with the development of what were called "ragged" schools in the slums of Liverpool.'

He was working in a parish in Sheffield when he married Constance Gage, always known as Bonny. Bonny was of rather aristocratic lineage as part of the family of Lord Gage whose country house was near Lewes in Sussex. They were a devoted couple and had five children – two boys and three girls. Carrying on the family tradition, all five children were imbued with a great desire to do something worthwhile with their lives, taking them into the church and missionary field, in the Middle and Far East and then to Africa.

Clara, the eldest, married a priest, Walter Rice, and they spent most of their time as missionaries in Persia (now Iran), writing several books about their time there. Emily, or Aunt Em, the middle daughter, married a banker who was for most of their lives in Shanghai with the Hong Kong and Shanghai Bank. The youngest girl, Dot, was a very dear person who spent her entire life running a Christian mission for the Jews. It was only years later, after John and I were married, that I discovered that Aunt Dot was the same wonderful lady for whom I had dressed up as a Zenana woman to do tableaux on Eastbourne Pier!

John's father, Robert Woodward – always known as Bob – was born in Liverpool in 1876 and brought up in Toxteth at the time his father was working with the ragged schools. He was educated at Liverpool College and then went up to Peterhouse at Cambridge to take his degree in ethics and philosophy. After that, he spent time tutoring the son of the renowned artist, Val Prinsep, in Pevensey at the same time as his best friend Keigwin was tutoring Osbert Sitwell. Anthony Prinsep subsequently became John's godfather, giving him a beautiful silver rose bowl at his christening. Prinsep was well off and well known and owned a couple of West End theatres and Bob's life as part of that family was peopled with such names as Dickens, Tennyson, Browning, G F Watt and Rossetti.

John met his godfather only once when he was asked along to a "very posh" restaurant. He didn't remember much about the meal or the man – except that he tipped the waiter enough to feed a penniless undergraduate for at least a week – but didn't give John a penny.

However, they did discuss Bob of course and Prinsep said he clearly remembered, as a very young boy, seeing him with two others, having just been recruited into the Imperial Yeomanry, preparing to go out to the Boer War.

The family never heard much about his war, but at one stage Bob was taken prisoner. As the Boers could not feed them all, 800 of them were released with a few bags of boermeal and told that if they were seen in the next 24 hours they would be shot.

Bob managed to meet up with English troops despite a fairly severe wound to the right arm and hand. The rest of his life was spent coping with indigestion as a result of the undiluted boermeal and doing most things left-handed.

After the war, Bob returned to England, taught at schools in Eastbourne and Hull and while in lodgings in London, met a determined wee Scots lass not quite five foot tall, Harriet MacEacharn.

...and the vivacious wee Scot

Harriet, or Harrie, MacEacharn had led a very genteel life – with the exception of the last few years. Her father was part of a large Scottish family with tenuous links back to Flora McDonald, the lass who helped Bonnie Prince Charlie escape and a suitably infamous sounding Black Baron of Kilravock – a supporter of Mary, Queen of Scots. They were undeniably tough Scottish highlanders mainly from the isle of Islay – home of the "worrrlds best whuskey …"

Harrie's father, John James MacEacharn was an artistic, creative man who wrote, published and produced with great success, plays in the style of Shakespeare. Early letters talk of him with great respect and affection. He went into the family's shipping business which shortly after he took it over, was badly hit by the Depression. The business went under. A proud man, John was shattered by what had happened. He managed to wind up the company and pay his debts, but didn't live long after that. There is speculation that he was so broken hearted that he took his own life.

Harrie's mother was one of six children – four girls and two boys – and they lived in comfort in Glasgow. Her childhood was filled with tutors, music masters, poets and writers – all of which she mimicked and took off with glee and considerable talent.

The mysterious death of their father and an invalid mother who could not cope on her own, meant that Harrie, as the eldest, was not only penniless but burdened with great responsibilities. At this stage the youngest, Eila, was still a teenager. Harrie did what many other suddenly impoverished gentlewomen of her era seemed to do (including my own great-grandmother) and opened a boarding house. This time, it was not for medical students in Edinburgh, as Anne had done, but for the sons of gentlemen in Holland Park, London.

Bob Hammond became one of Harrie's boarders at the time he was tutoring the Prinsep boys. He was seven years her junior and it was an immediate attraction of opposites. The tall, gentle, academic young Englishman and the irrepressible, artistic and tiny wee Scot. Their courtship continued for a couple of years, during which time Bob went off to the Boer War. She wrote at the end of 1900:

My own precious darling boy, I was so glad to have a long letter from you last week and the photo, which is simply splendid. Of course it is a wee bit dark but you do look nice. I haven't seen anyone half so nice since you went away. I am so thankful to know that you are safe where you are tho' I cant help being just a wee bit anxious…

Then just before Christmas of the same year, she wrote:

It is hateful to think of Xmas being so near and that I shall have to spend it without you. I wonder why there was no letter from you last week. I wish I could keep from feeling anxious and miserable when I don't hear from you as I know it isn't always possible for you to write – indeed it is quite wonderful how you have managed to do so… (Bother! Here's that Frenchman coming upstairs to give Madeline a lesson and her ladyship has forgotten all about him and gone out to dinner).

Harrie's strength and character is clearly reflected even in these short sentences and Bob was blissfully devoted to her from the time they met. When at one stage, he plucked up the courage to send Harrie a cable saying he had received a job offer in South America. Her rapid reply read, "Choose South America or me!"

When his next offer came to live in Africa – as Harrie had always nurtured a vision of herself careering wild and free on horseback over the plains of Africa – she accepted gracefully. Their marriage and partnership was to become one of the foundation stones of European education in the new country of Rhodesia.

A new life in Africa

Harrie joined Bob in South Africa in 1903. He had a job as a school-master and was the local magistrate in Amsterdam in the Eastern Transvaal. Two years later, his friend from university days, H. S. Keigwin, recommended him for the headmastership of Plumtree at £300 a year, plus board and lodging. It was £100 a year less than he had received at Amsterdam – but it held such a challenge! As such, it was irresistible.

In 1904, Harrie at the age of 38 had given birth to their first child, Ian, always known as Skinny, followed by young Bob two years later. Only six weeks before Bob was born, they left for the long trip up to Plumtree. It was a brave move for a woman who had not been in the country long, who was now over 40 and who already had one small child to cope with.

They were at least able by that stage, to travel by train rather than the more usual and much slower ox wagon. But even this was an exhausting, dusty trip. The line had not yet been metalled so the engine would stir up a cloud of dust, which would envelop the rest of the train as it went round corners. Even with temperatures well into the 100s windows and doors had to be closed to contain at least some of the dust.

History does not recall what her reaction was to seeing Plumtree in 1906 – but she must have been horrified. Whatever she felt at first, she set about her first priority, which was simply carving out for the family a comfortable and livable home in the original old thatched huts.

The village of Plumtree at that time boasted a lively social life with a great deal of to-ing and fro-ing to dinner parties and *braaivleis* (barbeques). Daylight hours were hot, but the altitude meant that evenings were cool and refreshing, with a chance to discuss the tales of the day and to cook a hunter's kills over an open fire.

As smoke drifted into the night, plans were laid and projects put forward for this new and exciting country of such opportunity. For more sophisticated entertainment, soirees, supper and smoking concerts were "the thing" and frequently held in the "refreshment room". Increasingly, and particularly with Harrie's influence, the school came in to provide entertainment – tackling excerpts from difficult four-part Handel and Bach oratorios to bits of operetta or Gilbert and Sullivan.

Once Harrie arrived, the village had not only a pianist but also, its first piano. She had brought over a little Collard and Collard from England and every time the family went to the farm, the first thing that was loaded onto the ox wagon, was the piano.

She played by ear and she played all the time. She only had to listen to something once and she could sit down and play it and transpose it up or down, as required. In Plumtree there always seemed to be someone who would join her – Joan Lee was an excellent violinist, Harry Rowe a pianist and music teacher and some of the girls who were there in the first ten years became excellent musicians.

Bob Hammond had a very difficult job and recent archives endorse just how hard it was – especially for someone with the ideals he held for the young of the new country. He was a highly self-disciplined man; passionately fond of the school and devoted to his family. He was also supremely idealistic, a great thinker and hard taskmaster. Reveille was blown at 5.30 a.m. each morning with inspection and duties starting straight away. He was determined to produce boys of well-rounded character, high moral fibre and resourcefulness.

He was a great believer in his boys finding out about Native customs and cultures, the bush, farming and nature study at first hand. He also believed all boys should do manual work and they soon built the school's first playing and rugger fields in this way. He insisted that every one had to find their own strength, whether it was taking part in sport, in the highest academic practices, cadets, learning bridge and chess, debating and drama societies, the annual Gilbert and Sullivans or other theatrical productions. Within his first 18 months, Bob Hammond formed a Cadet Corps, laid the sports fields, inaugurated the first school sports, speech and prize giving days, started up debating and literary societies and had many new buildings either planned or in the process of being built.

Bob was also prepared, in the interests of the boys' development, to take the risk of allowing them a tremendous amount of freedom to go out into the bush – it was never abused in the 30 years he was at Plumtree. They were encouraged to go out and fend for themselves at weekends – entirely reliant on their own initiative and resources. They had to let the school know where they were going and there were heavy penalties if that was not adhered to. The only other stipulation was that younger boys had to go with older boys who took responsibility for their welfare and there were protocols about when they were considered able to "head up" a group.

Before these bush trips, the schoolboys would do extra work in the garden or on the new playing fields in order to earn salt. The Natives didn't like or trust money at that stage but salt would buy the boys almost anything they needed – like goats milk or what was then known as Kaffir corn.

The first coinage that became common currency to the Natives, was "mascotjiman" which was a florin or 2 shilling-piece. It was so called from the habit of certain people known for their thrift, in passing off a coin worth 2/- (two shillings) as being 2/6^d (two shillings and six pence). Mascotjiman would, however, buy a bag of milled corn and that, in turn, became the name for a bag of corn or mealie meal.

Apart from that money was regarded as a poor substitute for trading with the real thing and they had little time for it. By the 1920s the Native women began to wear long skirts made of "Mjeriman" (German) – a hardwearing blue cotton with a tiny white print. The men were more reluctant to adopt European clothing and until the late 1930s they always wore a *beju* – a skin hanging from the waist down the front and one down the back.

The Plumtree boys grew up speaking the language – they learned to track animals and they understood the traditions and respects expected of them when they entered the villages. The Natives were quite interested in this school business but it made no sense to them at that stage when young boys were of far greater value being trained as hunters and herdsmen of cattle.

Plumtree has, as a result, produced by far the greatest number of Europeans who went on to work directly with the Natives, in education or as Native and District commissioners.

In the first and second decades of the century, provisioning a growing school so far away from a centre of civilisation was extremely difficult. Masters and boys had not only to grow all their own foodstuffs, but in the early years to kill for meat as rinderpest was still killing the cattle. To provide food for the school, as numbers grew, so far from anywhere, the headmaster had to become a farmer.

Bob bought a farm, Bush Hill, which was half a day's ox wagon ride away, as a means of growing crops and, once the threat of rinderpest had passed, of raising cattle. But it also became a great holiday home and every school holiday was spent down at the farm – saving the family the cost of going off on holidays elsewhere.

In later years, Bob developed this further and bought in cattle and pigs, fattening and slaughtering them for the school. In order to do so, he had to raise a personal mortgage on an extra piece of land. This became a troublesome financial burden to him for the rest of his life and he had enormous difficulties educating his children beyond Plumtree and keeping up with the payments. Fortunately, most won bursaries or he would not have been able to educate them as he would have liked.

In his attempts to mould his charges to become men of leadership, Bob tried at one time, to change the school clocks to "Plumtree Time" – an hour ahead of others in order to make the most of the daylight hours. After a few months of complete confusion, he acknowledged defeat turned back the clocks and changed the hours of operation instead!

In 1912, the school acquired a carbide lighting system to give "real" lights to the chapel and schoolrooms while candles and paraffin lamps were still used in the dormitories. This new machine had to be pumped up at certain intervals and boys were designated to take responsibility for this vital role. The lights would grow dimmer – the hope and delighted anticipation of the children being that they would be plunged into darkness – before the boy on duty started pumping.

During Evensong one Sunday that year, the lights dimmed alarmingly and Bob, in the full flow of his sermon, said very firmly in the middle of an important theological statement, and without interrupting continuity in the slightest… 'Pump, boy, pump!'

In 1913, it was decided to close down the girls department of the school with the few girls going to a school in Marula, a village nearby.

By 1915, the school's reputation was such that it was growing at a great pace with boys coming from all over Rhodesia and surrounding countries. As it grew, the problems caused by its isolation grew in direct proportion.

Water had always been a problem, with tank deliveries awaited anxiously. Baths were allowed to be only 1.5 inches deep with bath water used in turn for garden and fruit tree watering. The wells and tanks were under pressure and constantly running out of water. On one occasion, after desperate pleas to the education department, with no results or acknowledgment, a water tank was hijacked from a passing train to keep the school going.

A desperate shortage of money was an ongoing concern – and with it the ability to attract good teachers to a perceived "uncivilised" part of the world, *"with no guarantees of any continuous employment, no possibility of a pension and small opportunities of promotion."*

Things became particularly hard during the 1914–18 war as all male staff joined up. Bob had, to a large extent, to employ older retired men or women teachers who were not always the best at controlling wild young teenagers.

The famous benefactor, Alfred Beit died soon after Bob took over as headmaster. He had left £200,000 in his will, for "educational, public and other charitable purposes". There was a scramble from assorted power brokers – all with different ideas as to how this was to be administered. Bob played a pivotal role in persuading the Trustees to assign a fund to be put aside purely for the development of badly needed school buildings and infrastructure throughout the country. This was later on to be useful for Plumtree itself, as the present buildings could not possibly cope with the anticipated increase in pupils.

One of the first pupils at Plumtree in the days when it took both boys and girls, Muriel Baraf (then Furse) wrote, in her book *Recollections of Plumtree School*, of her return to the school in 1934 to take over as Matron of Lloyd House, after a gap of 17 years.

She relates some wonderful anecdotes.

My arrival in Plumtree as matron of Lloyd House… filled me with astonishment. When I last saw it, Plumtree was a dry, arid spot with a motley collection of buildings. Now, there were three houses for the boys, a dining hall with convenient catering department, a properly equipped hospital, bright airy classrooms, an administrative block, a fine Beit Hall with a stage and gallery, pleasant houses for the staff and studies for the boys; science and woodwork rooms, a well fitted-up laundry; three playing fields, several tennis courts, a squash court and a swimming pool, gardens, trees and lawns. These were the visible signs of an exceptional school, pioneered by a genius for making something out of nothing.

There was no water shortage now. Herbert Brooke, with a team of African workers was building the dam, which was named after him. The Hammonds now had a suitable Headmaster's house.

As an adult I came to know the Hammonds very well and felt part of the family. Things, which are now considered by many people as of prime importance, such as fashionable clothes and expensive, shiny cars, meant nothing at all to the Hammonds. They owned an ancient, derelict Ford and I think that every time I went with them in it something strange happened!

Mr. Hammond would always enjoy a joke against himself. One Sunday, during the evening service while he was giving his sermon, a "Christmas beetle" in a boy's pocket started singing. Mr. Hammond stopped and said, 'Will the boy who has a Christmas beetle kindly go out!' Whereupon the whole school stood up and trooped out of Chapel!

Mrs. Hammond was entirely without pretence; position and worldly possessions meant little to her. 'Och! What does it matter!' she would say.

As she grew older, she was given to little catnaps towards the end of the day. Bishop Paget had come to Plumtree and after dinner Mr. Hammond had work to do in his office, so left his wife to entertain the Bishop. As it was a hot evening, they took their chairs outside. When Mr. Hammond arrived an hour later, they were both fast asleep! The Bishop said afterwards that it was one of the most pleasant evenings he had ever spent.

Mrs. Hammond never worried about her appearance and I doubt if she ever troubled to look in a mirror. For a special occasion, she was once known to put on her dress inside out. When someone drew her attention to the fact, she replied, 'Och, never mind. The next time I'll wear it the right way out and people will think it's a new frock!'

In 1924, Plumtree was named by a leading educational publication in Britain, as one of the "top ten great schools of the Commonwealth".

Life in the Hammond family

John's earliest memories revolved around his beloved Didi. Didi Broomhead was the sister of William Bath, a man who was killed in the heroic but ill-fated Shangani Patrol. As a result she was given a 6,000-acre farm. Thinking in the early 1890s that the new railway line would come through Mangwe, thereby following the less steep route of the present wagon trails, she and her new husband chose a farm in the Bulalima Mangwe area.

No sooner had they done so, than the decision was made to bring the railway through Plumtree and they were left well off the beaten track.

They'd been married a short time when her husband, having got back from a day of shooting, tried to push some roosting chickens off a wire behind the house. For some extraordinary reason he held his gun by the barrel and used the butt of his loaded gun to do so – with the inevitable consequences.

Harrie now had five children (four of them born after she was 40), the demands of a headmaster's wife in an all-boarding school and her own substantial involvement in the music and theatre of the school. She was battling to keep up. She swept the unhappy Didi into the family in return for some help, particularly with the youngest three – John, Jean and Patrick.

By the time John was born in 1910, the family was large enough to have to move into all five of the original huts. In summer, as a very little chap, he would sleep out on the verandah of Didi's hut. He talked often of his delight at waking up outside the confines of a building, to the crisp cool air and increasing bedlam of an African dawn chorus. It was something he revelled in for the rest of his life.

The greatest sport for the five young Hammonds was the nightly ritual of chasing bats and catching white spiders which fell from the mopani poles onto their beds at night – gaining great satisfaction from the screams of terrified mothers, aunts and teachers alike.

At the age of four, John was sent to the village prep school with old Mrs. Cowling – known to everyone as "Ganzie". She scared the living daylights out of her pupils. Fortunately, their Aunt Eila was another of the prep school teachers and soon after John arrived, she took over as Headmistress.

Eila was quite a different cup of tea – she was loved and adored and the children probably got away with murder. She did have an uncanny knack of opening up the marvels of nature, the universe and creation to her young charges. She always had a chameleon hanging around on a branch, a "rikki tikki tavi", or mongoose being cared for and a warren full of assorted hares and rabbits. The children were encouraged to adopt *nagapies*, or night apes, as their pets. These were tiny little round-eyed possum-like creatures, which nestled neatly when fully grown, into the top pocket of a shirt. They'd mostly sleep during the day but would cause absolute havoc bounding about and catching insects at night. Most children had their own *nagapie* or "pookie".

In fact, the tradition spread into the highest grades of the senior school, and shirt pockets during the most formal of school Assemblies and events bulged with sleeping pookies. A spreading wet stain was often the only sign that they had been in there rather too long!

Books, other than pure schoolbooks, were very hard to find and in a country where, at that time, every penny had to be spent very carefully, they were considered extravagant and flighty. Harrie however had other ideas. On one of her trips "home" she "smuggled" in some illustrated children's storybooks and the telling of these became the nightly ritual.

Wee McGregor was the favourite. Wee McGregor was a Scottish lad who found himself in all sorts of very Scottish mischief. His tales of adventure were dutifully read to them each evening in suitably exaggerated Scottish accents. It kept their love of Scotland and things Scottish alive, but probably as a result of having such limited access John never really enjoyed literature or reading. In fact, he found reading tedious, difficult and laborious and preferred lengthy debates with a variety of opinions expressed as his way of satisfying his craving for knowledge and information.

As soon as they were old enough all four boys slept and ate at the boarding houses, but home was always accessible.

The boys all went around barefoot – in harsh countryside with its *wag-'n-bietjie* thorns, snakes and scorpions. They never appeared unduly concerned and learned to live with the dangers as the Natives did. John's memories of those times were never of there being any danger – in fact he was always surprised to think that there might have been. Except for one incident when he was 12 or 13. He hadn't noticed a huge black cobra lying across his path until he almost stood on it and it reared back ready to strike. John froze. He managed to attract his brother Bob's attention without alarming the snake any further and fortunately Bob's shooting was very accurate. The snake was duly dispatched and carried home in celebration.

The five Hammond children were growing up to be very different. Skinny was athletic, captain of cricket, ultimately head of school and more adventurous than the rest. During school holidays he'd take himself off at the drop of a hat to the Cape to see his Aunt Madeline at Seven Rivers… and his siblings regarded him with great awe as a result.

Skinny's great friend was Denny Rackham, whose mother had died when he was very young. Denny spent most of his school holidays with the Hammonds and he and Skinny were always off on some ploy or other.

Bob was more intellectual and had a great affinity for animals. He was always to be found on a horse playing polo or riding in shows and he knew from a very early age that he wanted to be a vet.

Jean, or Jinny, was the middle child, and the only girl. She was classically beautiful and a great gymnast. But she was also the only one of the family who was unable to attend school with the father she idolised and her wonderful brothers all around her. Instead she was sent off to school in Bulawayo, then to Roedean in Johannesburg with her aunt Madeline's two girls, Rose and Diana. She bitterly resented it. There was no alternative, but it remained a sore point all her life and she always felt she'd missed out. Her solace was her friendship with John and his loyal protection.

John was the tallest and biggest built. He was gentler and more serious minded than the others – and always the man with a mission. He found learning from the written word difficult and had to persevere at it, but he played all sports easily.

Patrick was bright and a good sportsman as well as an actor and eventually gained a Rhodes Scholarship. As a child, he spent his time with the two Watson boys, Eila's children Bobby and Hugh, collectively known as the three "nippers". Eila took responsibility for bringing these three nippers up together but they, like the rest of the family, grew up in and loved the wider community of the school.

The five Hammonds, Denny Rackham, Bobby and Hugh Watson together with assorted others, particularly in the school holidays, formed a little flock which swarmed together at all times and got up to all sorts of mischief and deeds of derring do.

An essential and integral part of this large extended family were two Natives, Gwanda and Magettis who would take their turn to be all things to the children throughout their lives at home. When Gwanda wanted to go back to his village and plough, Gettis would come in and help.

This flock of children would spend a lot of time – all barefoot – down at the rocks by the river, fishing and swimming. Every evening, Gwanda, or Gettis would come and herd them all back. The littlest ones would scramble to take pride of place sitting on their shoulders or necks whenever they could after an exhausting day of play.

Their greatest joy was to go early to bed – but only once they had been promised they could "sleep out". Off they would go to bed until later on when mosquito and other activity had calmed down. The two Natives would pick the children up, beds and all and put them out in the garden. There they would sleep seven or eight in a row under the black African night.

Again, this love of and empathy with Africa comes through every aspect of John's early life. The non-stop noise of an African night would paint an audio sound-scape for him.

He knew by the screams and roars of a kill, each of the animals involved... he'd lie awake waiting for the inane and hysterical laughter of a hyena, the cough of a leopard or the bark of a *bobbejaan* (baboon) stealing mealies in the fields next door. And he slept, once he had heard the low, gurgling, abdominal rumbles of matriarchal elephants as they fussily marshalled their young around them to move off warily and silently into the night.

It was a carefree life where the children grew to know and understand Africa and its people by walking and talking, tracking and hunting with them. They grew up strong, fit, tanned and healthy, independent and unafraid, both mentally and physically tough – and they were taught to cope in almost any circumstance.

It was a carefree life... in a huge family – with aunts, cousins and friends, Gwanda and Magettis as the centre of John's existence.

The only holiday away from the farm that John had as a child was when he turned nine in 1919. The family went off to stay at a friend's house in Scottburgh on the Natal coast, for three weeks. But none of these little "bush" children were particularly interested in the sea or the beach – there was far more adventure to be gained from chasing huge fruit bats under the house.

John remembered his father as "a gentle, thoughtful person. As a schoolmaster, he was strict, but with a sense of humour... never severe in the sense of being spiteful and always with a measure of understanding of the boys which was really quite remarkable... and which endeared him so very much to everyone who was there."

But, he was always very much the headmaster – particularly, to his own children. The only time the children had a chance to be really close to him was during school holidays, when they would all go off by ox wagon to the farm at Bush Hill, 50 miles south of Plumtree. As they left the fold, they grew to know him through a series of wonderfully loving, concerned letters he wrote to them all as they went through tertiary studies.

My dear old John, he wrote in September 1929 when John, on his way up to Cambridge, stayed for a few weeks first, with his Aunt

Madeline at their beautiful Seven Rivers, near Constantia:

I know you were sure to be busy at Seven Rivers, but I want you to try very hard old man to improve in the matter of letter writing. The Mater does sacrifice a great deal of comfort and things which most mothers have in order that it may be possible for you boys to get the best possible start in life and the least you can do is to write regularly and fully to her. I do not expect that you will disappoint me.

We were very glad to get your telegram and we miss you badly already old boy. I must make a real effort to get Jean and the Mater to England next year to see you and the other two (Skinny and Bob). I do not think that any father could feel happier about his son than I do about you… my blessings on you dear boy.
Your devoted Dad

It was not considered correct at that time for men to show emotion, so open affection was never shown in public – most particularly within the confines of the school. Young Bob confided to John one day many years later that "he often wondered about whether Dad really liked him or not… until one day he was walking along and Dad came along and took his arm".

Bob was able to be much more affectionate to his only daughter, Jean whom he adored. She was not at the school itself of course, and it was quite acceptable to show affection to a lovely daughter.

Their bright, rotund and no nonsense mother, Harrie, was the perfect foil to Bob – she was the yeast to the dough, the sparkle in the wine. She knew just how to pop in the apt and realistic remark that would make Bob's dreams achievable.

She remained loyally Scottish to the end. John recalled with great love: "She was a remarkable woman… widely read – musically very well educated – with a great sense of humour and an abundance of love and affection."

She was the ideal mother for a family of five – or, as was more usual, fifty. The huts simply expanded to meet whatever was asked of them, whenever Harrie was around.

From this outpost of empire, she was the one who negotiated the rights to perform an annual Gilbert and Sullivan production using the boys and staff of the school and also produced and accompanied the first production in 1912 of *The Mikado*.

Plumtree's Gilbert and Sullivan productions were at that time amongst very few amateur productions in the world permitted to be performed outside London. The tradition continues today.

Very few people in Rhodesia were well off at the beginning of the 20th century and a country schoolmaster was poorly paid. Harrie had to use all her canny Scottish ways and upbringing to make the budget stretch sufficiently to feed the family.

John remembers his daily diet consisting in the main of mealie meal (ground corn – staple diet of the Africans) and *maas* (sour milk not unlike yoghurt), with chickens, game and the luxury of milk and cream when they went away for weekends and holidays on the farm.

Harrie of course provided a daily ration of oatcakes and scones, steamed syrup puddings and pies – all good sound Scottish fare… in the heart of Africa.

They didn't eat much in the way of fruit and vegetables – because there was insufficient water to grow them in Plumtree and they were so remote, that fresh produce went off before it reached them. Oranges and naartjies (mandarins) were grown locally – but people didn't seem to have fruit and vegetables as part of their diet to nearly the extent they do now.

John was a good Bisley shot and he grew to be a good hunter, going off with the two Rangely boys, both of whom became Provincial Commissioners in Malawi and Benjy Williams, a well-known local character in later life. They would make up a scotch cart packed with provisions and regularly go out shooting stembok for the school pot.

Once when shooting near Tjolotjo, John had the misfortune to fatally wound a female roan antelope with calf at heel. As he approached her to finish her off, he saw great tears running down her face. He never shot another animal for the pot or anything else from that time onwards.

The boys all wore khaki shorts, shirts, pith helmets and no shoes – in fact John did not wear shoes as a regular thing until he was 13 or 14. It suited the practicality of life at Plumtree. Shoes were hard to get and they wore out too quickly in those harsh conditions. It was a lot healthier to go barefoot.

Wagon trekking during the holidays was also a great highlight. They'd use a huge old wooden wagon with 16 oxen in the span. Their driver was a great old character called Casimoro – and he not only knew every one of the oxen by name but also each of their idiosyncrasies, including their likes and dislikes.

Casimoro would spend hours each evening, gazing into their soulful eyes and stroking their noses – telling them what lay in store for them the next day. He was invaluable.

They trekked very early in the morning, outspanning at midday and then trekking again until late in the afternoon. At night everyone would cut huge piles of grass for bedding and shape it up under the wagon for shelter. The softness and smell of that grass was heaven – its occupants, sometimes, less so. Beetles were the least of the problem – snakes and hairy caterpillars the worst.

Harrie would make scones every time they stopped, to feed all the hungry trekkers. It was a leisurely life, close to nature and they'd take turns to walk or ride on the wagon – usually travelling about 20 miles a day. The greatest problem was ensuring that there was enough water for the oxen. On one occasion going to Tjolotjo from Plumtree, there was a spell of over 30 miles with absolutely no water. But they had prepared well and were carrying plenty of water in huge drums on the wagon. However, as they slept one night and silent as the dark around them, a group of Bushmen came and pinched all the water. Nobody heard a thing. Not the cattle, the dogs or Casimoro – who was distraught and vowed to catch them and string them up.

They then had to do a forced trek, which was very hard on man and animal alike. But with Casimoro having great discussions and many instructions to the oxen the night before, they made it, with the moon guiding them to the banks of the Gwaai River. The animals drank gratefully and the family sat on the banks in silence, watching every ripple on that water for crocodiles. It was too late to be watering the cattle safely and to lose one of the oxen at any stage of the trip was a disaster. They also had to keep an eye open for wild animals – lion and leopard mainly – but apart from a few scares, they escaped with oxen, dogs and people intact.

Aunt Eila and Jean tried hard to make the wagon more comfortable for Harrie because she loathed every minute of it. They would take the seats out of the old Ford motor car before they left and prop them up on the wagon, but unfortunately they didn't sit level on the floor and she kept falling off!

John remembers her trying to sleep with an umbrella positioned in such a way as to keep the moon off her face. None of this extreme pioneer activity matched her upbringing and she never quite got used to it.

Sport played a large part in John's life – he was bigger than the average and was in the rugby 1ˢᵗ XV for five years, starting when he was only 14 – a record, which has never been broken. He seems to have progressed through school in a fairly normal sort of way but it was music and theatre that dominated his life. Skinny played the banjo, Bob the 'cello, Jean the piano, John sang and played the fiddle and Pat sang and played the piano. At Christmas they'd scrape out the odd carol or two and sing round the village.

At the age of 11 John sang in an eisteddfod in Bulawayo and won the top diploma for his rendition of "I can hear the Mavis singing". He wasn't impressed, demanding to know 'What's a bloomer?' (a diploma). The following year, he was asked whether he would like to go to the show or sing in the eisteddfod, he chose the show... the eisteddfod never stood a chance. However, he did sing in church and school choirs to Harrie's satisfaction.

Being a good and very natural actor, John rapidly assumed the leading roles in the annual Gilbert and Sullivan. From the girls' roles of "Little Buttercup" and "Katisha, he progressed to the male roles of "Frederick", the captain of the *Pinafore*, "Colonel Fairfax" and "Giuseppe" in *The Gondoliers*.

As he grew older and increasingly better looking, the sighs of girls in the audience grew audibly louder. To this day memories remain of the time he had to step in and sing Marco's tenor aria "Take a pair of sparkling eyes".

The Hammonds were away on leave (reminisced Richard Holderness, later a priest in the Anglican Church) *Marco and Giuseppe were to be my cousin Cecil and John. Cecil had a beautiful tenor voice, but he couldn't read music, so he asked me to help him learn the songs. I could play the tunes with one finger, and in the process, learned them too. John had a strong baritone and was expert at reading music and singing in harmony. A sad thing happened. Cecil, who was always up to some silly prank, managed to unlock the tuckshop and steal sweets. The Deputy Head caught him and expelled him from the school. This seemed to us an excessive punishment (I always felt Mr Hammond would have handled it better!).*

Anyway, I was told to take Cecil's place as Marco. I did not have nearly as good a voice and had never anticipated such an honour. John was very good and encouraged me and I greatly enjoyed singing those lovely duets with him – "Buon Giorno", "We're called gondolieri", etc.

We had a hilarious time once, as Jean had been pulled in from Bulawayo to teach us the Gavotte. We were on the rugby field and had to leave pronto. So there we were with our hob-nailed boots on the beautiful polished floor of the new house, bowing and scraping, gliding and circling. The Hammonds returned from leave and of course Mrs. H. had to accompany it. I think she knew the score of most of the operas by heart!

Having performed at Plumtree, the production was deemed to be so good that we were asked to perform at the Allan Welsh Hall in Bulawayo. I'd had a bad throat infection and managed to sing most of the songs in a rather feeble sort of way, but it was thought that I might break down in my great solo, "Take a pair of sparkling eyes". So during the interval I was told John would sing instead of me. His mother simply transposed it down for him, and quite naturally he stepped forward and sang it and I'm sure nobody noticed. As far as I know, he'd never sung it before.

The boys at the school were always being encouraged to use their initiative and to be prepared to step in at the last moment, or follow up on ideas they had. John had just been made a prefect when he approached his father to ask whether they could have a common room.

'Yes. Good idea – what are you going to do about it?'

So John and his fellow prefects designed the building, made the bricks, and built themselves a common room, parts of which still stand today following a succession of fires, usually started as a result of the licence granted to senior boys to smoke.

John ended up as head of house, head of school, cadet lieutenant, captain of rugby and captain of the 2ⁿᵈ XI cricket team. He also won the individual grand aggregate at Bisley. Academically he could have tried harder. He passed with what he termed an "adequate" South African matric – and then thought he should try the London matric, which he failed miserably.

Bob and Harrie had taken a term's leave at the beginning of 1927 – the first time they had done so since 1906. John was at this stage, the most senior Hammond child still at school and as such, had the responsibility for reporting on and looking after the farm at Bush Hill. This he took very seriously, writing about the problems of lack of rain, missing pigs, dipping cattle and planting mealies and red beans.

For some reason, which nobody seems able to determine, the whole staff of the school went on strike while Bob was away – the children were just told to go and play. A strike at that stage in Rhodesia was absolutely unheard of. John's only comment was:

This place has calmed down considerably since the holidays, so it is now pretty obvious that it was J and B who were at the bottom of it all.

Just who J and B were history does not recall.

By the time he left Plumtree in 1928 pupil numbers were up to 150. He had done well enough to have won a bursary from his father's old college, Peterhouse, at Cambridge University and he left in September 1929, to join brothers Ian (Skinny) and Bob in England.

John travelled over to England on the *Edinburgh Castle* with a school friend, and wrote home a little sarcastically about what he saw around him:

We are shut up in our little space like a crowd of fowls and in spite of the fact that there are only about 150 passengers all told the first and second class are nearly all too snobbish to mix.

We have six Rhodesians at our table… and the rest can't make us out as most of our conversation is carried out in Si'Ndebele! We had a topping time at Seven Rivers (Aunt Madeline's home in the Cape) and were both very much struck by the beauty of the whole valley. Being winter, everything was green and the flowers were too wonderful for anything… and the various shades of green with patches of red earth and flowering orchards made a wonderful sight.

When he arrived at Cambridge, he was fascinated by the fact that nobody at the University seemed *"as fanatical about rugger as we are"*.

He loved the buildings and the traditions of Cambridge and soon fell happily into undergraduate life. But he was not all that impressed with some of the academics he had to deal with, they must have been very different from the down-to-earth teaching at Plumtree.

Most of our lecturers are the funniest old birds one would wish to meet. The Biology man looks so utterly scared of everything and any joke on his part is welcomed by loud applause, no matter how feeble it may be. The Geology man must have been lecturing here for about the last 50 years. He no doubt knows everything himself but he is most annoying when he puts a diagram on the board and then only half rubs it out before he puts another on top of it. The result is that before the lecture is finished there are 19 diagrams all showing through each other.

So far everything is much as I had expected – very green, plenty of water, huge trees and a tremendous number of people, most of whom are females. There is an atmosphere, which is simply wonderful and everyone seems to have a bike, generally with a basket on the front.

I rather miss the store of raisins and sultanas and also the occasional pumpkin fritter straight from the stove, all nice and hot!

His initial impressions about the English people are revealing and reflect many of the reasons Bob and Harrie fought so hard to give their children wider learning. After a term at Peterhouse he wrote:

I am already beginning to feel the effect of a Cambridge education. Things over here certainly do make one think a great deal more seriously about the world in general. I can't help feeling that out in Rhodesia we do miss a great deal that the average English schoolboy has and also that we are so very much more clumsy, or rather, not so refined (if that is the word) as the average man who comes up here.

Nevertheless, I don't for one moment envy them in any way; they are on the average absurdly narrow and appear to have very little ambition at all. They apparently have not the slightest desire to go abroad, but are content to stay in cold, damp, overcrowded, good old England for the rest of their lives without any wish ever to see any other country!

Rhodesia I suppose is really extremely insignificant, but one would expect men coming up to Cambridge to have some idea as to where it is; four out of five have not the slightest notion where it is, except that it's in Africa.

Rhodes also has hardly ever been heard of by some, in spite of the fact that he is one of the greatest Britons of recent times.

I suppose this sounds funny, coming from me, but I find I am going through stages of alternate periods of what I suppose is homesickness and what I know to be absolute happiness. I have come to the conclusion that I really want a vac to show me how lovely Cambridge really is and I have no doubt but that after the vac, I shall be simply longing to get back here again.

John gained rugger and rowing blues, but was undecided as to whether to do Forestry, be a teacher or go into the Church – having got involved in the Oxford Group. By the time he left, teaching – with a somewhat missionary bent – had won the day.

Like his father, John did some tutoring for the sons of the rich and famous, then got a job at Aldro in Eastbourne, where he made a great impression on his headmaster Fred (Crispin) Hill, an enthusiastic amateur thespian. One of his pupils for a term was Kim Philby, who was to be notorious later in life, as one of 'the five' in Britain's most famous spy ring.

Just a few weeks before he was due to return to Rhodesia, prompted and urged to do so by Hill, and following a request from Mrs. Gladstone, John reluctantly made his way up Milnthorpe Road in Eastbourne. He was bitterly regretting his stupidity in accepting the role.

He was welcomed at the door and ushered into a cosy sitting room with a roaring log fire, to await the arrival of the girl who was to play opposite him. He noticed a little fox terrier observing him gravely from the corner. He went down on his hands and knees to purse his lips and produce a high-pitched squealing sound, which he knew intrigued animals.

As the dog bounced at him, he rolled over onto his back laughing at its excitement and looked up to find a slim, dark-haired girl with sparkling eyes grinning at him. He felt a strange sense of expectation as he jumped up to greet her.

Chapter 5

Pith helmets, PKs
and the Merry Mess

London was looking at its most beautiful with grass and trees an extravagant backdrop of green to the blaze of early summer dahlias and geraniums. Despite the ominous gathering of war clouds and the death of our much-loved King George V, 1936 had been a halcyon year for Britain – but it had been a long, long year for me.

I thought I would burst with the waves of excitement and apprehension that shot over me as I clutched my purse, with its precious £36 and flew up the stairs from the tube station. This would buy me a return voyage from Southampton to Cape Town plus the train journey to Salisbury and back.

I had to pay by five o'clock or someone else on the waiting list would take my passage. The underground train had sat stubbornly in the tunnel for what seemed to be an eternity as two other trains took their time going past us. I prayed for movement to get me there in time. At last we gathered speed inch by inch, the whine of the motors increasing till we drew into the station. I was first at the door, then out and running up the stairs.

Now at only eight minutes to five, the Strand Palace Hotel was in sight. I rushed up the steps, arriving flustered and dishevelled into the calm of the elegant foyer with its footmen and its slowly opening doors. Observing all the niceties and walking as fast as I dared, I burst into the Thomas Cook office just in time to pay for my booking on the *Warwick Castle* leaving on Friday, 4th June.

What a year it had been. As John's last letter had said:

I do think that both of us have done well to have kept up the chain of letters and for my part, I feel so very glad that neither of us have tired of it or given up. Coming out on a holiday as you are, will not leave you with the strong feelings of a break in things, which I had on leaving. To you it will all be so new and I am simply longing to know what you will feel about it all. Don't let the train journey up from Cape Town influence you too far...

It had been difficult at first. Our early letters were full of the longing and anguish of a cruelly interrupted early relationship. We poured our hearts out to each other and John still pictured himself in, and longed for, the England I so loved. I dared to think that after an initial time back in Rhodesia, he would come back and we'd build ourselves a life in England. A life that revolved around my dream of John becoming the headmaster of a prep school of great repute – of course. I could see it all ... headmaster's wife entertaining graciously... a couple of beautiful children... both happy ever after.

That was 15 months ago.

Then came that awful middle period around Christmas when John was going to party after party and was quite obviously the much-favoured young beau of the city. Quite unmistakably and absolutely inexorably, I felt his heart turning again to Rhodesia.

The place is looking lovely at the moment and I feel my roots sinking more and more deeply into the soil of the country... but I never seem able to complete this picture without your taking the most prominent part in it. I often wonder if you will like it all...

He defined his growing interest in the massive task he felt had to be done in education of the Natives and of course, to the countryside. The countryside! It seemed to have an amazing hold on him and he wrote about it in almost every letter.

How I longed for you to see this evening my darling. We went in for sundowners with the Mylnes and sat on their front verandah. To begin with we had the charming evening light. Long shadows standing clearly out against a bright background. The stretch of lawn in front of the house cut up with cypress hedges against which some wonderful beds of cannas, zinnias, marigolds and petunias were growing. Looking straight down the drive, the rocks on the kopjes stood out wonderfully and some small birds with absurdly long tails squabbled in the gum trees… overhead small hawks were making their way westward one by one.

My hopes dimmed with each enthusiastic letter that came out of Africa. They died completely when he was offered a permanent job in Native education, which was exactly where he had hoped to be, at the Domboshawa Training Centre outside Salisbury.

When we started to write to each other, it took six weeks to turn a letter around – answers to eagerly asked questions seemed to take an eternity. Now it took only ten days, but even so, it was a disjointed communication – particularly when it involved details which would affect our lives. But as we came to know each other through the letters, the certainty had grown for both of us. As I began to know his strengths, his weaknesses, his insecurities, his determination and his idealism, I loved him more – even from this distance.

But now, as I paid for and contemplated the trip ahead I was very apprehensive about what I was doing and what it might do to my life.

Through it all, the overwhelming problem for us both had been that we were so short of money. John had to pay his father back for borrowings incurred during his time at Cambridge and then for a small car he had bought. He had decided he must help his parents with the extra mortgage on the farm at Bush Hill, which was a huge burden to them. Then there was always dear Didi, who'd buried her life to help support Harrie, John's mother, in the bringing up of the children… and who was now almost completely penniless.

Through this long, long time of writing to each other, we did manage to stay positive. John would let me know the smallest details of what things cost and how he was making out:

On Wednesday, I went into town to collect the month's groceries and to do one or two odd things. It is really wonderful how cheaply I seem able to live out here. The total cost to me this month, including clothes, drinks, smokes and a tennis racket restringing will be only about £8/10s… pretty remark-able when you consider that about 2/10s of that goes on booze and smokes! Another sweepstake is coming off soon…

Although he kept protesting that he was not trying to paint too glowing a picture of the country, I found myself swept up by his imagery. In March he wrote:

77

Slowly the moon came upwards, first a thin bright line along the top of the cloud and gradually climbing until its whole wonderful circle sat for a moment on top before leaving to turn the cloud top into a wavy and foaming sea.

It was one of those occasions when ordinary conversation seems petty and immaterial and even one's thoughts become atrophied in the intense sense of the realisation of the exquisite beauty of the whole thing. I longed for you then... because I feel you would not keep up superfluous conversation at the expense of such beauty.

I have always been a bit psychic, or perhaps intuitive is a better word, and I knew I'd be spending the rest of my life with John, so I disciplined myself to keep up with him in all regards – in my letter writing, my career, my descriptions, my learning.

Besides my full job at Rippingale with all the private lessons and classes of a music mistress as well as the boarding house and school games, our lives were extra busy, as we were looking after girl boarders, many of them with parents living abroad in India and the colonies. My day started off playing for assembly and ended late at night after prep, having taught all day. Often I would have to provide a shoulder to cry on for a homesick youngster or sort out more difficult and urgent problems for them.

The post arrived in the afternoon – after it had been to the two headmistresses – who must by then have had a pretty good idea of what was going on.

I'd occasionally go down to the front for a walk, or climb up Beachy Head, but apart from escorting schoolgirls to concerts and other outings, I led a pretty quiet social life at school. I would go home for the holidays of course, to our wonderful golf and tennis tournaments plus lots of dances and parties with all our friends. There was an absolute whirl of social activity in the Dengie Hundred every summer, but as winter closed in we tended to hibernate with only mixed hockey games to keep us busy. Daddy was not well and we no longer had as many concerts as we used to. The winter of 1935 seemed cold, bleak, cheerless and endless – except for golden moments when my "letter from Africa" arrived.

John on the other hand seemed to be on an endless round of parties all year round!

I have never known quite such a hilarious party – everyone was in just that mood which made things really enjoyable. The whole town seemed to go completely mad and many people from outside farms and districts were in. Some people never went to bed at all that night but went off to see the sun rise or went for a bathe in the very small hours!

I stayed in Salisbury the next day playing tennis at the Merry Mess and collected Mavis Nourse to join in with us. We were all very full of beans and I have seldom laughed so much before a few cool drinks cooled us down a bit and made us feel more like attacking the rather belated dinner which Miss Merry had for us.

When his letters arrived, I used to dread opening the envelope for fear of what it might contain. I must have expressed some concerns as his next letter said:

Your letter came this evening and what with your dreams of walking from Cape Town to Salisbury (1,600 miles I hope you realise) and your reactions to my little "nearly losing my heart"… I felt I must be more careful in future…

I am very sorry darling that I gave you heartbeats and misgivings but if anything serious crops up I shall warn you by putting a drawing of a "Ladykiller" on the back of the envelope. Quite how I shall represent it I don't know, but you will perhaps recognise it.

I only found out later that John was doing exactly the same thing and he would sit for ages before opening my letters, trying to gain a hint of what they contained from my habit of scribbling last minute thoughts on the outside of the envelope.

Our whole relationship had been made much easier for my wonderfully supportive parents, when they met up with an Essex cricketer and Secretary of the Essex County Cricket Club, called B.K. Caster. B.K. Caster was a well-known man of great integrity – and a friend for whom Daddy had great respect. Daddy often went up for key County matches to Leytonstone and did so specifically on one occasion as he knew B.K. Caster had just returned from coaching cricket in Rhodesia. There might be a chance that he had met the Hammonds, or at least knew of them.

Daddy was amazed to find that he had actually been coaching at Plumtree. More than that, he had just taken over as Chairman of the UK branch of the Old Prunitians Society (Old Plumtree Boys Club) and had even been persuaded to take over the role of "KoKo" in the inaugural Gilbert and Sullivan production of *The Mikado*. B.K. Caster couldn't say enough about the Hammonds and what they were achieving in that outpost of the Empire. With the ultimate accolade of the time, Daddy was repeatedly assured that they were a "tophole" family.

John and I had agreed before he left England that we must wait a year before becoming engaged or anything more permanent. However, because Daddy was ill and it was harder to raise the money for the fare, it turned into a long, long 15 months before we saw each other again. Mummy and Daddy knew that I was saving up to go out, but they hadn't yet actually heard from John until, thankfully, in January, he wrote:

Dear Mrs. Sugden,

I do hope you will forgive my not having written to you before this. I can offer no excuses except to say that I found it extremely difficult to know how to justify my attempt to get Nancy to come out here.

I want to ask you and Mr. Sugden if you will agree to her coming out here so that she may have a chance to see the country. If it appeals to her at all, could you consider the possibility of her remaining for an indefinite period?

So far as has been possible, I have tried not to give her an exaggerated view of the country's charm and I hope she realises that there are drawbacks to it. At the moment, I regret to say that I have not as much to offer her financially as I would like to have. But I have heard today that I shall very likely be given a permanent job in this department…

My chief regret is that her coming out will rob you of her and I can realise only too well what that will mean to you. I do hope you will forgive my trying to take Nancy away from you; but I shall do all I can to make her happy out here.

At about this same time, Bob and Harrie decided to leave Plumtree after 30 years at the helm. They knew it was time to move on, but they were both institutions of the school by now and it was a tremendous upheaval for them as well as for the people they would be leaving. Everyone tried to persuade them to stay "just a little longer…"

John went down to the annual sports day, held over Easter in 1936. For Bob and Harrie, it was to be the last of these memorable events and it became a formal *valete* to them both. Three hundred people attended from all over the country and in the time-honoured tradition, all the schoolboys gave up their beds and camped out in the grounds, while parents and VIPs slept in the dormitories. John wrote:

The weekend in many ways was rather trying, being the last Sports at which Dad and Mums will be there as the Head. There was much speechifying and several presentations from parents, old boys, school, staff, village and others. I shall send you a copy of the paper, which might prove of interest to you.

The journey down on Thursday night was far from pleasant. The train was packed and we had five in our compartment giving us hardly any room to move. We got down about 11 o'clock, swam, played squash rackets and caught up with long-lost friends.

On Saturday we had the first day of the sports in the afternoon and dinner in the Hall that evening, at which numerous and lengthy speeches were made preceding "The Gondoliers" put on by the school. It was well done, though the lengthy speeches left the wee brats dressed up on their war paint for such a long time that they were dead tired when the show started.

On Sunday there were the normal Chapel services for Easter Sunday followed by a presentation by the Old Boys to Dad and Mums. They gave them a lovely suite of office furniture which, as the family have very little in that line of their own, will come in very useful.

We followed this by a beer fight at which great quantities were swallowed and which put most of us into a state unfit for anything but sleep!

In the evening, Dad gave an address to the school and spoke better than I have ever heard him (see Appendix 1). *How they have managed to stop themselves breaking down is more than I can say as they are both feeling this departure very much. The Governor came down as a special effort as it was Dad's last… in the evening H.E. gave out prizes amid more speeches… all very moving.*

One of the country's poets, George Miller wrote a poem entitled "After 30 years… RWH":

and so the last hymn fades, and in the quiet he turns and moves away; there's an end.

so is the last word written when the book is done, so the last rivet driven and made fast;

so, when the agony of hand and spirit's over, is the last stroke made and

the wet brush laid by
    and while each maker knows the sober joy that bathes the spirit when the
task is ended
    in such simplicity, his heirs unborn enter their heritage. So man grows rich.

I began to understand what made my John when I read some of
the eulogies written by old boys and politicians, judges and priests.
One of his staff, Arthur Cowling, wrote:

*Hammond's main guiding principle was a belief in freedom for his boys in
both thought and action; and he was always prepared to defend this principle, which was consistently pursued.*

*   Boys were encouraged to take a close interest in and to discuss fully all
current affairs, not excluding political elections and any other local contro-
versial issues. He believed in taking a "Newspaper" period with every form
in the school for such discussions, which constituted a valuable training in citizenship. And he fostered self-government and personal responsibility in every
branch of school activity.*

*   He delighted in argument and had the faculty of not allowing the strongest
official disagreement with a master to affect personal relationship.*

*   We might feel at times that discipline was too slack; particular instances
would lead to an exchange of strong views, addressed officially; the correspondence would end with a note: Dear .... come and talk this over on
Sunday afternoon.*

*   The talk might go on from early afternoon till late evening, covering a
walk of miles and one came away feeling that even if all one's arguments had
not been adequately countered, one was assisting a sincere and lovable man
in an interesting experiment, in which his view might after all be the right
one.*

On a more personal note, I was interested to find this lovely letter
from the same B.K. Caster of English cricketing fame, who had assured
Daddy that by marrying a Hammond, I would be in good hands.
When he heard Bob and Harrie were leaving Plumtree, B.K. Caster
wrote:

*If any man and wife can leave a job (however much it hurts) with the
wonderful affection and love you two have earned, I do think they could
really in true sincerity say in so far as their work is concerned "Nunc*

Dimittus". This may sound effusive, but my dears, how much from my heart
it is meant.

May you both have many years before you. I don't wish you the love of
people because you have that in abundance. You made Plumtree and to many,
even those that never had the luck to serve or be at school under you, the
spirit of Plumtree is everything that the world and Southern Rhodesia so
badly needs. Humility, loyalty and the love of service.

I wish so much that I could be with you. I know how the whole thing
will affect you. You two taught me more than you and I will ever realise. I
do know there is a lovely warm feeling when I think of you and my life with
you.

I was looking forwarding to meeting this remarkable man – and his
equally remarkable and redoubtable Harrie.

John was concerned as to how they would adapt to life outside such
an institution as a country boarding school that demanded the whole
of their attention. His comment about the office furniture made me
realise that they had precious little furniture or anything else of their
own as they had lived in government houses with government furniture all their lives. It was going to be a major change for them both and,
sensibly, they decided to go off and catch up with their children in
various parts of the world before they decided where to settle. Bob to
see Skinny and Morrie in Sarawak and Harrie to visit Bob and Mollie
in Kenya before going on to England to see Patrick.

My letters still seemed trivial compared to John's, full of rather
meaningless chit chat, while his revolved around his present disillusionment with traditional Christianity and his philosophies on the
directions of the world and most particularly, the situation of the
Natives in Rhodesia. In passing, at the end of May he remarked:

Jack said that Brown of Tjolotjo will be leaving in two years time and he
seemed to think that I might get that if I cared to apply for it. Actually I
would not be at all keen on going there even as principal and more particu-
larly so if you were with me. It is miles in the wild and the rest of the staff
there are rather an unpleasant crowd, I gather.

Meanwhile as the time for me to leave England drew near, John's
letters from the school at Domboshawa became more excited, yet
oddly cautionary about what I might find.

It is all so marvellous that I find it hard to think coherently… next term there will be several houses on the place empty and I may manage to get one of them and have Jean here… Mylne will almost certainly ask you out… with the car down in Bulawayo… large party have arranged a four- or five-day camp in the Matopos… a bit concerned about your line up in Salisbury… might take in the Falls on the way… don't come out here prepared only for hot weather… bring tennis kit and golf as well… must tell Patrick to see something of you before you leave…

Unfortunately my arrival was going to be about six weeks after Bob and Harrie left Plumtree.

I do so wish you could have met them this time. They are a dear couple and I am sure you will love them when you do get to know them. You must be warned, of course, that in Mother's eyes, there is no one like her family; but fortunately she is now used to them getting married.

And now at last, as I waved my dear family goodbye, I was on my way… and in two and a half weeks time I would see my beloved John in Bulawayo.

When I arrived at Southampton, I was delighted to find I had a four-berth cabin, with a porthole, all to myself – the other three people had cancelled at the last moment and they had been unable to fill the places. It was very lucky as the boat was packed. I thought the whole thing was stunning, I'd never seen anything like it. The sheer size of the ship, the palatial, sweeping staircases, huge dining rooms, the meals and sports rituals – and the non-stop parties.

Within a day or two I had made firm friends with a South African girl, Stanser Wilkinson, who had been training to be a doctor in England and was now on her way home again. We played every deck game there was, entered the fancy dress and crossing the line ceremonies, danced the night away and spent long hours pondering and fantasising about what the future might hold for us both.

My first step onto foreign soil was at Madeira. The ship anchored in the bay and we all stepped into precarious little boats to go ashore. While waiting to leave the ship, young men and children shouted up at us to throw coins into the sea. 'Small boy dive,' they said. When you threw the money, they'd dive and catch the coins as they sparkled through the water – holding them up in triumph, with a great grin.

Madeira seemed to be an island of cobblestones. When I stepped off down the road, the buckle on my shoe promptly broke. We then climbed up endless steps, step after step after step – almost impossible with a broken buckle. We did end up at a magnificent hotel with a fantastic view and I found a Portuguese family who sewed it back together again. They didn't want any payment but I gave them a shilling in gratitude.

We had a lively crowd of young people on board and one of them, who lived in Natal, was on his way out to take over the headmastership of a prep school in Bulawayo. I hoped he might be going up on the train – but no luck. In fact, there didn't seem to be anyone else who would be going up on the train to Bulawayo and I felt the first qualms of panic.

Several of the other passengers seemed to think I was undertaking rather a tough journey on my own, and were not slow to paint the risks inherent in going to or living in such an outlandish place.

There was very little sleep that last night before the ship docked at Cape Town. Everyone was setting alarm clocks so that they could be sure to be up on deck in time to watch as the "fairest cape in all the world" came into view. I was up at dawn with the rest of them and will never forget my first impressions of this beautiful land. I had never seen a mountain of that size and was stunned by its purple presence – a massive backdrop for the emerging city clustered between its arms, its twinkling lights fading as the sun rose.

The bustle of finding luggage and disembarking, clearing customs and immigration and taking in all the strange noises, the smells and the completely different panoply of people was utterly bewildering. I looked around desperately for a face I knew. Nobody! Not a soul I recognised, not even a friendly face from the voyage. I panicked, then, thank God, out of the chaos and clamour came a wonderful, gentle man in a Thomas Cook's uniform – he had found me and would extricate me from the chaos, clearing my way and escorting me safely to the station, and on to the train bound for Rhodesia. It was a great relief to be on board and wave him goodbye.

This train was *very* different from the Southminster train. It was enormously long and I could only just see the steam swirling around what must have been the engine way, way down the track. Each carriage had eight compartments with six bunk beds and two with only three bunks. Each had a basin and a pull-out table and we all shared toilets at each end of the corridor which ran the length of the carriage.

We left at 4 in the afternoon and I found I was sharing the compartment with a missionary from Tegwane, quite near Plumtree. She was able to fill in a lot of detail about Plumtree – and the Hammonds. She was also able to interpret for me when the little mixed-race (coloured) man came in to make up the beds that night. I simply could not understand a word he said – in fact I really didn't think he was speaking English!

A four-note gong played up and down the corridors by a smiling Native man summoned us to meals and we would bump our way down the swaying corridors to the restaurant car where superb silver service meals were served – even to us in second class. This was rather different to anything I had known on the LMS, GWR or SR rail systems in Britain!

It was the perfect way to meet other people and we all sat playing card games or making up quizzes to while away the time. We occasionally had the opportunity to stretch our legs for a brief few moments at some of the stations we passed through – many of them little more than a concrete platform and a sign. With a great whistling from the conductor and a hooting, straining, puffing and shrieking from the engine, a reckless game was played, particularly among the younger men. They'd stand around on the platform, looking debonair and casual then at the very last moment, trying to be as nonchalant as possible, swing themselves up onto the now moving train. I hardly dared look – certain someone would be left behind, crushed by the wheels.

The train wound its way through the magnificent Hex River Valley, clinging to the mountainside and overlooking the vines, the magnificent great trees and the spectacular colours of the Cape's wine and fruit growing areas. I kept imagining Aunt Madeline's beautiful farm Seven Rivers, which John had described so graphically and which I knew was somewhere in this area.

Gradually the countryside changed and flattened out into the grasslands and veldt of the Africa of my imagination. Great miles of empty grasslands seemingly always with a line of blue hills in the background and with Natives wandering about usually with their herds of cattle. Another change – this time to the saltbush and scrub of the Karoo and the utterly endless and absolute dryness of the Kalahari Desert.

I prayed that Rhodesia was a little more attractive than this.

The train stopped, it seemed, at any excuse – miles from anything or anyone. Sometimes a person would appear tapping the wheels of each carriage – or the engine would fill up with endless supplies of water, shoot off steam and hoot a lot.

Sometimes it shunted back and forth picking up other carriages. This always seemed to be in the middle of the night. The engine would go past the window, waking everyone up, going choo choo choo choo chooo chochochochochochochocho. Then just as you were dropping off back to sleep, you'd be rattled and rocked in your bunk as it bashed and crashed into other carriages either picking them up or dropping them off. On other occasions it stopped for hours for no reason. It was always a relief to feel the gentle swaying of the carriage and the clicking of the wheels again not least because it would quickly send me off to sleep.

It didn't seem to matter where we stopped during the day for within seconds, there'd be a horde of little black children shouting and laughing. 'Penny penny penny, pliss… Penny penny penny, pliss… Penny penny penny, pliss… Penny penny penny, pliss…'

I had only ever seen one black man in my life before, one who came to Daddy's surgery with a dog when I was about ten years old. I remember being fascinated at the time… now I was surrounded – and having terrible difficulty telling one from the other.

We didn't see many wild animals unfortunately, but one day there was great excitement as an ostrich pounded along beside the train. It then moved right outside my compartment, for at least a good ten minutes – having no trouble keeping up with the train, and with its huge long-lashed eyes looking right at me. Fantastic!

With John and Rhodesia now so close, this last bit of the journey at the end of a 15-day voyage was almost unbearable in its slowness – the waiting and the anticipation was like a huge empty hole in my stomach. We started to climb up to what was known as the high veldt… and relief! It was a lot prettier.

Very tall, flat-topped thorn trees, plenty of grass, but with the countryside cut up by substantial ranges of hills and hillocks of huge granite rocks all tumbled one on top of the other. It seemed impossible that they didn't all cascade to the floor like marbles.

Three days and three nights after I had left Cape Town, at 6 in the morning, we would be getting into Plumtree. It was the first stop as the train entered Rhodesia. My excitement was so great that I was already dressed and staring out of the window as the dawn started to lighten the skyline, bringing the trees and huts into sharp silhouette in front of the train.

I had been up since 5 but it was now quite light enough to see… as the sun rose about half an hour before we were due in to Plumtree. The engine was working hard to pull us up quite a long steady rise and I had to slit my eyes to avoid flying smuts from the engine. John had told me that as we left the station, the train would run along right beside the school. Elise popped her head in just before 6, as she knew how excited I would be – and she was pointing things out to me as we drew to a stop.

Well! It wasn't much of a station! In fact, like many other places we had been through, there was nothing to see except a dusty old siding, the name "Plumtree" and a tiny little ticket shed. At this time of the morning it was deserted, except for the railway official who was walking up to the engine looking important, and a dog lying asleep by the fence.

Oh no, I was wrong. There was one man on the platform. He seemed to me to be typical of the white man in Africa that I knew from books and films. He was standing under a tree, wearing khaki shorts and a shirt, with a white pith helmet, or topee, on his head, and deeply tanned arms and legs.

As the train stopped, the man moved towards us and my heart nearly jumped out of my throat. It was John!

'But you're supposed to be in Bulawayo…' I said.

He just grinned as he reached up and gave me a rather embarrassed and very quick hug. I had to make arrangements to get off quickly. The important man told me I couldn't take any of my luggage as it was in bond for customs clearance in Bulawayo – still another 75 miles on. I pleaded for some overnight clothes at least.

Elise found a rather tatty old paper bag. I stuffed in a few essentials and as the important man was whistling and waving on the platform, rushed down the corridor with Elise promising to tidy up the rest of my baggage for me to clear and collect in Bulawayo. John thought it was great fun to see me coming off the train clutching only an old paper bag after such a long journey.

He gave me another quick hug as I jumped down onto the platform. I looked into his dear face and his eyes… and all I could think of was that I hadn't remembered how blue they were – or how thick and black his eyelashes were. Despite all, we felt very shy and formal.

I couldn't believe that I was at last seeing him again in the flesh. I was face to face with the real person... not the person I had created through months and months of letter writing. Suddenly, I sort of knew him again.... and recognised and understood why I had been so immediately attracted the first time we met. My fears about creating someone so perfect that couldn't possibly exist started to dissolve.

We knew each other far better than most people who were with each other all the time – for nobody would be able to talk, in the middle of running their lives, to the depth, or detail we had achieved through our letters. I felt overwhelmed that he had chosen me.

We walked slowly up the dirt road to the home of some old Hammond family friends, the Forresters. They welcomed us with open arms and had laid on a huge breakfast of fried eggs and bacon. I was very sad that I had missed the Hammond era at Plumtree by only six weeks but intrigued to hear all about them as this was, of course, their main topic of conversation. It was very obvious how dearly loved John's family were.

The Forresters offered me some toast. 'Have some butter,' Sheila said. I refused politely. 'Don't you like butter?'

"...you never eat butter with fried eggs and bacon – in England,' I said, rather lamely. They howled with laughter. John squeezed my hand and I knew he'd help me cope with these trivial cultural differences!

After all his descriptions, most things seemed comfortingly familiar. My exhilaration at being here kept me sparkling although I was overcome with nervousness. I felt they must all think I was pretty different and probably a bit pampered coming out from England and I wanted to show I was just as tough as they were and that I could cope with anything. Oh Nancy! Little did you know!

Sheila asked whether I'd like to "tidy up" and pointed to an outside toilet way down the garden path or the alternative, an enamel potty behind a screen in the spare room. I was secretly terrified that I'd meet a lion en route, but I couldn't quite bring myself to use the potty or let her know my misgivings either. So I declined the offer.

John had recently bought a smart little car with a dickey seat. Two of you could sit in front under the hood and two could sit in what was essentially the boot, but that meant you could sit out in the open. It was very fashionable and great fun. I hadn't any luggage so that was not a problem and off we set with lots of promises to come back again soon.

John had planned to show me round the school before we left for Bulawayo. After all the photographs and word pictures, it was remarkably familiar. I could imagine the childhood that John had had, and where certain events took place, and could see the enormous strides that had been made since his parents had first taken over in 1906.

It was now nearing midday and I felt I really should try to find a toilet. I found out that this was called a PK in Rhodesia – short for *piccanini kia,* or little house. I spotted one under a nearby tree and discreetly took my leave. To my horror the seat was running with fierce-looking, inch-long ants. I couldn't!

We were due to have lunch with a housemaster, Eric Turner, and his wife, so I thought my chance would come there. They had a solid-looking house but again she pointed miles down the garden. No thank you, not after seeing those ants. I decided to wait until we reached civilisation, or perhaps ask John to stop on the way so I could pop behind a tree.

Off we set. I soon realised that nothing was going to persuade me to get out of that car! No gracious elms or friendly hedgerows, no green fields or country pubs, this was wild animal territory and I was filled with stories of adventure and near misses in the three-hour journey to Bulawayo. The road was pretty rough – no more than dirt and very corrugated. I felt every increasingly uncomfortable bump. Then bliss. We moved onto a real Rhodesian "special" – the strips.

These were amazing inventions, unique to Rhodesia, and were designed to keep men in employment during the depression. The government couldn't afford to tarmacadam the whole road in a country of this size, so it simply tarred two strips of about 12-inch width – one for each wheel.

As something approached from behind or in front of you, you took your life in your hands and lurched off the edge of the strips – hanging on for grim death with two wheels on the outer strip as you passed in a great swirl and rush of dust. With the torrential rainfall they have in Africa there always seemed to be a drop of at least six inches between the tarmac and the dirt road. John was as skilled as the other drivers hurtling past and he chuckled at my, not quite so tough, alarm.

We arrived in Bulawayo just as it was growing dark. I had been astonished at the speed day turned to night as we travelled farther and farther north in the train. It was a case of sun-up one moment and pitch-black the next. Soon our lights picked out the name of John's sister's house, "Azulikit". I sighed with relief. After all the raw Africa I had just been through, this was a very English suburban name. It held endless promise.

A most attractive young woman came out to give me a warm welcome. Jean was dressed in a tailored pink jacket and skirt. She had lovely dark wavy hair with John's blue eyes fringed with dark lashes. Her John was very like mine, albeit a little rounder and rather jolly with a sparkling good humour and wit. We were ushered in and I was shown my room.

But by this time, I was in extremis!

'Could I go to the toilet?' I whispered as soon as politeness allowed.

'Of course,' she said and led me down the passage. She opened the door at the end and pointed out into the dark!

I couldn't believe it! Added to which, there is nowhere as pitch-black as the black of an African night. It was now a nightmare.

'I can't see it,' I said in as brave a voice as I could muster.

'No problem,' she said. 'Sixpence will show you.'

This was now a nightmare with indignity thrown in. Sixpence came with a little tiny lantern and I followed him, feeling vulnerable and stupid, down to the end of the garden in the blackest night I'd ever seen, stumbling and barking my shins on every conceivable object. I didn't dare look in case there were worse than ants on the seat, but by this stage I had no choice. Sixpence waited patiently outside while I finished. I looked for some sort of flushing mechanism but there didn't seem to be one anywhere.

I was very relieved, in many more ways than one, to be back inside the house!

The next morning, I was woken before sun-up by the shrill of the dawn chorus. I had never heard anything like it, from a deep booming echo, to complex whistles and twitters, which joyfully welcomed the growing light. I was fascinated by the fact that I didn't recognise one single birdcall out of all this panoply of African sound.

June was actually a wonderful time to arrive in Rhodesia. It was mid-winter – but a mid-winter unlike anything I'd ever seen. Every day, it would reach a maximum temperature around the mid-twenties, but was quite likely to go down to zero at night. Best of all – it never rained. It seldom rains in a Rhodesian winter – there are just a succession of endless clear, clear blue skies and crisp sunny days, for at least four months.

I was struck by the immensity of the space – the horizons with no end – you could literally see forever even in the slightly dusty air of the dry season. Distant views were fringed with deep blue hills – and every tree, apart from the ubiquitous gum trees seemed to be thorny and flat on top or drooping with heavy bunches of exotic daffodil-type yellow flowers.

From the beginning I related well to Jean and John. We laughed easily and often. My John had come out to be best man at their wedding and they had now been married just under a year. Jean was so like her brother – the family resemblance was extraordinary – the eyes were the most striking similarity and the finely chiseled features.

The house was very English in style except that it was a bungalow, which was unusual for me, as every home I had lived in and most of the houses I had ever visited were double or triple storey. It was spacious and airy and Jean left the windows flung wide open all day and nearly every day... even in the middle of winter.

My trip had been designed to coincide with the beginning of the school holidays. I soon felt quite comfortable with the two Johns and Jean, or Jinny, as she was known. We'd go into Bulawayo almost every day. It was a very typical colonial town of mostly single- and double-storey buildings but with immensely wide streets, designed to be able to turn an ox wagon and full span of oxen and with huge dips in them. It was like riding a roller coaster. I was told these were stormwater drains to carry the rains away. They were so huge that I couldn't believe they would ever need them. I was introduced to Dalton's tearoom and other local haunts and we went out for sundowners every night to meet their friends.

The women of our age all drank a lot of spirits! They swigged down their brandies and whiskies as fast as the men. There was no refined little glass of wine and I was at a complete loss. I was so determined never to be seen as a feeble, sissy Englishwoman or let John down in any way, that I had to try to drink something! The truth was that I had only ever had a mouthful of sherry in my life before. It took a lot of getting used to.

Rhodesian women seemed to me at first to be very tough and self-assured – with no "side" to them. But it didn't take me long to understand that their confidence and open mannerisms arose out of having to be pretty strong and independent in a tough country – and that underneath, they were very like the wives of some of our Southminster farmers. Most importantly, they all seemed pleased to see me and were very easy-going and welcoming.

Within a couple of days, we were off on a camp to the Matopos. This is a wonderful National Park 30 minutes south-west of Bulawayo, which is full of enormous granite hills and *kopjes*. World's View, as its name suggests, is one of the highest points in the park and was chosen by Cecil Rhodes as his burial site. I could imagine it as John described the scenes that took place, with the bravest warriors, the Matabele Impi carrying his coffin up to bury it in the hole carved out of the rock at the top. The area was full of interest and there was a lot of game around.

Just before I left England, I had bought a pair of special blue trousers as I had always seen pictures of women in Africa in trousers. I had never worn them before and felt very avant-garde. But my jaunty new self was short-lived as just after the camp started John told me that the Native people did not like to see a woman in trousers. He felt they were not suitable wear for a headmaster's wife in a Native school. Ah well, I was quite happy to give them up!

I had never been on a camp before – it wasn't the sort of thing we did in England, unless you were fearfully hearty – but it was all so easy in Africa. We slept on the ground in a row – about 12 of us – with Natives keeping watch all night and stoking up the fires to ward off leopard and hyenas. We didn't seem to need mattresses. I was a bit alarmed by the coughing of the leopards – they were very close, or it sounded like it. And we were pretty far away from civilisation. But, there was great comfort in numbers.

Something I hadn't expected was the noise of an African night. I didn't think I was ever going to be able to get to sleep with the constant scream of crickets, and the startled barks and coughs of wild animals.

It was amazing to lie out under the huge bowl of the sky – to see the nearness of the stars, which seemed so much brighter than they ever were at home – and to see the moon, hanging like a great lantern and flooding the veldt with light. John had written about it so often – now I saw what he meant. There is nothing, anywhere, like an African night... a huge moon, enormous stars – and noise.

After two hectic and sociable weeks in Bulawayo, we said goodbye and started our drive up to the country's capital city, Salisbury. The road was strips or dirt all the way and it was going to take us a couple of hard-driving days.

We spent a night near Fort Victoria, as John was keen to show me the Zimbabwe Ruins (later renamed Great Zimbabwe) and to catch up with friends, the Rothmans, because they had just tragically lost their 12-year-old schoolboy son due to a shooting accident.

They didn't know we were coming and we just arrived... but they were delighted to see us. I realised this was a feature of this country – just arrive and the last crust will be shared with joy and celebration.

Because they didn't have enough beds, John and her husband slept on the verandah floor while I shared Mrs. Rothman's bed. I woke up on several occasions to find her sobbing inconsolably. My heart broke for her. I was so glad we had come.

The Zimbabwe Ruins are quite extraordinary. At one stage, this was obviously the centre of some considerable regional significance. Now, it was merely a sizeable "village" of ruined three-foot-thick, dry-stone walls and conical monoliths. Nobody seemed able to pinpoint why it was there or when it was built. Speculation remains rife on dates, with some still believing in the romantic notion it might go as far back as the Phoenicians and the Queen of Sheba – others feeling quite sure it is a relatively recent Mashona tribal settlement of the Monomatapa era. There was an eeriness about the place which bothered me. I felt it had been a focal point for something frightening, or that tragic events had taken place there – and it was most noticeable that no birds whatsoever sang... anywhere near the Ruins.

Salisbury, by comparison, was the height of civilisation. A lot bigger than Bulawayo, it actually had one fully tarred road right through the middle of town – First Street.

We went straight through Salisbury and on to Domboshawa in our little car – which had done jolly well by then. I stayed with the acting headmaster and his wife, as John had to go back to work almost immediately. I liked the feel of this agriculturally based school and enjoyed finding out what they were achieving. But I felt a little ill at ease for my first few days, trying to find my feet and because I didn't want to get in the way.

From the moment I arrived it was as though John and I had known each other forever. My music and laughter seemed to do for my wise and rather more serious John, very much what the irrepressible Harrie had done for Bob. Although we had come from such extraordinarily different backgrounds, I realised there was a strong thread of shared outlook, moral values, love of music and acting and a determination to make something of our lives. I also realised our families were really very similar – just living in two different countries.

I began exploring the possibility of finding a music teaching job in Salisbury to keep me occupied while John was working. But within a couple of days of my arrival, a short man with a strong accent came knocking on my door. It was Albert Claer, the building teacher and he had come to ask me whether I would be able to teach his wife English. He had been in the country for a couple of years, from Germany, and had sent home for a wife a year beforehand. Mia was now eight months pregnant, could hardly speak a word of English and was very lonely. On top of all that, Albert spent most of his time out in the Native reserves nearby, teaching them a variety of easily adaptable building techniques. This was heaven-sent as it meant I didn't have to trek into Salisbury every day and could be near John at all times.

So I moved across and stayed with them. Mia and I related very well and I managed to communicate somehow. It made a huge difference to her. I couldn't believe that she had accepted this arranged marriage, never having met Albert before. Now she was pregnant, and largely because she knew so little English, had found life very lonely.

Domboshawa School had been named after Domboshawa Rock – a massive granite rock 18 miles from Salisbury. It was on the edge of the tribal trust lands and had been designed as a school where practical agricultural and technical studies could be combined with academic work to give the equivalent of eight years' schooling. It taught its Native students some vital new skills… crop growing and animal husbandry suitable to the region, carpentry, building, tanning, leather-work, metalwork and community health.

The facilities were magnificent. The school was well laid out with beautifully maintained buildings, plenty of gardens and lawns, sports grounds and a model farm. The school had become something of a showpiece not only for its physical attractions, but also for the excellence and calibre of the students it was producing.

They had recently been having problems with a real troublemaker on the staff and shortly before I arrived, John had written:

The Governor was out here again yesterday only a week after his last visit and brought with him two more of the English Peerage, Lord and Lady Manners. He has taken up the cudgels in Mylne's scrap with Edwards and

I gather that Mylne has won the first round and at last managed to get an assurance from Head Office that Edwards will be transferred.

Fortunately, Edwards had just been transferred to Tjolotjo and left at the beginning of term. It seemed to be a welcome move for everyone concerned. There were several young people on the staff of ten or so Europeans and we spent the evenings having sundowners and *braaivleis* (barbecues) round the staff houses.

Almost every weekend John and I would drive into Salisbury to stay at the Merry Mess – a huge old house with about ten beds, run by Miss Merry for Old Prunitians, or old Plumtree Boys. It was inexpensive and clean and he always knew somebody there.

We played a lot of high-standard tennis at Government House because John knew the incumbent, Sir Fraser Russell. They had found he was related to Harrie in some way. Sir Fraser held open house for a circle of acquaintances every Saturday so, again, we used to just drop in. No pomp and ceremony – just excellent tennis and very good company.

We'd often make up a party to go on afterwards and dance at the Grand Hotel or go to a film. Then, very daring, we'd visit the Ace of Spades, a pleasant nightclub – and a "topping" place to go at 3 in the morning. All very sophisticated!

One night, about six weeks after I had moved over to the Claers, there was a tap on my door. 'Ve go to Salisbury,' said Albert. Mia was in labour. I packed her up in the middle of the night, wishing her well and was thankful that she had learned quite a bit of English in the time I had been with them. She was terribly grateful and hugged me like a long lost friend.

I was due to travel to Northern Rhodesia to stay with Olive and Molly, the children of Mummy's sister, at their home in Mufulira. Mummy's sister Maud died in Malta when the girls were tiny and as a result they were brought up as an extended part of our family and were very dear to me. The train from Salisbury would take three days.

We were due to stop at the Victoria Falls on the way so I took the opportunity to see the Falls for the half-day the train was in the station. The spray, even at this dry time of the year, shot up into the air twice as high and twice as fast as the curtain of water that fell into the abyss. The Natives had very aptly called it "Mosi oa tunya", the smoke that thunders. I kept imagining what the explorer and missionary David

Livingstone's reaction must have been as he realised just what this "smoke that thunders" was. It was the most humbling experience to feel the might of all that rushing water – to see the placid beauty of the great, wide Zambezi River upstream and its frothing, wild turbulence as it squeezed and shot itself through rocky gorges downstream.

Mufulira was a small copper mining town at that time but, as always, with towns built and sustained by mines, it was beautifully laid out, with high-quality homes and gardens, leafy streets and wonderful clubs and facilities. Olive's husband Floyd Brooks was the Mine Manager and we'd go on jaunts into the Congo to have a drink in some little pub or other over the border – mainly for the novelty of hearing the Natives speak fluent French. Molly took me out on a boat on one of the country's biggest rivers, the Kafue, but I didn't really enjoy it as I was mesmerised by the enormous crocodiles snapping and surfacing all around us with menace in their lizard-like eyes. I began to realise I was not as intrepid as I liked to make out and this side of the country would always make me a little uneasy.

I was away from Southern Rhodesia for a whole month of my precious four months away and found myself impatient to get back to John, not wanting to waste another second of our precious time together. The time so far had been so busy that we hadn't really talked about any more plans for the future.

On my first day back, 1st October 1936, John met me at the station and we went to have tea at Sanders tearoom. He asked me again if I would marry him, and if so, what kind of ring would I like. I said, 'Yes,' and 'oh, something small and not too expensive!' I saw the relief in his eyes as I confirmed that he could go and choose something he could afford. It was the tiniest possible solitaire diamond, but to me it was priceless.

Next day was the annual sports day at Dombo' and Native parents were walking, bussing and riding their way in to the school from all over the country. It was a wonderful day that ran like clockwork with some good athletic performances – particularly from the runners – and demonstrations of gymnastics and dumb bell routines from the younger ones. After the prize giving, we all went to the Mylne's house to enjoy the increasing congratulations of our friends and acquaintances as they spotted the shiny new ring on my finger.

Mummy and Daddy had given their approval to our engagement, but asked me to come home again for a time to make sure that I was fully aware of what I was doing.

Another family, the Roelke's, asked me if I would teach their daughter Shirley correspondence school for the last couple of months of the term before I went home. So this fitted in perfectly and I loved teaching her in the gentle atmosphere of their home. It gave John and me plenty of time to see each other, to go out and enjoy just being together, to be thoroughly sociable and to start planning for our future together.

I assumed I would be coming back to live at Domboshawa. Now that I knew the place and its people, plus its easy drive into the city of Salisbury, I was thrilled at the whole prospect.

But while I was in Northern Rhodesia, John had been offered the chance to take up the position of acting Principal at Tjolotjo School. This was the place he had mentioned to me while I was in England, but he'd quickly dismissed it because of its location and other unnamed difficulties. Now, he had to cope with Edwards as well. But he didn't seem too bothered by that, as he had actually developed a reasonable relationship with him.

Tjolotjo was a similar school to Domboshawa but with the teaching of cropping and animal husbandry geared to the different soils and drier conditions of Matabeleland, south-west of Bulawayo.

John knew the area well, as it was not that far from Plumtree and as children they had frequently gone on hunting trips to Tjolotjo.

I had become a little wary through the references John had made to the place in his letters. As we talked about it more, it certainly didn't sound particularly attractive. Tjolotjo was in a very hot and isolated part of the country, riddled with a particularly virulent form of malaria. But the school needed the energy of a young man to get it moving after many years of changing principals and teachers and generally inferior performance.

We discussed it at length and I felt it was a case of "whither you go…" So in the week I left to go back to England, John accepted the position.

We agreed that waiting another year would give John time to become established at Tjolotjo and that I would be back in Rhodesia, ready to be married, in December 1937.

Chapter 6

Feuds, floods and
a sixpenny bride

I arrived back in England on 6th December 1936 to find placards and posters screaming, "The King to marry Mrs Simpson". It took me a few moments to realise what it meant. I had been so out of touch that I knew nothing about it and had come home thinking that the next major British celebration would be the coronation of Edward VII.

Trish and Mum met me at Victoria station. Oh! It was lovely to see England again – it looked so lush and familiar. What mixed emotions there were! Daddy really wasn't at all well – he had been diagnosed with pernicious anaemia and for such a debilitating disease, I was surprised to see him looking his usual, forthright and jovial self.

As I got home, there was a phone call from my old headmistress, Bert Brown. Would I be interested in taking up a music teaching position back at my old school, Hillcote, for two terms? Fantastic! I was delighted. I loved the thought of being able to while away the time working with her again – at Eastbourne – by that wonderful sea.

We had a constant stream of visitors bursting with questions about my adventures – and of course, whether I really was going to leave them and go out "to the colonies".

In January, John wrote rather apprehensively about Tjolotjo:

I seem to be hearing odd reports about that place. Edwards and Searson apparently do nothing except under Brown's orders, which seems an odd state of affairs. I don't want to add yet another breath to the somewhat troubled atmosphere already there and I shall wait to see what is in store for me when I arrive, as these rumours frequently require a lot of discounting. Must stop as a swarm of locusts has just invaded the place and we are all going out in our cars to chase them off the lands.

The next week he had arrived at his new post. He was excited by the challenge of going in as deputy… but had *very* mixed feelings about what he found.

Oh! My darling its blery 'ot. Compared with Salisbury, it's simply awful and any energy one has is simply sapped. It doesn't require any exertion to induce a trickle down the old spine… one only needs to sit and small artesian wells spring out all over one's person! I'm told that I am unlucky coming to heat as intense as this…

The road here was no pleasure… many bumps and dips on a very undulating track with all the ruts washed out by the rains.

I arrived about 6'30 and beyond the outstanding impression of flatness, I was quite taken with the place. There are some very lovely native trees about and the paddocks give very much the impression of English parkland. When the veld dries off and becomes its winter brown, this impression will be harder to maintain. Very few of the trees that have been planted have come to anything… I cannot make out why they have not yet started planting more native trees…

So far my darling, it looks as though Mather (Native Education Department Inspector) is going to be right and that I shall have a hard job here. However, I feel that there is an important job to be done and I can tackle it with a fair degree of success. Mr Brown has a passion for hard work and so far seems to be giving me as free a hand as I had hoped for. In fact it is very apparent that I am here to learn how to take over the reins when the time comes. The only problem is that they eat mountains of food and seem to imagine that a plate's edges as well as its bottom should be covered with food… I face gargantuan meals with a sinking feeling.

I have met the Agriculturalist, Searson and his wife, as well as Davids the clerk. He seems pleasant enough but is one who (I gather) has a high opinion of his own position and ability. He and Brown are not on social speaking terms. The Edwards household constitute feud two with the Browns… but they are away at the moment so I am unable to form any opinions of my own, other than those everyone is keen to feed me. The Native teachers are not back yet, but I gather they are a good lot, mostly from South Africa… it does seem quite extraordinary that in such a minute white community there is so much infighting.

Mather tells me that Brown will be unlikely to go on leave this April, but will probably wait till September pending retirement. The job will then fall vacant and it remains for me to do it well enough to make them want me to succeed him.

John's new house was being built and until it was finished, he would stay with the Browns and cope with their meals. It was a small cottage with a steeply thatched roof. It had only one bedroom, but was apparently very cool – the most important thing of all.

I am not yet sure if they are going to net it, but a mosquito net and an ample supply of flit will probably prevent the bugs being too much of a trial.

The "bugs" were obviously going to be a problem. The area was notorious for its ghastly tropical diseases – three virulent types of malaria, typhoid, hookworm and cholera were all prevalent at various times of the year. Keeping staff at Tjolotjo had been a nightmare so far, as they would get one of these diseases and never return.

John's first recommendation was for Sister Weir to be transferred from Domboshawa to Tjolotjo to prevent the schoolboys (who came from every corner of Rhodesia and its neighbouring countries) taking these virulent diseases home with them. She was a talented and dedicated nurse from the northwest of Scotland. We always likened her to Albert Schweitzer and she did just as important a job.

Boys have already started turning up, trying to make sure of places in the school and I can see that we are for the first time going to have almost as many as we can accommodate with some trouble selecting them. Brown has got the place going well now and it should not be difficult to carry on provided the staff work together.

Do try to see Mrs. Swanson – I gather that everything was a bit of a shock to her when she arrived, so you may find her rather prejudiced and not much in love with Tjolotjo. She paints by the way, so that will give you some point of contact.

I looked forward to meeting Mrs. Swanson and hearing what she had to say! Apart from all the work of starting up a new school year, there seemed to be plenty of time for the small white community to play golf, tennis and bridge. John didn't write as much about the

101

school's problems as I would have liked – I think he was concerned that it might put me off. Occasionally, however, I gained a glimpse of what he was trying to do.

We have some 84 tests to go through tomorrow and it looks as though we shall have record numbers for the coming year. I have severe concerns about our ability to equip them properly. There is a great deal to be done and I can see that much of my time will be taken up trying to get hold of equipment to fit out the classrooms to a decent state.

It will be a good five years before this place is decently fitted out with classrooms and dormitories and the building department will be taxed to its utmost capacity.

Mrs. Brown dropped a word today, which has made me think – though she may have spoken earlier than she ought to have done – to say Brown is so fed up with Edwards that they will probably leave before their time. She told me he was going to talk to me, but so far this has not come up. It looks as though they will go on leave in April and not return again… in that case I stand the chance of being in charge from April onwards…

He did seem pre-occupied by the feuds taking place between people on the staff and had been apprehensive about Edwards being on staff after his short experience with the havoc he had caused at Domboshawa. Mylne, the headmaster, had threatened to resign if he was not moved – it became such an issue that the Governor had been asked to sort it out. It seemed quite extraordinary to me from such a distance.

To steer an even course between the various people in the place is not easy and I have come to the conclusion that the only way to do it is to have ones friends outside the school altogether and to treat everyone within it as equally as possible. I have seldom seen such bitter hatred as the Browns have for the Edwards. I feel very sorry for the Browns. They have put their life's work into this job and have done some really fine work. Until the Edwards arrived, they were happy doing so – now they are completely miserable about it all.

I shall have to start taking regular doses of quinine with my sundowners, as the coming three months are the worst for mosquitoes and malaria. A bottle of quinine is on the sundowner tray as regularly as the other bottles in this place…

I am agitating hard for another teacher as it will be quite impossible to do full time teaching myself.

By February, it was apparent that the Browns were going to be off as soon as possible.

It looks as though I am to be left in charge of this place sooner than I had anticipated. Whether the same difficulties will come my way I can't say. So far everyone has been very affable, but I can see that one will have to follow a very careful course if trouble is to be avoided. I can now see Stark's point entirely, that it would be quite impossible to appoint any of the industrial instructors in this department to the position of Principal. They simply have not the background socially, educationally or culturally to carry out the job.

If only I could get old Choogie (John's cousin Hugh Watson) out here in Edwards's place I would be quite happy. Unfortunately he will be a hard man to move...

I am so tired of the discussion of personalities that I groan inwardly every time I feel the conversation going round in that direction... and it is distracting me from the really important work. Everyone here has cursed and criticised everyone else until I'm sick and tired of it and am longing to be in a position where I may be able to do something towards stopping it.

I had been back about a month when I received a letter from Harrie who had just arrived in England from her time in Kenya. She was now on her way to London for an operation and she had written suggesting we meet. I was very apprehensive. I knew so much about her and she seemed such a formidable character. She was mad about her sons and very fussy about who they married. Meeting her expectations for this particular son would be a major test. One Sunday about a week after her operation, I was to meet my prospective mother-in-law.

The morning dawned as a typically bleak January day. It was cold, dark and pouring with rain. As the train pulled into the station, it grew darker and more hostile. I nervously made my way up to the hospital, then started to try to find her ward.

'Nancy. I'm over here.' She spotted me in an instant probably having had her eyes fixed on the corridor for hours! I would have known her anywhere from all the descriptions and photographs I had seen.

She was just getting over a pretty big op but her eyes sparkled and you could feel her vitality almost before you said hello. I found she was much, much nicer than I could possibly have imagined or hoped. She was in a private room so I was able to stay for a good long time and we had a great afternoon roaring with laughter. We had such a lot in common – we were both very musical, from very similar backgrounds and both able to see the positives and the funny sides of life.

She had been staying with her sister Madeline south of London and was a bit bothered because she was due to go up to stay with one of her daughters, Rose, in Derbyshire. I asked if she would like to come down and stay in Southminster which was not quite such a major journey. She was happy to do so – and when the time came, Mummy and I went up to London to collect her.

She was supposed to be the one who was recuperating – but she was an absolute tonic. We had a wonderful time. She and Daddy played music non-stop in the evenings. We had all the Dengie Hundred farmers in to meet her – and many of them were Scottish, which thrilled her. She was a tremendous hit and they all got on like a house on fire. It did Daddy an enormous amount of good having her infectious personality around – in fact it was a golden, happy time for us all.

Harrie was so enthusiastic about everything, whether it was driving down to funny old Southend, or off to bridge afternoons. Mummy and Daddy felt even more comfortable having met her and I was touched when she announced that she would be cutting her trip short in order to be back in Rhodesia for our wedding. It meant a lot, as it was unlikely that my family would be able to be there.

I realised how much I had changed after my short sojourn into the colonies, when at a party, shortly after I had returned, my dear old friend Dick asked if I would like a drink and I said, 'Yes please – a whisky.' He was shocked! He covered it up by trying to say rather nonchalantly, 'Oh, I suppose you drink a lot of that sort of thing out there.'

But – back to reality: John's next letter was very depressing. Brown had applied for leave – but so had Searson. That meant that John and Edwards would be the only two Europeans on the place. He was under no illusions that the ingratiating manner in which Edwards was treating him at the moment could turn in an instant. He again lamented his inability to be able to get on with anything "important" because of the constant distractions of these personal issues. But, at least, his impressions of the pupils were encouraging:

The boys look a good crowd, very much smaller than they were at Domboshawa, in fact, much more of the schoolboy type and not so many men among them. There is an excellent coloured teacher here, Guinche, who has been in charge of the Academic side of the school and I don't feel he has been getting nearly enough support. The Native teachers seem a fairly good lot now that they are all back… some of them are grousers, but I am particularly impressed with Ramushu and Mothobi.

As John began to feel the isolation of Tjolotjo, he would slip into introspection and lacked the confidence I knew he would need to lead such a troubled school. I kept writing encouraging letters in an attempt to boost him. But they were not really much help.

Although I longed to go out and give him some moral support, the decision was made to marry on the 11ᵗʰ December in Bulawayo. It would mean another long year apart so I kept him in touch with my daily trivialities to buoy him up and keep him positive.

The rains had set in around Tjolotjo and seemed to bring another whole set of problems.

We left town at 2'30 and found the road very wet. In places we drove through water for hundreds of yards and some of the wee spruits were running fiercely. We only just made it across the drift and the whole trip took three hours, which was pretty good considering the state of the roads.

That evening, the Swansons and Von Memerty came in to supper and to play bridge. Jack (his cook) did very well though he was a bit slow in getting things on the table. He gave us such a spread that few of us were really up to playing bridge after it. He is a true bachelor's cook and likes to have his own way in the kitchen – and he suits me admirably.

A funny wee piccanin aged about 9 or 10 is also on my domestic staff, or rather he was until yesterday. I am not sure whether he is or not at the moment. On Friday he came to ask for a shilling to go to the store to buy a shirt. I sent him off with a note to Hawkins asking him to fit the wee chap out in something rather smarter than the things he was wearing. The pic was thrilled with these and yesterday morning at half past five, he crept into my room and asked if he could go on leave for two days. I grunted agreement, and the next thing Jack saw was the little nipper running away as fast as he could. When hailed he lay in a gutter and tried to hide. Jack swears he will not return… we shall see tomorrow whether he does or not!

Fortunately the footbridge across the river makes it possible to get mail, as I couldn't stand it if your letters were cut off for any length of time.

The next day the rains came down again, and this time the Edwards were nearly swept away themselves as they miscalculated the depth of the water. The Searsons had gone in to Bulawayo and now had no hope of getting their car back for as long as the rains continued. So, they had to leave it on the other side of the river, and cross over a perilous suspension bridge made of paraffin tins, carrying vast numbers of boxes and packages containing rations for the school. The lorry went to meet them.

The river was not passable for three weeks. This seemed to increase the isolation and with it the ridiculous feuding of the white staff.

Brown wants me in the office whenever he foresees anything, which might lead to a contretemps with Edwards. It might make for some sort of peace, as they don't get very violent when I am there, but it is rather embarrassing for me – and a dreadful example to the Natives.

I am beginning to realise that unfortunately, none of the European staff here are really schoolmasters. We have a cleric, a bricklayer and a farmer and they don't seem to have picked up a great deal about actual school life

A flock of inspectors will be out in a fortnight's time and I must bustle round in that time and get things shipshape. But we have been told to cut estimates – so what can a bloke do? There is so much to be done and now they will not allow us to use pupils on any of the permanent building – we will have to get round that somehow or, not only will we be unable to house the present complement of boys, but there will be no hope of expansion. Demand is increasing all the time...

Despite all that, I am getting quite fond of this place and with so much to be done, I cannot be bored. Being here in my present position has given me a great deal more self-confidence.

I also know that much of my changed attitude towards things is due to you. I can't really explain this, but you can have no idea, my darling, how it has all helped. Just knowing that you love me and that I love you, seems to have brought everything and anything within the possibility of realisation. It is a wonderful change from my old outlook and oh my darling, I do thank you for it.

But it seems odd to me that I have to take charge of this place when I

106

am so young and it needs a lot of thinking to make me realise that I am old enough to take it on.

I have had a minor tragedy this week, I bought rather a nice-looking kaross (animal skin rug) the other day and Jack planted the thing straight on my bed without first hanging it out in the sun. The result is that the night before last I was inundated with LICE above all abominable things and this has not made life any more comfortable. We also had some excitement when a buffalo bull appeared from nowhere and came right through the school grounds breaking down three fences en route. The staff and pupils rushed off with spears and knobkerries to try to run him down but without success.

I must awa' my pet to deal with the very antiquated lighting system – few of the lamps work properly and there are not many of them at that. I anticipate a laborious and very messy job. I will then go over to Brown's for a bath as Jack is off this afternoon and I have let the bath fire go out, so my two paraffin tins of water have not heated up!

Oh, how I longed to be with him, mosquitos, malaria, buffalo, paraffin-tin hot water heated on a bath fire or antiquated lighting systems – though I was not too sure about the lice or all the feuding going on. Time seemed to be crawling past, but I was thankful that I was at Hillcote and not back at Rippingale. I suddenly found I was in demand by groups like the WI (Women's Institute) as a speaker on my experiences in wildest Africa.

By April, Brown's resignation had been accepted and speculation was rife as to who would succeed him. It had still not been formally announced that John was to act in his stead, which was making things pretty difficult for him.

They can't help having a fairly good idea as I had to spend all Monday and Tuesday in the company of the inspectors. I don't suppose they will give official intimation of it all until a day or two before I have to take over.

I intend to take Mum's advice and scrap for the things I want. I have it fairly clear what I do want and don't intend to give them very much peace until I have got it. It is a sad indictment that they have not had a single principal in this department who has not either been kicked out or left because things were made too hot for him. The fools at the top have been to blame principally and I hope, by now, that they have learnt sense and will give me the powers without which no one could possibly run a place of this kind.

This afternoon after lunch I lay down and read "Goodbye Mr. Chips" and it made me realise the drawbacks of this work compared to a similar job in a European school. From this place, I can't hope to get the satisfaction that Dad must have had out of Plumtree.

Any intimacy or real friendship with the boys is practically ruled out. So there could never be the same satisfaction on retiring from here, of the feeling that homes exist throughout the country where one is not only welcome, but where the person occupying that home would be definitely annoyed if it were not visited. It is very sad.

I am alarmed by the state of things in Europe. Ye Gods, what are we coming to? It makes me shudder to think of it and you must get out of England before the storm breaks. There are few things, which escape the Natives at the school – they are avid readers of the newspapers and enjoy our current affairs sessions. I find it hard here to justify the actions of Europeans and if the real truth were told there are cases where no justification could be found.

One day, a woman with a very South African accent phoned up and introduced herself as one of the staff wives at Tjolotjo. It was Mrs. Searson. She wanted to come and meet me and take me out to tea in Eastbourne. I was rather pleased. But when she and her family arrived, I found that they had such strong accents that I couldn't understand them.

They seemed so terribly out of place that I was aghast – and so was Miss Brown when I tentatively introduced them on our return.

'Your future staff…?' she asked with an eyebrow raised.

Oh dear. There was going to be more adapting required than I had really thought about – my focus having been simply on being with John – with little consideration for anything else.

John wrote on 1st April:

Well darling, today I took over from Brown and am now the blooming Principal! Tomorrow I make my first public exhibition by taking prayers and Mather will probably say a few "appropriate" words to the school on Saturday. It's all very exciting and I feel horribly important, though I'm trying hard not to appear so, but to be as much the same as ever.

Thank you, thank you and thank you again my sweetheart for sending that cable. The strain of being Princ was just beginning to make itself felt when the postmaster rang and said I had a cable from Eastbourne. Pessimisti-

108

cally I thought of tonsils and road accidents and a variety of other possibilities when he went on "Good luck from Nancy." For the first time in a year, the Principal's office rang with song!

I had a very charming letter from Stark (Director of Native Education) in which he says all kinds of flattering things:

"...and now Brown has gone and you are saddled with the responsibility. It is a big task you have to face, but the Government has every confidence in you. I wish you every success in your new job. The Prime Minister, the Secretary for Native Affairs, the Public Services board, to say nothing of your humble servant are expecting great things of you. Good luck in it all!"

It makes me realise how very important this position is and I can only take a large gulp, plunge right in and trust that I live up to their expectations. Stark was probably rather clever in sending a copy of his letter to Edwards.

If variety is the spice of life, my present existence must rank with the Indies. During the day, I have taken stock on the farm, counting cattle, sheep, goat and fowls; I tried to diagnose some ailment in a sheep's foot; I gave orders for the slaughter of two oxen for meat, and distributed some vegetables; I acted as paymaster and discussed hospital and equipment; I chatted on the relative merits of native poles and sawn timber for roofing and gave orders for the construction of two new verandahs; I reviewed the possibility of increases in pay for some boys and took in complaints about housing conditions; I made arrangements for the loading and dispatch of our lorry to town, had to refuse five boys permission to go off to act as choir at a wedding... and on top of all this I am supposed to be a schoolmaster.

Then on Friday, Rev. Fish was to have come over to take the service. The rains of the last few days stuck him in the mud and the job fell to me. My sermon did conform at least, to my idea of a good sermon in one respect – it was all over within ten minutes, interpretation included!

Yesterday when I should have been writing to you, I went over with Searson and Mather to Ihlobo – the school farm on the other side of the Gwaai – to look over boundaries and to get the hang of the place and know, more or less, what land we have over there. We went over in the school lorry which has a hard seat – no more than a board with about half an inch of very squashed-down padding, and bumping over the very bad roads there sent us back with seats on which it was very painful to sit!

I am a wee bit distraught at the moment. One of the standards has just given me a list of complaints against their (Native) teacher and I have had to give them all a sound ticking off. He is an excellent fellow and I have *hopes for him. I'm afraid I almost lost my temper with their demands… and do hope it has the necessary effect.*

I was having increasing bouts of tonsillitis – something that had started while I was in Rhodesia. Eventually my doctor said they had to come out. I arranged for this to happen at the end of my two terms of teaching at Hillcote. I wanted to be fit again, as John had given me £50 to spend on things for our new home – and I wanted to be able to enjoy and savour every second of doing so.

The next letter from Tjolotjo was much more pragmatic.

I have now been in charge for a fortnight and things are settling down more to the way I want them. I am scared of being too new-broomish and am trying to go carefully and to make improvements more in the less conspicuous, but nonetheless important parts of the place which are in such a shocking state of affairs. Things seem to be getting a fairly good move on and I hope they will continue to – above all, we have so far avoided any open conflict on the staff. I have felt that my first job has been to get the blighters to work together. So far they are doing it and I hope will continue to do so. One has to tread carefully and draw upon amazing reserves of tact.

Edwards, who has been the thorn in the side of so many people in this place and at Dombo, is so far doing fairly well. He is one of those unfortunate men who want to try to run other people's jobs as well as their own and who before very long, almost certainly runs up against those over him. He may now be disposed to go more carefully, as he got a letter from Stark which, as good as said "any more trouble and out you go".

I am now simply itching to get hold of another teacher. Treasury has authorised his appointment but it's a bad time to get anyone. I want to change the whole timetable to what I consider will be an excellent one… and am fortunate in having seen Dombo and this place in action and to find the weak points in both and try to put them right.

I had now had my tonsils out and was heading towards the final few days at Hillcote. England was gearing up for the coronation of King George VI and the red, white and blue was in evidence everywhere in flags, bunting and celebration. Everyone was taking the day off to celebrate the coronation and so, funnily enough, was John. His reports about the events, which would be taking place in Tjolotjo, were amazingly different from mine. I loved every thought of it.

Once our sports day is over, and replies are now pouring in, we will have a huge Native dance at night. Beer and beef will flow freely that night and I hope that they will succeed in keeping away axes and knobkerries from the party as they are rather liable to be put to use when the party gets warmed up a bit. It would be a pity to have a number of cases of culpable homicide following on to what ought to be a day of national rejoicing!

It looked as though he really was going to have to take Harrie's advice and fight tooth and nail for everything he needed. Tjolotjo seemed to be pretty far down the list of priorities as far as the head office of the Native Education Department was concerned.

Isn't it amazing? After all the good reports by the inspectors and assurances from head office about the importance of this place – a letter came today cutting our estimates for the coming year to shreds and we shall be unable to have much on this place that is not absolutely essential. I have been simply furious all day.

A young heifer from the farm was brought in this evening, cut about horribly badly by wild dogs, and the poor brute had to be slaughtered. The only bright spot in an otherwise awful day was your letter… and your poor throat was so sore and you were bored stiff and longing to get out. I longed to be with you…

How wonderful it is to think of you, when these darned fools in Salisbury put clumsy boots on top of one's pet schemes. If only we were within 20 miles of that place things would be so much easier.

We are such a convenient distance away that we can be easily quashed by the use of terrifying official jargon and any further correspondence leaves one little better off.

I am longing to have Stark in my sitting room for an hour or two… I have spent the last two days writing letters and minutes to Stark and am expecting to get some real raspberries back. However, I have covered them all with a private letter and hope that will ease the tension a bit. I have tried to make so many requests that he will feel bound to come down here to talk things over!

I am going over to Plumtree to fetch Sheila Forrester who is coming to help out with all the celebrations of the next few weeks, and the Mylnes (the previous head of Dombo' and now headmaster of Plumtree) *will also come and stay a few nights. 12th May is Coronation day and the*

following weekend we have the show and the sports against Tegwane. Prepa-
rations for that will be going on all this next fortnight.

By now I had completed my two terms of teaching at Hillcote. So
I was preparing for the next great adventure in my life. But first I had
some money to spend.

At that time every single thing in Woolworths cost 6d. So I managed
to get wine glasses, china, cutlery, kitchenware, great china vegetable
bowls and serving plates – everything I could possibly think we might
need – and nothing for more than 6d. each. Then of course, they all had
to be packed up and sent off in two huge tea chests. It was great,
because Mummy and Trish were able to share the excitement with
me. I was very conscious that they might not be coming out – and
secretly panicked at the thought that I might not see them for years if
we were too poor to be able to afford to get back.

Wedding presents were flooding in by this stage and they also had
to be packed up and fitted into tea chests. As time drew near for me
to leave, it became apparent that Daddy was far too ill to come out for
the wedding. Although Mummy would have given almost anything to
come, she didn't feel it would be right to leave him. Dick was at veterinary college in London by this time and Trish was still at school. So I
was going to have to go out and be married on my own.

John was getting close to the staging of his first speech and sports
day. In fact, it was the first of its kind as he was determined to try and
introduce much the same feeling as at the Plumtree sports weekends.
It did seem to me to be an amazing undertaking in such an inacces-
sible part of the world.

Jinny will be out to act the hostess and there's a busy time ahead for us all.
On Sunday I have to give a sermon, on Wednesday a Coronation address
and on the following Monday a speech to the assembled guests at the show.
At the show of course, I shall have to spend my whole time with H.E. trot-
ting him around the place and showing him everything. Perhaps we shall
manage to get some things done; it's wonderful how things move when
Governors are hovering around the place!

I must try not to drop any bricks and to speak circumspectly, but I fear
that it will be hard for me to keep in some of the things that I really feel.
With luck H.E. should come by air and that will be an added excitement
for everyone.

The programme is roughly 10'30 to 11'00 tea at my house. From 11 to 1 some sports events and exhibits to visit. Boys will be working on their ordinary tasks so that people will be able to see what goes on here in the normal course of things.

There will be a class going to school, the tanners will be tanning and leatherworking, carpenters, builders and farmers will all be at their respective jobs. From 1'15 to 2'30 we have lunch and after that the last of the sports events takes place, ending up at about 4'00 when most of the people will disperse and return to town, leaving us to get down to a good old sundowner party.

We have at least eighty VIPs coming, which is really quite exceptional considering the distances they have to travel. We have issued them all with a road map warning them of the areas to avoid – I tried to make it comical, but was afraid that it might succeed in putting everyone off coming. However, they seem prepared to tackle it.

You'll be interested to know that a wire has just come in from Stark to say he will be coming down from Saturday to Tuesday or Wednesday. Evidently my various letters have taken effect and I shall be able to let off steam in good style.

John was horrified at the lack of facilities for the boys, the poor hospital and medical areas, the dormitories and classrooms. He was also amazed at the level of illness, which was now a very real problem with an exceptionally high absentee rate from malaria. Sister Weir desperately needed an orderly or assistant to cope.

I was constantly amazed at how he was able to get anything done at all. It was particularly hard to find teachers as Rhodesia had very few black people qualified to teach at that level – so most of the Tjolotjo teachers were South African or had qualified in South Africa. The increasing pupil numbers were proving difficult and a lack of seating for evening work and prep meant Standards IV, V and VI were able to go into the classrooms only three days a week and Standards II and III for two days. Every boy had to rise at 5'30 for 20 minutes of drill and John would set off each day on his bicycle to take it. The show and sports day was going to be a real opportunity for him to tell a wider audience what he felt should be happening. When it was all over he wrote:

Sheila, Hugh and I went into town on Friday last and had a very hectic day, going round making purchases and arranging the hire of crockery etc. The sports against Tegwane started on Saturday afternoon and we lost I'm afraid in both the athletics and football – but we hope for better things next year.

While still rushing off last minute details for the show, people started turning up and left us all in rather a flap. The Gov. turned up by air much to everyone's excitement and we had a short trip round the school to see things going on. It was hard to tell what he thought of the place as he is a master at concealing his feelings – however he said pleasant things in the speech he made following my report and I hope he went away well satisfied.

The Bulawayo Chronicle gave a full two-column account of the day's doings and that must have played a part in putting the place on the map. Stark stayed on until Wednesday and Mather came out on Tuesday to have a general discussion of things. This made a lot of things much clearer for both of us and I will be going up to Salisbury next month for a week to attend the Inspector's conference.

Owing to my youth (he was 27 at that time) *and to Stark's going on leave in August, they may postpone my permanent appointment until January or February. This is rather a snag from the financial point of view, but must not interfere with our plans. If I am then appointed and Stark says that he has no one else in view at the moment – the appointment would be made retrospective as from October of this year.*

I think he was sincere in his confidence, and his desire to help.

Now that the hue and cry is over everything seems very flat and it is an awful sweat clearing up all the mess. We have been packing up the crockery to go back to Bulawayo and the last of the guests will take it with them. Then we shall be back to normal…

John sent me a copy of the report he had given at the sports day and I felt proud to be able to give it to my family and friends to read, so that they too had some idea of what he was trying to achieve. (See Appendix 3.)

After this, the time seemed to start flying past – everyone wanted to see my dress and I had to put it on every week for somebody or other. There were literally dozens of farewell parties, plus a "mock" wedding with cake and champagne for my family and dear friends who couldn't attend the real event.

By now it was November and the last-minute pace increased. The day before I left I received a beautifully drawn card of a little Scottie with a note in its mouth. I opened it to find a note from Dick Castle, which said, "I have heard that you are going far away and won't be

114

coming back. Is it too late to ask you to change your mind?"

Yes dear Dick, I'm afraid it was – but you and your family would always remain "almost family" to me – even 6,000 miles away in the heart of central Africa.

The reality that I was just about to leave became clear when I heard our darling old vicar, the Reverend Scadding trying to read our banns of marriage – he stumbled and fell and picked himself up and tried again! "…of the parish of Southminster" was of course, no problem, but "…of the parish of Tjolotjo, Nyamandhlovu" was really too much to handle despite several careful rehearsals with me first. He twinkled at me sitting in the front pew as he battled to pronounce his words with the children giggling and tittering at his efforts.

The Union Castle boats docked in Cape Town every Friday, so I timed my arrival for the Friday before the wedding, still on schedule for 11th December. This would mean that the train would arrive at Bulawayo on Monday 6th. It was almost exactly a year since my return to England. What a long, long time it had been – but again our letters had carried us through. Growing to know each other by pouring out our feelings, our love, our hopes and uncertainties on paper had helped us set the firmest of foundations.

Jean met me off the train, as John was busily involved in wrapping up the end of the school year. I stayed with her for a couple of nights before she drove me out to Tjolotjo.

The build-up to the wedding had, up to this point a rather dream-like quality – but not once we started driving down that Tjolotjo road. Help! It was simply awful.

I had never imagined heat like this. Great swirls of the finest choking red dust swept round and into the car, covering our faces and caking into mud in the perspiration round our hair. We looked as though we were wearing masks – with white holes for eyes. We were reduced to less than walking pace on several occasions as we negotiated huge holes, old washaways or rocks in the road. My apprehension increased as we dropped in altitude. It seemed to get hotter and hotter with every mile.

It was also very dangerous. We'd turn a corner to find a huge group of cows just standing in the middle of the road, their heads hanging low with, it seemed to me, the sheer effort of staying alive. The country-side was parched with great cracks running through the soil. There had been no rain at all for nearly nine months. Apparently any moisture there was would gather at the edges of the road so the grass was vaguely green and therefore attractive to the cattle. But they were so hot that it took a lot of persuasion to get them to move off the road. In fact nothing moved – there was not a breath of wind – leaves just hung as though they'd just given up on life.

For the first time a wave of real fear swept over me. I could see Jinny watching me rather anxiously.

We dropped down and down to approach the great, flat slow-flowing Gwaai River and I almost imagined it looked greener and more pleasant – good-sized, flat-topped shade trees everywhere and still quite a bit of water in the river. It wasn't imagination. The countryside was definitely more attractive here than it had been on the way and my heart started to beat faster as we turned into the drive of "our" house.

It was just indescribable seeing my wonderful John – and the fears of the journey vanished. I thought my heart would burst I was so happy – and so was he!

He enveloped me in a huge hug as I jumped out of the car. We just hugged and hugged and wept with happiness. Harrie came running out behind us, tears of joy running down her cheeks to see me safely there. It was the most wonderful welcome.

Dear Harrie had been at Tjolotjo for two weeks preparing the house for me. Oh! The joy of just being here at last. I looked at the garden and over towards the school, and realised that Tjolotjo *was* a more beautiful place than I had imagined after all the horrors I had just been through and read about. As John had said, it was pretty flat but with big open grassy spaces and trees. The Gwaai River being so close helped to keep everything looking comparatively lush.

I was curious to see a group of Native children milling about on the front verandah of our house. They suddenly struck up a very noisy and boisterous song.

Harrie whispered to me, 'It's a song for you, welcoming the Principal's new wife.' John said I must go round and shake hands with every one and thank them for their kindness. He showed me how to *hombera* – the African way of clapping cupped hands in acceptance of a present or a greeting. There is one way for women and another for men.

Shortly afterwards, some fearsome warriors came sort of sashaying down the drive in a threatening manner, carrying big sticks and dressed in skins and headdresses. I was a bit alarmed, but John assured me they

116

were bringing presents of welcome and that I was just to accept them gracefully, make a short speech and *hombera*.

John had tried to cover every contingency when he described what I should expect, but these spontaneous gestures of affection and tribute, he had not expected – and I was certainly not prepared for them. We were both very flattered and delighted. I found I was being closely scrutinised . After everyone had looked me over quite openly, they spoke to John in Sindebele and announced themselves satisfied with what they saw.

Once they had left, I went into the house. It was much bigger and roomier than I had imagined with a huge verandah enclosed by gauze netting.

Harrie had done a great job and it was looking clean and welcoming with fresh flowers on the few pieces of rather scant furniture we did have. The cupboard and dressing table John had so lovingly and carefully made for me gleamed with polish. I couldn't have been happier.

Then I met his wonderful old retainer, Jack. I rushed over to shake his hand and say how pleased I was to meet him.

But he was definitely not so pleased to see me.

He thought I must be a very poor creature, unworthy to be the Principal's wife, because John had not paid my father any *lobola* (bride price). In fact, John had not bought any cattle or ordered any festivities to honour my father. Instead, I was the one sending out huge trunks and tea chests full of presents. This was not right at all and he was deeply suspicious.

Harrie had left all the tea chests intact so that we could have fun together unpacking once the wedding was over. But we couldn't resist opening first one, then the next and ooohing and aaahing over everything we found. Jack watched uneasily from a distance and John was unable to mollify him.

The next day, Mrs. Edwards had a tea party for me at which I met everyone I had heard about in John's letters. Notable for her absence, was Mrs. Searson. There was now, apparently, tremendous antagonism between Edwards and Searson. To make matters worse, they shared an office. They had shared this office for nearly two years by that stage, but because they were now no longer talking to each other, they sat back to back and passed notes to one another. John had to act as interpreter. It was a ridiculous situation, which he had been unable to resolve because the government department concerned would not take any action. The whole situation made him simply furious because it distracted everyone from the work at hand.

We sat chatting until well into the night, revelling in the cool evenings that are such a bonus in that part of the world. After we had all gone to bed, there was a loud knock on the front door. An agitated man was standing outside saying someone had been attacked by a lion and needed help. John popped his head round my door and asked if I'd like to go out and pick him up. Off we went into the blackest African night, with no moon at all.

We went bumping along in the infamous truck with its inch-thick padding on the seats, on increasingly small and bumpy dirt roads in search of this poor fellow. Our lights picked out the track ahead and sometimes the startled round eyes of a buck or the cat-like slits of a lion. After about four hours drive, as the sky lightened in the east, we headed for a camp fire surrounded by people and there he was, considerably the worse for his experience, but alive.

He had been badly bitten around the head and shoulders and seemed to have lost an awful lot of blood. He lay there, quite conscious, and seemingly completely unworried about the outcome, as we decided how to move him. It was the first time I had seen the amazing fatalism of the Native and I was staggered by his acceptance.

We made him as comfortable as we could in the back of the truck and arrived back at the school just as the sun rose and in time for John to go straight to inspection and morning drill on the football field. Sister Weir was waiting and took the poor fellow off to her little clinic immediately. I was astonished to hear that within a couple of days he had recovered enough to go home.

The Wedding

The whole wedding had been arranged for me, through letters with Jean and John. And it was as special as I could possibly have wanted. Daltons, a tea room in Bulawayo, were going to do all the catering for five shillings a head and it was to be held in the lovely garden of a great friend of the Hammonds called Roger Gibbs. We were to be married in St. John's Church, Bulawayo, by Canon Gibbon, who also happened to be from the Dengie Hundred, and who, incredibly, had a sister living in Latchingdon, a couple of miles from Southminster.

11th December dawned as a boiling hot day. I was thoroughly spoiled with breakfast in bed. As the sun poured through my window – relentlessly hot even now, I thought of home – mid winter – and all that mid-winter meant on those Essex flats.

How I wished they were all here – Daddy, Mummy, Dick and Trish. My eyes filled up and I had to swallow a big lump in my throat – stupid girl, you're about to be married to the most wonderful man in the world! I knew it, but I also knew how much I missed them all already and what a lot of changes there were going to be.

Jean's houseboy was designated to iron my veil and was told to do so very carefully. Jean asked him if he knew what it was for and he nodded wisely and said, 'Yes – for the moskeets…'

We had decided to be a bit extravagant and bought some mud face packs for "the day", so that we would both look radiant. It was some terribly exotic and expensive mixture, which smelt revolting and Jinny and I were almost hysterical as we put it on and turned into mud monsters with white eyes and lips! We carefully took it off, as instructed, one hour before the service. She looked wonderful. But it must have been on too long for my delicate English skin as I looked like the rising sun. I was absolutely scarlet and swollen! We were appalled – but time had run out.

I put on my, by now, much-worn wedding dress for the last time. With my face slowly returning to normal but still, thankfully, hidden under my "mosquito" net, I walked up the aisle, at last, to marry my beloved African.

Chapter 7

Oh! Tjolotjo

The wedding was, of course, superb. How could it be otherwise after so long? A sincere service in the lofty St. Johns Church, built of local Bulawayo stone. As I walked up the long aisle on John Swire-Thompson's arm to join my darling John, it was humbling to see so many faces I had come to know when I was here a year ago. John Swire stood in for Daddy so kindly and gently – and Jinny, a good six months pregnant, Ann and JJ (Skinny and Morrie's two children) were my bridesmaids and pageboy. People came all the way from Mashonaland to see us married. They must have begun to wonder if it would ever come off!

The Gibbs' garden looked stunning – they had gone to so much trouble and it had responded joyfully with the first rains a couple of days before. It was the happiest, most carefree occasion and ended up with my dear husband wandering around with my mosquito net on his head! The wedding was exactly as I would have wished it and could easily have taken place in my own hometown – except for the lack of my own lifetime friends and family – and, of course, the heat. December was very different in Africa!

We set off that evening for our honeymoon and I re-discovered an endearing feature of early Rhodesian life – we didn't have anywhere planned to go! It certainly made life interesting. John had a vague idea of where we were heading, which was towards Fort Victoria. We spent the first night in Gwelo then went through the mountainous Selukwe area to the Glen Livet hotel. This was a gracious building backed up against a pine forest, with only about ten large, beautifully furnished rooms. We had two nights there as we couldn't afford any more. But it was a wonderful time of being able to just be together – I don't think a single minute was spent without our arms round each other. The need to keep touching each other was irresistible after all these years of being apart. It had really been too long.

We spent the rest of our honeymoon week in other people's company. The only way we could afford to do so was to stay with various friends before making our way up to Salisbury. John's father Bob was due to return home after nearly two years working in Sarawak, then touring in Russia and all sorts of other exotic places. I had been looking forward to meeting him for years. So we designed the trip around all of us arriving in Salisbury at about the same time.

As we drove towards Salisbury, I seemed to be developing a slightly painful jaw. I went to bed that night thinking nothing much of it – but next morning, as I woke up, I thought, "something's not right". John's face confirmed it.

I had a swelling the size of a small apple on my face. It was some sort of abscess on my tooth. I was thankful it had not appeared the week before. But it meant an emergency trip to the dentist before going off to the station to meet John's father. After the visit to the dentist, where the tooth was removed, I not only had a very fat face but I couldn't speak properly from the anaesthetic. A great way to meet a new daughter-in-law!

Fortunately, I didn't feel too bad in myself as I sat entranced by this gentle, intelligent man as he described the extraordinary trip he had just completed – sometimes in the most hostile and difficult conditions. Coming home had buoyed him up, but I could see he was tired – and I was pretty sore, so we didn't stay too long.

It was now a few days before Christmas. As we left Bob and Harrie, we felt there was no alternative but to postpone Christmas with Jinny and John in Bulawayo as the dentist wanted to see me for the next three days or so. Morrie's brother Arthur Cowling and his wife Gertrude invited us to share Christmas with them and their two little girls. Arthur had been at Plumtree with Bob and served as Deputy Head for a time. He was a very funny man – with a droll and cynical wit. He took great delight in pulling my leg from the moment I arrived.

I came down to breakfast on Christmas morning to find a little clay model of a cow on my side plate. It had a mournful look on its face and a big lump on its jaw. It was peering over a label that said "Lopsy from Essex"!

Apart from that we had a great Christmas – but in all my time in

Africa, I never quite got used to eating a full-blown Christmas lunch – turkey, ham, bread sauce, plum pudding and brandy butter – in all that heat. This was definitely a cold weather meal – but the ties to England and English traditions were still very strong in this colonial outpost.

John was anxious to spare me as much of the heat as he could in this first year so he had arranged to take another week off before we left for Tjolotjo just after New Year. We took the opportunity to head out to Dombo and spend a night with Dudley and Edith Hampton. They were very interested in what John was doing at Tjolotjo and the problems with Edwards were no surprise whatsoever. Dudley was now Deputy Principal at Domboshawa so the two boys had a lot to discuss. I enjoyed catching up with the Roelkes and the Claers and seeking out our old haunts in Salisbury again. We carried on the practice of just dropping in on people and having great meals and wonderful chats and laughs – they always seemed prepared for visitors and I realised this was something I was going to have to get used to very quickly.

We had to be back at Tjolotjo in early January as the term started in three weeks' time, so in what was John's relatively new car we set off. It took us three days to drive to Dembo and do an enormous shop designed to last us for the next month, before we set off on the last leg..

No sooner had we crossed the Gwaai, and turned into our drive than we were greeted with the latest saga in the Searson/Edwards feud. Jack couldn't wait to tell us the blow by blow details. One of Edwards' chickens had wandered unwittingly into the Searson's garden. Mrs. Searson had picked it up, held it by the head and swung the poor bird round till it was dead... before throwing it back into the Edwards' garden. I was astounded!

We were just settling in from the journey and unpacking our cases and huge quantities of food, when Mr. Swanson, the Assistant Native Commissioner, popped in. I invited him to have a cup of tea, but he declined, asking me instead if I would be interested in joining him on a hunt to go and shoot a rogue elephant. I really didn't want to – but I was not going to let anyone think I might quail at this sort of thing, so, ever anxious to please, I politely said, 'Yes, I'd love to come along.' After all, I was a country vet's daughter and quite used to seeing animals put down. This would be just the same – after all, the beast had been killing people and trampling their corn.

But, as I went through to tell Johnnie about the invitation,

123

he suggested I think twice about it. He was quite sure I wouldn't like it.

He went on to describe how the animals would be butchered as the Natives would traditionally climb right into the belly of the carcass. They would be seeking totems and bits and pieces for witchcraft and medicine as well as just cutting off hunks of warm flesh, eating it and drinking the blood as they did so. Oh boy! It sounded horrific to my delicate little English way of thinking. I was only too happy to take his advice and change my mind on Chummy Swanson's offer.

The place was aptly named – Nyamandhlovu means 'meat of the elephant' and Tjolotjo itself – 'the skull'. Even the names seemed ghoulish – what a lot I had to learn.

I was used to living in a relatively small community in Southminster, but of course in England you are never far away from the bigger communities like London. I was soon to find this small community at Tjolotjo was very, very different indeed.

Over the next week I had every wife, black and white, come in to meet me. I was very touched. I particularly liked Mrs. Bulle, Mrs. Ramushu, Mrs. Koti and Mrs. Dabengwa, four of our Native teachers' wives. The Kotis were Xhosas from the Eastern Province in South Africa and he had been having trouble with the boys for some time. John felt it was completely unwarranted, and felt it was simply because they were South Africans from a different tribe. Mr. Dabengwa was a good local teacher, a strict disciplinarian and a Matabele, although he had been trained in South Africa. To find teachers for the upper classes of the school, John still had to call on South Africa as there were very few of our own Rhodesian Natives yet trained to that standard.

At that stage the staff consisted of three Zulus (who mixed very easily with the Matabele locals as they all had the same origins and spoke a very similar language), two Xhosa, one Tswana, one Matabele, one Shona, one Englishman, one South African and my Rhodesian-born husband.

Most of the European wives were, unfortunately, all too keen to bombard me with their various alliances and stories. Each of them was trying to encourage me onto her side. John advised me to have nothing to do with it and reinforced the fact that we must keep friendships with Europeans, to people outside the school. It was still the custom at that stage for everyone to call everyone else by Mr. or Mrs., or among the men, just by their surnames – until you got to know each other better. John was absolutely insistent that this remained the rule in perpetuity among the staff at Tjolotjo.

Dear little Sister Weir, whom we later came to know as Lalan, was a blessed exception to all this. She invited me down to see what she did at the hospital.

We walked off through the bush that first evening with Tan, her dog, and a tiny little paraffin wick lamp, which threw out the smallest imaginable pool of light. On the way, she regaled me with a story of how one night she had to keep calling Tan because he was being slow. 'Och, coom along Tan, you're being very slow tonight.' She couldn't see her dog in the poor light of her lantern. 'Coom on now, Tan,' she called in her strong Scottish brogue. It was only as she neared the hospital that she realised the panting presence behind her was a slavering and opportunistic jackal – not Tan. Tan was sensibly cowering under a table at home.

So I was more than a little disturbed at the prospect of just what we might meet on the way – people here didn't seem to think twice about it. But my eyes were wide open!

We arrived at the hospital safely and in we went to the first thatched mud hut. In the dim light of a hissing hurricane lamp, I saw it was filled with people lying on the floor in blankets. As we passed each one Lalan gave me his or her medical history and we solemnly shook hands. It didn't seem to matter how sick they were, the men were full of jocularity and the women a bit more retiring, but full of smiles.

We moved on to the second hut. 'These are the VDs,' I was told. Amazing, I had never really known what VD was in humans! On to the third hut – I tried to shake their hands… but they had funny bunched up fingers.

'These are the lepers,' Lalan said.

I tried not to recoil in shock but everything I had ever heard taught me that you should not go anywhere near lepers – certainly not touch them. In England, we never saw lepers and to me, I suppose, they were still poor unwanted people in Biblical stories. Here, they were very real and looking at me with dark, uncomplaining eyes in bodies with noses, lips, ears and fingers bunched up, distorted or missing. Lalan knew them all, understood their backgrounds and their problems and cared deeply for each one.

Then off we went to the next hut. 'You'll enjoy this one,' she said as her eyes twinkled in the lamplight. 'This is the maternity wing.'

125

In we went to a hut where there was only one woman obviously in advanced labour, and wearing her very best straw hat for the occasion. She greeted me with laughter and much clapping before she started bearing down again.

'She's going to need some help soon,' Lalan said, palpating her distended stomach, ' …but I think I'll get you home first.' I was very relieved. These were enough revelations for one night. My respect for this diminutive and plucky wee Scot grew out of all proportion – but after all the excitements of the day, I was very glad to get home.

I was of course, rather interested to meet these fearsome trouble-makers, the Edwards. Having done so with due ceremony, I formed an early opinion that she was possibly the more venomous of the two. One of their many daughters was now causing havoc of her own, by chasing a bachelor in the Native Department – a debonair and most attractive German called Von Memerty. He just wasn't interested. She threatened suicide and all sorts of mayhem, but old Von wouldn't have a bar of it. To slight him, she had found herself another man and got engaged. Von was so relieved! Unfortunately, only a few short months later, she broke off the engagement and hotted up her pursuit of poor Von. When we eventually met him, he was looking hunted and fed up with it all.

My greatest immediate task was getting to know – and mollify – John's cook, Jack. He was suspicious of me and of every single thing I did.

He grudgingly gave me a shopping list on our first trip to Bulawayo four weeks later – huge quantities of course, designed to last us – and countless "droppers-in" for the two to three months necessary before the next trip. And all before fridge's or freezers – in that stinking heat.

It looked as though the rains were setting in, so this was an especially big order in case the Gwaai cut us off. It required a lot of planning and organisation and at first I doubted I would ever get used to it.

On my long shopping list was "blue soap". This was a mottled, recycled soap that everyone seemed to use for laundry. It was sold in long, squarish bars separated by paper and was very soft. When we arrived home, the bars had to be cut up into usable sizes and dried in the sun to harden them off so that they lasted longer.

'Have you counted?' Jack growled behind me.

Well of course I hadn't. Later, when I had plucked up courage, I asked him why he had asked.

'You must count,' he said, 'because if I know you have counted, I will take what is right. If you haven't counted, I will take what I can!'

I felt that this held some strangely wise and ancient philosophy – but I was not quite sure what.

Mrs. Searson came over on my second day at Tjolotjo to welcome me like an old friend after our meeting at Hillcote. She said she would like to send me a special treat. I was very grateful and thanked her profusely. She wouldn't tell me what it was.

A few hours later, a huge, brown paper-wrapped parcel arrived sitting on a tray, which was about an inch deep in blood. I unwrapped it very cautiously to find it was the most disgusting looking lump of bloody fat covered in dirty fur. I was horrified! I'd hardly ever seen raw meat in England, because the maids always cooked it first. This piece was particularly unpleasant and the flies swarmed round it in a second. Was it some form of curse or nasty omen, which had been sent to us?

'What is it?' I blurted out to Jack.

He looked at me scornfully and said, 'Sheep's tail – is very good.' He knew exactly what to do with it. It was only later that I found out how how useful it was. By rendering a fatty tail down, you'd get basins and bowls-full of very good cooking fat – the only sort of fat that was available to us. But it was a nasty shock when I first saw it.

Didn't count the blue soap… didn't know what to do with a sheep's tail. This was a poor wife that the Principal had married. Jack's respect for John started slipping as well.

Two weeks later, I had to face my first "drop-in" dinner party as the headmaster's new wife. Four inspectors, including Mather, had announced that day that they would be coming down to see the school, arriving in the afternoon and staying a couple of nights.

I spent hours preparing the table and making a fairly exotic pudding, while Jack cooked a roast and vegetables. In order to make it a bit special, I polished up some silver candlesticks that we had been given for our wedding and put them on the table, lighting them just as we went in to eat. The atmosphere was perfect and John gave my hand a squeeze as we walked into the dining room. We seated everyone carefully and enjoyed a little toast and pate first. Jack came into the dining room bearing the great roast and vegetable dishes – and saw the candles. He dropped the tray as a look of utter horror crossed his face.

He looked at me knowingly and shaking his finger at me, roared, 'Ah, ah, Roman Catholic,' as if this explained everything!

Then he left and simply disappeared into the night. Fortunately, everyone could see the funny side, but I felt mortified and worried about the future relationship between Jack and me, as I picked up the roast and the smashed vegetable dish and tried to retrieve at least something for us to eat.

The next day, he took John aside and said he felt he had taught me enough and it was time for him to leave. Poor Jack, John had gone down substantially in his estimation. I was heartbroken – and felt I had failed my first real test. I had also become rather fond of the old rascal and felt very let down. It took John hours of talking to persuade me of the nature of bachelor boys, none of whom liked interfering new wives anyway!

Despite Jack's disapproval, the first few months were filled with happenings as more and more boxes and presents kept arriving. At last I had the house looking somewhere near what I had hoped it would be. John was amazed at how far his £50 had stretched and what I had been able to buy for 6d apiece. We didn't have much in the way of furniture except for items John had lovingly made for me before I came out. Our bedside tables and other cupboards were made out of paraffin boxes with pretty curtains hanging over them. They looked fine and lasted years. John's beautifully made dressing table and cupboard worked superbly and, in fact, lasted over 20 years. I somehow couldn't bear to throw them out.

Just before I left England, my Auntie Annie had phoned to say that she wanted to give us a canteen full of real silver cutlery. I thanked her very much, but wrote back to say I felt this was possibly not suitable for the Gwaai Reserve. If she had not yet bought the canteen, I asked if she would mind giving me the equivalent in money so that I could get myself a piano once I arrived. This had been agreed, so once everything had been unpacked and I was pretty well settled in, we planned to make another trip to Bulawayo in about a week's time, to try to find a piano.

By this time, it was the end of February and ooh! It was hot. I had never imagined anything like this energy draining and stifling heat. We moved our beds out onto the verandah to take advantage of every cooling breeze, but it didn't make much difference. The rains, which had started just before our wedding, had stopped entirely for the rest of December and the whole of January and we were now on the edge of a drought.

The extreme heat and a feeling of almost suspended animation would precede the rain in this part of the world. Looking out across the lawn the day before we were due to drive to Bulawayo, with my head throbbing from an unexplained migraine, it seemed as though the world had stopped as the heat was just too great. Even the crickets were silenced. Mac, our huge old Rhodesian Ridgeback, panted slowly, eyes half-shut, under a shady bush. The gardener sat with his head in his hands, under the fig tree.

John sent all the boys to their dormitories early, because it was too hot for them to concentrate.

It had taken three days to build up – days in which I found myself unable to do anything, except lie on my bed with a cold flannel across my eyes, praying that the excruciating headache would go or the heat would break somehow.

Then – there was a sudden swirl of wind and a rattle of leaves.

Another gust – followed by the violent slamming of a door.

Then – the thudding rumble of distant thunder. Something was up. My headache started to clear almost immediately and I moved to the door to see huge black cumulo-nimbus clouds racing towards us, spiked with fierce shards of lightning. John came running in over the lawn as huge drops bulging with water, plopped into the dust at his feet. The fresh smell from the cracked and parched earth as it absorbed the precious moisture, was indescribable. I had never smelt anything like it, as I had left before the rains came last year.

'Why are you running?' I asked.

'Just you wait,' he grinned.

I ducked involuntarily as the most cracking explosion of lightning and thunder burst around us followed by an absolute sheet of water. We sat on the verandah and watched the incredible pyrotechnics display all around us. It poured and poured. Little puddles formed – then burst out of their confines and ran down any slope they could find – till there was water gushing everywhere.

It poured and poured and poured – solidly, for three hours. It was amazing to watch. My headache lifted as though it had never been and I watched the Africa John loved so much coming to life. Frogs appeared in puddles, ants started flying out of the ground and birds sang their little hearts out as the rain gradually fell away. What a sight, and how different from the gentle mists and drizzle I knew. We watched as the night fell and the storm moved on towards the Victoria Falls.

John had a great deal of school shopping to do as well so we decided to go to Bulawayo in the truck. The Gwaai was twice its normal width by the time we arrived at the drift.

'Mmmmmn, hope we don't have any more before tomorrow,' John said, 'or we'll never get back.'

We stayed with Jinny and John and they had friends round for a very jolly evening, uncomplicated by the innuendos and hidden agendas of the people we mixed with on a daily basis. Jinny was by now eight months pregnant and hoping her bundle was going to decide to come early. Next morning, we set off to "Knights", the only piano shop in Bulawayo, to see what they had in the store. We actually found a very good little upright with a pleasant tone and good keyboard action for the £18 we had been given. So we paid it out and arranged for the piano to be packed up ready for collection by the school lorry in a couple of weeks' time.

'Time to go,' John said as we finished our lunch at the Swire-Thompsons. 'I hear it has been raining again, so we must get back before dark.'

Off we went on roads made slippery from all the rain, and as we turned the corner to approach the swirling Gwaai, Johnnie remarked that it was fortunate we had not left it any longer ... but he felt we should still be able to get through.

I was scared stiff and clung white-knuckled to the seat as we edged down towards the water. You couldn't see where the edge of the drift was and it had no side rails... it was just a slightly raised, rickety row of logs and wood, strapped together to allow you to drive across the riverbed. There was a slight ripple in the fast-flowing water to indicate the upper edge of the drift and John had to drive across using this as a guide.

We went in deeper and deeper.

'It's OK, these trucks have overhead something-or-others,' I was assured, 'which means that you can go in pretty deep before they conk out.' Nearly through – about 50 feet to go. We "conked out".

After a couple of gentle expletives, John tried to open the door, but the water by this stage, was well over the running board.

'Now just stay here, darling, I must find help.'

The next thing I knew, he was climbing out through the window! I couldn't do anything else but wait and watch as he struggled to the bank with water swirling and tugging at him as he went. 'Oh Johnnie,' I prayed, 'be careful.'

The river was running very fast by now, and great roaring currents eddied around the truck.

Some Natives came running down the bank and they were full of shouts and joy at this new excitement. They all rushed into the roaring water quite oblivious to any danger, it seemed to me, and came to say "hello, hello, hello"… and assure me that I was all right. The water kept rising. It was over the top of the wheels now.

Then, everybody disappeared up the bank into some big old thorn trees at the top − including John. Where on earth had they gone? Should I get out? Surely John would have told me to do so if that had been the best move. The water kept rising. Now it was well over the arched bit that covers the wheels and only about four inches below my window. I really was terrified, especially as the truck, even with a heavy load of pig iron railings on it, was beginning to feel decidedly unstable.

Slowly, slowly, I saw a team of oxen approaching. 'Oh, thank God!' Slowly, slowly, for oxen cannot be rushed under any circumstances, the span was backed into the water and hitched up to the truck.

It took them nearly 20 minutes of heaving and straining, slipping and sliding and general commotion and exhortation by the now quite sizeable group of Natives, but gradually the truck started to move. It sprang clear as the drag of the water fell away from the back wheels and we drove away to a chorus of laughter and goodbyes.

Once again, I was very glad to be home.

After Jack left, Hanleck arrived. He was a good chap − always smiling and pleasant. But I did find it difficult being left alone in the house with a manservant. We had always had women servants in the house at home. So it was strange enough having a man in the house all the time, let alone the fact that I couldn't understand one word this one said. I would far rather have done the housework myself, but I knew that this would not be seen as correct procedure. I sometimes felt like hiding under a bed just to have a little place to myself.

I had been bitten to death by mosquitoes. It was fortunate that because the rains had only just set in, the malaria season was later than usual. But now they were out in force and they certainly sought out my new blood. We had to sleep under nets as well as the gauzed-in verandah and these had to be put down over the beds by about 4 o'clock and the room well "flitted" to make sure we were able to sleep.

During the day I would sit fascinated by the perpetual buzzing and singing of insects and beetles in the veldt; by the sound of the Africans singing in the distance, by the heat and always, by that breathtaking midday stillness.

I started having the staff back to morning tea and getting to know them in return. I boldly invited Mrs. Searson and Mrs. Edwards together, but of course it did no good and I had to sit between them and talk for them. Nothing would persuade them to speak to each other. Each family had several daughters and even the daughters wouldn't speak to each other. It really was ridiculous.

Some of the Native teachers' wives asked me to go to their houses and visit them. I found it so interesting – they were such lovely gracious women and I became familiar with all their various children. Lalan knew them very well and she was a great help in introducing me and breaking down barriers.

In fact, everyone befriended me, but I didn't really have any "soul mates" who understood my background. I felt the European staff didn't approve when I went to visit the Native teachers' wives and worse, when I sat playing the piano – they thought I was just messing about as none of them had any background in classical music.

The piano became my solace in those lonely early years; I was able to lose myself in performance and music. But often, just when I was struggling to get some great work right, Edwards would pop his head round the door and say, 'Oh, stop that awful noise and come and have a cup of tea.' It was utterly deflating.

I found myself getting very depressed and missing my dear England so badly.

Lalan became a great friend in need because she was not on the teaching staff. So I tended to spend more of my time with Lalan or with people from the Native Department. Chummy Swanson, as the Assistant Native Commissioner, was head of the Native Department in Gwaai Reserve. His wife Tessa was also English and an artist and we had some lively evenings with them – until I made a bit of a faux pas!

One afternoon, there was a knock on the door. It was a Native with a stick in his hand. Stuck into a slit in the stick was an envelope – it was an invitation from Tessa, hand-written on expensive looking paper and headed "The Residency". I responded with an acceptance on similarly expensive looking paper which I headed "The Kremlin". It was dutifully wedged into the cleft in the stick for its homeward journey.

I recounted this tale when John returned for lunch and was rather pleased with my return address. He quickly disillusioned me. "The Residency" was the official name of the NC's house! I was aghast as I honestly thought she was just being funny. I wrote a quick note of apology, but despite a little frost, it was never mentioned again. Secretly, I did feel it was a bit pompous for such a remote outpost of Empire!

We had some very enjoyable tennis parties on Saturdays for the younger men and women of the district, mostly at the Native Department tennis court. This was a rather ropey old thing made of red ant heap and the lines were whitewashed into place. Very different from the lush grass courts of home I also couldn't get over the speed the balls came off the surface – helped apparently by the fact that the air was thinner at 4000ft than at sea level.

I thought they all played rather lazily. They all thought I was a bit odd because I ran about the court so much chasing that speeding little ball. However, we eventually compromised and had some excellent games.

The neighbouring dogs would all trot along too. In fact, even when it was pouring with rain and tennis was cancelled, they would trot off by themselves every Saturday, as regular as clockwork to meet their doggy friends. It was priceless! They'd then realise we weren't coming and droop home, tails between their legs, all doggy-smiling in their embarrassment.

We also had a little nine-hole golf course. It had sand greens which were a bit of a challenge! These would be doused with used diesel oil and we would scrape a path for our balls with a toothless rake-like object. It was pretty rough, but it was certainly something to keep us occupied.

I had to admit that although I tried hard to keep busy, it was boring by comparison with what I had left. Not many people I could really identify with, no music, no theatre – I was thankful I could play a reasonable game of tennis and golf. But always, the draining and soul destroying nightmare for me by far, was just coping day to day with the heat.

That first year, and despite its late start, instead of the usual 22 to 23 inches of rain, Nyamandhlovu had a total of 48 inches. The drift was torn away only three days after we had managed to ford it – and even the ghastly suspension bridge was washed away. This had been my absolute nightmare. It was made of rope and beaten-out paraffin tins supported by rope under your feet. But often, there were bits of paraffin tin missing and we looked down on this voracious, roaring river just a few feet below. I was delighted to see the suspension bridge go. But it meant we were completely cut off for over a month. That did pose difficulties, but fortunately, we were in a better situation than many, because we had our own milk and butter, vegetables and meat – all grown by the school.

A rope was eventually pulled across to the other side and secured. The post boy would put all the letters in a leather satchel on his back and cross the river holding onto this rope for dear life. I thought he was very brave and he was regarded with great awe. Many young Natives were only too keen to cross the river hanging onto the rope. It was wonderful to get the letters through – but they always required a lot of drying out and de-smudging before they could be read.

Unfortunately, my migraines became a regular feature of the hot six to seven months of each year. They were shocking, three-day headaches which almost blinded me with the pain. At this time of the year, I seemed to have a couple of headaches a week, so there was precious little time without them.

The first day I would be prostrate with a brain-numbing ache which followed the first telltale dazzles; the second was just a heavy, horrifically intense headache and by the third it was beginning to ease off, but it left me feeling stupid and dazed. I would do weird things like putting the letters in the meat safe, or newspapers in the fridge, because my brain was just not functioning properly.

It was not easy, coping with the endlessness of it all. If I hadn't been married to the man I loved and admired quite so much, I would have been hard put to stick around. But love and admire him I did and there was no way I was going to give in.

The good old colonial tradition of having an afternoon rest in the tropics meant I was able to do a lot of reading. It also gave me the chance to read some of John's reports and gain a better idea of what he was trying to do.

I had been fascinated to see the schoolboys arriving from all over the country that first term, with their shoes hanging round their necks having walked all the way from the train at Nyamandhlovu. They would walk miles and miles… some, well over 100 miles from Bechuanaland – and regardless of the heat. A lot of them were much older than I would have expected – they looked like grown men. In fact, I found out some were married with children and older than John or me.

They all wore khaki shorts and shirts that were provided by the school. They paid £4/10s a term and there were two very long terms a year. For this sum, they were fitted out with uniforms, food, board and books, tuition and sports. It was astounding value by comparison with costs in England. Everything possible was provided, though in the early days they had to queue up to share their classrooms and equipment.

The sports and speech days had grown in splendour and were now a great feature of the annual calendar with people coming huge distances to attend and all the local people watching what went on. The Governor, Sir Herbert Stanley would come all the way from Salisbury each year. I always put a Royal Purple potty in his room in case of need – but despite the suitability of its regal colour I don't think he could bring himself to use it.

John tried so hard to encourage parents to attend, but only the Malabas and Kumalos, parents of Griffith and Gwin respectively, felt confident enough to do so. It was early days.

At 5.30 every morning John would leave the house on his bicycle, dressed in khaki shorts and shirt, wearing a white pith helmet, to take drill out on the square. He'd be back to put on his gown for Assembly and school inspection. The boys had one lot of lessons starting at 6.45 in order to overcome the heat, before going to breakfast at 7.30. John would come in for breakfast at the same time, then cycle off for the rest of the day.

He seemed to spend most of the morning teaching or supervising out on the farm and would be back in time for lunch. In the afternoons when the pupils had a rest and time off reading and lying down after lunch, John would catch up on office work. The boys would then do their elective programs such as agriculture, leatherworking or carpentry and would play sport from 4.30. Prep was done after supper in the evenings, presided over by their prefects and housemasters.

Every evening, we would have a sundowner – and our quinine – sitting out on the verandah and chatting over the day's events. I always had to wear mosquito boots, which were just like riding boots, under my skirt to protect my ankles from being bitten.

Tjolotjo School was established in 1921 in fulfilment of a promise made by the then Native Commissioner in Tegwane, H.S. Keigwin. Keigwin was one of Bob Hammond's close friends and they had tutored together on leaving university. He had been responsible for implementing the government policy at the time of settling people into the Gwaai Reserve from an area just behind Plumtree, which had been allocated for commercial farming. He always hated this policy and had promised the people he moved that he would provide training in agriculture and allied building trades in the area, to show how they could live and prosper in that part of Rhodesia.

He was as good as his word and within two years the school was started. 600 acres of land for the school itself and a 4,000-acre farm four miles away across the Gwaai River were made available.

By the time John arrived at the beginning of 1937, the school had been going for 15 years… but there had been 13 principals in that time!

Until John's arrival, the school had considerably more capacity than students. Many of the Natives hadn't yet caught on to the idea of schooling and there was great suspicion, particularly from the Tjlotjo people about the relative merits of sending a son to be educated when he was far more valuable tending the cattle.

John would spend days meeting with the local chiefs to persuade them, that like it or not, the changes in society meant that if their people were going to survive and eventually run their own country, they had to be educated.

Eventually, the Chiefs and Head men agreed to let us have a few young men for school. But at the end of term, it was all undone. The boys would go back to their villages and immediately of course, they assumed new stature! They knew things nobody else did – so they were treated like celebrities. Unfortunately this did them no good, particularly as the Chiefs decided they had now had their education and sent a completely different batch of young men for the second term.

So, the school was still very much in its infancy when John took over.

The soils in the area were mostly sandy loams or typical mopani soils – and both absorbed water almost instantaneously – so the 22 inches of rain had to be carefully conserved and managed. The Gwaai River was full of bilharzia, the debilitating scourge of Africa, and the land was too flat to dam easily, so the water supply had to come from boreholes. Three boreholes had been put down to 70 feet and met all the needs of the school until 1936 when one dried up. A second had just gone dry and with only one dubious borehole for about 250 people, John was in the process of putting down a fourth borehole – this time to 120 feet. It looked encouraging. But the water from the boreholes was not suitable for large-scale irrigation because of a high level of magnesium salts. This itself provided considerable training in, as the school vegetable garden had to be carefully rotated to keep the soil useable and sweet.

It was not until the early 1940's in fact, that John at last got his first class of pupils through for a full eight years of primary schooling. This was a triumph! But they were still young adults and not the children he was keen to see in greater numbers. The curriculum embraced vocational training in agriculture, building or an allied trade, run concurrently with their last three years of academic study. This meant they were readily employable when they left.

Practical work took up about a third of the time devoted to vocational training and the school was built, the furniture made, and a good percentage of the meat and vegetables grown, by the pupils themselves.

All the time this was taking place, local Natives were brought round the school and farm to be shown how they could benefit by doing the same sorts of things. John was keen to introduce two more years, post-Standard VI, as he felt the time was coming when there would be a need for more specialist knowledge.

On the agricultural side, the main emphasis was on animal husbandry. Dairying, beef, sheep, pigs and poultry were all on the curriculum as well as such things as dry stone-walling, fencing, black-smithing, training and handling of trek oxen. The equipment and techniques used had to be readily available and easily adaptable to local conditions because it had to fall within the capacity of the local Natives to buy for their own use. Cow byres were simply constructed and feed for cows was limited to fodder and grain grown on the school farm.

Every year, about 50 acres of crops were grown, half to be used to feed the animals, the rest to feed the school. All sorts of things were being tried, but John was not impressed with the yields produced by the new maize varieties. In tough years, they didn't produce at all – or were so inferior they were only suitable to be turned into silage. He was much keener to try to develop the native corn, or millet, as it would produce yields as good as maize and what was more important, it would produce some sort of grain even in the worst of seasons.

Demonstrating the benefits of two-, three- and four-year rotations was one of the most important elements and demonstration plots included cotton, pearl millet, finger millet, monkey nuts, *makomane* and other types of melons. The aim was to grow as wide a variety of crops as possible and show how these could be fitted into crop rotations.

John was determined not to use expensive or sophisticated techniques; boys had to learn to compost and manure the lands, rather than buy fertilisers, and seed was selected from their own crops to ensure sustainability. Oxen undertook all the traction and everything was transported on wagons and Scotch carts.

Provisioning the school was, just as it had been in Plumtree, always a problem. They had to work towards self-sufficiency. In 1937, a local farmer named Hawkins supplied the school with meat at 2d a pound. By November that year, he was asking 2.7d and after another six months 3d a pound – and costs kept rising, due to our isolation.

I was intrigued to read John's first ever report from Tjolotjo when he was Assistant Academic Teacher. It was a very different document to what was happening at the school now that there were more applications than places available. The rules had to change:

Now that the School has reached its present size the selection of pupils in future years will have to have a definite policy to follow. I would make the following recommendations:
a) aliens except in special cases should be excluded.
b) younger boys should be given preference to those who are past the school-age.
c) preference should be given to boys wishing to enter the lower standards so as to ensure that they will be under its care and influence for longer than is now the case.
d) local boys should have the right to enter before those from areas already served with central boarding schools.

He also felt it would be useful to start a pre-school for kraal children in the Nyamandhlovu area as they were so much further behind than those coming from other areas of the country. The government, felt it had enough on its hands at this stage, and refused. John remained concerned about the issue, as the local boys were markedly disadvantaged when they came in to Tjolotjo.

The school also battled with a severe lack of seating and had to "hot seat" classes at different times of the day, so that each standard could get at least three mornings and two afternoons on academic and industrial work.

A series of weekly debates was introduced to improve English conversation and general knowledge and this was an enormous success. However, John found some of the books they had to use were singularly inappropriate for his pupils.

I would like to see the Michael West readers used in the school; for nearly all purposes they are preferable to the Longman readers now in use. The latter contain many stories and much subject matter which has no appeal to the boys and which is quite outside their sphere of experience and imagination. They do however, contain much which is of value for history and geography and I would like to see them used as supplementary readers for those subjects.

There was also a need to provide more sports facilities:

New football fields have been pegged out and will be put into use during the season. It may be necessary to have two more and this will mean the clearing of additional hay fields to make up the loss to the farm.

Tjolotjo was building itself a good, solid reputation – serving its original purpose to show that crops and animals were viable in the area if the right methods were followed. Several pilot schemes were set up with the local people, to try and help them improve their own crops and livestock. These were meeting with varying degrees of success.

John was increasingly concerned about the fact that the school was drawing boys from every corner of the country and, with no immunity, they were taking particularly virulent strains of malaria back home with them. In addition, it was almost impossible to keep staff or boys for any length of time, because once they had contracted malaria, particularly if they survived the malignant tertian variety, it was considered too dangerous to allow to them to come back into the area. Local-area children seemed almost immune to the disease but this did not extend to pupils from other parts of the country.

As 1938 moved toward an end, and after two years of battling with increasing malaria and ever-greater difficulties with staff, it was obvious the school had to be moved to a better site if it was humanly possible. John knew he really would have to justify his case to reassure Keigwin.

He could see what excellent work was being done and the wonderful calibre of boys the school was producing, but again and again, he would be defeated by malaria – and then by the lack of water. The new borehole was producing 1,000 gallons per hour but there were fears it would begin to dry up as the others had done. The huge distances was another negative factor – everything was moved by ox wagon – and this meant delays of weeks on end. There was no bridge (and at the moment, not even a drift) over the Gwaai and the road from Bulawayo was quite one of the worst in the country.

John's background growing up at Plumtree had been of great benefit to Tjolotjo. He was used to making things happen in situations that seemed almost impossible. He was known as a tough disciplinarian – and he was – but he was also immensely fair. There had been considerable apprehension about appointing him Principal of the school at the tender age of 27 but with almost 18 months under his belt, he was confirmed as Principal and then made a member of the permanent staff in December 1938.

Like his father at Plumtree, he would always take time out to listen to any boy or member of staff who wanted to discuss a point with him.

'You see Nan, we have a dilemma. I feel we should be building on the disciplines and practices of Native tribal life. Those old chiefs and headmen know what they are doing – they have this amazing ability to gain consensus among their people, allowing everyone to make a point, allowing everyone to feel important – yet they maintain the utmost discipline. Every member of that tribe knows his place in it and would never dream of changing or challenging it.'

'It sounds an ideal system,' I said

'It is. It's a very good system and we cannot be responsible for breaking it down.'

'Why should that happen? Government must recognise its strengths as well, doesn't it?'

'Well – it does to a degree – but government feels we should be equipping the people for a future based on the European way. But the people themselves don't help – they think they can be like us if they learn English and behave like us. That's why we have such a need to act with the utmost propriety all the time.

'When I was at Dombo, Jack Mylne wrote to the Governor and he said, "I am running an African school. What should I do ... should I try to build on an African culture or teach them what I know of my own culture and interpret it in that light?" The Governor was unequivocal in his response –

"No, no... give them what you have got."

'I cannot be convinced he is right – we have to build on their culture – not ours.'

'Can't we do both?', I asked. 'Layering ours over the base of theirs?'

'Absolutely – that is the ideal. But already the way we do things is influencing relationships in the kraals. I am worried about it. I've found that when we remove Native disciplines and impose our own freer society, they find it very hard and see it as great weakness in us. They laugh at this weakness, but also find it very confusing. They respond much better to strictly enforced guidelines and rules.

'Another thing worries me, and I know it is not a conventional view, but I really cannot believe there is a long-term future here for the whites as rulers – this country's future will be in the hands of a mixed race or a black race. If their culture is destroyed – what do we leave them with? What I don't seem able to do is to get them to understand that their way of doing things is good. Couple their confusions with the government's attitude and I believe we are fighting a losing battle.

'My problem is that there are such great day-to-day pressures in just running this school that I don't have the time I'd like to be able to think this through more clearly. I have to try and do the best I can within my experience and understanding, to get them to accept responsibility and learn leadership for the future – whatever it might be.'

One of the things John still enjoyed was going off for an *indaba* with the local chiefs and headmen. He would do this whenever he felt he could. He'd spend hours sitting with them debating issues and trying to understand those that caused them concern.

In turn he would discuss with them the things that were bothering him and then translate what they had said into ways in which those

141

concerns might be discussed or implemented in school. He gained great respect for doing this and in turn grew really to understand the way things were done in their society. Similarly, he gained tremendous respect for the Chiefs.

Kayisa Ndiweni was a pupil at Tjolotjo, although he was of similar age to John, and he was the heir apparent for that area. John watched him growing up with great interest, convinced he would turn into a fine leader.

Because of all this, we had to be conscious of setting a good example. So I was extra careful in everything I did. The length of my skirt, the cut of my top, the way we conducted ourselves. John knew everything we did was watched – and copied. That was why he was particularly distressed by, and intolerant of, the infighting and feuding of his European staff. Time and again he tried to have the troublemakers moved to other places… time and again head office fobbed him off.

Although it did not look as though government was going to move on the issue, the school had to be moved. We started going off during school holidays exploring sites that might have the potential for a move. Time and again, head office fobbed off the recommendations. John wrote report after report, sent medical experts out, talked to inspectors, demanded action and understanding.

He received very little.

By the middle of May in 1939, a delightful man was appointed to the staff as an academic teacher, Maurice Mills. His wife was due to follow him at the end of the year. He was a straightforward, uncomplicated person and shared an enormous amount in common. What was most important was that Maurice had a sound teaching background. He became an enormous support to John.

We managed to persuade the clerk, Davids, to move on and now had a 22-year-old Englishman in his stead, Charles Wilks. He was so refreshing with his great keenness and willingness to work. The staff were beginning to knit together.

But now, war clouds were gathering over Europe and I was anxious to get back and see the family. Daddy didn't sound at all well and I was pretty desperate in case I didn't see him again, or worse, that John might never get a chance to meet him.

We were due four months leave from July 1939 and had been saving hard to afford the passage. Dudley Hampton offered to come down and act in John's stead, so with Maurice on staff, John felt able to leave the school in good hands. With much excitement, we planned to leave Cape Town in time to catch the English summer.

It was sheer heaven taking the train and feeling it drop down from the Transvaal highveld to the sea. With every click of the wheels as we steamed into the Hex River Valley I felt the heat of Tjolotjo recede – and with the first glimpse of the sea, we could both look forward, not back.

It was wonderful actually being on a ship with Johnnie this time. Together, we shared the romance of it, the fun of shipboard life and the luxury of having a whole two weeks to relax. Apart from the first two days of talking about it non-stop, we chose to forget about the increasingly difficult situation at Tjolotjo.

We arrived "home" on a sparkling July day. Again, I had forgotten England was so beautiful. We both revelled in it. Daddy was back from hospital, but oh, he was so frail! My heart clamped with fear when I first saw him, but he had lost none of his robust Yorkshire humour, or his interest in the world around him. The very best thing of all was that he was absolutely intrigued by what Johnnie was doing at Tjolotjo – and John loved having an objective, but captive audience. The two men related so well and they would talk for hours. Daddy was much brighter and more enthusiastic about life as a result.

Almost as soon as I arrived, I remember asking Mummy,

'When do you think the war is going to start?'

'War?' she said. 'There won't be a war.'

The tables had turned. This time, unlike the time when I had heard nothing about Edward and Mrs. Simpson while in Rhodesia, we in the colonies, had heard far more about what was going on in Europe than they had. Here, there was blind acceptance of Chamberlain's assurances that war had been averted.

We had been there only three weeks, when in early August, we had a letter from Rhodesia House telling us to have our suitcases constantly packed, to be no more than a day's journey from Southampton and prepared to leave at a moment's notice. It was most distressing and unsettling.

It was not just the uncertainty of our situation but the anxiety of what on earth was going to happen to Mummy and Daddy, Dick and Trish. It certainly cut short our chance to see friends and some of the northern parts of England that we had hoped to visit.

However, we were able to catch up with some of John's relatives in and around London and with my friends in Essex. We were due to leave during the middle of October but as we got towards the end of August – the newspaper placards were beginning to shout "War Imminent".

It was a glorious autumn morning when John and I decided to go down to Burnham for a game of golf. We had just finished the first nine and went into the clubhouse to have a cup of coffee. Everyone was gathered silently round a radio. We joined them, just in time to hear the shattering confirmation that war had started at 11 o'clock that day. We couldn't stomach the thought of playing the second nine, so we got into the car and went home, our emotions churning. As we arrived, the almost deathly hush of disbelief was split by the raucous howl of the first air raid siren.

War was declared on 3rd September. It was obvious that Mummy and Daddy could not stay at Southminster after what they had been through in the First World War, particularly now that Daddy was so ill.

Within two days, the Army contacted us, wanting to commandeer the house once again, so the decision was made to rent a small house in Budleigh Salterton, near Exmouth in Devon. Fortunately, Mummy had had a delightful Catholic nurse, helping her with Daddy for the last few months. Nursey had been smuggled out of France in a laundry basket when things started getting tough over there a few months before. She had become absolutely indispensable. She was very much a part of the family now and it was a relief to me to know that she would be there to help.

We had to leave the Army some furniture at Oakleigh so Mummy and Daddy took the things they really loved or needed, and at least we were there to help them move.

Dick had decided that however attractive taking over the family veterinary business might be, planes were his life – not animals, so he had given up his veterinary training and joined the Fleet Air Arm up at a base in Yorkshire. He would be going on active service almost immediately.

Trish had only just left school and was due to start a dress-designing course and take up a job at Lilleywhites in London two weeks' later. But even before we left, she had had to abandon thoughts of dress designing to take a shorthand and typing course, as she had been called up as well.

The rush to leave England was on. There was no chance of our getting away any earlier than our planned booking and it suited us not to do so anyway. We were able to see Mummy and Daddy safely ensconced in a pretty house in Budleigh with their furniture unpacked.

As time drew near for that awful sailing date, we heard of shipping being sunk close to the very routes we'd be taking; and as I sadly acknowledged that I would be unlikely to see Daddy again my stomach seemed to carry around a perpetual and very heavy lump of lead.

Saying goodbye to Mummy and Trish on Budleigh Salterton station was one of the most agonising things I had ever had to do. We were determined to keep it short and sweet and unemotional. The reality was anything but. There was just too much at stake – none of us knew whether we'd ever see each other again… we didn't know if we would make the voyage – they didn't know if they would survive the war.

I was so numb with anguish that I don't remember the train even leaving the station. I only seemed to "come to" as we approached Southampton and saw the grimly boarded-up buildings, the army vehicles rushing about and the crowds and crowds of people trying to get away on any ship they could find.

We would be joining a convoy to the Cape and at least that gave us some consolation. After hours of painstaking checking and re-checking, of additional military searches and clearances, we eventually managed to get to the boarding line.

As we queued up the gangway, I noticed ladders hanging over the famous mauve sides of the Union Castle liner as painters tried desperately to camouflage our civilian passenger ship by painting it North Sea grey. There was none of the gaiety of leaving port – no visitors were allowed on board, no bands played.

John and I had been fortunate to be allocated a two-berth cabin. It was very small, way down below decks and with no porthole, but at least we were together and not sharing.

We steamed out of Southampton docks at 5 o'clock in the evening and I watched through tear-filled eyes as the lights of my beautiful country fell away behind us. It had been such a breathtaking autumn – almost as though God was giving us something extra special to remember it by.

As we cleared the Isle of Wight, the ship began to turn sharply. I thought we had left something behind. It was too dark to make anything out clearly. But no, after a few minutes it turned the other way, just as sharply… then again, back we went. We realised this was going to be the pattern of our trip – zig-zag all the way to Cape Town.

John and I were both early birds, so the next morning we were up at crack of dawn, keen to get some fresh air. The ship was rolling heavily as we started to enter the infamous Bay of Biscay and combined with the zig-zagging it was pretty uncomfortable.

But it was peaceful up on deck. John held me in his arms as we stood gazing at the stern, with the huge wake beneath us. The sun started to lighten the darkness around us and we felt some calm after the frights and frenzy of the last two months. The huge, empty sea and the thrum of the ship's engines became almost hypnotic. We saw a little gun on the very back of the boat above the screws.

Empty sea – and one pathetic little gun!

The realisation hit us both at the same time. We rushed to the sides and looked to the front of the ship – there was no convoy. They had sent us out – a huge, lumbering, unprotected passenger ship – with no convoy. I looked at John absolutely stricken. Our chances of surviving the trip had just dived ominously.

At breakfast, the bad news was confirmed. There was no convoy – they simply couldn't provide one – England's naval resources were far too busy fighting for their lives and were tied up elsewhere.

The captain was excellent and as soon as people came down for breakfast, he immediately put several routines into place. Every able-bodied man had to report in order to be allocated four-hour watches. We would have emergency drill every single day and we had to sleep with our lifejackets on our beds. In fact they had to stay with us at all times.

John went off to report and sure enough, he was on that night. He had to climb right up into the crow's nest on a mast, way above the funnel and peer through special binoculars the whole time. There were four of them up there, each surveying a quadrant of the sea for torpedoes or other ships.

All the doors and windows had heavy black material over them because lights can be seen from extraordinary distances when at sea – so much so, that we were not even allowed to smoke on deck after dark.

But it made us a very intact group of passengers. We were all "in peril on the sea" together and there was one delightful woman who soon composed a song for us to sing to keep our spirits up.

Zig-zag, zig-zag, zig-zag, zig-zag, zig-zag all day long
Zig-zag, zig-zag, zig-zag, zig and nothing will go wrong
In every sort of weather we'll zig-zag together
Zigger-zagger, zigger-zagger, zigger-zagger, zig,
We'll zig-zag to Hong Kong.

Some people somehow wouldn't believe the danger we were in, until we were told one morning that the German Pocket Battleship, the *Graf Spee* was loose in the South Atlantic and that we would have to change our route. The Captain and crew would never disclose where we were. It was only afterwards we discovered we had gone almost to America before crossing back towards the African coast.

The ship's siren would go off at any time of the day or night and we had to move to our stations as fast, and as silently as possible, clambering up into the life boats – never sure whether this was the real thing or not.

Despite this, we had wonderful evenings of singing and dancing and tried to make as merry as the situation allowed. But there were always a few of us with husbands "on watch" and we would become furious with the "languid lilies" who would stand holding the blackout curtains open while chatting to their friends smoking down the corridors.

News of the war was grimmer and grimmer and we were all very anxious. There was also concern that, as the trip would very likely take eight to ten days longer than had been planned, the ship might run out of water. Within a couple of days, water and food rationing were put in place.

One morning, nearing the end of the trip, we were sitting reading in the lounge, with our lifejackets beside us when, very quietly, the crew came round, telling us to put the lifejackets on and motioning us to move with as little noise as possible, up onto the decks.

This was different. Where was the siren? Suddenly, all music was stopped. No loudspeakers! Nothing! Yet the crew's voices and actions were urgent and brooked no argument. We went up on deck.

Every passenger and most of the crew were standing along the deck in absolute silence gazing at the horizon. There, like an ugly lump of grey and packed with menace, was the notorious battleship.

'The *Graf Spee!*' was whispered round the deck. The noise of the ship's engines as we turned in order to present the smallest possible target, seemed terrifyingly loud.

They must hear us. They must see us if we could see them, so clearly.

Slowly the battleship came towards us… slowly, we tried to run away – but it was very evident that it was a lot faster than we were.

An hour passed as we prayed and stared in silent disbelief, imagining the crunch as the first torpedo hit. Visualising how we would cope. We had all heard horror stories about the passengers on the *Graf Spee's* other victims and of the appalling conditions they had faced being crammed like sardines onto its fellow raider, the *Altmark*. This would be our fate too.

We clung to each other, praying the men would be allowed to come in the lifeboats with us. Oh, Johnnie, how cruel it would be – after we had had but such a short time together.

'It's turning away,' – the whisper grew.

'It's turning away.' And it was. This great ship – this prizefighter of the German navy was turning away. It hadn't seen us! Or had the Captain, after sinking so many ships, decided he couldn't face another one… or that the sinking of a passenger ship might disclose his position?

It was turning away.

After that, nobody opened blackout curtains or smoked on deck. We were a much more subdued lot as we contemplated the five days of the voyage still left to us.

We now had to start drinking foul-tasting liquid called condensed water, which was made from treated seawater. Apart from the condensed water, our food lasted remarkably well.

Our voyage had lasted for 22 days (nine days longer than normal) when at last with enormous relief and gratitude, we saw the "Fairest Cape" once again. The ship hooted and hooted as we entered harbour, as news had got out about our narrow escape… and the dock was alive with people, bands and welcoming ribbons and banners.

Once again, I was very glad to be home – even if that home was still Tjolotjo – at the hottest and driest time of the year.

Chapter 8

Of antbears, malaria and feuds galore

John and I were emotionally worn out by the trip – the ongoing tension over those long three weeks had brought with it, the special relationships that build up in shared adversity. But it was all the other emotions, which had been the most draining. It was the sorrow and anguish at leaving my family to the nightmares of what lay ahead for Britain. It was time standing still as the *Graf Spee* moved closer and closer to our ship. Finally, it was the exhilaration of the moment when we realised it was turning away. Experiences nobody in Rhodesia could possibly understand or empathise with.

October to mid-November, before the rains really set in, had been a nightmare the previous year – a nightmare of brain-numbing migraines and trying to speak sense to the stream of official visitors. I was dreading it, but as we made our way back, I kept my thoughts to myself and sat quietly. My concerns seemed so trite by comparison with John's now urgent need to move the school. Being a Commonwealth country, we would shortly be likely to lose most of our expertise and skills to the war effort anyway, so this was becoming ever more difficult.

As we drove on, the road seemed more welcoming, the Gwaai more forgiving and the lawns and grounds of the school greener than I remembered. Perhaps it was purely by contrast with the anxieties of the last three weeks. John's gentle squeeze of my arm as we approached made me realise that my sensitive and understanding husband knew and understood, my mixed emotions.

It was good to be back after all. The war suddenly seemed far away. There were anxious letters from Mummy, of course, as she had heard that the *Graf Spee* had been seen in the vicinity of the route our ship was taking.

Hanleck had gone back to his farm and we had a new houseboy, Aaron. He was excellent – a hard worker, always full of laughter. Aaron had excelled himself and the house shone like a new pin. There were presents and letters of welcome, flowers throughout the house and a pantry full of food. Yes, there was kindness and generosity here too – I had to keep reminding myself of that.

We unpacked, then lay on our beds and settled back to read and catch up on letters. We fell fast asleep in the heat of the early evening and decided we didn't feel like anything to eat. We slept the sleep of the really worn out on our huge and airy, wire-netted verandah –with the mosquito nets rolled and knotted above us.

Next day, we woke early to that thrilling African dawn chorus. The bird song had never seemed more brilliant or melodic and the greyness of the morning was crisp and fresh before the boring eye of the sun rose up inexorably to claim another burning day.

Despite the gauze netting we had both been badly bitten by mosquitos, but fortunately it was not really malaria season.

Dudley Hampton seemed to have done a good job. Searson and Edwards were still not talking to each other, but at least their relationship was no worse. The sad news was that once again, there had been a "no" from Head Office regarding any thought of moving the school.

We were delighted when Sheila Forrester said she would like to come over from Plumtree to stay with us as she was battling with the after-effects of an operation and badly needed a break.

About ten days later, a visiting parson arrived to preach at Sunday service and John and I sat him down with a cup of tea before heading over to the hall. I was busy choosing the hymns and John was preparing for the service. I noticed him suddenly disappear. When he hadn't returned ten minutes later, I went to see if he was all right. He was lying on his bed with sweat pouring down his face.

'I can't go back,' he said. 'I feel ghastly.'

I cranked the handle on the party line phone we had just had installed – two short rings and one long one. After what seemed an age, Lalan answered and promised to come over immediately. As I hung the phone back onto its hook, I felt myself go cold. Within seconds I too staggered to bed.

It was malaria.

Not just any old malaria, of course, but the malignant tertian variety. We were both *very* ill indeed.

John slept almost continuously for ten days – the sweat poured out of him and he had to have his sheets changed constantly. But he was barely conscious through it all – just rousing sufficiently to take massive doses of quinine.

I was too ill to know what was happening to John. Lalan asked the clinic's Orderly, to be with us all day. She was with us all night despite running the clinic. Poor Sheila ended up taking turns to look after us as well while Aaron kept the house neat – and our various carers well fed.

I tossed and turned feverishly for hour after painful, dizzy hour but I could not sleep or sweat. I seemed to shake and shake with the ghastly rigors of the disease, having the most terrifying "coma" nightmares. It was ten days of being unable to see because of the worst headaches imaginable, unable to sleep, and either boiling hot or shaking with cold.

The only treatment in those days was to "blitz" it and we both had to take up to 60 bitter 0.5 mg quinine tablets per day. They made you feel ghastly – deaf, nauseous and thick in the head. I went bright yellow to add to my misery. We were unable to even contemplate getting up for the first ten days… and it took us at least another ten to regain any energy.

Lalan's careful treatment saw us through – although it had been touch and go on several occasions apparently, with our temperatures rising so high that there was the chance of damage to our internal organs. John couldn't finish off the school year as he had hoped to do but fortunately Dudley was able to stay on.

John never had malaria again. But I was not so lucky. I had two bad relapses and for several years, seemed to sustain a type of fever every time I travelled down to sea level. Having had this virulent strain of malaria, we would be unlikely to survive a second bout.

We had to decide whether to take the chance and stay – or to leave. Headmasters and staff, as well as boys, who had survived the disease before us, had been only too pleased to go. I confess that I saw it as a blessed chance to move up to, perhaps, Mashonaland… but understandably John wanted to finish what he had started.

'I really don't feel it is going to take very much more for the Government to agree to the move, darling,' he said. 'It is so important, and the teachers and boys are doing well – I can't let them down now. It would be an awful thing to do after building their hopes up over the last three years…'

Fortunately, Tjolotjo had taken on a completely new atmosphere with Maurice and now Daisy Mills on the staff. Mrs. Mills (who I only came to know as Daisy many years later) and I would go off on long walks and we became the firmest of friends. She loved my music, I loved her art and Mr. Mills understood exactly what John was trying to do.

Daisy was one of the very few people who seemed to understand so much of what was left unsaid, she knew what I was going through leaving Mummy and Daddy behind, and my daily battle with the heat and the headaches of Tjolotjo. I loved her whacky sense of humour and appreciated her considerable artistic talent. When John and Maurice were off at work we would play golf and tennis, or play the piano with no fear of remarks about "stopping that awful noise…"

Christmas 1939 was a happy occasion – the Mills, Guests and Swansons came round for the usual traditional lunch. I knew that Dick and Trish had been able to take time off and that the family was safely together in Budleigh Salterton. I'd been in Rhodesia for two years now and my visit to England had settled me down a bit and given me a greater sense of belonging in Rhodesia than had been the case before.

1940 dawned, with news from England looking more and more frightening. The Mills, John and I would walk down to Lalan's after supper to hear the world news as nobody else had a radio. They were companionable, but tense evenings. More particularly, because communications with Britain had become so difficult.

Every letter we wrote was photographed and sent as a small postcard – open for all to see. As a result, not much was said – and I didn't know what on earth was going on at home. Dick was by now on active service and Trish was in the WAAF. Mummy didn't know where they were. All Trish had been able to say was "where Auntie Craig used to be". She guessed it was Yorkshire and possibly Harrogate – and gained a bit of comfort from that.

But agonisingly, Daddy was failing fast.

The new school term started. There were 163 applications from all over Rhodesia and South Africa – for 54 places. The demand was now so great that this became an even stronger argument for a move – the water resources would not cope with these numbers.

The school had a mid-term break in March and Bob and Harrie said they would like to come over and spend a week or so with us. They loved popping out to see how their schoolmaster son was doing and John always valued time with his father – gaining such pleasure from the depth of the relationship they shared. Father and son would go off round the farm seeing the agricultural projects, as well as the building and other electives. They'd sit for hours over their sundowners discussing matters of policy and discipline – and considering possible solutions for the problems John faced.

Bob's wisdom and experience after all those years at Plumtree was invaluable and he was, in turn, intrigued and interested in the dimensions added by the education of Native as opposed to European boys at that very formative time. Bob and Harrie were living at Shabani, where Bob was involved in the local Native primary school although he was thinking of standing for Parliament, which might mean a move to Salisbury.

While the two men were off round the school, Harrie and I had the greatest fun together. She would teach me bridge and cooking – we'd play duets and discuss the pros and cons of all her children. Skinny and Morrie were thinking of coming back from Sarawak and although the two Grans, Harrie and Ganzie, had coped well with Anne and JJ for the last five years, they were beginning to feel the children needed a more traditional home life. Bob and Mo were happily settled in a veterinary job in Kenya although they had been terribly saddened by the death of their little boy, Nigel.

Jinny and John now had Anthony to look after – he was a jolly, rollicking and good-humoured little two-year-old and the absolute apple of their eye. John was doing well in the bank and his career path looked very promising as he took on bigger and better things.

So it was only Patrick, Harrie's very special last child who was a worry to her. He was in the Army somewhere in North Africa. Harrie's worry about him was intense. What an intact family they were. I was so glad and privileged to be part of it all.

Daisy would enjoy popping over while Harrie was there and the three of us would spend the time in fits of laughter. One day as we were sitting out in the garden enjoying some afternoon tea, Harrie looked at us and said,

'Now look here you two girls, it's high time you thought about starting a family. My annual baby was as good as a trip to the coast!'

We laughed and promised we would think about it.

John had been disappointed by the end of year exam results and felt some blame was due to the fact that the education department insisted on having written exams in the hottest time of the year. In pleading for re-think of the exam timetable, he wrote to them:

Many of the boys suffer from excessive exam-phobia and it is hard to see how this can be overcome. The Departmental Examination this year was easy and I am sure that standard VI are able to average higher marks than the 44% which they did get. The mistakes made were frequently very elementary.

It is a very great pity that the school year cannot or is not changed so as to bring the examinations in May or June. The heat this year has been intense. September, October and November are all bad with temperatures up to 106. I cannot see the sense of having the examinations at the very worst time of the year. We are not linked up with any external examination system… and it seems we are simply clinging to an unsatisfactory timetable because it has always been the custom to hold examinations in the summer in England…

Poor results in arithmetic proved to be a constant problem. John couldn't believe the department's dogged insistence that examinations be based on the English system.

…one is undoubtedly faced with problems which are not met in schools for European children. The chief of these is the lack of background. In their own homes, the boys have little need to calculate; a small knowledge of money and an ability to count the numbers of their cattle suffice. They cannot yet appreciate that if they are to become really good workers their ability to calculate has to improve.

Next year I intend to throw some of the onus for the demonstration of the practical use of arithmetic onto the Industrial Teachers. An attempt will be made to get them to point out exactly where and how arithmetic comes in the practical work they are doing. In the past, the industrial men have been rather too inclined to treat arithmetic as a purely academic subject, which is no concern of theirs.

Otherwise, he was quietly pleased with the way the boys were developing real leadership and responsibility.

There was still however, the major area of concern. They seemed more than ever, to want to discard anything and everything that involved their own native way of doing things, in favour of the European way. This was now causing enormous strain between pupil and parent – with parents regarding the school with increasing suspicion as their sons discarded traditional disciplines – and courtesies.

John tried to deal with it by preparing sermons and initiating discussions around the need to sustain their own systems and culture. But it seemed to fall on deaf ears. He was frustrated beyond belief.

'I sometimes feel,' he said over sundowners one evening 'that they think I'm trying to disadvantage them in some way by saying, "hold on to what you have". They don't seem to realise that what they have is so good – and I cannot be convinced that replacing it entirely with what we are offering, is in their best interests.'

'Perhaps they feel we are denying them something which would provide an entrée into our world,' I ventured.

'You're right – but how can we convince them otherwise? The European way will become dominant in time. I'm afraid that's probably inevitable. But if we can only put what we can offer on top of a solid foundation of respect for what they have already… somewhere there must lie an answer.'

'I thought back to a conversation I had held recently.

'Mrs. Malaba was talking to me last week about Naison's parents who are disturbed at the way he is treating them. She doesn't seem to have the same problem with Griffith – but then he is an exceptional kid.'

'Yes Naison is a problem – I'm going to have to watch him. But this is why it is doubly important. If they understand the importance of their own culture, they can then advance in the European way, while retaining a pride in who and what they are. But, somehow there always seem to be mischief makers around, determined to misconstrue what I say – and all too often these are misguided Europeans.'

'…I know,' I said ruefully, 'and I hate to say it, but they are usually recent immigrants from England. I'd like to shake the lot of them sometimes. They get so tied up with "do-gooding" in a situation where they have no background or understanding. I'm only just starting to get to grips with the complexities of it all – and I am lucky enough to have you beside me all the time to explain and teach me. But even so, I don't think I would ever have presumed to make the statements and take the actions they do, without finding out a bit about it first. It really makes me mad.'

155

'My darling girl – you can't take the blame! I suppose the thing that really worries me about these Poms, is that after about two years they seem to switch and become rabidly anti-black. I find that equally, if not more difficult to understand.'

'Yes, I know duckie – I've watched that happen too and can hardly believe it. You're lucky to have grown up in this country – it's almost as though you don't see a difference.'

'Well, I think I see and understand the Natives' great strengths,' John said, 'as well as their real weaknesses – we all have them. It's just that at this point those differences are sometimes quite great. The English immigrants seem to think they are exactly the same people, but just with different coloured skins. They're not. They're highly individual-istic and very different people with a well-considered way of social interaction – which works beautifully in most cases. But that's why I get so cross when white people condemn – or equally when black people condemn – on superficial knowledge. We are here to live and work together. We're educating these boys for the time when they will lead this country and we must be able to teach them the skills to do so, without turning them into black Europeans.'

He was always urging his staff, to cram in as much extra background and understanding as they possibly could in the short time the boys were within the influence of the school. Trying to keep them focused on schooling and practical work was not a problem.

Edwards had refused to take part in his duties for morning drill or attendance at Sunday activities. We privately rated him the laziest man on staff. Now he was protesting that he was working too hard and nobody should be expected to do these extra things.

'That's the other thing I do hate about the Poms,' John said. 'They bring their "me-first" attitudes with them, in a situation where we have to set extraordinary examples and where we simply don't have enough staff to cope in the first place. I never get these attitudes from the Native Teachers... they must think we are a very odd lot.'

In amongst these social problems, we had another, more urgent problem. A lion had killed two people in a nearby kraal and badly mauled another quite close to the school. As well as its obvious taste for humans, it had previously taken cattle and goats and was causing widespread fear and anger.

Something had to be done about it so we organised a shoot with four of the staff and two from the Native Department with guns and old Bembi as the tracker. Bembi was a great character – he had 27 wives and had lost count of the number of his children! I often spent hours with Bembi saying it was time to stop – but he would just grin with his much-wrinkled face creased in disbelief that anyone would want to stop having children. They were his wealth and his assurance for the future. Bembi was a marvellous tracker and he asked whether he could bring his son Enos with him to start learning the trade.

John and Maurice were going along with two of the guns, together with Teacher Ramushu and Teacher Mothobi… Daisy and I asked if we could come along. We were given very strict instructions as to what to do and were to stay close beside them at all times, unless there was a charge in which case we had to scatter and climb the nearest tree. As most of the trees in that particular area were thorny, I didn't fancy the thought!

Just before dawn was the time to go, when the lion would be out and looking for a kill. Days of planning went into the hunt with Bembi tracking and watching where the lion rested and what his movement patterns were for each day.

We woke early and dressed in khaki clothing to merge as best we could into the veld. Then we drove considerably north of where the lion was thought to be, as there was a strong southerly breeze that morning and we had to be sure the lion did not pick up our scent.

We started creeping through the bush. I was fascinated by the concentration on old Bembi's face. We watched him like a hawk. Occasionally he would signal us to stop. He would slowly turn his head in otherwise frozen mobility to try and pick up the slightest sound from the direction the spoor was headed. Daisy was a bit worried that Enos was being a bit too clever and showing off – but Bembi seemed able to control the boy.

An hour later we were still stalking – walking a few steps – stopping – listening – changing direction.

'He's here,' Bembi signalled to us to be quiet. 'And he knows we are here. He has just moved round us so that our smell is coming to him. He is very clever and his marks show he is very big and very heavy. We must be careful now.'

Chastising Enos for stepping on a twig, Bembi moved off ahead. I suddenly saw what Daisy was worried about. The boy looked sullen and defensive.

We moved as quietly as we could. Suddenly – a noise to our left. Enos had thrown a stone into a clump of thorn bush and the lion was coming out at him at a huge speed. As I turned to flee, I saw the old man rush in front of his son. I heard the lion's roar and actually felt the rush of air as it went past. It was horrifyingly close. I heard a scream of agony.

A shot rang out – then another. And the hideous growling and muffled roaring cut off as the lion was thrown to one side by the power of the bullets which hit him just behind the head and through the heart.

I turned to look. It had got Bembi. Brave old Bembi. Enos was howling in a corner. While Daisy tore off her jumper to put round the dying man, I ran to Enos and slapped him across the face, demanding more respect.

'Stop that ridiculous noise. Your father is seriously hurt – get over there now and tell him how sorry you are. He needs your help and your care, not your cowardly crying!'

The boy looked at me with hate-filled eyes, but then realisation of what he had done dawned fully and he stumbled over to the old man. Despite Daisy's jersey, the old tracker was shaking and trembling uncontrollably. He managed to speak a few consoling words to Enos… and to stumble out a few sorry words to the rest of us before his life drained from him and he quietly slipped away.

We stood absolutely stunned at the ferocity and horror of it all. Then as one, we bowed our heads and John said a prayer asking God to look after this brave old man.

I was rather appalled by my actions, but Enos turned to me as the men started to make a stretcher to carry Bembi home. The lion would be left where it was.

'Thank you *Inkosikaas* – I was able to say sorry and my father forgave me.'

Twenty-seven wives and all those children… what on earth were they all going to do? Enos was the oldest of the family and Daisy and I talked to him as we walked back to the school. There were several other little Bembis at the school and I knew John would do his utmost to ensure that they were able to stay. When we neared the school, John asked Enos to go ahead with him to find the senior wife, so that she could be told what had happened.

The school was abuzz with the drama of it. Give him his due, Enos came up trumps and looked after that family superbly. John managed to find a position for him helping with one of the farm projects and a year later he proudly showed me his first-born son – there was satisfaction in the fact that he had called him Bembi.

John had not been allowed to enlist as he was in a protected occupation. But our fears about others were realised; Maurice Mills and Wilkie (Charles Wilks) were called up. In addition, one of his best teachers, Herbert Ramushu decided to go to South Africa for further education. John asked him to return to the school as soon as he had completed his training and Herbert was keen to do so. But in the short term, the loss of these three men was going to be hard – particularly if approval to move the school came through.

The good news was that Searson had been transferred to the Native Department and would leave at the start of 1941. At last we could look forward to the moment when the embarrassing feuding amongst the European staff might stop – although with Edwards still around anything was possible.

He was a strange man. He would never let John know where he was. For some extraordinary reason, he seemed to feel he didn't need to abide by normal rules or courtesies. He would disappear for days sometimes and felt no explanation was needed.

John had been horrified to find on going in to the office early one morning, that Edwards was there, going through the personal staff files. He hadn't heard John come in and was absorbed in what he was doing.

'What on earth do you think you're doing?' John thundered.

Edwards paled and tried feebly to find some excuse, knocking the files over in his haste to explain. But he had been caught red-handed and from that day on, his hatred and vindictiveness turned against John as well.

He had to go – nobody on the European staff – or even our local Presbyterian minister would have anything to do with him. John wrote to Stark, head of the Native Education Department:

There is no need for me to retell the disputes which have arisen about the duties of the European staff, as you are familiar with all the details. I only need add that such disputes have had a very bad effect on the working of the school and that they are most unsettling and distasteful to those concerned. I have been conscious all this term, that the Native staff have been watching very closely the disputes which have been going on and since one of the teachers was directly concerned in one of them, they have no doubt drawn their own conclusions as to the causes.

Daisy was downhearted at the thought of Maurice going and she came over a few weeks later, to say she was feeling depressed and sick. It was only when I said I was feeling just as sick, that we realised that Harrie's words must have had an almost instant effect! Shortly afterwards it was confirmed – we were both pregnant. We were due within two weeks of each other – Daisy on 12th December and me on Christmas Day!

She decided to stay on at Tjolotjo for a few more months as John had asked her to start teaching a bit of "proper" art. The only art of any kind that had been taught so far was technical drawing and John had felt for some time that the boys seemed to have a natural aptitude, particularly in modelling and sculpting, which ought to be encouraged. Mr. Koti had been teaching singing and this was very popular. He had reached a very good standard in some of the choral pieces that that the choir had learnt.

On 20th June, the phone rasped out our code – three shorts and two longs. I went to answer it. Telegram for Mrs. Hammond – *"Daddy died peacefully at 4 a.m. this morning".*

Oh, how I wept. How I longed to be at home. There is nothing more intense than that feeling of helplessness when a loved one dies far away. Dear Daddy – I relived my wonderful times in the surgery with him, when he would allow me to mix up medicines with pestle and mortar and the wonderful musical evenings – I felt so guilty at being so far away.

John was wonderfully supportive and concerned – suggesting I go home to be with Mummy… but there was too much against it. At last, I became more reconciled and was glad he had gone "peacefully". I prayed for him – and for Mummy now left on her own, in a country fighting for its life – and with two of her three children on active service.

In the meantime, the school had started more advanced current affairs classes for the upper forms, which John enjoyed taking personally. He was fascinated by how the boys simply soaked up every scrap of information and asked more and more relevant questions. They were particularly interested in the developments of the war. His end of year report to the Department, in December 1940, says:

Boys as well as the Native teachers have shown great interest in the progress of the war. They have been kept up to date with the news by regular reading of the bulletins from the "Bantu Mirror" and the Information Office.

The questions they have asked show that they appreciate the issues involved, even though they seem unable to realise that they themselves could ever be seriously affected. Few have been sufficiently influenced to want to offer their services. There can be no doubt that the younger generation that is now growing up, is pacifist in outlook.

Few of the appeals to loyalty or upholding of justice affect them very greatly. This is, of course, understandable. Their present goal is the achievement of a higher material standard.

They quite honestly think that this is the only standard which rules among the European population and I can't help feeling that they are inclined to consider our emphasis on the spiritual and mental values in life to be very hypocritical.

It is a phase in their development, which is bound to appear and must therefore be treated much as one treats and understands the growing pains of children. They want to take all they can get with as little trouble to themselves as possible. They have not yet realised the need for giving.

John was now even more determined to move the school. He kept pounding Head Office with facts. One of the visiting soil conservation officers provided further ammunition, saying that when he employed men to make contour ridges, they could manage 40 yards a day in Fort Vic, 25 yards in Plumtree and only 15 in the Gwaai Reserve.

He began to feel the only answer might be to get H.S. Keigwin, the man who started the school in 1921, back to see just what they were coping with. Keigwin had to date, been the most ardent advocate of the school staying where it was, but he promised to come out and see us in August of 1940.

In the meantime, the climate of uncertainty was very difficult – prompted by the war and underlined by the question of whether or not we would be moving. John decided to continue as if the school was not moving. So when the need to build new stone kraals and sheds was raised, it was decided to go ahead, for if the school moved, the buildings would be a valuable legacy for the local people.

He was also trying to improve the quality of life for the Natives by encouraging them to work together on joint projects – but he was frustrated by how difficult it seemed to be to make them really successful or even to just keep them going. In the first scheme, the school bought milk from the local Natives to make butter, which was in turn, sold to the teachers. The cash would go back to the milk suppliers and they would learn in turn, to make butter. It started with great enthusiasm. He said in his report to the department that several milk suppliers:

> ...benefited quite handsomely. But two of them got tired very quickly. They didn't like having to get up early – one landed himself in prison and the fourth became ill. We helped him even to the extent of sending schoolboys to help him with his milking, but having once sampled this easy way of making money, he failed to put himself to any further trouble when he recovered from his illness.

The other scheme involved trying to improve the village sheep herd by putting the local farmers' ewes to the school rams. But the Natives found it difficult to regulate their breeding seasons.

> They undertook to castrate all their rams and to make some attempt to prevent their ewes being covered. Again, they were greatly enthusiastic, but their keenness must have waned because when they came in with their ewes in the middle of September many of the sheep were either in lamb, or had lambs running with them. The result was that we were only able to select 24 very poor ewes and as Mr. Searson says, three of these lambed while they were here. Both schemes were most disheartening.

John really was disappointed in the results of these schemes, as they were fundamental to Keigwin's promise. I could feel his idealism slipping.

'Sometimes I feel like shaking them Nan... it is such a tremendous opportunity – what do I have to do, to get them to stop being so apathetic? I really can't believe it – their lives are so difficult, yet when we offer them a chance to change, they can't be bothered. Perhaps they really aren't interested – perhaps it's the heat, the bilharzia or malaria... I don't know.'

As he had promised, old man Keigwin came down to the school in early August. It was a difficult situation for him. He had made a promise to the local people of the Gwaai Reserve that he would provide training and education for their children. And now we were asking him to let us move that facility.

He agonised over it during that first meal – particularly when he heard of the disappointing milk and sheep projects. He said we must understand that he would be letting the people down by moving the school away. He was such a straight, honest man, that he couldn't live with that broken promise. It did not look encouraging.

Keigwin and John spent two days going round the farm and the school. They came in weary and troubled. They talked long into the night.

By the end of the second day, as he realised the full extent of what everyone at the school was actually trying to cope with, he was visibly upset.

The transmission of virulent malaria strains to other parts of the country, constant high levels of absenteeism because of illness amongst the boys, difficulties in keeping staff, the isolation during the rainy season and finally the inadequate water situation were all very clear. He eventually had to agree to the move.

By the end of that last evening, John had promised that in the couple of years it would take to move the school he would do everything he could to leave a lasting legacy behind him, in the shape of improved herds and flocks, improved skills in building and agricultural under-standing.

Keigwin insisted that boys from the Gwaai Reserve area should receive preference in entry considerations. The Native Department had by now started a small school to take them up to Standard I and therefore the local boys should be able to hold their own.

John held a special assembly to thank everyone at the school for their patience and good humour over three difficult years when it was never certain whether there would be a move or not.

'I want to pay tribute to you all,' he said. 'You have, with very few exceptions, displayed infinite patience during this hiatus in the school's progress. You boys have uncomplainingly put up with considerable discomforts and you will, I feel sure, be overjoyed at the prospect of moving the school elsewhere.'

He outlined the shape the move might take and gave everyone a bit of an idea as to how they might be affected. The excitement was intense.

That day, as I was teaching Aaron a new recipe for some department visitors, I heard a strange hissing noise in the kitchen – like a kettle boiling. I looked around – but couldn't trace it. After a while, I went over to run some water into the sink to fill a mixing bowl – and saw

163

something shoot up out of the plug. I looked closer – then shrieked – loudly! We sometimes had lizards and things that would make their way to the kitchen. But this was no lizard. It was an enormous and very angry snake.

Aaron was amazingly quick and dispatched it with a well-aimed swipe of the broom taking the head and about 12 inches of snake off completely. It was a boomslang – very poisonous and a very nasty customer. I was completely unnerved at the thought that it could get up the drainpipe and into the sink so easily and wild horses were not going to get me back into that kitchen in a hurry! Eventually, we managed to close off the opening to the drainpipe with small-gauge wire netting to prevent any further invasions.

My pregnancy was progressing without any problems and it was wonderful to have Daisy in exactly the same shape. We read book after book about the state of our babes in-utero and gained some appreciation of what motherhood was going to be like. Keeping fit was obviously an important ingredient in our present state.

We fell into the routine of going for a daily walk round the school. One day, we were walking down by the Gwaai just as it was getting dark, when Daisy caught my arm.

'Look out!' she said. 'There's something coming towards us!' Something certainly was coming towards us – it was lion-like in colour and after the last episode, we didn't wait to ask questions. Hanging onto our growing stomachs, we ran for our lives.

We just managed to gain the shelter of one of our guest huts and pull the stable door firmly behind us when the creature rushed past. It was a very large ant bear. Then we realised what was happening – for the ant bear was being chased in turn by a group of highly excited schoolboys wielding knobkerries.

I don't know what happened to the ant bear – but Aaron, who watched the whole thing, was aghast. He shook his head gravely.

'Very bad to be chased by ant bear… with baby coming. Very bad.'

'Why Aaron – what will happen?'

'Very bad for baby…' was all he would say.

As the heat started to build up in September, I was increasingly prostrate with migraine and to my horror found I had picked up hookworm. Daisy had gone to be with her family in Johannesburg. I missed her zany, good humour and hardly a day went by without a blinding headache as the pregnancy progressed.

164

By mid-October and now nearly seven months pregnant, as John came in to lunch one day, I admitted how hard I was finding it all and said I just couldn't go on. I felt I should go to Salisbury for a break before the baby came. The heat and headaches had beaten me. Daisy and I had joked about having long-nosed babies because of being chased by the ant bear, but I was a little unnerved by Aaron's remarks and wanted to be nearer to civilisation.

Poor Johnny, he was overcome with remorse at not seeing how hard I was finding it.

He arranged for me to go as soon as possible to stay with Harrie and Bob, who had moved to Salisbury while Bob was getting ready to challenge the sitting member of parliament at the next election. Fortunately Sister Weir was planning to go up at roughly the same time.

Before I left, Johnny took a couple of days off and we spent precious time together quietly planning and chatting about the move, and enjoying the excitement of the imminent addition to our family.

In the first week of November he took Sister Weir and me in to Bulawayo and put us on the train for Salisbury. I hated leaving him and had to fight down my resentment at being apart at this most important time in our lives.

Oh Tjolotjo – you are not a kind place to live.

Dear Harrie was waiting, and I fell thankfully into her arms for a great warm hug.

But when Johnnie's first letter arrived, it felt like old times seeing that familiar writing on the lined beige paper:

Darling old Nan,
What a miserable hole this is without you! Getting home and finding the house all locked and looking very uninhabited made it very much worse – I felt once again the pangs which I used to suffer before you came out here to be married!
…a letter from Stark awaited me when I got back – it summons Edwards and me to appear in Bulawayo on Wednesday week for a pow-wow. I have just written to him again pointing out that I don't really think that there will be much hope of settling the business amongst ourselves, and that I am not prepared to abandon the stance about the necessity of removing the source of the problem. Stark will have to argue very hard to convince me on this point. Aaron is experiencing a bout of energy such as I have never seen before… he had all the washing done by tea time and had swept the dining-

165

*room and cleaned the bathroom! We have ten new baby chicks out of the
second batch of eggs...*

Harrie was not keen on my going into hospital for the delivery. She
had had all her children in the most primitive conditions and didn't
really approve of any extra fuss. She had arranged for a nursing friend,
Sister Ponsonby, to look after me at a sort of private nursing home in
North Avenue.

I began to enjoy my time in Salisbury, catching up with my friends,
thoroughly enjoying being pregnant and planning for the future.

Five days after I arrived, I woke up feeling a little strange and realised
I was haemorrhaging badly.

'Harrie help,' I cried. Poor old Harrie, who had never had a day's
illness in her life, was simply horrified at what she saw. She rang the
doctor urgently.

'Get her to lie down with her feet above her head – I'm coming.'

I was in a dreadful state by now – I had never seen so much blood.
How could the baby survive ?

'You're going to have to hang on to this baby – every extra week it
has will give it a better chance' Mr. Honey said. 'but I have to tell you
that you have a condition known as *placenta praevia*, which means that
the placenta has attached itself across the mouth of the womb. And in
addition, your baby is still in a breach position.'

Thank God I was in Salisbury. I sent a telegram to John letting him
know what had happened and reassuring him that I was all right. But
the haemorrhage did not stop. Mr. Honey felt it would be sensible for
me to go into the Lady Chancellor Hospital straight away.

John's letter came straight back, bless him:

My darling old girl,
*I do really think it wise that you should go to the Chancellor... just in case
of any mishap. As you say, it would be dreadful to lose the babe now.
Somehow, this indaba seems to have given it a more vital meaning. Already
I feel it is a more definite personality that it was before.*

*I am glad that you have been so philosophical about it all. Doctors, of
course, are anathema to Mums and always have been, with the result that
she sometimes speaks out rather too abruptly!*

*I love to hear that everyone has been so kind to my old darling, you are
such a dear thing that people can't really help it.*

166

I am sitting on the sleeping porch, sweating and feeling I should go back to the office. The absence of rain is getting serious. Yesterday looked more hopeful, but the clouds soon scattered towards Bulawayo. I'm so glad you have not been here to undergo the heat of the last few days.

Dropped in on Fish last night (the local parson) and brewed ourselves some tea in his study. He suggested that, as we had known each other four years, had we not better drop the Mr. or take to Christian names! So now it will probably be George and John! Not that I mind with him. He is proving a perfect mine of information about Edwards and seems to be almost more angry with him than we are!

I was now in the Chancellor and unfortunately the haemorrhage still wouldn't stop. The bleeding had damped down a bit, but there were now lumps of tissue coming away.

I was very worried but tried to be as light-hearted as I could in my letters to him:

My hair has been super since the perm and am wearing my best pink bedjacket, but all to no avail and all wasted! The only male I see is the doctor – handsome enough and plenty of scope there, but our conversation consists of awful details about discharges – black or brown and whether my bowels have been opened and so on! In spite of the bedjacket – too bad!

Having seen through my flippancy and also having received first-hand details from Lalan, who had gone home the week before, John replied:

My poor wee darling
Your two letters have just been making my heart ache for you. Oh my sweet-heart, I do so wish we could be together through all this. I know it is better for you in Salisbury – nicer place, nicer people, nicer doctor and oh, better everything, but I do just wish you were not nearly 400 miles away.

You are such a brave wee darling and even though you say you feel quite fit, you are wonderful the way you are going through all this business and still remain so cheerful. Oh Bunny, I do admire and love you so very much for it all…

Today is the last Sunday of the term – how very glad I shall be to see the end of it on Thursday. You alone, probably, will fully appreciate that.

I lay on the verandah this afternoon, sweltering and sweating. I slept in

fits and starts but had to arouse myself after each half-hour to mop up the sweat which streamed off me in buckets-full. Its only consolation was a snuggle with you in a dream…
Lalan thinks you should stay in the Chancellor till the baby arrives.

For some time John had been worried about one of his teachers, Bennie Musasiwa. He was going about looking very "hang-dog" and unhappy, but no matter how John enquired, he could not get to the bottom of it.

While I was away, and in the middle of the night, another of our teachers, Cyril Mhlanga appeared at the door saying Bennie had beaten him up. John went off to sort it out and when he came back an hour or so later he wrote:

Poor old Bennie, he suspected that Mhlanga had been sleeping with his wife, which is why he's been so unhappy. This evening, he told everyone he was going to Nyamandhlovu, but instead, he hid in the woodpile… and sure enough Mhlanga showed up. Unfortunately, Bennie let fly at Cyril – and his wife, so heaven knows what might happen now.

I was horrified as I had a lot of time for Mrs. Musasiwa and privately felt Bennie treated her pretty badly. I was not altogether sure John was reading the situation correctly.

How horrid about Cyril and Bennie – especially poor Bennie's kids – I fear he may be the greater skellum – in any case, one can't blame them when they see Europeans fighting in front of them all the time. Yes old duck, I think, like you, we must just stick it out a bit longer – bearing in mind the possibility of getting out into something else. It will be fun making plans…

I was allowed out of the Chancellor that weekend, but was as weak as a kitten and had to be wheeled out of the hospital in a wheelchair. Mr. Honey had told me to go home and build up my strength, but to take it very quietly and when I felt better, to take a few steps round the garden.

Harrie and Bob needed no more convincing that I should go into the Chancellor to have the baby and in fact, they wouldn't leave me on my own for a minute. Fortunately, there were lots of good friends around, prepared to "baby-sit" me if they went out.

It didn't last unfortunately and the next week I was back in hospital with my feet up in the air again. However, it seemed to clear up quite quickly this time and when Mr. Honey came in to see me on Monday night, I was hoping to be let out the following day. I was feeling a bit odd, but didn't let him know in case it stopped me going out. But by the following morning, I had to acknowledge it. I had fever. By lunchtime it had come on full force – a relapse of malaria.

Leaving hospital was out of the question as I battled with the fever. I was absolutely fed up. Honey immediately put me on 30 grams of quinine, knowing it would make me feel worse and warning that it might bring on premature labour.

Sure enough, after I had had only 20 grams, I woke up with an unmistakable tightening and thought – 'here we go'. I wrote to John:

...these went on all day – they all pooh poohed me, but I knew what it was, as they got worse and worse at shorter intervals. Mums thought so too and, of course I felt doubly rotten with fever and all the quinine as well.

At 4.15 in the morning after a tremendous battle, as weak as a kitten, having been in bed for nearly three weeks with no exercise, and now with a raging temperature and fever, our first child, a girl, was born. I had felt like a sailor pulling an enormous boat up a beach for hours, as I was given a sort of loop to pull on hard in order to help push. The next day my hands were raw and red.

I woke up (after some chloroform) just before 5 to hear the babe yelling and couldn't help laughing when I saw it – such a fat chubby, puzzled-looking little bundle with crowds of hair just like yours. It is the joke of the Home as no one will believe it's premature – it's the biggest, fattest and most intelligent-looking of the lot they all say!

Despite being the last day of term, Johnny was on the train from Bulawayo that night and came in to see me on Friday afternoon. He managed to stay the whole weekend although he had to return to close up the school. When he arrived back at the school, he wrote:

Only another ten days and we shall be together again and will then have the pleasant prospect of watching Jill (I think she must be that) grow up.
I really think you are a wonderful pair. I hope you were not too put out

by my surprise when I saw her first. She looked so wee and black and odd that I had rather a start. It's only now thinking back and comparing her with the other babies that I begin to realise what a very fine cheeild (sic) we have and what a wonderful little girl her mother is!

I was in the Chancellor for a full ten days, and confess I really needed it after all I had been through. Everyone kept suggesting names for this wee mite with the most extraordinary crop of black hair... but somehow we kept coming back to Jill. By the time we finally decided we were back at Tjolotjo and too far away from a registry office to add her name. So to this day, she has a birth certificate with no name on it! The heat in Tjolotjo was simply dreadful – it had ranged between 104 and 106 for over ten days and I just prayed that by the time we returned the rains would have started to cool it down, but not in such force as to flood the Gwaai.

John had a couple of possible new school sites he wanted to see early in the New Year – in addition, he had initiated discussion with the Roelkes and asked Head Office if it would be possible to have him down to oversee the building of the new school. They had agreed. The plus was that this meant Roelke and Edwards would be changing places. It really looked as though John's dream of being able to design a school and a curriculum that was relevant and accessible, was about to be realised.

In fact for us both, as we neared the end of 1940, things seemed bright and promising.

Chapter 9

Pick up your school

What a welcome home! I found myself sitting under a thorn tree, three days before Christmas 1940, trying to feed my tiny, two-week-old baby, with the Gwaai River in full flood once again. John hoped the water level might start to drop in a couple of hours time. As we sat chatting on the bank of the river I felt we were, at least, initiating our little creature into the ways of living in a very remote corner of the world very quickly.

We had not seen each other for months, and it had been a difficult time for us both. With John's arms round me as she fed, I felt that once again all was right with my world. The flood did at least, give us a chance to catch up and get to know our new babe.

Jill was a contented little person and she fed and slept quite happily most of the time, but we were having to fan flies off her face constantly and keep a lookout for big, aggressive Matabele ants which give a painful bite. John was absolutely fascinated by his new daughter and as we waited for the river to go down, he examined her fingers and toes and gently, gently touched her sleeping face.

These were new experiences for us both. We felt suddenly overwhelmed by our new responsibility and the dangers of bringing this precious little person up in Tjolotjo.

Like it or not, there was still a job of work to be done – particularly with the school move. I was going to have to be extra careful to make sure her nappies were ironed so that she didn't get maggot flies and that she would never be bitten by mosquitoes, for a start.

Maggot flies – I'd never heard of them until I arrived in Tjolotjo. These were great fat buzzing black flies, which would nestle into something damp and lay their eggs. If that something damp just happened to be an article of clothing which was left unironed, the

171

moment it came into contact with the skin, these eggs would assume a life of their own and burrow under the skin to turn into maggots. They were utterly revolting.

What would start as a pinkish and sore place would become larger and larger, developing a blackish "head". This "head" would be a real head – the head of the maggot! After a week or so, when it had fully developed, it would be ready to come out and become a fly. Once you could clearly see the head, with a push and squeeze this fat maggot – at least an inch long – would burst out leaving a very painful and deep hole, which was, of course, open to infection.

The only thing you could do was to smear Vaseline over the spots at a certain stage and this would mean the maggot couldn't breathe. With luck you could force them out a little earlier, which meant they were smaller and didn't leave quite such a hole behind them. I had seen some babies with eight or ten maggots in them, so meticulous ironing of all washing for the household and particularly for babies, was absolutely essential.

After about four hours of waiting beside the swirling, roaring river, with the heat of the day growing more and more menacing, the extraordinary high-pitched buzz of insects in the surrounding bush increased in intensity. It was like perpetual tinnitus.

John felt at last, that it might be safe to cross over the new drift. We were being extra careful of course and made sure we could see the outline of the drift pretty clearly before we attempted it. After a great lurch as our back wheels left the pull of the water, we were, at last, on the final lap home.

All the staff, teachers' wives, and people from the Native Department came over during the next week to see our new arrival. It was the happiest time imaginable. There were no other European babies around, but Mrs. Bulle had just given birth to a little boy, Ernest, and on the same day Jill was born, Mrs. Dabengwa had Dumiso, whom she used to call "Dumisani", almost singing the name as she held him in her arms and spoke softly and lovingly to him. We compared notes about how beautiful our babies were and how they were growing and I wondered what Mummy would be thinking about her grand daughter growing up as the only white child in the area.

Every day I would wheel Jill out under the trees in her pram to sleep, making sure that the mosquito net was securely tucked in all round her and checking overhanging branches to make sure they were clear of snakes or animals that might pounce. I mused over how even in my wildest imaginings as a schoolgirl in Southminster and Eastbourne, I'd never have dreamed I'd be bringing up my first child in this sort of environment.

Lalan also had a surprise for us. Two weeks earlier, a young mother had died in labour and produced a two-month premature baby. The father was nowhere to be found, so this minute scrap of humanity, weighing well under a pound when he was born, became her next challenge. It didn't seem possible that the tiniest baby I, or anyone else, had ever seen could live… but this was one fight she was determined to win.

Daisy and Maurice Mills were coming over to spend Christmas and the next three weeks with us, mainly of course, to introduce their new arrival, Jenny. What fun we had with our little "twin" girls.

Every gory detail was exchanged as we compared notes and looked on in awe at the new little humans we had all created. Lalan came over with her little bundle while the Mills were there. She hadn't given him a name yet as she had been too busy saving his life. But now, she reckoned he would probably make it, as he was nearly two and a half pounds in weight. Maurice looked at this tiny, shriveled little babe and said, 'Poor wee mite, he looks just like a prune.' And so "Prune" he became! He was also to become one of Jill's best early childhood friends.

The demand for enrolments for 1941 was going to be bigger than ever – with over 200 new applications received well ahead of the deadline. This didn't count the 75% of places taken by pupils already in the school who would obviously have first preference. Tjolotjo could only cope with around 200 boys. This year, it might be possible to increase numbers slightly because they would be building the new school and would effectively have two campuses. Everything was dependent on how many staff were available and at the moment, it looked ominously as though they wouldn't have nearly enough to cope with one school, let alone two.

During the year, an avenue of Cedrella Toonas, which are large leafy, shade trees, had been planted along the roadside through the teachers' village and round the main football field. Now that the rains had come and term was about to start, 1,200 gum trees and 600 jacarandas, all pricked out into tins, would be ready for planting. But with the go-ahead to move the school this was one of many aspects which had to be re-thought and discussed as to whether they should now be kept here or planted in the new site. Eventually a compromise was reached – 400 gums and half the jacarandas were planted at Tjolotjo, with the rest to go with the move.

Almost as soon as we got back, there was another issue to be faced. Thankfully, and as part of an ongoing battle with Head Office about the "legacy" to be left behind for the local people, John had been able to persuade Government to maintain an agricultural development post within the Gwaai Reserve Native Department. This was most important in that it would build on the relationships and joint ventures already established with the school. He had, at last, been able to persuade Head Office to move Searson off the school staff and into this position.

To sweeten the pill, and it had taken some arranging to do so, Searson could continue living in the school house until the move had taken place completely – probably a good year to 18 months away. All of a sudden, he said he wasn't prepared to do so because white ants had infested the house. It was made of pole and dagga – very pleasant, airy and cool with wide verandahs all around. The real reason for Searson's complaint however was that he wasn't prepared to continue living next to Edwards. They were given a couple of options and Mrs. Searson objected to both. John wrote to head office:

> *I fully realise that the Government cannot give consideration to the idio-syncrasies of wives of officers when arranging housing… I have endeavoured to find the most suitable solution. Owing however, to the attitude adopted on this occasion…*

With so many people away because of the war and with resources becoming scarcer almost by the minute, there was nobody else around in the School or the Native Department to be able to do anything about the house – which we all knew was perfectly habitable! John eventually told Mrs. Searson that as the Clerk to the Assistant Native Commissioner had been called up he would to do some minor repairs to his house in the short term. A few "bloomings" escaped his lips when he came home that night!

Although Edwards would also be moving on shortly, John had had enough of them both and wanted a clean sweep before the school finally moved away from Tjolotjo.

174

At long last, things seemed to be moving on the curriculum front as well. At last the Head Office was going to allow him to introduce two years of academic study – post Standard VI. The demand for the pupils graduating from Tjolotjo was already so great, that as soon as they left the school they were snapped up – but in the longer term, the opportunities for them would be limited by the current narrow curriculum. It was vital it was more applicable to the needs of the pupils in either getting decent professional jobs or in being able to contribute in a more direct way to the improvement of overall standards of living in their local areas. This meant that hand in glove with the industrial training there had to be a strengthening of the academic.

The present school curriculum was still very much based upon the English standard, where it was, of course, expected that every pupil would stay at school for the designated period of 10 to 12 years.

But this did not happen, at that time, in Central Africa.

Native families had many children. It was difficult enough for them to decide whether they even wanted education, let alone to educate them all. It was even more difficult to decide which child would be the chosen one to benefit from education. So most decided to send all their children along, for perhaps two years of schooling each. The fathers made all the decisions in those days as women were regarded as second class citizens. They found it difficult to understand why it was beneficial to their sons to stay any longer than two years, as they were still impressed by the seemingly vast knowledge their children brought home.

Parents were still pretty suspicious of the school, as pupils being what they are, they would laud it over those who knew less. Fathers felt that this "education" had the potential to break down the disciplines and cultures of their own society. John felt they were quite right, unless it was carefully handled. Yet in the new situations confronting them, they would also simply be left behind unless they understood and took advantage of the benefits of good education.

He in turn would use everything he could to get the pupils to understand that with this increased privilege came, not dominance, not pride, but greater responsibility to those who had not been fortunate enough to be educated.

John spent an awful lot of his time talking to parents, encouraging them and convincing them they were doing the right thing for their children. Then he'd come back and fight with the Department, using every possible argument to try to make them understand the parents' various concerns and his own difficulties with the present curriculum. He had to make the curriculum more relevant.

It was tough going and it was only the really far-sighted parents or the families of chiefs and headmen who really understood the importance of it all and the benefits to their sons in the light of the huge and now unstoppable social changes taking place.

From the beginning, there had been some outstanding families, the Malabas – parents of Heyi and Griffiths and the Khumalos, parents of Gwin in particular. They would attend every speech and sports day or other important school occasion, watching the development of their offspring with pride, and encouraging or chiding their children as needed.

Griffiths Malaba was the smallest boy in the school when he first came and at one end of year play, he had to sit, dressed as a pretty little girl, in a half rubber tyre which had been suspended over a tree branch and decorated with twigs and flowers. As two other "girls" swung him to and fro singing a song about "lovely water... precious water..." Griffiths beamed with delight at seeing his parents in the audience and would look at nobody else.

Both these families gave John great hope that in time they would see speech and sports days packed with parents. At this stage most parents, particularly the mothers, found the school environment too daunting to participate very much themselves.

In his attempts to gain the confidence of more parents John had to improve the skills of those who could only stay a couple of years, yet cater for those who could stay for the whole period.

By introducing additional academic years, it was now possible to concentrate on fine tuning the teaching of "industrial" work (agricultural courses, leather and tanning, metalwork, blacksmithing and building courses). This would mean that boys, who could not stay at the school for the full period, would have some practical and relevant teaching, enough to give them an advantage after only two years or so. Those able to stay for the whole eight years would move on to more theoretical and academic work in their final two years.

Underlining it all, there was still an urgent need for more local teachers, as there was no doubt that the pupils "played up" with teachers from South Africa. So there was an additional benefit to adding those last two academic years, as the senior boys would be able to start teaching some of the lower classes themselves, thus relieving the local teacher shortages and earning money to keep up their own education. John knew he would be able to employ as many of those who had completed the whole curriculum as he needed – but the demand for well-educated boys with the potential to move into other better paid professions was growing every day.

At last, after four unforgiving years, it looked as though my dear husband was going to have not only a new school in a much healthier location, but replacements for Searson and Edwards and a revitalised, more relevant and more practical curriculum as well. In addition, he was going to be able to design the school exactly the way he wanted it – because there was nobody else around to do it – or perhaps more important, to interfere!

An other aspect of school life that John always felt was important in providing a balanced education, were the lessons to be learned in the playing of sport. Sport underlined the importance of keeping fit, of learning how to win gracefully, to lose philosophically and to play as a part of a team for the advantage of the whole.

Before his call-up six months earlier, Maurice Mills had spent time introducing and coaching cricket. There had been some initial grumbles because everyone just wanted to play soccer but by the end of his last year there had been some excellent batting and bowling figures presented and a new enthusiasm for the game. Inter-house matches were hotly contested and the highlight was the school versus "the rest". The rest being anyone who could play any sort of cricket – from the staff, the Native Department or anyone else close enough to co-opt. The school usually won quite easily!

In 1941, it was hoped to start an inter-school cricket competition. Pride in the school and its achievements reached a peak when, for the first time in ten years, Tjolotjo, while narrowly losing the athletics to its arch-rival, Tegwane, won the football convincingly.

In fact, the school was feeling rather proud of itself. As the term started during the third week of January and after four years of waiting, the pupils were coming back to take part in "the move" – at last a reality after so many expectations. Enthusiasm and motivation at every level, was sky high.

As we entered the new term, things started to move quite quickly. Mr. Roelke joined us from Domboshawa in February. It was wonderful to see these old friends who'd looked after me so well when I first came out from England. Their daughter Shirley had gone from strength to strength at her boarding school after my early correspondence teaching and was turning into a most attractive and vivacious person.

For the first time, since he'd come in 1937, there was the prospect of peace among the European staff. John was almost light-hearted at the thought of being able to build a team of people around him, all heading in the same direction.

But it was not all going to be smooth sailing – of course.

There was a world war taking place – and beside that, it was still difficult to persuade Rhodesian Europeans to teach Natives. Unless they were missionaries, or among the very few that understood the importance of well-directed and balanced Native education to the future of the country, John was frequently made to feel he was "the wrong side of the fence" in the eyes of his contemporaries.

With the demands of the war and the lack of qualified Native Teachers, the school looked as though it would end up having no agriculturalist until at least halfway through the year. Even worse, it was unlikely to have a European academic teacher (to replace Maurice Mills), an African academic teacher (to replace Herbert Ramushu) or an office clerk. Little did we realise then that this situation would last for the whole year. To top it off, Lalan was off on six months' leave from mid-year.

The shortage of staff would have been difficult enough, but now in each term, some of the staff and whole classes of boys would have to go over to a new site to start building the school.

However, approval to move had been finalised, so a site could now be chosen officially. In the first two months of the year John looked at a number of places and rejected them all for one reason or another. Then, when Jill was about four months old, he asked me to go with him and look at a place called Essexvale just south of Bulawayo.

The site John was looking at was at Mzingwane – about three miles from Essexvale. It lay at the base of a large hill called Isi'Koveni where open, undulating grasslands gave way to a good perennial stream. This meant that with two excellent boreholes already in the area, there was a constant and secure water supply.

Although there was no electricity yet, the site was also on the route of the water main and the new power line, which was being installed between the Ncema Dam and the city of Bulawayo. So the chances of bringing electricity to the school in the next five to ten years were good.

One of the most interesting things was that there seemed to be good rapport between the Europeans and the Africans of the area. There were in fact, some very interesting Europeans around Essexvale – they seemed ahead of their time in their vision for the future, but were down-to-earth realists as well. We found the Natives worked more easily with the European farmers and the Native Department there than they had done at Tjolotjo or Domboshawa. You could almost feel the tangible warmth and respect between them.

The piece of land in question was large enough to take the school buildings, but it was nowhere near enough for the farm and the agricultural training side. In order to maintain the farm, it would be necessary to negotiate the purchase of additional acreage from the Native Purchase Area. This would need difficult policy changes and even more difficult acceptance by the local Natives.

It was potentially and politically very sensitive. But within weeks, local farmers, the Native Commissioner, Mr. Fletcher, and the local chief had held meetings and they were all excited by what the establishment of the school in Essexvale would do for the whole district. We were almost overwhelmed by their interest in seeing the school established there – as well as their reassurances that they would help make it happen. John decided Mzingwane was to be his only recommendation to Head Office.

I thought it looked wonderful. The school would face the blue Bushtick range of hills, which swept down towards Balla Balla and eventually to Shabani. The altitude was nearly a thousand feet higher than Tjolotjo and *much* healthier. As for the village of Essexvale – well! It was a town by comparison – with the choice of *three* grocer's shops within a ten-minute drive of the school. I also felt the name was rather appropriate and the contours of the valley did remind me very much of my home county of Essex. We went home very excited by what we had seen.

Having decided this was to be the site, it then took another agonisingly slow four months to secure the myriad of necessary government approvals and extract a promise from the department that they would ensure that there was enough land for the farm as well.

It was going to cost almost £10,000 to build the new school – about £7,500 of this to come out of a loan from Government. There was no question of any Government grants. The rest would have to come from revenue earned.

At last, in May 1941, John was able to go over to Mzingwane offi-cially, with Roelke, Dabengwa, Mothobi and Bulle to pace out and position the school buildings. It was important to include features that would make the Native youngsters unused to the European way feel more at home, as they often felt alienated in their first couple of years.

So John and Roelke worked closely with the three teachers to try to achieve some sort of middle ground, particularly for those first few years.

They all felt it was important to encourage pupils to stay in the school for as long as possible. Those first impressions and the way they settled in often made a critical difference to their attitude throughout their school life. Making them feel at home meant the pupils them-selves would demand to stay longer.

A lot of discussion went on, particularly into the design and posi-tioning of dormitories. Eventually, it was decided they would all be thatched and smaller than the normal boarding school dormitories of the time. They would also be built in such a way that they were clus-tered around the housemaster's quarters. This would mean that boys could approach their housemaster in the same way they would approach their Chief or elders at home and gain the sympathetic ear and consensus decision-making processes they were used to.

The Second World War meant that there were pitifully few building materials anywhere in the country – everything had been comman-deered. As much as possible was going to have to be made by the boys themselves even down to the metalworking of door handles, fence posts and chains. It was going to be quite an exercise.

For sometime now, a man called Mazorati had been visiting Tjolotjo as a guest of the Native Commissioner, Chummy Swanson, to play golf on our funny little course.

He was a wonderfully flamboyant character – very good-looking and immaculately turned out in perfectly pressed linen slacks, worn with fine cotton shirts and an expensive cravat. He brought a rather devil-may-care exotica to our funny little society. He was also an exceptional pilot and would fly onto a little gravel strip at the end of the playing fields, waggling his wings at us to ask us to come and fetch him as he zoomed in over the school. There was never any shortage of people to meet him and pick him up.

He suggested that John and I come to a flying day at the Bulawayo airport to have a flip as he had taken John up on a previous occasion. Well, this could not be refused! We picked up Jean and John and set off for the airport. It did look a very small plane, but there were lots of others buzzing around and nobody seemed to be particularly concerned about anything. His plane had double wings and two seats one behind the other – both open to the wind. Having assured me he would do no "tricks", Mazorati put on his flying helmet and goggles and gave me the same items to wear. I found he could talk to me quite clearly which was reassuring, as I was definitely nervous!

John waved me off as we zoomed into the air.

Oh! This was wonderful. We swept down low over the suburbs of Bulawayo and I was sold on the whole idea. Then two other aeroplanes zoomed up beside us and we flew in formation waving at the pilots on either side. Great fun! I heard Maz say, 'I'm just going to do a loop the loop.' Fortunately we were over and back again before I realised what was happening.

'Now I will do a slow roll,' he said.

Blast the man, I thought. He said he wouldn't do any tricks, but it seemed all right and in any case I didn't have time to protest before we were climbing up and up – and up – and up.

As the plane started to go over onto its back I felt myself lifting from the seat. Too late I saw the straps hanging beside my seat – I had not been strapped in as this was going to be a straight flight. I spotted a tiny little hook on the floor, managed to curl my fingers around it and hung on for grim death. It seemed to take an absolute eternity before I started to fold back into the little space behind the pilot, screaming all the way.

John standing below saw the plane going into a loop and knew I wasn't strapped in. His heart stopped as he saw my legs hanging out. He was utterly helpless. He could only watch as the plane completed its loop and pray we'd come back as soon as possible.

Thank God Mazorati realised with horror what was happening! I fell back into my seat awkwardly, knowing that I could never survive another manoeuvre of this kind. He reassured me that we were going straight down again and I just clung on until I felt the wheels bump along the ground. Never, never again! I was shaking so much I could hardly haul myself out of the plane – yet at the same time I couldn't escape from it fast enough. Willing hands reached in and I was soon sobbing in John's arms. I couldn't speak from the shock of it all. Poor

Mazorati – he felt absolutely dreadful and didn't know how to make amends.

He'd always been very interested in the school – and particularly in its projected move to Mzingwane. Whether it was because of the aeroplane incident or whether he was genuinely keen to help, Mazorati became our saviour. He was a most enterprising man and was with the Rhodesia Air Force Training Group in Gwelo at a time when a large number of British pilots were out there, being trained up for the war.

He felt that as they all came from such differing backgrounds, there was likely to be a good reserve of skills among them, which might be put into effect for our benefit. He returned to Gwelo and asked if there were any volunteers with the appropriate drafting or surveying skills who would be prepared to give up their spare time to help.

Many came forward, delighted to be of help to the country that had befriended and taken them in for this important training. Between them, they drew John's plans to scale and started to source some of the more difficult material needs.

Roelke and John spent hours working out how on earth they were going to be able to maintain the teaching programmes, both academic and industrial, with such restricted teacher numbers – on two campuses.

In July, Roelke and Bulle travelled to Mzingwane, accompanied by one senior class of building boys. They were to be there for one term and in this time they'd be doing some academic lessons but the main focus would be their practical work, overseeing and working with local labour in making bricks and laying foundations. At the end of the term, they'd return to Tjolotjo to catch up on their academic work requirements and another class of boys would be sent over to Mzingwane to continue the work.

The boys and staff camped out while they built the first dormitory – then they'd move into that and the next lot would camp out – and so it went on. As soon as they had completed dormitory space enough to house them, they'd start on the first classrooms – quite a step up from the large marula and m'futi trees they had used for this purpose for so long.

Together with the second lot of building pupils, went a class of agriculture students. Their job was to plant vegetables and fruit trees so that the school could be heading towards self-sufficiency in meat, milk, butter, cheese, fruit and vegetables as soon as possible.

Each mid-year break, John drove to Kumalo near Bulawayo for army training. Although he was in a protected occupation, he still might have to go to war should the need arise. I took the chance to go over to Shabani to spend some time with Harrie and Bob. Anne and JJ were staying there as Skinny and Morrie were in the middle of establishing their new tobacco farm in the Umvukwes. They were growing into lovely kids and they really took to Jill – I hardly had to worry about her at all. It was good to feel that she would be growing up with lots of cousins round her.

Before he went off for his army training, John had been asked to send in a report on a disciplinary matter which had arisen at Domboshawa and which was causing the Native Department concern.

After much thought, he decided to write unofficially to the head of the Department, George Stark, as in this way he could say things which needed saying, much more frankly and without having to be too bothered about the politics of it all. He wrote at some length and was delighted, on his return, to receive a very complimentary letter back from Stark:

Dear Hammond,
Thank you for writing privately rather than officially about the Disciplinary Committee at Domboshawa. I found your letter most interesting and illuminating. I have always held that you have the makings of a good headmaster, but this judgment has been based on the attitude, which you have adopted in the hundred and one things, which go to the running of a school.

Your statement concerning the philosophy of headmastership does my heart good and confirms my view that your appointment as Principal of Tjolotjo was a wise move.

I liked very much your statement that, "invariably it is the moral tone, which they (the Headmasters) have introduced, which classes them above others". There you've struck it! That's the kernel of the whole business. I am delighted with your reaction. It is that of a healthy headmaster.

I am not going to try to answer your letter because I do not want in any way to even seem to suggest that I do not most heartily agree essentially with your viewpoint. I shall therefore leave the matter over for discussion with you when an opportunity of meeting occurs. It will make a very good subject for discussion.

This was encouragement indeed as John still felt his lack of years, having only turned 31 a few months before. I, of course, knew how exceptional he was, but he didn't accept my praises as being quite as objective! Despite the positives, there were always critics of course.

John's report at the end of 1941 says:

I feel well satisfied with the progress made at the New Site. The delay in starting has put us behind the schedule, but Mr. Roelke hopes to cover the major part of the programme for this year.

The most pleasing features... are the progress made with brick making and the supply of labour, which has always been available to us there. The bricks are of excellent quality and we are now well on the way to making the 300,000 at which we aimed.

While progress has been good, it has nevertheless been seriously held up by the difficulty in acquiring building materials and by the inadequate facilities for transport and water supply. I would like to endorse the urgent plea, contained in Mr. Roelke's report for the speedy provision of these facilities and of the water and power scheme in particular.

It is difficult to visualise the completed project when all one can see is the bare veld, but as the first buildings go up we shall be able to clarify our ideas and to make such amendments to the plan as may be necessary.

Criticism has been levelled against us particularly in regard to the site selected for the accommodation of pupils and African staff. Our critics, as far as I can judge, would wish to see dormitories and African staff houses tucked away in some remote corner, hidden and unobtrusive. They would have the whole plan designed simply to give the European staff houses all they would require and would ignore the fact the Natives also appreciate pleasant views and the fact that it is a school for Natives. In drawing up the plan the main concern has been for the efficient organisation of schoolwork and I do feel that the present arrangement will make for that.

Any perceived privilege for the Europeans, simply because they were Europeans, had always worried John.

'It irritates me when people assume that Europeans must automatically receive some sort of privilege over Native teachers,' he said one night over our regular "sundowner". 'They're excellent blokes these teachers – they've worked hard and given up a lot to reach their position. They deserve proper recognition for that.'

'What are you going to do about the houses?' I asked.

'Take no notice, just build and let them criticise later. I'm not going to put up with it. It's good for the boys to see that the initiative and enterprise of their Native teachers attracts real reward.'

'Do you think any of the European teachers might leave?'

'No, I don't think so. If they do, perhaps we didn't want them anyway.'

He sighed. 'But you're right, Nan. I do have to be careful to make sure that it is still attractive enough for European teachers to want to come here – the salaries certainly don't offer any incentive and these boys must have the best teaching possible, it's a fine line to tread.'

One of the things which was stopped very quickly at Tjolotjo was the free milk, butter, eggs, vegetables and meat which were enjoyed by the European staff at Domboshawa. At Tjolotjo and Mzingwane, these things were available to all staff – at a small cost – with the earnings going back to school funds.

Jill was walking by the time her first birthday came round and I gave her a little birthday party under the trees. The Mills were back in Salisbury as Maurice was headquartered there, so there was only one other little European child around and he was visiting his grandparents, the Gavins, at the Native Department. Dumisani, Ernest and Prune, plus all the other teachers' children were invited and a great time was had by all.

Mummy was fascinated by the photo I sent back to her and she showed it to Dick and Trish, the Castles and everyone else she could find! I still couldn't believe I was living such an utterly different life to the one I had expected.

There were highlights, but I confess I mostly found Tjolotjo an absolute nightmare – but I'd never been more in love with my dear John nor more determined to stick it out for his sake.

We were both so pleased with, and proud of, our dear little "baba". She was a bright little thing and would keep herself occupied for hours playing with Prune and with the little mud oxen that Aaron or Bessie, her nanny, would make for them. She had very few toys, but it didn't seem to matter one iota.

I was always insistent, however, on reading her at least one story every evening. She soon picked it up and would recite the best loved ones back to me. I also played and sang nursery rhymes to her. She would sing and clap in time. I was delighted to see that she was obviously going to be musical.

And so 1941 came to an end. It had been tough – a drought, bad malaria and not enough staff, but we had struggled through it and Jill didn't get malaria.

If we thought malaria was bad in 1941, we had no idea of what lay in store in 1942. It was as though the area was not going to allow us to leave without serving up a huge backhand of troubles. In April, with quinine almost impossible to get, John wrote to the Health Department:

> *I attach a brief report from Matron. The figures she gives demonstrate all too clearly what a small part of her time is devoted to schoolwork in comparison with the time spent on the patients from the Reserve.*
>
> *This is a point, which the Medical Department appears to have been loath to appreciate.*
>
> *Malaria in the first term of the year was even worse than in 1941. Nearly half of the boys contracted the disease and many of these had two and some three periods in hospital. There were times when as many as forty boys were absent from school on a single day. The difficulty of obtaining quinine was one of the main causes of the large number of re-admissions.*
>
> *There is one aspect of the school's health, which I cannot stress too strongly; that is the debt we all owe to Miss Weir. In the six years she has been at Tjolotjo only one boy has died and his death was due to heart failure which would have been hard to cure under any circumstances.*

While Lalan was coping with the malaria in April, George Fish our local Methodist minister sustained a bad dose of malaria that turned into Blackwater Fever. Europeans seemed more susceptible than the Natives, to the really bad variants of the disease. "Blackwater" was particularly nasty because it caused internal haemorrhaging and the breakdown of the red corpuscles. In most cases it was fatal.

He had to be moved – and fast. Johnnie took our trusty old green lorry over to his home where the poor man was by now, in a critical condition. He had great respect for George Fish and it was vital to take him into a hospital immediately.

It was 75 miles away, and the dark was already setting in. Fish was on the point of death but for some extraordinary reason, his wife didn't seem to realise this and she was fiddling around packing up this and that with John in an agony of apprehension.

The rain came pouring down as they were leaving and the road was probably in the worst condition it had been for some time. It was very, very rough at the best of times. After a horrendous storm, on a nightmare road, with a man so ill that every minute counted, John eventually arrived at the Memorial Hospital in Bulawayo and thank God, George Fish recovered. He was a much-loved figure in the community and he would have been badly missed by everyone.

I was now becoming paranoid about Jill getting malaria in that dreadful year – everyone you saw had it, or was just recovering from it. She fretted in the heat terribly. From the time she was about eight months old and could sit up on her own, I'd pop her under the garden sprinkler to cool her down. She loved it and would shriek with glee. But it only provided temporary relief and I was now constantly anxious about her welfare. I had breast-fed her for over a year, but once that protection was removed she seemed to suffer more.

As she grew, she became pale and thin. In fact, she was frighteningly so by comparison with the red-cheeked, chubby babies I was used to in England. Underneath as cheerful an exterior as I could manage, I was worried sick, but I didn't want to bother John, because now he really was right in the thick of things.

The realities of coping with short staff numbers and the terrible malaria of that year was making what was always going to be a difficult time, even more so. It didn't take much stirring of the pot, just when the malaria was at its height, to persuade the boys to be troublesome. They went on strike ostensibly because of "unfair" treatment by one of the teachers from South Africa. John's report on the incident reads:

Full reports were sent to you… unfortunately, I can add little now to the surmises made then as to the real cause of the disturbance. Being the first situation of its kind with which I have had to deal, it may be that I was not sufficiently severe. I have, however, now made perfectly clear to both boys and staff, the steps that I intend to adopt if such indiscipline is repeated.

I feel satisfied that a small number of malcontents were the ringleaders. Eight of these left at the time of the strike; two applied to return but were refused. The real measure of the discontent is, I think, indicated by the fact that only ten boys failed to return at the beginning of the second term and I know that at least four of these would have done so had they found the fees. There has been little evidence of any further discontent, or of any resentment of teacher Koti.

Several cases have been reported to me of minor squabbles between the boys and prefects. At present, discipline within each house depends rather too largely on the personality of the prefects of the house and insufficiently on the Housemaster. There is a notable exception to this in Jackson House where Teacher Dabengwa has had great success in instilling the idea of House Discipline and unity. Teacher Nthlobo, on the other hand, has been particularly weak in this.

I very much hope that when the rearrangement of accommodation for both pupils and teachers is introduced at the New School that Housemasters will be able to exert greater influence on the boys of their houses than is now possible.

Privately, John was furious. Teacher Koti was an excellent man and he was being victimised purely because he was a Xhosa – the Zulus on the staff were sufficiently tribally close to the Ama'Ndebele (who formed the great majority of pupils) to be acceptable – but the Xhosas – no. They were too different. The strike had been stirred up because Koti had disciplined a couple of real troublemakers.

It became more and more apparent that more Matabele and Shona boys had to be trained to become teachers as soon as possible. In the meantime it was equally vital to make sure that the excellence of the work Koti was doing became the criterion – not the tribe to which he belonged. Fortunately, he was well liked by most of the other teachers.

Then another concern started to rear its head. As 1942 drew on, it appeared that the Government was going to do absolutely nothing about the existing buildings at Tjolotjo but let them sit and rot.

This seemed ludicrous and was an enormous waste if they weren't going to be used for some useful purpose. John presented ideas for further uses but there was no response from any of the Government departments concerned. In yet another report he said:

I have on several occasions had to justify the decision to move the school. Many outsiders are critical and I am not sure that all are convinced of the rightness of the decision. Criticism comes mainly from Native Department officials and Missionaries.

The former are usually convinced by the arguments I have been able to put to them, the latter are less easy to persuade and some have warned me that the Government may be called upon in Parliament to justify its action.

Criticism centres not so much on the decision to move as on the apparent waste in abandoning the present school at Tjolotjo. Persuasion would not be difficult if they could be presented with a scheme for the disposal of existing buildings here.

During this awful time at Tjolotjo, the development of the new school at Mzingwane was steaming ahead. For the first time:

...each industrial subject will have its own classroom. Here we have had such limited accommodation that the question of whether teachers or pupils should change rooms has not been an issue... in most weathers, the shade of a tree serves just as well as that of a roof.

The carpentry shop had been completed by the end of 1941 and a class of boys had gone over early in 1942 to start making roofing timbers, window frames and doors – and most important in the light of moving the animals across, fencing posts. The mid-year report to Head Office stated:

In January all the post-Standard VI builders and final-year carpenters went to the New Site. They were joined at the beginning of the second term by Standard V. There were 76 boys and three teachers in residence there. Next year it is hoped to move Standard VI over there at Easter, leaving only Standard IV and the specialist in Tanning and Farming at Tjolotjo.

When this move takes place I shall transfer the office to Essexvale. It is to be hoped that when this happens, some clerical assistance will be available to ease the situation.

This January move sounds so easy when merely written up in a report – but this was actually an enormous undertaking – we immediately labelled it our "great trek".

One teacher and 52 boys herded almost half of all the four-footed animals at Tjolotjo, the 100 difficult miles across to Mzingwane. The preparations for it all were enormous. Even the local community got involved when they were commissioned to make dozens of plaited basket carriers for the chickens. These were tied onto the ox wagon and would give them all eggs en route. They had to work out, in conjunction with the staff, exactly which animals they could slaughter for food and which they could milk in the estimated four to five weeks it would take to trek that distance.

The ox wagons were loaded up with masses of educational necessities as well as building and carpentry needs. The boys were responsible for keeping the materials intact, for the planning of each day's trek and for ensuring there was enough water and food, not only for the trek oxen, but also for all the herds of cattle, pigs and sheep as well. Herding pigs is a talent in itself! What a sight it was to see them leave at last – there was much farewelling and scampering along of the local piccanins who followed them until they crossed the Gwaai and were lost to sight.

John was doing for his boys what his father had done for Plumtree – giving them the responsibility to undertake huge tasks… but before they went, he let them know that he trusted them and had no doubts that they were quite capable of achieving it.

They did – and he was immensely proud of them – as they were of themselves. It was an enormous achievement. The excitement when they were first spotted as they turned into the long drive up to the new school was absolutely intense – Europeans and Natives alike lined the route to cheer and follow them all the way down that final lap home.

While things were on the whole going very well at Mzingwane they were a still difficult at Tjolotjo. There was not only the feeling of having been left behind and away from the excitements, but there was the debilitating depression, which always followed malaria. The actual statistics of boys absent due to malaria are astonishing.

The average number of boys away per day was 3.2 in February, 7.8 in March and 13.5 in April, falling back to 7.1 in May. Few of these patients were re-admissions, and you will be able to judge how large a number of boys had to miss work in school because of malaria. For the whole year a total of 1,064 days were spent in hospital through malaria alone. An average of 8 boys a day in the first term. I sincerely hope that the better drainage and more open country of the Essexvale site will see a large improvement in this aspect of the school's health.

Apart from malaria, the general health of the school has been good. Early in the year we had several cases of scabies. In October and November I was worried by the appearance of three cases of dysentery.

I have always been haunted by a fear of an outbreak of this type because our sanitary facilities are not of a type which makes for the easy control of this disease. Several boys were treated for venereal disease – none serious. A pleasing point to note is that boys now come forward of their own accord if they suspect VD infection…

It was still amazing to me, that the greater percentage of pupils in the school were still in their mid- to upper twenties – some of them married, and even some with their own children. Each year the average age was coming down, but it was a slow process.

Gradually the boys themselves started to take the initiative in projects that encouraged John enormously. One evening he told me how two of the most senior boys had come to him with a request.

'They told me they'd like to learn to write English really well and could they start an essay competition? I asked them how they would go about it and felt it should be open to anyone who wanted to try and write, not just the senior boys.'

'Were they happy with that?' I asked.

'Well, they didn't suggest it, but they agreed readily when I said I felt it should not exclude anyone. They've asked if I'll set the subjects and mark the essays, then give a short critique at Assembly. I think it's a great idea.'

I knew how pleased John was by this rather surprising initiative, but I was bowled over the next night.

'During the prefects meeting this morning,' he said, 'I was asked how the boys could help the local people in the reserve due to the terrible rains we have been having.'

'What did you suggest?' I asked

'Well, we threw around a whole lot of ideas and they have settled on putting on a concert to raise funds. I've agreed to invite people to pay five shillings each to come and see it. It's a bit expensive, but because it is for a good cause, initiated by the boys themselves, I reckon we'll be able to fill the place with people from Bulawayo and a couple of bigwigs from Salisbury. We'll tag it on to Sports Day and make it the first evening's entertainment.'

Three hundred people came to that concert, every one of them paying their 5/- a head and when we totted up the takings at the end of the evening we found there was a total of £103 in the till! So there had been some generous 5/- entry fees paid.

'Many of the people would not let us give them change,' they were excited to report.

John was able to announce at Assembly that once expenses had been

191

deducted (which he insisted on doing as a learning process in running fund-raising or other commercial ventures) they had made a hand-some profit of £91. As he was going over to Mzingwane that week, he also announced it there with great ceremony.

It was a great success. We were thrilled to see that the boys who initiated it were treated like heroes when they went out to present the money to the Chief.

The annual report at the end of 1942 is a fascinating glimpse of the school in microcosm. It was able to show 12 months of sound achievement on both sites, despite the lack of teachers.

The Academic work of the school has been more seriously affected by short-ages of staff than any other area. With only four teachers I took on rather more teaching than I should have done and left myself insufficient time to give full supervision to the teachers.

A fair standard has, despite this, been maintained though the percentage of failures is undoubtedly high. A tightening up of our entrance tests will, I think, help to reduce this figure to its right proportions. In Standard V, for instance, half of the failures were boys who entered the school in January.

In Standard IV we realised that many boys were very weak when we admitted them and they were considered to be more in the nature of a Standard III. Most of these boys themselves realise this and will probably return next year to take Standard IV again and they should then have little difficulty.

Arithmetic is still the weakness... following the marking scheme set down for the departmental examination, credit was only given for correct answers. If we only took off a proportion of the marks for a wrong answer if the boy showed that he knew how to do the sum but merely made a slight error in working, our percentage of failures would have been about halved.

Serious consideration is being given to the possibility of reducing the amount of manual work which the boys have to do (at Tjolotjo itself)... we are still demanding a lot of these boys and a reduction would have beneficial results on the academic standard.

English maintains a high standard. Several of the senior boys took turns to read the daily lesson in morning prayers and gave a very fair rendering. Teacher Ngcobo has done some good and quite ambitious work in Hygiene... Teacher Tjuma is proving himself an excellent man for the more backward pupils in the lower standards. He has infinite patience and has achieved good results from very poor material.

At the boys' own request a monthly essay competition is thrown open to any boy in the school. I set the subjects and mark the essays and usually give a short criticism of them to the whole school. The results are very promising.

The year has afforded us plenty of variety, counting on the debit side a strike, a bad malarial season, excessive heat at the end of a very dry season and a rather high proportion of failures in examinations; but more than balancing these we have the opening up of new prospects at Essexvale, a good crop in a year when crop failure was the rule and above all, peace on the staff.

Nothing disturbs the work of the school more than staff squabbles and this year has been delightfully free of them.

The boys also show an appreciation of those other values in life which education alone cannot give. I have started a fund for the building of a school chapel at the New Site and boys have done what they can to raise money. They have organised a concert party and several have approached old boys of the school with a view to raising contributions. Their desire to raise funds for the alleviation of famine amongst the indigent natives gives an indication of the growth of the realisation of their responsibility to the community at large.

It was all the more pleasing in that it needed no prompting.

The report concludes:

At a time such as this, the mind of each member of the school and particularly of the staff looks ahead to the time when the school will again be altogether. 1942 has I hope seen the worst of the "Great Trek". In 1943 we hope to see the growth of the new school. By 1944 we should all be together again and able in 1945 to return once more to normal, ready to go ahead in the pleasant surroundings of the new School site and endeavouring to spread our influence in this new area for the benefit of the Native population.

It will be strange to feel some sense of permanency. This move has been in the air since 1937 and even now with the visible evidence of bricks and mortar it is hard to realise that it is actually in progress. How delightful it will be to feel again that projects can be put into being which will be lasting, how very pleasant not to have the feeling that any new venture would be a waste of time because "the move" lies ahead.

How deep a significance this move has had for us, no one who has not spent a period of his life at Tjolotjo will fully appreciate...

By the beginning of 1943, more thought than ever was being given to the legacy that would be left behind once the school had gone.

Although the milk-to-butter scheme had failed, the sheep breeding project started in 1940 had grown enormously. Only 24 ewes were brought for servicing by the school's rams in 1940. In the following year, 36 came along, but last year the number had risen to 104.

John wrote to Keigwin, as he knew he would be particularly pleased about it:

This is most encouraging and the scheme now has the active support of the local Chief who has instructed his followers to castrate all their young rams. When we leave Tjolotjo we shall be able to leave a number of young rams to carry on the scheme and we could also leave a few ewes to form the nucleus of a stud flock.

The pigs have flourished since we acquired new breeding stock…

Poultry has done fairly well, though the excessive heat makes breeding difficult…

Artificial incubation is proving very popular…

But the heat has been too great for successful vegetable gardening and forestry has had little success.

The Native Department had, at last, agreed to support a small preparatory school with its own teachers, and raise some money to help build it. This meant that local children, who would be getting preferential entry to Mzingwane under the Keigwin scheme would now be able to compete perfectly adequately with those from the rest of the country.

The school agreed to build this school for the Native Department as a building project – and motivation – for those pupils "left behind":

Standard V has undertaken the building of the Preparatory school. It has afforded them an excellent project with plenty of practice and any of this class who go on to specialise in building will have the benefit of a very good grounding. Teacher Bulle has supervised this work almost single-handed and has done very well.

The experience of the teachers and the training that was taking place at Tjolotjo meant the school's crops were much more impressive than those in the reserve. The difference excited the Gwaai Reserve

194

boys at the school who were now very keen to take their new expertise to teach their parents and friends new and different ways of doing things. In particular, the making of compost and the results this achieved impressed the boys enormously and it was satisfying to hear of parents already adopting the practice as well.

The school was almost completely independent of outside suppliers in terms of meat, milk, eggs and vegetables. This was another great achievement and John was determined the same would be the case as soon as possible, at Mzingwane.

For the first time, my husband began to feel that what the school was now doing was going to have some tangible benefit for the local people of the Gwaai Reserve. On the wider scale, there also seemed to be far less suspicion about the school from parents all round the country – and from South Africa – with growing recognition of the benefits when their children stayed at the school for more years.

Perhaps the greatest satisfaction was the fact that the boys them-selves were gaining employment in places many people had not dreamed would be possible. They were breaking the mould. John had argued strongly that the school should not be educating simply to improve conditions at the boys' homes which was certainly the pref-erence in direction from Head Office when he first started. It was a good starting point but it was more important to ensure their ongoing employment. It was beginning to pay off handsomely.

> *Teacher Mothobi continues to do good work in the tannery. Two of the final year specialists this year were the best leatherworkers we have yet turned out and they have both gone on to the Bata Shoe Co. in Gwelo. I foresee a great demand... and I feel the time has come for us to include machine work in the Post VI course...*
>
> *The three crippled boys to whom special bursaries were given are all doing well. They are showing outstanding aptitude for this work and the bursary scheme has much to commend it...*

But I now had another worry – this time about John. He didn't seem to have the reserves of energy he once had and grew very despondent about things – much more quickly than normal. He came back from a trip to Mzingwane a month later, overly concerned it seemed to me, because the condition of the working oxen had deteriorated so rapidly. There had been no delineation as yet of what was to be farming and what was to remain Native Purchase Area land. As a result, they couldn't buy hay for the oxen, they couldn't grow food, because they didn't know where to grow it and now only a few oxen were fit enough for work. So they had to use petrol at a time when the country was being urged not to use a drop more than it had to. It was frustrating, but I would have thought less so than some things he had faced.

To top it all off, dear old Tjolotjo was dealing us another bad hand. During the whole of 1942 we only had eight inches of rain, most of it in two raging storms. In the ten months between February and November, three inches fell. All the crops, except for some Native-base millet, failed completely.

As 1943 approached there were more staff changes in sight. An outstanding teacher, Roger Malusalila had joined us to take over from a bright youngster and former pupil of the school, Joshua Nkomo. Joshua had been helping to teach carpentry. And at last, after a year of waiting, there was going to be a temporary replacement for Mr. Ramushu until he was able to return from his studies.

Eighteen months ago, in desperation at not being able to find another agriculturalist, John had begged a nice old chap, Mr. Hodgson, who had been retired for some 15 years, to come in and help in Searson's place. This he did, very creditably, but now he was tired and simply could not continue.

Just as John was wondering what on earth he was going to do, Roy Alvord, son of a well-known American missionary and visionary agriculturalist, applied for the job. Alvord would be joining us in the New Year and he came highly recommended.

There had been no school clerk at all that year. John had to write all his own reports, cope with all his admin and with only three Europeans on the staff – one of these constantly at Mzingwane – the responsibilities had fallen heavily onto the Native staff, and they had coped extremely well and very cheerfully.

No administrative staff for over a year, having to do teaching himself, planning and supervising the move, and managing the day-to-day disciplines and policy-making required of a headmaster – it was little wonder John was exhausted.

As he faced 1943, he had nearly 500 new applications for admittance to the school – and this was already a qualified number from the applications that had been coming in throughout the year. The selection process was becoming almost impossible.

On top of all his own problems, he found his irritation with some of the Mission schools increasing. They seemed to be reluctant to pass their boys on to Mzingwane – despite the fact that none were teaching to this level. Several would not give him accurate assessments of the boys who were applying for places, to their disadvantage of course. As a staunch Christian himself John found it hard to justify their position.

On one occasion, two boys from one mission applied for entrance and were accepted. The mission had asked him to send acceptances or refusals through them – which he did. Neither boy turned up. They applied again in 1941 and the mission failed to report on the two boys until late December. Because of this and because they had not come the previous year when they were accepted, they were both refused. Now they had applied again, saying they couldn't understand why they had been refused twice. John explained it to them and found that the Mission authorities had never passed on their acceptances for 1940. His comments to the Department were:

I am being led to the conclusions that we may in future have to ignore those missions, which will not co-operate. Not unnaturally, the Native is beginning to wonder if Christianity does inspire truth amongst those who profess it.

'The only answer Nan,' he said to me, 'is to insist that new entrants only come in at the bottom of the school – then we can make our own assessments and not be held responsible for other people's failures.'

Just as the schoolboys were returning for the beginning of term in 1943, Jill was not well. She had just had a smallpox inoculation and had suffered some sort of violent reaction to it, ending up with what was virtually a mild dose of smallpox.

We agreed that I would take her down to the coast for six weeks to try and build her up and, at the same time, avoid the worst of the malaria season. I hated leaving John when he was so exhausted, but we both felt we couldn't risk her getting malaria while she was so run down. I was also worn out and fed up with the migraines, which had dogged me for the nine months of summer, striking almost to the day every year, as the heat started to build up in September.

But before I could leave, Jill's condition suddenly deteriorated and I had to rush up to Salisbury to be near hospitals and doctors. John followed me at the weekend and we then decided Jill and I would go straight down to Bonza Bay and not go back to Tjolotjo.

If anyone needed a holiday, it was John and I begged him to join us. It was too difficult for him to leave the school at that critical point and he was really much more concerned to see his girls fit, than he was about what might lie ahead for him.

John was due to see me off on the last Saturday of January, but he had this awful habit of turning up late to catch trains. It was something peculiar to the European men of this country, which I had noticed when I first came out from England. Somehow, living at Plumtree where they could almost dictate the departure time of the trains had entrenched the practice a little too well. John would walk beside the moving train, swinging nonchalantly onto the running board as it gathered speed – and always at the very last possible moment!

Well… we missed the train! The next one was three days later.

At least it meant we had eight days together. A letter was waiting when I eventually got down to Bonza Bay.

I still feel very apologetic about your missing the train on Saturday, but I was jolly glad that we were able to have the two Mondays together, particularly as they saw Jill picking up again so much. I do so hope the wee duck is quite OK again. I'm simply longing, already, to be with you again…

The back of the letter was covered in baby talk especially for Jill, with a picture of a baby hugging its mother. "*Did you like puff puff?*" it said. "*It's rather like wow wow with smoke from nose! Tah tah from Dah Dah.*"

What an extraordinary man he was – the complete headmaster – strict, fair, immensely hardworking – doing a job which most of the European population still considered was pretty odd and a waste of time… yet he was also the most sentimental, loving husband and father. It didn't matter in the least if he couldn't catch trains on time!

I was lucky – and the very thought of him immediately made my eyes fill up with silly tears and emotion.

Jill picked up almost immediately we arrived at sea level. We had taken Bessie with us to this wonderful retreat, near East London, that was primarily for army wives. Bessie was one of our old tracker Bembi's, daughters and was a super girl.

As we arrived, Bessie looked over my shoulder at the sea. She was absolutely thunderstruck – she'd never seen or imagined anything like it.

Eventually she asked me in a very little voice, 'Is it deep?'

After we had unpacked and put away our things into our little cottage, I took Jill – and Bessie – by the hand and we walked slowly down to the beach. By the end of an afternoon of timidly dipping their toes in the water, both of them were completely in love with the beach – and the sea.

It was the greatest joy imaginable for me to see our precious little girl come alive again, literally within days of arriving on the coast. I seemed to thrive there as well – throwing my head back into the sea breeze – and for the first time in months I had no headache. I re-lived my glorious walks along the front at Eastbourne... I climbed up above the cliffs and I was once again on Beachy Head. Tjolotjo seemed a long, long way away.

There were no men at the resort and I was the only one there who was not an army wife, but we all had children of a similar age and they had the most marvellous time. I swam and walked, made new friends, played bridge and tennis and felt the years slipping off me. Not only did I not have a headache but I did not have a single migraine in all the time I was there.

I hadn't felt so well for a long time. Jill was growing fast, she was tanned and sparkling with health, and Bessie was in heaven. There were a large number of nannies there as well and we could hear them singing and dancing and howling with laughter together – so we were all well catered for.

But I missed John so much. I absolutely ached to see him and wished we were sharing this experience. I could only write describing it in as much detail as possible, and despite his incredible workload his wonderful letters kept coming back. Concerned, caring, thrilled to hear that we were both so much the fitter and enjoying it all.

The six weeks passed like lightning and I suddenly felt I couldn't face going back yet. But how could I leave John on his own any longer? I quailed at the thought of asking him if we could stay on... we'd be heading straight back into that awful March/April malaria time... I couldn't bear to see Jill so ill again... the resort would allow us to stay for another month at substantially reduced rates... So eventually and after much heart searching, I wrote:

My darling one,
I wrote to you yesterday saying I was swithering about when to come home.
During the night, I thought it all over and came to the conclusion that all

this week I have thought only of you, and wanted to get back so that you should be alone no longer – I hadn't thought as much of my other responsibility – Din Din, and for her sake, I really do feel I should stay the extra month. (For my sake too, I suppose, but I really was thinking only of you and then her.)

She is so absolutely wonderful here, so well and happy every minute of the day with the sand, sea and "other babas" that it seems awful to take her back to the heat of Tjolotjo with the constant fear of fever (especially now that she stays up later and runs about more into the long grass etc.).

There is also very little for her to do there, she is so limited having to stay under cover from 10 or 11 a.m. onwards and here she has become used to running wild over vast stretches of sand and in and out of the water and so on.

Since deciding to stay, I have felt heartbroken for you, my precious. It is a terrible time in which to leave you still longer alone, but if you can just bear the other four weeks, I know it will be worth it. It would be worse for you to see Jilly losing condition as she does in the heat… it was 21st April when George got blackwater… and me getting all headachey and crotchety again… whereas, if we return for May, it will be colder which suits me so well – the worst of Tjolotjo will be over and I should be in fine fettle for another baba and Essexvale.

One sees things in perspective here – Tjolotjo seems a terrible little spot in which to have raised so precious and perfect a baba as Jilly, and the Rhodesian women all look so much more worn and tired than these South Africans.

Oh, but I do feel so sad for you – please darling tell me honestly if you really can't face these four weeks alone (indispensable am I ?!!!I). I will leave my train booking as it is until you've answered this, I had to tell the Nichols though, as they've held my room pending my decision. Bookings are coming in fast as April is one of the best months here. They make a reduction for three months, am not sure what, but think (and hope) it should be quite considerable.

PLEASE take care of yourself. Is Cookie Flitting? The whole house should be sprayed at 5'30 p.m. daily now. Do hope the days won't drag for you – they go awfully quickly here. Jill and I don't wake till 7 when tea comes (still not quite light). As soon as she wakes, she says, "nice little walkies" then, "koshy with other babas".

Please don't think I haven't thought about you over this extra month business – I can think of nothing but you my precious one and do so hope you are OK and not worn out and despondent. All my love dearest – it is rotten we have to be parted so much, but it really is for the best.

200

We stayed the extra month and I went back feeling quite, quite different. In fact, so different, that within three months I was pregnant for the second time and quite ready to cope with packing up the house for the move to Mzingwane. In fact, I couldn't wait.

Then out of the blue, one young pupil died of malaria. Within two weeks a second boy had an accident and died when a cement carrier crushed him. It was shattering. There had been only one death in the seven years before that, when a boy died from inherited heart disease.

This was Tjolotjo's final curse – but it unnerved everyone in both places – particularly the superstitious Natives. Morale dropped like a stone.

Discipline in both camps had been remarkably good but now it threatened to fall apart. John felt sad about the fact that his workload meant he had been forced to neglect a most important part of his work as a headmaster.

I have felt this year, more than ever previously, that pressure of other duties has made it difficult for me to get to know the boys individually as well as I should. To my mind, this is the most important part of my work here and the past year has been a lesson to me not to neglect it again to the same extent.

The full realisation came to me when I had to make out school reports at the end of the year.

I found that I knew very little about some of the boys – admittedly this was primarily with those who were at Tjolotjo and whom I had been with for only one term, but it has been a warning against filling up too much time with other duties and against the temptation to make the school too big.

The only offences of any note have been the kicking over the traces of healthy youth...

There was one aspect however, which try as he might to overcome it, just would not improve – and he would come home and discuss it with me regularly. His report to Head Office sums up his concerns:

This question of lying is one of the most difficult which faces us in the schools today. Some of the boys lie with such facility that within a very few minutes they firmly believe their own lies.

The African Teacher or parent would punish merely on suspicion. The European has a dislike of presuming the lie without adequate proof and as a result will often let the boy get away with it.

201

If we could but get to the stage where boys would tell the truth and take the consequences, Native Education would need no other justification.

As a means of combating it, I am seriously considering allowing House Masters to cane boys up to a certain number of cuts. This, however, would only be put into practice if you raised no objections.

The main difficulty is that, once started, the practice would be difficult to remove without making the teachers lose face in front of the boys. I think that it would be worth trying. It would, I know, be running counter to all modern theories on the subject, but I sometimes very greatly doubt if the theories would be the same, if the theorists had to deal with those who had not had generations of caned ancestors preceding them.

On the personal front, we were beginning to hear some discomfiting news from Shabani. Harrie phoned us a couple of times saying that she was concerned about Bob. He seemed terribly tired and lacking in energy, often taking to his bed in the afternoons, which was most out of character.

At the beginning of May, the time came for John to do his military service again so I took the opportunity to go over and give Harrie a little support at this worrying time. As I arrived, the local doctor was in seeing Bob. Harrie's dear face was lined with anxiety.

When the doctor left, I popped in to see the old man. Bob did not look well but he was his usual gentle self and as always, full of lively interest in what was happening at Tjolotjo and Mzingwane. He simply loved Jill – an all too rare girl in a very male family.

The local doctor couldn't identify the source of the problem and said Bob must stay in bed for a week or so. This gave me the chance to sit and chat with him and I was able to give him a very good idea of all the excitements and disappointments of the move so far.

I'd been there about ten days when I was woken one night by a real commotion in the house. Bob had woken up with a tearing pain in his chest. We drove him to the local mine hospital and rang to ask Dr. Standish-White to come down urgently from Bulawayo. He promised to be there by lunchtime the following day, Friday.

Harrie and I felt we should contact all the family and let them know what had happened. John immediately applied for compassionate leave from the army and drove down with Jinny that afternoon. Skinny and Morrie would come down over the weekend. Bob was grey with pain – it was most upsetting for everyone. Standish-White was a little delayed, and he arrived at Shabani hospital at about three in the afternoon. He took one look at Bob and ordered him into theatre.

At 11 o'clock that night, Standish-White came round to the house and we all stood out in the garden in the dark to hear the result. He told us that Bob had a burst aneurysm and he could do no more for him. It was a terrible shock. Bob had never been robustly healthy because of the regular relapses of malaria – but he'd always recovered.

This time, he was not going to do so. As we stood around talking and taking comfort from all being together, the news came that he had gone. He died in the early hours of Saturday morning, 17th May 1943.

We were able to take a lot of the inevitable post-death organisation off Harrie's shoulders – Bob in Kenya and Patrick with his army unit in Mogadishu had to be told and the funeral arranged. Harrie wanted the funeral to take place the next day so we had to alert specific people at Plumtree School, in Government and other professional areas, as well as his several close friends.

For the last few years, Bob had been working with Garfield Todd, a New Zealander and minister of the Church, helping him with the mine's Native preparatory school.

Bob and the lanky New Zealander had become firm friends. As the next day was a Sunday, it was decided to ask Todd if he would take the service when he visited that afternoon.

Plumtree School held a memorial service at the same time. As Sunday morning dawned, we were amazed as car after car started to drive down the roads to Shabani. As they came they passed people walking in twos and threes – along the roads and through the veld. People, European and African, came from all over the country. Some must have dropped everything to set off the moment they heard of Bob's death. They were determined to bid the old man farewell. It was tremendously heart-warming and wonderful for Harrie to witness these demonstrations of affection.

The service started at the hospital and led to the graveside. John, Skinny and John Swire-Thompson were all pallbearers. Garfield Todd led the prayers

We give Thee thanks our Father, for the life of him whose body we are laying to rest… for his courage, his integrity.

We thank Thee that his life was lived unselfishly for the benefit of our country

and our Empire. We thank Thee that thousands of the young men of our land have a clearer vision of right and duty because they have dwelt with him.

Sanctify, we pray Thee, his memory to us, that we, remembering his faith in his fellow men and his unwavering enthusiasm, may be more worthy of our own station.

The tributes paid to Bob were extraordinary. The *Herald* and the *Chronicle* ran full pages of editorial on his life and achievements; the British Press ran column after column. "Hammond of Plumtree", they proclaimed, classing him among the great headmasters with Sanderson of Oundle and Way of Grey. (See Appendix 3.)

We just remembered the gentle man whom we had loved so dearly and who had been such a guiding light in all our lives.

John had to go back the next day, very reluctantly, to finish his army stint, but at least it gave me a couple more weeks to be with Harrie and help her get over the shock of it all.

John came to collect me at the end of May, and we dropped in on Mzingwane to see how things were going. It really was moving ahead quickly and now several of the staff houses had been finished. It actually began to look as though our time at Tjolotjo was growing short. On present achievements, we could reasonably expect to move across to Mzingwane round about September. We arrived home to find a delightful letter from Wilkie – he had heard that we were moving on and said:

… memories of the congenial atmosphere that existed (at Tjolotjo) linger on. So often in a small community this is lacking and this has been of great importance to me now that the responsibility for "harmony" is mine. Only now do I realise the part you both played in keeping us on talking terms with one another!

We were amazed – and gratified – to think that this had been Wilkie's impression of the place. After all the nightmares with Searson and Edwards we wouldn't have thought the atmosphere the least congenial! The only good thing was we must have somehow taken the brunt of it and kept it to ourselves, John just hoped that the Natives had also been less aware of it. This was always the main worry – setting such an awful example.

The beginning of the last term of 1943 saw a wagonload of books and academic material going over to Mzingwane. The new Agricultural staff member, Alvord, was proving to be quite capable enough to look after the one class that would still be left at Tjolotjo for the last six months. All the rest of the staff had now moved across to Mzingwane.

So it was time for us to go too. As I started putting everything into piles for packing up, Jill became fractious and difficult. Oh dear, I had enough on my hands with packing up the house and feeling sick from the new pregnancy. I prayed she wasn't sickening for something. She cried a lot. What was it? Bessie came in.

'Ah! Ah! Jilly has got many putsi.'

I couldn't believe it. Maggot flies. I had been lulled into the comparative safety of the coast and had obviously slipped up on the ironing. Twenty-three fat, revolting maggots I squeezed out of that poor little girl, who was too exhausted with weeping to protest any more by the time I removed the last one.

I confess that as we packed our things into the car and drove off to cross the Gwaai for the last time, I didn't give Tjolotjo even a last backward glance.

Chapter 10

…and plant it deep and well

The old green truck smoothed out the miles as though they didn't exist. It had done us good service over the last five years. It had been stuck in the Gwaai, been out on lion hunts, carried people to hospital, picked up supplies for the school on a regular basis… and it was still serving us well. What it lacked in comfort it made up for in practicality.

Our new nanny, Cecilia, was in the back of the truck playing with Jill in a space we had managed to create amongst all the paraphernalia – room enough for a playpen and a place to sleep. The green canvas flaps were tightly buttoned down along the sides and the back to keep out the dust, but when we stopped in Bulawayo to give them a cool drink, Cecilia was hardly recognisable. She was covered in dust from head to foot with only her eyes and teeth shining through. Jill looked like nothing on earth. She had been crying and was hot and perspiring, so she was covered in streaks of mud and dust – she looked absolutely exhausted and was very cross.

Huge ice-cold glasses of cold water and lemon revived us all, as we set off for the first and last time, in the opposite direction to Tjolotjo. This time, we were heading due south, past a rather sophisticated looking hotel and pub called the Round House then winding on and down through heavily treed ironstone hills. We emerged onto the plain of Essexvale. It was fringed by these dark blue hills and heavily wooded with very African looking flat-topped acacia trees. The road was good quality strips all the way from Bulawayo, with a few miles of full-width nine-foot tarmac round the bends.

What a long way I had come – thinking that strips were such a relief! They were – particularly after the Tjolotjo road. It seemed too good to be true – the truck purred along – life was going to be sheer bliss!

We were bursting with enthusiasm and optimism… Jill was getting on towards three now and chattering nineteen to the dozen. We were completely besotted by her and her funny little ways. As we drew nearer we opened the little window that connected the cab to the back of the truck and all sang nursery rhymes together.

Packing up the last bits of the school had been a nightmare and wagonloads of materials and other school paraphernalia seemed to have been leaving for weeks now. Loading up our own few possessions seemed ridiculously easy by comparison. Our old Rhodesian Ridgeback, Mac, was coming through with one of the wagons and acting as guard dog en route. It was so exciting seeing it happen at last – but it had been a long, long time coming. The war had extended the projected 18-month move into almost three years.

John, who was normally given to considered, rather quiet, well thought-out statements, was almost chattering in his excitement as he described to me the progress that had been made both at Tjolotjo and Mzingwane.

Mr. Alvord, Teacher Dabengwa and the last classes of agriculture and building students had been left at Tjolotjo for the last term to finish up the cropping and to put the final touches to the Native Department primary school. They would be handing over all the joint projects to Searson, now safely ensconced in the Native Department – in a new house! John hoped to have the whole school together by the end of 1944.

There had been some heart-warming farewells – particularly from the local Chief and headmen who were very sad and understood all too well the implications of seeing the school go. John promised that he would go back as often as he could to see them – and reiterated his promise that children from the Nyamandhlovu area would always receive preferential treatment for places at Mzingwane.

'I think we have been able to make the best of a bad job,' he mused. 'It really was an unfortunate place to choose to put a national school. At least, I suppose, we've left some sort of legacy for the Native farmers, and now that the National Park is under way, there should be good opportunities in the Game Department conserving the animals.'

'Oh Johnnie, you really had no alternative. It was by far the best thing to do for the boys as well as for the teachers, particularly until something is done about the malaria.' I felt horrified that he might even have doubts. 'You'd never have been able to keep attracting the sort of staff you need... and now the demand for education is increasing so much, you have to be in a position to provide the best.'

'I know, Nannie, you're right,' he grinned ruefully. 'But I don't really like having to admit to being beaten by anything – it's that old Plumtree ethos, I'm afraid.'

We laughed. I now felt quite ready and able to cope with the new baby which was due in April. This was something I would not have thought possible six months ago, before our trip to Bonza Bay when I was tired, worn out, worried about Jill and coping with endless migraines. Fortunately, I didn't seem to be getting anything like the same number of these intense headaches during my second pregnancy as I had with my first.

We dropped in to see Mrs. "Tookie" Richardson on our way. She was a wonderful person who was entirely sympathetic to the cause of the African and had great influence in the area among black and white. She'd been very supportive of the school moving to Essexvale and had helped to remove all sorts of barriers that were in our way. She swept us along with her warmth and delight at seeing us.

'My dears – how wonderful to see you at long last.'

Her husband, nicknamed Tookie, had been with Rhodes in the very early days of the colony and his Native name was Mehlu kwaZulu – "the eyes of the people". After the Matabele rebellion he was given the responsibility of re-distributing the cattle which had been taken from the people and making sure they were all given back. At his funeral there were many Africans from all over the country who trekked for days to attend.

Mrs. Richardson was very keen to call the new school Mehlu kwaZulu. It was going to be a bit sensitive, but John intended to stick to his guns, because he did not feel that it was right to do so, and that just Mzingwane School was preferable.

We were shown onto the shady verandah of her house for after-noon tea. It was a wonderful old place, built entirely of stone with a deep verandah around all four sides. Her daughter, Stella Fynn, was with her, accompanied by her own daughter, Diana, who was just a few months younger than Jill. I was delighted to hear that she was also pregnant again, and that her baby was due at about the same stage as mine.

Mazorati had managed to find a store of old corrugated iron at the Air Force Training Centre and in the last month this had been nailed onto a wooden frame, pre-fab style, to give us some form of shelter while our own house was being finished. Even though it was going to be rather primitive, we felt the time had come to move to Mzingwane even if this meant we had to suffer a little discomfort.

We reached the school and oohed and aahed at the developments that had taken place since we were last there. The boys were singing and dancing as we arrived and the teachers waving. With John now ensconced at the new base everybody felt the school had really moved!

As we drove up towards the house, my heart sank. It was a gloomy looking place – all tin, very small and very green. It seemed to glower at us with its very small windows. I could already feel how hot it would be. It was tiny – one sitting room, one bedroom, a bathroom and kitchen, with outside PK. I just knew it would house a multitude of skellums – scorpions, snakes and spiders. Oh how to be positive faced with this little treasure!

It did have a huge old native fig tree in the garden and with another between the tin house and what was to be our new house. When I wandered over to see how the new house was progressing, I was delighted to see that there was an even bigger fig tree in what would become our front garden. They were huge umbrella-like trees with small leaves and dense, dense shade.

The row of staff houses was on a ridge looking down over the school, with Isi'Koveni, covered in flat topped trees, standing about 1,500 feet high directly behind us.

There was no point in unpacking too much of our furniture as we would be moving again in a matter of months, so we made ourselves as comfy as we could with Jill sleeping in the sitting room and Cecilia in the kitchen.

That first night it was as hot as Old Nick!

'I thought Essexvale was 1,000 feet higher and was going to be much cooler than Tjolotjo,' I protested. 'This is terrible. Jill's come out in a dreadful heat rash.'

'It is the hottest time of the year my duck, and this tiny little room is pretty airless. It has been lovely during my visits over the last few months. It will get better – I promise.'

I hoped so – because that endless heat did depress me terribly. It was something I never seemed able to come to terms with. However, only a few weeks later, by the middle of November, the first rains had come and everything started to take on a new hue. Green grass spread

210

through the valley – particularly in those fields where the cattle spent all day lazily munching and ruminating... keeping the elephant grass down. It almost looked like an English park. Oh yes! This was going to be a good place to be.

I would spend the last, cooler hours of the afternoon each day wheeling Jill's pram down to walk round the new school and to meet John on his way home. He still went everywhere on his bicycle – sitting bolt upright and pedaling very slowly... I'd have recognised him from almost any distance, anywhere.

The school buildings were quite splendid. John's office was just being completed and had been sited right in the middle of the classroom complex, which was designed in an E shape. The classrooms seemed huge – light, bright, airy and, for the first time, with ample space to take a desk for each child. It was Rolls Royce stuff by comparison with Tjolotjo.

It was marvellous seeing the staff, the teachers and their wives safely set up in their own new houses at last. They were so pleased with them. There were some promising new teachers who had joined us to cope with the extra pupils at the new premises – Roger Malusalila, Dennis Moyo and Allen Kumalo. John hoped to be able to attract additional European staff as well for 1944.

We'd walk up the gentle incline towards our house as the sun set, looking up at lovely Isi'Koveni which so dominated the background. It was a pretty substantial hill made almost entirely of ironstone, which meant the fertility of the surrounding red soil was very high. It was certainly very red! One step outside would cover your shoes in a light fine dust and it took a bit of getting used to the fact that white clothes became lightly pink after only a few washes.

We'd arrive home at dusk and the singing would start.

I still thrill to the sound of Africans singing in the distance, they would sing whenever they had the opportunity – sometimes when they were working, often when they were sauntering down the road and always in the evenings. Those African evenings were just glorious. The height meant it was cool, even on the hottest day. Malaria was not nearly such a problem here so we were able to sit out under the fig tree for our sundowners, always to the accompaniment of drums and song.

We woke every morning to find little buck, called duiker, on the lawn. It meant that vegetable gardens and certain plants didn't survive very well – but the duiker were so dainty and sweet and Jill so loved them, sitting watching them for hours until they melted back into the bush. She came to know each of the families and when a new baby was born she would whisper very softly so as not to disturb them. In fact for years afterwards, whenever we talked about duiker, she would whisper very, very softly.

We were just settling in when Stella Fynn, her husband Kim, and Diana popped in to see how we were doing. She invited me along to a Women's Institute meeting the next week as a good way of starting to know some of the local people.

I was full of expectation when the day for the meeting arrived. We were to meet in the Heany Hall, which I thought looked a splendid place after what I was used to, and was located just across the road from the church and the village's single, main street.

I had already been to the Heany Hall once to go to a morning market. This was held every Saturday morning and organised by two sisters, Miss Bell and Mrs. Welby. All proceeds were in aid of the new church fund and all the farmers and mining wives around brought home produce, cakes, jams, marmalades and plants for sale. It was excellent value and a great social occasion. The Christmas's who were mining near Bushtick, the McLeods from the Native Department, the Phillips from the police station and the Booths who were farming nearby, soon became good friends.

Mrs. Tookie was chairman of the WI at that stage. During that first meeting, I had to stand up and introduce myself, painting a bit of a picture of my background and of what was happening at Mzingwane. The Institutes were mainly concerned with African affairs, health and cultural arts. By the end of that first meeting I had decided to join. It seemed to be a worthwhile organisation and would give me some purpose and direction as well.

We all stayed on for tea and I met about 15 women, all around my age and many with young children and babies. I was just about to leave when a very large woman, Mrs. van Blerk, approached me.

'So you're the ones from that Kaffir School down the road,' she said.

I was amazed. I'd never heard anyone speak in that way before. I was so shocked that I kicked myself later for not coming straight back with some clever retort.

'Don't worry about Mrs. van Blerk,' Stella said. 'That's just the way some of the Afrikaans people talk about the Africans. They don't really mean it, I don't think. In fact I've found that the African people respond well to them. They seem to understand them better perhaps than we do. I don't know... but it is very confronting isn't it? I have had many arguments with them with no luck. I'm afraid you'll find others like that here.'

Well, we certainly did. When I returned home that evening, I said to John, 'I couldn't believe what this woman said to me at the WI.' I related the tale to him and also Stella's comments afterwards.

John smiled wryly, 'I've just had a rather similar experience today... one of the most senior people in the Native Commissioner's office has just told me he doubted my sanity trying to educate Africans. It certainly doesn't make it any easier does it?'

He looked sideways at me. 'Did you say that the morning market earnings were going to a fund for the building of a new church?'

'Yes, why?'

'Well, we're going to need another building project fairly soon – and it might help to overcome some of these ideas if we were able to build them their new church.'

John contacted the local rector, Maurice Lancaster, to find out about their plans and offered the expertise and pupils of the school to build it for them. Well! Suddenly the local population began to look at us very differently. There would have to be a charge, of course, but as a government contract, it could be built cheaper than if they had done it any other way. In fact, with the money already collected from morning markets, the plans and costings for the building could start much sooner than expected.

The school was actually a very useful addition to the population of Essexvale – all the retail and farm stores benefited enormously from this huge influx of people and from the requirements of the big farm attached to it.

Now that the weather had broken I was able to spend time developing the gardens, planting daffodils out under the big fig. Daffodils! Somehow these flowers were the epitome of everything English to me. How I had longed to grow them at Tjolotjo. But they couldn't cope with the climate there. A couple of pathetic, stressed little leaves would make it through the soil – but no flowers – never any flowers. I had great hopes that the climate here would allow them to burst through with just one golden trumpet.

A large, thatched rondavel with stable doors was being built between the tin house and our new home. It was designed to take the rest of our furniture until we moved but after that would serve as a guest hut or playroom for the children. It was just under the outer branches of the second great fig tree and became one of our favourite places.

The new house was coming along slowly. There were many much more important tasks to be undertaken at the school first and I had to squash my impatience and grin and bear it in the tin house. John did promise me it would be finished before the baby arrived, but already the "couple of months" in the little tin box looked like stretching to at least six.

As the house took shape it did look as though it was going to be superb. It was on the highest spot of the ridge with two wings at each end, which were set at more than right angles to the main section. This created endless possibilities and certainly enhanced the views from all the rooms. We had a huge sitting room, quite able to take the boudoir grand piano my great aunt had promised me, a big dining room next door, which was connected by a passage to the kitchen – and four bedrooms. So for the first time, Johnnie would have a study to himself. The view looked out beyond the third of the great figs, over the school to the rolling line of blue Bushtick Hills which I so loved, in the distance.

How different it was from the flat surrounds of Tjolotjo. I felt my heart sing and my babe seemed to jump for joy. John was delighted to have most of the school together by the beginning of 1944 and was in the thick of coping with registrations flooding in from South Africa as well as from every corner of Rhodesia. He could now take 320 pupils although he was reluctant to push class sizes above 25.

'It is so tempting just to put 40 into a class and simply cram them all with facts.' John was reacting to a hard day of trying to be fair in his assessments of who should attend. 'They'd probably get through their exams all right, but that would give them expectations they'd be ill equipped to meet in other areas. I cannot believe that is the right way to go.

'We have to insist upon teaching the whole person... so that he understands he can certainly expect more as a result of his education, but that with those privileges come big responsibilities to those who have not been so fortunate. If we just create a sausage machine and churn them out, literate, numerate and precious little else, I'm afraid there could be absolute anarchy in 50 years or so, as everyone jostles for power.

'We have to remember that we're teaching the leaders of the future – sometimes I find that responsibility almost crushing.'

Poor old Johnnie – this did worry him. He became more and more concerned about it – feeling that this educative role was the pivot round which the country might succeed or fail. As a result he drove himself, his staff and his pupils hard.

He'd leave the house just after five each morning, after a quick cup of tea. Off on his bike down to the sports field to get them cracking with PT, drill and inspection. The boys hated it – just as John had done when he first returned back from England. Many times, he was tempted to give it up. Many, many years later when he was still at it, taking early morning drill at Goromonzi, he received a letter from David Zamchiya, now one of the country's top lawyers. This delighted him beyond measure. David wrote:

There is one feature of the school's daily programme, which had a great effect on me and, as my observations later showed me, on other boys. This was the morning inspection for which I always prepared and in so doing grew into the habit which I hope not to grow out of – the habit of tidying myself up the first thing in the morning before I appear to the public.

Admittedly to start with I made myself neat and as presentable as I could because I feared your scanning eye and reproaching voice at parade, but this soon helped me and I know many otherwise dirty and shabby boys to be smart and help themselves.

I would listen to the crack, crack of the dumbbells wafting up on the early morning air as we prepared a good helping of mealie meal porridge in winter, or maas (made of sour milk) in summer. I'd switch on the BBC news at eight for his arrival back for breakfast, having already taken his first class of the day.

After breakfast, it was back to assembly, prayers for the day, a hymn and time to praise or remonstrate. John held two non-denominational services every Sunday and house prayers were taken every evening by the housemaster. The boys themselves would organise their one evening of the week which was set aside for denominational group meetings, and which was always a great success.

But they were no sooner settling into being a fully integrated school again than disturbing signs and attitudes began to emerge amongst the students. Sadly, these came mainly from those boys emanating from the Mission Schools. John described it as the "poor blacks" syndrome which was shortly to be followed by the "everyone should do what he likes, when he feels like it" scenario.

He was both irritated and beaten down by it. Just when everyone had been working way above and beyond the call of duty in the last few years to improve things, particularly for the pupils, this attitude had crept in and threatened to cause division and upset.

It showed up with the boys slacking off in those aspects of the school's activities not related to the earning of marks. This was the very thing John was trying to avoid with his "whole of life" education. It was worst in pupils new to the school, but was infectious. At the end of a year of working this through with the boys, everything would be splendid again and pushing ahead – just in time for a new intake to "re-infect".

'It's amazing Nan,' he said, with his head in his hands. 'The Africans themselves don't come up with these ideas – they're basically as keen as mustard. But my goodness they are quick to learn and it spreads through the school like wildfire,' he sighed.

'These idealistic ruddy whites,' he continued, 'don't seem to understand that we cannot be paternalistic and just give them everything on a plate. They'll be running the country one day. These guys just cannot be looking ahead, otherwise they'd understand that the only outcome of this sort of unthinking idealism is that the African will think he just has to sit back and do nothing. He will feel the country will just run itself and we'll always be there to do everything for them anyway. It'll be a very rude shock for them – both black and white.'

John became more determined than ever that the age of entry had to be reduced as quickly as possible and a minimum of six to seven years within the influence and environment of the school was critical. The current average of three years was not enough.

With these new influences of course, came a high degree of disillusionment from the staff and teachers. John found he had to keep boosting them up, assuring them that they were doing the right thing and it was all going to be worthwhile in the end.

'Is Mr. Hammond here?' I heard a gentle voice at the front door one Saturday afternoon. It was Teacher Bulle. He was a delightful man, always with a ready smile and a great roaring laugh. Today he looked worried and anxious.

'Yes, Teacher Bulle – he's in the study. Have a seat and I'll go and get him. Would you like a cup of tea?'

He nodded his head and gave me a half-smile. I went down the passage to call John. 'It's Teacher Bulle...but I think something is wrong, he looks concerned.'

John raised his eyebrows and went straight though to the verandah to talk to him. I brought the tea in a moment later.

'Ah Mr. Hammond, what do we do about these boys?' Bulle asked. 'I am so fed up. Sometimes I think you have a charm.' He laughed and looked at John, hastening to explain, 'because you just have to come into the room and you don't say anything and the boys will work and work and work and work and work. But with us, they are veeeeerrrrry lazy. How can we catch this charm? We are becoming very angry with these lazy boys.'

'We have worked so hard. Why are they now so cheeky all the time and why do they keep wanting to have more and more things, without helping us themselves?'

I left them to it. The discussion went on for hours. John, finally, came through very bothered about it all.

'Bulle is on the point of resignation. I think I've managed to persuade him that it is worth hanging on. He has done so much. He's taken so much responsibility in the last couple of years. The Department doesn't seem to recognise it and now the boys are being churlish. No wonder he's depressed.'

'Do you mean the Department still hasn't done anything about his salary?' I asked. John shook his head.

'Really they must take some responsibility,' I said. 'It's like beating your head against a brick wall trying to press them to take any action. It must be 18 months since you first wrote about the need to increase Teacher Bulle's salary.'

'It's at least that. I sometimes feel we have no support from them whatsoever. It doesn't seem to matter how many letters I write, how strong the reports are; they are all too feeble to take any action. That business with Searson and Edwards was a classic example – and now I might lose good staff because they will not recognise their worth.

'Mothobi is another one who must have a rise, but they have taken no notice. Then there's Roelke as well – he's been working under intolerable conditions.'

He was very depressed by it all when he wrote his annual report that year:

The thoughts of a European child in this country are disciplined by the compelling fact of the necessity for earning a living. He realises that his success or failure in life depends primarily upon himself and consequently spends less time blaming the already rich for the poor remuneration of the occupation he elects to follow.

The Native on the other hand, ignorant of the conditions under which other races work, can only look upon the European as the barrier to his own progress, envying him the position he has gained for himself in life yet not prepared to take active steps to achieve that same position; hoping and believing that the European who is thought to be infinitely wealthy, can with a stroke of the pen bring the Native economic standard up to his own.

John was particularly sad because he had been both astonished and delighted at how well everyone had coped with the move – each working with commitment and enjoyment. Mr. Roelke had been amazing in the work he'd done to keep the building going. Teachers Mothobi, Dabengwa and Bulle had not only built the school, but kept their departments running without a hitch – and almost single-handedly and Mr. Alvord had tied up the Tjolotjo end well. The boys had been inspired and enthusiastic and hard-working.

His summary to the Department in that end of year report that year, had a very positive note to it:

The general progress of the School has been satisfactory in view of the conditions under which we have had to work. As always, of course, one cannot help feeling that we might have done better.

The results in schoolwork have been the best on record for this School and there seems no real reason why these should not be maintained. Many years of hard work remain and although at present our African staff are up to required numbers, any assistance in the way of additional European staff will be welcomed.

It can I think, be said that our achievement here over the past four and a half years has been unique. With a depleted staff and working against all the adverse conditions which a war imposes, a Boarding School of 250 boys has been moved over a hundred miles to a new site. The new School has been entirely built by the School staff and yet the normal working of the School has continued throughout without being allowed to suffer unduly, even during the three years when part of it was at Tjolotjo and another at Mzingwane.

I know of no parallel case; I hope no one will be fool enough to repeat the performance.

In the face of this, it is not surprising that resentment should be felt against the people for whom this is being done, when they make things more difficult by their persistence in the belief that they are badly treated and because of this, do more to hinder than to help.

I must admit there have been times when I have given serious consideration to the whole aspect of this work and have wondered if the effort put in here has been worthwhile.

Each member of the staff of this School has done their full share during the war years; they have persisted in the face of difficulties and of an apparent lack of interest and appreciation of the difficulties from outside the School. They cannot be expected to continue carrying the burdens of the past six years indefinitely. Assistance both within the School and from sources outside is urgently required and should immediately be forthcoming.

It is felt that this has been well earned.

When negotiations on the placement of the school first started, John had been assured by the Reverend Herbert Carter, the Chairman of the Board of the Native Purchase Area, that as soon as the school was ready to make application for the additional land for the farm, it would be considered favourably. The time had come to make that application.

To John's utter astonishment it was turned down, with no satisfactory reason given.

This was a major blow. How could an agricultural school be successfully run without the ability to grow demonstration crops or to house sufficient livestock to become not only self-sufficient enough for the demands of over 300 people but also to demonstrate the strengths of the various varieties of cattle, native-versus-exotic breeds, for instance?

After six months of trying to gain agreement with patently no success, John approached a European farmer whose lands adjoined the school. The owner, who was involved in other things besides farming, did not appear to be utilising the land. Would he be prepared to sell the acreage required? Yes, he would!

But, there now was another, bigger, problem. Use of the land as a farm attached to the school meant that it would now be used for African, not European, advancement. As such, it would therefore cross over line of the Land Apportionment Act. This would make it that much more complex.

219

But something had to be done – and done soon.

Eventually, John decided after many more months of negotiation, that although it would take a week to complete the round trip, only a visit to Salisbury was likely to convince the Government to accede to the request, allow the purchase and empower the Department to buy the farm. It did. An exception was ultimately made to the Land Apportionment Act – an amazing breakthrough at the time. The neighbouring European farmers had no objections and by the end of the year, the Government agreed to buy the land.

By the end of March 1944, I had grown pretty large and was longing for our second babe to be born.

News from England was depressing. Dick had been involved in some amazing escapades, flying one of the old Gladiators named "Faith, Hope and Charity" in the defence of Malta. More recently, he had taken part in some extraordinary bombing raids such as breaching the prison walls at Amiens in order to release hundreds of French resistance members.

Then a telegram came from Mummy – Dick was missing.

I couldn't believe it. This war had been going on so long and there were glimmers of hope that it might be winding down. Our family had seemed to be wonderfully and almost miraculously intact. Trish was involved in some top-secret stuff that she could never talk about, but at least she was in England. Now Dick was missing and nobody knew whether he was alive or dead. In the emotional last stages of pregnancy, the news hit me very hard.

The first crisp nights of the approaching Rhodesian winter signalled the start of April. At last we were going to be able to move into our new house. It was only just in time because the baby was due in three weeks. But my daffodils were growing strongly.

Jill had settled in well, she loved "the hut" as the big rondavel came to be known and would happily sit and play there for hours with Prune and their farmyard of clay cows.

Sister Weir had come to join us on the staff again by the beginning of 1944. This time Lalan would be employed by the school itself, doing some outside work for the village, but also giving First Aid and hygiene lessons to the boys.

During this last year, the staff had all been particularly impressed with a young chap called Joshua Nkomo, who'd been helping out as carpentry assistant at Tjolotjo.

He had really come up trumps during the move and early in the year he said to John that he wanted to try and do his Cambridge School Certificate. This could be done, but it was going to take some organising to have him enrolled and find the money to enable him to do it. But he was bright and likeable and John was impressed with his drive and tenacity. So he created a position and put him on the staff as an assistant teacher in carpentry to Roger Malusalila, and also as a part-time lorry driver. He was a tall, slim young man, good-looking and smart. Joshua's younger brother, McKenzie, was also at the school.

Jill loved Joshua as he would drive us in to Bulawayo, then stay in the truck looking after her while I went round the shops. 'Joshua tummin, Joshua tummin,' she would shout as soon as she saw the truck appear. She'd rush out and clamber up into the cab to chat to him, knowing that this would probably mean a trip to town. He was very good with her.

April was always a busy month at the school and this year, Morrie and Skinny were due to come and stay with us for a couple of nights. We were so looking forward to it as it was years since we had seen them. They'd just been down by train to collect JJ and a school friend from Plumtree for the Easter holidays. John went in to fetch them from Bulawayo station and they returned just in time to enjoy one of the highlights of the year, the inter-school sports day with Tegwane. Skinny and John were always the visionaries of the family and they shared many ideals. The two of them, plus the two youngsters, all had a marvellous time watching the sports, enabling me to take life a bit more quietly and catch up on the family with Morrie.

They were well established back in the country now with a farm at Umvukwes. They had just built themselves seven pole and *dagga* huts, incorporating a sitting room, dining room, kitchen, bathroom and three bedroom huts all round the base of a pretty little granite kopje with the hills of the great chrome dyke rising behind them. The huts were designed to take advantage of the climate. The bedrooms had windows and stable doors, but the dining room was all open, with great curving arches instead of windows and wide sills that the children loved to sit on.

Carving out a tobacco farm from that bush was tough going, partic-ularly as the area was sparsely populated and it was extremely difficult to find farm workers. They eventually managed to get enough by bringing them in from Nyasaland on our easter border. This year, they'd

221

managed to plant their first ten acres and were very pleased with how it all looked.

Skinny had just had the unfortunate experience of discovering he had a borer in his ear – and once there the bug thought it was a great place to keep boring! Poor old Skinny was in agony and the borer required removal as soon as possible, but all the rivers were up. So eventually in desperation, Skin had swum the Msengedzi and walked to a nearby farm, asking the farmer if he could drive him to town. Not content with that he had also had to swim an even bigger river, the Tsatsi, and negotiate another ride the rest of the way. It had been an adventure in itself, but at last he was admitted to hospital and the borer was removed. Skinny arrived back at the farm keen to relate his rather hair raising story only to find it well and truly trumped.

Morrie's mother, Ganzie, had been staying with them at the time and that morning her early morning cuppa had not arrived. Tut-tutting away, she hauled herself out of bed and went over in her nightgown and slippers to find out what was going on. The cook boy and Maradzikwa the garden boy were in the kitchen with the door shut. She asked what was happening and received a muffled reply. With more tut-tutting away she turned back past the dining room hut to return to her room. Half an hour later, there was still no tea.

This was too much! Ganzie, always a fearsome figure, strode past the dining room hut and burst into the kitchen. 'Where is my tea?' she asked.

'Look, meddem, look!' stuttered a terrified Maradzikwa, pointing through the open arch of the kitchen window behind her.

Ganzie turned.

A fully-grown leopard was sitting snarling on the step of the dining room. It had been drowsing in the early morning sun as she had walked within three feet of it, three times. It was drowsing no longer!

After much shrieking and performance the Boss Boy arrived and he was able to persuade the leopard to move on. Skinny's story paled into insignificance by comparison! He did make us howl with laughter describing both stories, and confiding that such was Ganzie's awesome presence, that if she had actually seen the leopard first, he was quite sure she would have rounded on it with her finger pointed and commanded it to "sit"!

We had such a lot of laughs together. John was now due to take them back the next day, but Morrie offered to stay and help with Jill as the baby was due any minute.

'I'll be back in a couple of hours,' John said, as Morrie and I turned back to the house having waved them all off down the drive. They were still going down the road with the dust swirling behind them when I felt the first tightening round the tum.

I wasn't particularly worried as it was obviously very early in the process and Morrie and I went in to prepare for my departure and finish our breakfast. By lunchtime the pains were strong and regular – and there was no sign of John. By 3.30 I was getting worried. I didn't know whether to borrow the Roelke's car and head into Bulawayo, or to wait for him.

By six that evening, I had decided I had no choice and was about to go over to the Roelkes when John arrived. He had been unavoidably delayed with a breakdown, and was appalled to find how advanced I was by this stage. We took everything out to the car and were just loading it up when we saw... a puncture.

This time it had to be Roelke's car – and quickly. We didn't feel we had time to change the wheel. Jean had suggested I go into a private nursing home, the Monica Maternity home. It was a welcome sight – very prettily painted, lovely big rooms and attractive bed covers. We arrived there just after eight in the evening. John hurriedly kissed me goodbye and rushed off because it was obvious that it was not going to be long.

As he left, the owner of this expensive home changed from a smiling and benevolent helper into a malevolent, mean-spirited fiend.

'Now you get into that bed,' she ordered. 'And I don't want another sound out of you until morning – or you'll wake my husband.'

I crept, crushed, to my bed. But I was in a terrible state of anxiety, as I knew there was no chance I'd make it until the morning. After another seven hours of agony trying to hold everything back – the urge to push was absolutely irresistible. I staggered up to phone the Lady Rodwell, the government maternity home, pleading with them to come and fetch me. The woman woke up and was furious! She cut off my phone call as I gasped, 'The baby is coming and there is nobody to help me.'

'Oh, that's all right dear.'

She suddenly changed her attitude as she realised what trouble I was in... and snip, the waters burst and a huge baby boy came rushing out.

He should have been born hours before. Despite the immense relief, I was deeply angry. The baby was nearly eleven pounds in weight and far too long for any of the cots she had in there. No wonder his birth was such a battle. I was almost too tired to think – although as I drifted off I panicked about the effect that long labour might have had on the babe.

When I woke from a deep sleep a couple of hours later, Richard was brought to me. We had decided that if it were a boy (we still had no news of what had happened to Dick) he would be called Richard.

He was quite different from Jill – golden haired and looking rather like a contented old farmer. He was absolute ravenous and looked none the worse for his impeded progress into the world… and I certainly had no trouble feeding him. John popped in at visiting time that afternoon, with a beautiful little Omega watch. I wept quite unashamedly as soon as I saw him and longed just to go home with him. The prospect of ten days to two weeks in this place was daunting.

I wrote the next day:

Gosh darling, that is a most lovely watch and so tremendously sweet of you to think of it and get it for me. I keep looking at it with such pride and will take very great care of it and hope it will last me all my life.

It was lovely seeing our nice little notice in the paper this a.m. I expect Sister gnashed her teeth to see both births in today's paper were at the Monica, but neither thanked doctor and nurse!! It is too funny – Sister is sucking up to me right and left and is, I am sure, scared stiff that I am going to report her to the doctor.

The other girl in here is tickled to death as she hasn't had so much attention since she's been here and Sister was awful to her until I came in.

Sister is really a terrible woman though and has been in a foul temper. And today (we hear her going on at everyone, but us) the houseboy just picked up her own child which was climbing off the verandah… and she yelled at him, "Damn you, that's not your work – you're not to touch the child you stinking munt." I couldn't believe it.

She has to pull herself together and put on a sweet honeyed face when she comes in here at the moment, so for our sakes, I think it is better that I don't tell the doc. Then I can hold it over her head while I am here. Her eyes flashed when I dared to ask about the baby's net…

Next afternoon I woke up and was preparing to feed Richard when a baby was literally plonked into my lap. When I looked at him it wasn't Richard.

'Sister – this is not my baby!' I shouted at her retreating back.

She laughed unkindly. 'I just thought I'd try it, to see if you knew your own baby.'

She was an absolute sadist. There were only two people in the hospital and we had both had boys. My mind quailed to think what might have happened if there had been many more in there. The place was condemned and closed down a few months later.

Richard was a contented baby and just ate and slept, ate and slept. When I arrived home again, Jill and I kept surreptitiously waking him up so that we could gain some reaction from him. Jill "adopted" him immediately and couldn't do enough for him. She insisted on her baby coming to listen to the stories every evening and she'd talk to him and ask him questions about what he had heard! Poor old Prune seemed to fade into the background for a while, as Jill became absorbed in this living "dolly". But eventually Richard didn't react enough to interest her and Prune was back on the scene.

To my joy, on my return home, there was a daffodil in bloom. I wept unashamedly. Somehow this little flower symbolised a move away from the harshness which I had found so difficult in Tjolotjo. The perfectly crafted little golden trumpet spoke to me of an English spring, of fresh new beginnings and of things finally coming to fruition. I picked that first daffodil, popped it into a long-stemmed vase and willed it to live as long as it could.

Lalan came in one evening a few months later, looking a little anxious. 'I think I've got a typhoid, Mr. Hammond,' she said.

John groaned. Typhoid was a horrid thing and a notifiable disease. This meant the school would have to go into quarantine.

'I'm taking myself off and away to the hospital and I won't come back in case I act as an intermediary,' she said. 'But absolutely everything is to be boiled... all the milk and particularly the water – even the water that the vegetables are washed in or that dishes are washed up in... and keep the flies down wherever you can.'

She gave John a clear list of instructions as to what had to be done to notify the authorities and to keep the school as safe as possible.

The hospital was just behind our house and I was in an immediate agony of anxiety and apprehension in case either of the children caught the disease. We'd always boiled our water anyway, but now that water was boiled a dozen times a day – in fact, there was always a great pot bubbling away on the old black coal stove.

The kids seemed to be fine and we were almost out of the danger period when I awoke to find myself covered in pink spots and feeling like hell on earth.

'Get Lalan,' I called to John through parched lips, 'and don't let the children come near me.' I was right – it was typhoid.

Fortunately I don't remember much about it as I was rapidly moved to hospital and was delirious for several days. But it was a real problem for Richard as he was still being breast-fed. How they coped I don't know, but by the time I "came to" in Bulawayo hospital, I found Richard was also in the hospital. He had been admitted so that he could be near me as he was still less than six months old and he had been brought to see me two or three times every day, but was only able to look at me through a window. When I called out to him, he didn't know me. I was simply shattered. John said he had found the same withdrawal and lack of recognition almost from the first day.

'It's had an awful effect on him, I'm afraid,' the doctor said to me. 'He just lies in his cot all day and won't cry or do anything. We've been concerned in case he had it as well, but we don't think so now… it's just a very bad reaction to being parted from you.'

I was in hospital for about three weeks and when I took Richard home, it was like taking a little stranger with me. It took months of tender love and care before he would respond to us again.

One thing that did help during this awful time was that, shortly after I came out of hospital, a neighbour of ours near Southminster, Mrs. Sinclair, had phoned Mummy to say she'd been listening to the radio and by chance heard a German broadcast saying Dick was a prisoner. He was alive! There was great rejoicing as at least there was some hope of making contact with him and finding out how he was. By now the war really did look as though it might be in its last stages and, hopefully, Dick would make it safely through.

I had my hands very full with the two children, so I was not quite as in touch with what was happening at the school as I had been but it all seemed to be settling down and consolidating well and certainly the results were improving all the time.

The Department had just approved John's request that Mrs. Roelke be allowed to be his clerk in the office. As a general rule, women, especially the wives of staff members, were still not permitted to work in these roles and Head Office took some convincing. But it was a good move and by the start of 1945, he would have a full-time clerk again.

Although there were vague promises made around the possibility of a couple of new immigrants from England, it did not seem likely that we would be allocated any more academic staff.

The dormitories seemed to be working well. The pupils preferred to sleep on the floor to begin with, but after a few weeks were happy to try out the beds and then there was no looking back. There were only ten boys per dormitory and it certainly helped that they had the ability to access the housemaster quickly and easily if necessary.

John's overwhelming concern now, within this scene of seeming peace and achievement, was that the tide was turning so rapidly that the race was now really on to do everything European-style. As always, he was very sad about it.

'It's the negation of everything that is important to them Nan, and I don't seem able to stop it. The parents must be very concerned. There is steadily decreasing respect for the elders and it has been replaced by this overwhelming desire to learn so that they can have access to what they perceive to be the might and wealth of the European.'

He wrote to Head Office expressing his concerns saying the push for Europeanisation was exacerbated by the ridiculous curriculum he was having to adhere to:

There is little learning for the sake of learning as one can find in schools for European children. As a result, no matter how interesting a subject may be made, these boys like to feel that anything that they learn is going to be of some practical use to them in after life. They can see the value of Arithmetic and English but are inclined to discount the value of History and Geography and General Science.

It may well be that these subjects could have been better handled than they have been here, but it would be of assistance if the boys thought that results in these subjects went towards their final certification, as well as those in English and Arithmetic.

I am still concerned that the two-year courses in carpentry and building are sufficient only to turn out something, which is half-baked. At least another year is wanted if the boys are to go out to undertake any form of advanced work on their own. They are getting jobs all right, but they are disappointing their employers and finding it absurdly difficult themselves as a result.

There has been a tremendous influx of boys to take the builders' course and this is due to the present boom in wages – a boom which may not last many more years. I have done my best to warn the boys against the possi-

227

bility of their finding difficulty in getting employment in a few years.

These increased numbers are going to present some difficulties next year as we try to find projects for the building specialists. It is proposed to put Standard V onto the construction of temporary dwellings to house the labour. These will be constructed of green brick under thatch and will be of very simple design. The first year of the Post VI class will erect the main dormitories in burnt brick while second year pupils put up the new teachers' cottages.

We shall, I know, have to resist the temptation to use the pupils to too large an extent on pure construction work.

'You know what we are battling with Nan? It's a scary combination of a breakdown in tribal disciplines, which are no longer taken very seriously… undermining of the disciplines of Native Commissioners, because some of them insist on their over-strict adherence to laws made for a completely different society… and now the added difficulty of maintaining discipline here, particularly if we are given teachers from another country who don't have a clue how to handle Africans.'

'Duckie, you are still doing a wonderful job.' I used my most encouraging voice, knowing full well the extent of his concern.

'You may be the only person that thinks so,' he smiled wryly. 'No, I don't mean that… when I see how good some of our boys are, I do take heart.

'The African cannot yet have an understanding of the concept behind earning a living. When learning only to achieve results are encouraged, he will tend to see the European merely as a barrier to progress. As a result, it becomes destructive.

'He ends up envying the position the European has, yet is not prepared to take active steps to achieve that same position. I sometimes believe that they think Europeans are infinitely wealthy and with one stroke of a pen can bring the African's economic standards up to his own.'

'Johnnie, it can't be that bad…'

'Oh yes, it is – sadly. I cannot believe how difficult it is to teach the boys that the ability to write a cheque is the end product of having money in the bank. It's only when they have been with us three or four years that they understand that we don't just write a cheque and an infinite stream of never-ending money flows at our command.

'How are we going to put this message across to the millions who are not at this school or the very few others like it? They simply don't believe it, unless they're in this sort of learning environment where through experience and communicating with us, they grow to trust us and believe what we say.'

There was, however, one positive outcome at this stage – the parents. They were becoming more and more involved in the school lives of their children and John was determined to start a parents' weekend as soon as possible.

There is a great need for a closer link with the parents and I feel the best way is to have as many as possible meet here for discussions. It is very gratifying to see the increased interest and sense of responsibility which parents have for the school. Today the majority of boys are sent to school by their parents and the boy who has to find his own way through school is becoming almost a rarity.

There was a strange sense of anti-climax once the move had been completed and as Roy Alvord at last moved the rest of the farm over at the beginning of 1945. This final move had been delayed because of the land acquisition problem. But now, the move was complete, the farm secured and everything was, so to speak, under one roof again.

As early as 1945 and 1946 John thought things were moving too fast and that this was bringing with it, a recipe for trouble. The "young" colony of Rhodesia was caught in a pincer movement with increasingly insistent calls to resist and to shake off the shackles of colonialism. Interestingly, these coincided with a visit from a team of international educationalists – one of whom was Russian. He seemed particularly interested in Rhodesia's ability (or otherwise) to educate the bulge of black youngsters created by the highest population growth in the world. John felt very uneasy about their visit.

'It is inevitable of course, but we really haven't had time to lay down the level of education required to cope with a sophisticated western society and economy and to cater for the vast number of children produced because of the country's increasing prosperity. It's asking too much. I wonder if they have the slightest idea how hard it is.'

Just as John was concerned about turning out half-baked builders and carpenters, he was even more concerned about turning over a half-baked country, which had had only 60 years of European contact and only half that of exposure to education for very few in number. It was not enough to build the foundations necessary for such an utter change in society and to leave that society able to fend for itself in the brave new post-war world.

John wrote in his report of 1945:

Only an educated people can make democracy work and where there is an uneducated race the only effective means of government is an autocracy. If we are to leave the Native with his present freedom to work or play, only the minority will elect to work. This is bound to have, in fact, it is having a markedly bad effect on the Native population now growing up. It can be checked by introducing a more autocratic form of government with a curtailment of present liberties, or by the expansion of liberties to include the freedom to starve. This has been the greatest disciplining force in the world in all past ages. The Native has neither of these.

He comes to school with an inadequate background of discipline and has no outside forces compelling discipline. The School is the only place where he cannot do what he likes, where he cannot leave without suffering for it in his later life, where he us under strict control as to behaviour and freedom of movement. He chafes at these restrictions and it is fortunate for schools today that pressure to enter them is so great, otherwise the situation would be very difficult.

Poor Johnnie – I did feel for him. He had battled for years with only one or two other European staff because everyone else was tied up with the war or wouldn't have anything to do with teaching Natives. He had absolutely nobody to talk to who seemed to have any understanding of his concerns and fears for the future, and he received absolutely no support whatsoever, it seemed to me, from Head Office. It was a typical government department – lots of nice words, but precious little action.

In these bigger-picture scenarios, he seemed very alone – and I could only listen.

Mostly the problems of 1945 were not terribly serious – just wearing and time consuming, requiring,

…infinite patience to change. I do not despair of improving this state of affairs, but I hate having to run a school while it is suffering from this mental indigestion.

The one case of active disobedience to authority occurred with the Demon-

strators in training. Towards the end of the year they were set revision papers in order to brush up their theoretical knowledge before their final examinations. The first of these they refused to do.

When they persisted in their refusal to write anything in answer to the questions, I threatened to expel them. This had little effect and I duly sent them away. Certain members of the African staff thereupon made representations to me on their behalf and I recanted.

Several different punishments were devised for them and his report concluded:

As four of these men were holding bursaries from the Native Reserves Fund and as they were all within two months of completing their course, I was glad of an opportunity to allow them to go through to the end of the year without allowing them to feel that they had come off best.

But absolutely inexorably and more obviously every week, the Natives could see no good in their own culture. It was being over-turned slowly but surely. In searching for reasons to combat it, he felt that perhaps part and parcel of it was the "careless" teaching of certain subjects like history:

I feel it is imperative that the teaching of history be put only into the hands of men whose knowledge is such that they can arrive at fair judgements and present unbiased cases. History teaching in the hands of an unscrupulous person may do infinite harm to the future peace of this country; handled with care it should go a long way towards improving race relationships.

As 1945 came to an end, John felt a little more encouraged. He'd now been promised three new European members of staff – two of them unfortunately, straight out from England now that the war was over and neither with any experience in boarding schools. Still, having extra hands on deck would help – and they would learn. The third was a man he knew and liked, Mr. Murton, who'd come as second agriculturist to Roy Alvord.

But he was still desperately short of African teachers to cope with the extra numbers the school was now taking, and the effect this would have on the good people he did have on staff already was a huge concern.

His final word to Head Office was:

It is hoped that we shall open 1946 with sufficient African staff to ensure that no one man has to carry any excessive burden any longer. I am sorry the Government could not see its way to the opening of a school for the children of teachers.

At Tjolotjo it was a strong factor in keeping the staff stable and contented. Two of our senior men have applied for transfer because of the lack of adequate facilities here for the training of their children. I shall not be surprised if two more follow in the near future.

As we celebrated Jill's fifth birthday, I said to Johnnie that I thought the time had come for another holiday at the Cape. I was worried by how depressed and anxious he had become as he faced the fact that, although he felt time was running out, he was unable to increase the pace or quality of Native education, particularly with all the impractical idealism around him sowing seeds of unrest and discontent. He had no time for it and felt it was just time-wasting and should not be part of the fabric of a school like Mzingwane.

In February, he came home one evening and I could see something was on his mind.

'What is it?' I asked.

'Well…' he started slowly. 'I haven't known whether to tell you or not because I have been a bit disturbed by my own reactions to it and really needed to sort that out first.'

'What is it Johnnie?' I cried, imagining the diagnosis of an illness or worse.

'No, no,' he reassured me. 'It's nothing like that – but it has probably shaken me almost as much.'

'I received a letter from Pat Pattison last week to say he had applied for the headship of REPS, which will be coming up sometime around mid-year. I think he'd be a fine man for the job so he'd certainly have my backing, and I should think he has a pretty good chance of getting it. Then he asked whether I would be interested in taking over his job as housemaster of Milner as he said he would love to have me there with him.'

'Would he love to have you there for you – or for the "Hammond of Plumtree link?"'

This had been a subject of discussion many years ago and John had felt that it might not be a good idea just because of those very strong links with his father. I had not agreed as I felt that John was such a fine headmaster in his own right. But it was a point that needed consideration.

'No, I asked him that and said I wanted him to be absolutely honest,' he smiled and looked at me '...I think Pat convinced me that it was because of me – and my ability to do the job. Here's his letter.'

I took it and read:

Dear John,

Maningi indaba! (Plenty of trouble!) *Southern Rhodesian Education is a great mass of rumours but before long a few facts might emerge on the question of appointments. There are headships coming up at Plumtree, REPS and Guinea Fowl. You may have applied for some of these posts for all I know.*

For some time there have been continuous rumours that I was being shifted from here to REPS. I have applied for it this time. I don't mind which way things go. I am just determined to stay in Boarding Schools of this type as it is the type of Education that I have real faith in. If I got REPS it might mean leaving this term, but more likely now it will be August.

If I had to go, I would be very worried as to who would be coming into Milner. I look around and see no one whom your old man or J.D. Lee would choose to come in here. Then I heard that you had been feeling a bit down and at once thought gosh! If John has not already had a crack for one of these Headmasterships, I wonder if he would consider his old House? We need you John!

Plumtree must get in more men who believe in this type of education and can handle boys. I would be terribly interested to hear what you are thinking about things. I certainly think it is time you took a rest from what you are doing, you have done more than your fair share now.

Another section is wanting me to apply for Guinea Fowl where some people are hoping a second Plumtree might emerge. I went into that with the Department, but I don't trust them a yard at the moment. Plumtree is the complete "ugly duckling" as there is really no place in this State system for a purely boarding school as things stand. They don't like it because they can't control it as easily. Unless they give the person starting Guinea Fowl almost complete freedom, free of all their regulations and restrictions, I defy anyone to produce anything more than an Enkeldoorn.

They may be proud of Plumtree, but Plumtree is here in spite of State policy, not because of it. They may change their outlook and you may be interested in that sort of thing too with your Dad's history behind you and your experience in these things.

Let me know what you are really feeling. I'll let you know of the first appointments and with some pushing we might find something will work out. Keep it under your hat… it's damn unsettling here and one does not now what is likely to happen anywhere.

'Well, that's a super letter,' I said. 'What's the matter with that?' I had always known how marvellous it would be for Johnnie to go back to Plumtree, with all its very happy associations. He looked at me…

'You're right. There's nothing the matter with it but I have just turned it down. The real matter with it was my reaction to the whole thing. I have been so sure for so much of my life that the only important job in this country is the education of the African people – so driven in my desire to see it happen properly – and yet latterly, I have been so saddened and, I suppose, disillusioned by what is going on, that I found myself actively considering leaving.

'In fact, in the last few days, all I have been able to think of is how much easier and more pleasant the job of housemaster at Milner would be. That's shaken me… and I'm finding it hard to come to terms with.'

I didn't say anything because secretly I would have loved to have followed in Harrie's shoes – all that music, the shows… although I was happy at Mzingwane and it was so satisfying to see John's dream come alive. If only the Department would give him more support… if only the boys would show some appreciation of what was done for them…

I couldn't let my feelings influence him at this critical moment.

I just reached my hand out and held his for a very long time. I hoped our holiday at the Cape would allow him to come back at peace with himself – and with what lay ahead. I prayed that he'd gain the strength and desire to meet whatever those future challenges might be, head on, with his usual dogged determination and enthusiasm.

More than anything, I prayed that this disillusionment was only temporary and merely the outward sign of an exhausted man.

Chapter 11

The Plumtree passion
and a magnificent Messiah

The flaxen-haired little boy had his head down as he barged along with his favourite trolley at great speed on the walkway to the beach. He made vrooming motor car noises as he went – oblivious to everything else. Jill and I rushed to catch up to stop him charging straight into an elderly man taking tentative steps in the same direction.

Richard had turned into a great chap – a thatch of golden hair, dimpled cheeks, chubby and bewitching in his gentle, considerate little ways. Jill adored him – although I had noticed the first signs of a little sibling rivalry, probably because our rather good looking little boy tended to receive an undue share of attention.

Oh how wonderful it was to be down at the Cape. It was our first break since our holiday in England in 1939 when we had the escapade with the *Graf Spee*.

What a lot had happened since then – two children of course, and for us both sporadic bouts of malaria, with me contracting typhoid as well. But for John… he had had the almost impossible task of moving the whole school, with only a few loyal helpers. But it had been done, and when we left in the middle of March 1946, Mzingwane was a hive of activity, with new buildings going up and the farm lush with crops and animals.

The very best news of all was that Maurice and Daisy Mills would be coming back onto the staff at the start of the second term. Our friendship had grown from the time of our "twin" pregnancies and the chase by the antbear, and even though we'd been so far apart some of my happiest memories were of times we had spent with them in Salisbury. Jill and Jenny were also very good playmates.

Just before he left, John felt he should write to George Stark, Head of the Native Education Department to let him know about the offer from Pat Pattison. We had just received a long letter back from him. It encouraged John enormously and made him feel Stark understood the position and was not critical of his frustration and disappointments:

You have of course, had an overdose of things during the war years and it is just possible that with Mills' return and after your change to the coast your reactions may alter, although I am doubtful of this unless it is possible for you to put on that protective covering and refuse to allow yourself to be upset by what has been happening.

I should miss you from Mzingwane. It's your school and you are making a great success of it. I should hate the idea of your leaving. But there are larger issues involved. I hope that all will yet come right, but if they don't then please be assured of my utmost sympathy and support in any move, which will make for the happiness of yourself, your wife and family.

'Oh well, that's good of him,' John said. 'I feel I have got it off my chest and now I can relax and enjoy the holiday.' John had been very tense when we first arrived but now, after a week at the coast, with the children and me, he was beginning to relax and return to his old self. He actually hated the sea and I was always rather surprised to see him take the plunge. It was only when the kids were in the water, that he would even consider it. Only then, and after a long time of making up his mind, would he run down the beach, take a huge dive into the waves and emerge spouting and protesting. The baldness, which had been threatening since before we were married, was now much in evidence. Reluctant to admit to it at his young age, he had one long, thick lock of hair, which he carefully nurtured across the top of his bare head. When he emerged from the sea, this would be glued to the side of his face. The children loved it. I loved to see him able to relax and be himself – not constantly having to stand on his dignity or feel he was having to set an example.

I loved seeing the kids getting to know their father better – and vice versa. The evenings were the best times when we would all sit round and play card games, charades, "I Spy" or word-association games. Jill and Richard were always very quick at these and loved "trumping" the grown-ups.

Richard had a best friend who was two doors away – "Big" Fynn. He was Kim Fynn's father and we had met him several times with Kim and Stella. Rich would suddenly and solemnly announce he was off to see Big Fynn. I'd find him happily sitting on Mr. or Mrs. Fynn's knee eating all sorts of treasures and entranced with their stories. The Fynns loved having him. And he loved having a cuddle with them. He came back and announced that he liked going to see them because he was a "kissy, lovey boy".

The Homestead at Fish Hoek was a very happy place to be with children, it was close to the sea and we'd go down each morning, walking under a railway bridge on the way to the beach. If a train came along, the beach would empty of children as they raced to get under the bridge as the train went across, all shrieking "sailor, sailor, sailor". Most of the trains were full of sailors on their way to, or from, the naval base at Simonstown.

The children's meal times were packed with over-excited but fit, happy and healthy kids, and we could put them both down to sleep after a few card games and jigsaw puzzles to have some precious time to ourselves.

After a couple of weeks away, John arranged to go into Cape Town for a meal one evening to meet his best man Norman Bibra. Norman was doing a post-graduate degree at Cape Town University. I thought it was important for the two men to have some time together so we all waved him off on the train one afternoon. He gave me a big hug and promised to catch the last train home. It was wonderful to see him looking so carefree and full of fun again.

When he hadn't returned by 11 o'clock that evening, I started to get anxious. All I could think about was Cape Town's renowned "skolly boys" and the murders and mayhem they had been causing at that time. As the night wore on, and I heard nothing from him, I was quite convinced something ghastly had happened and I wept for my two sleeping and, by now I was sure, fatherless children. I dropped into an exhausted sleep around five in the morning. Shortly after six there was a gentle knock on the door. It was John!

I should have remembered his inability to catch trains on time. He had arrived at Cape Town station to see his train pulling out and he couldn't run fast enough to catch it. As he stood around on the now completely deserted platform, another train backed in. John jumped on and waited. It was only when they put all the lights out that he realised it wasn't going to move until the morning. There was nothing he could do by this stage as he was locked onto the platform, so he slept in the train and woke up to find it moving out of the station just after 5'30 that morning!

We now had only two weeks of our holiday left and I was beginning to count off the days very sadly. Leaving the sea was always a great deprivation to me. John fetched the mail and among a good batch of letters, there was one from his eldest brother, Skinny.

Dear Johnnie,
You have become notorious in your absence. Herewith all the "bumph" relating to the affair and there are possible repercussions to come. I have asked A.G.C., to whom I have sent a copy of my letter to the Branch Secretary, to show it privately to the Chairman of the Public Services Board and John Cowie, head of the Education Department, which I think will clear you of any question of implication in the affair. You'll have to come and deal a raspberry or two yourself at the OP weekend in June…

John's face dropped when he saw the bumph Skinny had sent. It included an article from the Rhodesia Herald of 17th April, headlined "HEADMASTER OF PLUMTREE" and saying that:

A proposal that representations should be made to the Government to secure the appointment of Mr. J. M. Hammond as headmaster of Plumtree School was carried at a meeting of Old Prunitians held in Meikles Hotel last Thursday. It was pointed out that the present headmaster, Mr. J. E. Mylne, would be retiring this year and the meeting was in favour of the appointment of a young man, capable of devoting many years of his life to the school. Mr. J. M. Hammond is a son of the late Mr. R. W. Hammond, first headmaster of Plumtree.

John was aghast.

'Nobody has approached me about this. What on earth do they think they are doing?'

Skinny enclosed a letter he had written plus a published letter to the editor and two editorials which had been written as a result of all this. One letter to the editor was headlined "Protest on Principle" and signed by someone calling him or herself "Vigilant":

No doubt there were many who, like myself, rubbed their eyes at the idea of any society wishing to discuss a Government appointment, who not content with just discussing the matter, actually had the impertinence to recommend to the Government who should be appointed.

It is an admirable virtue to be proud of one's school, but it should be remembered that Plumtree is only one of seven High Schools in the Colony and although one can excuse old students for claiming it to be the best, they must not expect the rest of the community to think so or to acquiesce in the implication that without the assistance of the Old Prunitians' Society a wrong choice of headmaster would be made.

There is a principle involved.

John groaned. 'That sounds horribly like a Departmental response in disguise...'

The editorials were both rather positively taking the side of the Old Prunitians:

...there is something to be said for Old Boys and parents having a say in the appointment of the headmaster of such a school. True it is that the man who pays the piper should call the tune, which means that as the school is a State school, it is for the State to make the decision. But it is also true that no small part of the revenue, which supports the school is derived from parents, many of them Old Boys...

We see no reason why principle and sentiment should not be reconciled...

The other editorial said:

We publish today a letter from one Old Prunitian, which advances the idea that the time is now ripe for amending the system under which appointments to headmasterships are made, to enable younger men to be appointed. The idea is to get men who can plan with enthusiasm over a long period. A point of view well worthy of consideration.

The editorial went on to suggest that such had been the success of Plumtree that it was time for the foundation of a second Plumtree and just how that might be done. John's face was ashen as he turned to read the letter Skinny had sent to the OP Society:

Sir,

I must enter the very strongest of protests against the way in which the Salisbury Branch has concerned itself publicly with the appointment of the next Headmaster.

It is a gross presumption on the part of your committee to have considered the meeting an official one whose findings should be the subject of public comment. This is, of itself, deplorable. The Society is a private body, in no possible sense a political one and for your committee to dare on its behalf to make recommendations to the Government is a rank impertinence, not only to the Society itself but to the Public Services Board.

My brother, Mr. J. M. Hammond, is at present on leave and therefore unable as yet, to comment personally on the publication of his name. It astounds me that you should have considered it other than ill-mannered to have proposed his name without having first consulted him, or having done so, to have deemed it proper to have published it, thereby placing him in a position of great embarrassment. He is not, as you should know (being so evidently familiar with his capacities) a member of the Education Department, nor had he entered an application for the Headship.

I consider therefore that I have the right to demand on his behalf a letter of apology, which, I trust, will not be published outside the Society – from your Chairman to Mr. J. M. Hammond.

Thank God Skinny had responded so promptly as the letters and articles had taken nearly a week to arrive.

'This will almost certainly guarantee that I never get a job again, and what on earth will Stark think now? He'll think I stirred this up as he knows how unsettled I have been, but it will be awful for the school to read all this nonsense too.'

John sat down immediately and wrote to Pat Pattison, to John Cowie, Chief Education Officer of the Education Department and to George Stark, head of the Native Education Department, assuring them that he had known absolutely nothing about the move.

He also sent cables to the *Bulawayo Chronicle* and the *Rhodesia Herald*:

Please dissociate my name from consideration of appointment of Headmaster Plumtree and emphasise that proposal from Salisbury was made without prior consultation with me.

A week later we received the first response… from Pat Pattison. He agreed that the OP show was "shocking" but felt that all had been done to put it right. His news was that the chief posts had now been filled, and only elections might change those decisions if Sir Godfrey Huggins was elected as Prime Minister:

I have heard completely confidentially that B… of Umtali is coming here. He has a few more years to go and I gather is a very suitable man. That looks as if in four or five years they will reconsider the question of an HM and in the meantime watch some of the numerous names that have come forward.

John, it makes it absolutely imperative that you should come here. You know the ropes, you know the tradition … you will slide into it as easy as hell. Your old man took a plunge and put me in here over the heads of five men who had been here longer than I had – it was a bit unpleasant, but the compensating thing was I knew the troops were all for it and so I did not give a damn and it could be the same again.

There is the precedent of Mylne coming from Domboshawa to the position of Headmaster! Mylne is I believe, in Cape Town at the moment – what about your contacting him? I have mentioned my hopes to him already… can assure you all I do will be most circumspect.

Your Missus might like to follow on with the musical side that Mrs. H started and Mrs. P has continued?

Dear old Pat, he was very encouraging, but it really did not help the situation. However, John was happier with the next letter from Cowie, head of the Education Department:

I thank you for your letter from Fish Hoek and I can well appreciate your worry and anxiety of the action of the Salisbury Branch of the OP Society. It may comfort you to know that my first reaction on seeing the newspaper article was to say to myself that whoever was responsible for it, John Hammond was certainly not that person and I can assure you that my reaction was shared by all your friends in Salisbury.

We have had a sincere apology from the OP Society and so far as the Department is concerned, the incident is closed and your reputation has not suffered in any way.

No decision has been arrived at by the Public Services Board on the reorganisation of the Education Department… even if this does not take place, transfer from the Native to the European sides of Education has been made easier already by the grouping of all teachers in the Schools Division for salaries.

John sat for a long time, with his head in his hands. 'Oh Nannie, what should I do? I have felt so strongly that my role is to work in Native Education, to try to bring them balance with practical discipline and a broader based education. With all this "do gooder" idealism around, it could be the decider between giving boys the ability to become real leaders of this country or simply creating expectations which cannot be met and which must ultimately lead to disaster.

'I know that this is one of the most important jobs in the country… I know that we are over the worst and Mzingwane should be set fair from now on… but it is so relentlessly difficult… it is so unforgiving… I get so little support… and now the boys themselves seem increasingly deceitful and ungrateful… I feel very despondent about it all.'

My mind was whirling. We kept going over and over the same ground. What advice could I give him? We were very happy at Essexvale and Mzingwane was doing so well. Yet, perhaps the constant letdowns were too much for him.

'In the letter Stark wrote to you after you told him about Pat's initial approach, he said something, which I thought was very true.' I took the letter out and read:

> *…my recent correspondence with you has revealed a sensitiveness of spirit which is too vulnerable for your own peace of mind.*
>
> *You have served the Department well – excellently well – and your going would be a tremendous loss. You have not spared yourself for the school of which you have been in charge. You have more than justified my confidence in you when I recommended that you should succeed W. G. Brown at Tjolotjo. I am deeply grateful for what you have done and for your loyalty. It is because of all this that I shall so fully support you.*
>
> *I feel that you deserve by your idealism combined with practicality, by your enthusiasm and thoroughness, a role that will give full scope for your belief in human nature.*

John thought about it for a moment. 'Yes, I think he is probably right. Sensitiveness of spirit! Yes, I suppose I do allow myself to be hurt when people let me down – I expect the best from them at all times

– perhaps that's wrong and although in a less obvious way, I probably am as idealistic as the rest.'

'Johnnie, it's only wrong because it causes you so much pain. Your high expectations have been the very reason your boys have always done so well.'

The discussion went on for hours. I knew that if it had been any school other than Plumtree, John would never even have entertained the idea of leaving Mzingwane or Native Education. But Plumtree meant so much to him. I tried to explain this to him, but he could only see it as a weakness in himself, and of not having the strength of character to stand by what was important. I asked if he would apply for the headship of Guinea Fowl, the school, which was to be established under the same lines as Plumtree. No, he wasn't the slightest bit interested.

'There you are, you see? It is only because it is a Plumtree position Johnnie, otherwise I don't think you would have any doubts about where you should be.'

Whether we liked it or not, it had cast a sombre note over our holiday and despite all the assurances, John was apprehensive about what he might find when he returned. By the end of the holiday, however, he was firm and positive in his decision that Mzingwane really was where he wanted to be and we were both glad to be packing up again, refreshed and ready for him to get on with job.

The welcome from staff, teachers and boys at Mzingwane was heart-warming and dispelled most of John's uncertainties. Our two months away seemed to have made quite a difference and they were glad to have us back.

I was so thankful. Johnnie went off with a new spring in his step to cope with the shortages of materials and the buildings which still had to be completed as well as the development of "useful citizens". He came back at lunchtime that first day.

'You know, it is funny how things change. D'you remember that hue and cry at Tjolotjo when I first suggested that the African staff houses should be near the boys' dormitories? I found today that the system is working so well, that they are now volunteering to have their private quarters under the same roof. The effect on the younger boys has been marked, they have settled down so much more quickly having their sleeping quarters in a grouping similar to what they're used to at home. It is very satisfying to see it working.'

I smiled. Good!

The next day, he came bounding in to say that they were planning to have the first parents' weekend next Easter now that the school year fell into three instead of two terms.

'I've always wanted to be able to invite the parents to a major function and we'll do the same as at Plumtree, the boys can give up their beds to the parents for the weekend and they can rough it as we did. It gives me so such pleasure to see how much more interested they are in their children's progress. In fact, I am almost at the point where I can actively give priority to those applications for admission to the school made by the parents... there will always be the exceptions of course, but it is an almost complete turnaround by comparison with what we had before.'

Even better! He was settling down again and his bounce was back. But he had come back knowing he had to cope with one matter that had occurred while we were away.

Several students had gone on strike ostensibly because there were too many flies near the dining room. It became fairly obvious when John did some research into their complaint, that it had been a "put-up job". It was complicated further because the boys had walked off the school grounds, had been arrested, and then taken to the District Commissioner for punishment. John went to ask to have the boys back saying he would administer his own punishment as he did not want them to end up with a criminal record. He told them that he did not want to expel them but that this was unacceptable behaviour. The alternative was for them to spend the next three days digging the main football ground. They agreed to do this and set to with a will.

When they finished, prayers were held and the boys were given soap and towels to go and wash, ready for their lessons. Several of the staff members came up to John to thank him for giving them a second chance and the boys themselves came up after school that day to say they had learned their lesson and would not be doing that again.

'I find it encouraging that they accept discipline and punishment so well, particularly if they can see that it is fair. It gives me great hope for the future. The boys seemed impressed that I went and bargained with the District Commissioner on their behalf.

'Interesting isn't it? I think I know them, then I realise I really don't.'

Maurice, Daisy, Jenny and their new babe Robin, joined us on the staff again, and I found my social life improving out of all recognition.

In addition to which, now that the war was over Trish and Mummy were thinking of coming out to visit us.

A continuing problem was that there was no school nearby for the children of his African teachers. He arranged for the school lorry to bus them all in to Essexvale. We soon found that this was going to affect us as well, as there was no school at all for Jill to go to except in Bulawayo.

As soon as she turned six she should start school. Jill was far too young to send in to Bulawayo as a boarder, so I found out about correspondence school and started teaching her myself. This turned out to be an ideal solution. The course was based on the Australian "school of the air". There was great excitement every two weeks as the lumpy, brown paper parcels came in packed full of new things and with all the corrections and marks for completed exercises.

Those were some of the best moments, I was back teaching my own daughter, with Richard always a "hanger-on", demanding to do what she was doing. I taught Jill for two years and when she went to school she was well ahead of the rest of her class. She didn't take too kindly to learning the piano with me unfortunately, as she always seemed to think it was just having fun, not serious work.

There were increasing demands on my time to entertain visitors keen to see how the school was doing since the move. Sir Otto and Lady Beit came out and said they would be keen to see a Beit Hall built at the school. The Governor, Sir John Chancellor, came out frequently and many others from South Africa and from countries north of us. The reputation of the school and the excellence of the boys graduating from it was spreading

The WI was also taking up a lot of my time and I found myself helping out more and more in the Cultural Arts area. I longed to put on a play but felt I should only do so once the children were off my hands.

John was going down to the Plumtree Sports in the middle of June, as he had been asked to present their sports cups. I was a little wary of the trip, as I worried that it might unsettle him again, but he seemed so much happier at Mzingwane that I put my concerns aside and we set off to enjoy a good weekend away, leaving Jill and Rich with the Mills.

I hadn't counted on the pressure that would be put on John – almost from the moment we reached his father's old school.

It seemed that everyone wanted him to take Pat's place at Milner. Pat had been confirmed as the new head of REPS and he would be going there at the start of the third term. Johnnie laughed it all off quite happily.

It was wonderful to see how well the school was doing and for me to see it in action. The Old Boys wanted to put up another boarding house as the demand for places was so huge, and they were keen to ensure that their sons would be admitted to the school. They had just announced that they would like it to be called Hammond House. To me the atmosphere at the school was like the best of the British public schools. The sporting and academic achievements of the boys were spectacular, although there was great sadness at the huge numbers of Old Boys who had lost their lives in the war.

We had a very happy weekend – until the last afternoon of our stay when Pat asked John to come and have a chat. He said the swell of support for John's appointment to Milner House was so huge that it could no longer be ignored. Would John agree to his name being put forward to Cowie, the Chief Education Officer of the Education Department. John agreed reluctantly, but he did agree, simply because he so loved Plumtree and everything it meant to him.

I loved it too and would have been quite happy to take up the music and Gilbert and Sullivan's where Harrie and then Vangie Pattison had left off. At the beginning of August, Cowie's reply came back to Pat, with a copy to John:

I thank you for your letter of the 22nd July on the subject of the appointment of your successor in the Housemastership of Milner House.

I must admit at the outset that I have a great deal of sympathy for your point of view and the point of view of the school but I regret that your suggestion that Mr. John Hammond be appointed cannot be entertained by the Department.

Mr Hammond is not a member of the European Teaching service and no matter how strong his claims may be on personal and traditional grounds, it would be quite impossible for this Department to justify his immediate appointment to a post which must be regarded as one of the prizes of our service.

Mr. Hammond has not applied for a transfer to our Teaching Service… liability to transfer is one of the conditions of appointment and I am afraid that in the first instance Mr. Hammond would have to accept this condition.

Once he is settled in our Service and has proved himself he would be given consideration for any post for which he was qualified.

John was absolutely furious. I had never seen him so angry. He wrote a scathing letter to the General Secretary of the Rhodesia Teachers' Association, of which he had been a member since he started at Tjolotjo:

As things now stand, it would appear that my nine and a half years' experience as a Principal of a Native School for 250 boys count for nothing when I apply for a post in which I would have charge of 70 boys in a European School. Yet there appears to be no quibble when a man from the European Teaching service, with no experience of Natives or of School administration, is appointed to be Principal of a Native School.

I would also point out that in applying for this post I would be looking for a smaller "prize" in so far as prizes are measured in pounds, shillings and pence, than the one I now hold. Had I been appointed to the housemastership it would have left a Principalship in the Native Education Department vacant, and past experience has shown that officers of the European Teaching service would have considered it a "prize" for which it would be worth their while to compete.

It would now appear that the official attitude is that European education is something vastly more difficult than and superior to Native education. I find it hard to believe that this is the viewpoint of the Association. I would like to know however, whether or not I am right in this belief.

John was incensed to think that the attitude prevailed that the teaching of Africans was less important and difficult than the teaching of Europeans. Yet in his ongoing interaction with Government, he had increasingly come to feel that this was the case as he was consistently given so little support.

Cowie's reply gave cold comfort:

Your frankness in explaining your attitude is appreciated but I am afraid that you have erred in assuming that this Department is operating a "colour bar" to the detriment of members of the Native Education Department.

There are many people who, on personal grounds (quite apart from traditional grounds) would like to see you in an important post at Plumtree, but your progress to such a post can only be achieved by your establishing your capabilities in teaching and residential work in the European service.

'Well at least that has finally made up my mind. I'm not interested in going to any other school and I would not be the slightest bit interested in transferring to their blooming European service under those conditions. The Plumtree chapter is closed.'

So that was that.

I was very happy at Essexvale and the staff and boys all seemed to be pulling together well since we had been away. Several teachers and boys had specifically spoken to John and intimated that they were extremely pleased to see him back.

A couple of months later, John felt he had buried his fury sufficiently to contact Cowie about another matter. He had felt for a long time that Europeans were missing out on the sort of education Mzingwane and Domboshawa were providing and he sent in a detailed report about the desirability of opening a school within the European Education System which was run on similar lines. It makes for interesting reading:

A number of things have gone to convince me that there is a considerable demand for such a training particularly for that type of boy who can see more beauty in a bull than in a line of Latin verse or the one who gets greater satisfaction out of building a vertical wall than he would from learning an abstract definition of the term "vertical":-

There is a persistent demand from the farming community for the establishment of an agricultural school.

Never has the country been so much in need of practical farmers, able to support their practice with theoretical knowledge.

There is some exploitation of the average European's lack of practical knowledge by the semi-trained African artisan, particularly in building and carpentry.

The modern conception of an apprenticeship takes little account of the duty of the master craftsman to assume responsibility for the apprentice's moral and spiritual wellbeing. The apprentice today is little more than a source of cheap labour in the eyes of his master...

Many people feel this type of education would be admirable for European boys, while a number of young men who have been here have expressed regret that they did not have the chance of a similar training.

One of the greatest shortages in the country today must be school accommodation and combined with the present shortage of labour it would seem that it will be years before you will be able to make up the leeway. Do you not think that the boys could go a long way towards building their own school and love doing it? We have done it and after only six years can now deal with 260 boarding pupils. There was nothing but veld when we started.

The response was, perhaps predictably, lukewarm.

Immediately however, important things were happening for me. I had to arrange another trip to the Cape in October – this time to meet Mummy and Trish at the boat. Dick had been released from prison camp and was trying to adjust to civilian life again, though quite what he was going to do with his life, nobody was sure. Shortly before he was captured he had married a lovely girl, Betty Wills, who was a veterinary surgeon, and they were now living in Bristol. But Mummy and Trish had endured a very stressful war and they badly needed to come out and have a complete break from England.

With great excitement I set off on the train, waving goodbye to my precious family. We had decided it would be too disruptive to take the children down again. How lucky I was travelling down to sea level twice in one year! At the Cape Town docks I looked up at the *Carnarvon Castle* seeking a face I recognised – then I saw Trish looking distracted. She gave me a delighted wave then signalled for me to come on board. There was a lot of waving going on – a young man dressed in uniform pushed his way down the gangplank and made his way towards me.

'Your mother has collapsed I'm afraid. It's probably just the excitement of it all, but I am getting special dispensation for you to go on board.'

I was panic stricken. 'Please Lord, don't let her die after all this'. I flew up the gangway and found my way to their cabin. I hadn't been prepared for what I saw – they were all in dormitories – 30 people squeezed into what would normally be space for ten or twelve. The boat was still configured as a troopship. Mummy was conscious but looking ghastly.

'Oh Nancy, it's so wonderful to see you... we've had the most terrible trip.'

There were 1,500 women and children on that boat, double its normal capacity and Trish had been seasick for the whole three weeks. It was all catching up with Mummy now.

They were so thin. I had to make sure I didn't reflect my horror. I was staggered. Thin and pale – Mummy with white hair – she had aged before her time. They both looked like walking skeletons. I was as fat as butter by comparison.

At last we were able to take them off the ship. It seemed to take hours and poor Mummy threatened to faint every few minutes as we tried to clear customs and immigration in the chaos that was Cape Town docks with an overcrowded ship in port.

I took them out on the little train, which runs beside the sea to Muizenberg. I had decided to take them to a hotel right on the beach looking over the sea and as we walked to the Balmoral Hotel, I knew I had made the right decision for them – and me.

It was delightful and couldn't have been closer to the sea. I'd decided to stay down with them for a week before setting off up to Rhodesia. We left Mummy to have a rest and Trish and I sat in the gardens chattering nineteen to the dozen. Neither of them felt like lunch and Trish went off for a rest. We went down to dinner and ordered something very simple, as they didn't seem able to face much food. Hotel rooms were so hard to come by that we were all sharing a room. Suddenly in the middle of the night, Trish was violently sick. She was so sick in fact, that we had to call in the hotel doctor. He was not particularly concerned, as he had seen this before.

'They've lived on so little for so long that their stomachs just can't take it. They are both malnourished at the moment and these are the steps you will have to take to get them eating properly again...'

I began to realise how lucky we had been in Rhodesia. As they talked, I became more and more horrified to hear of the risks they had taken, the secret areas Trish had been working in and the canteen Mummy had run single-handed in Bournemouth. They were amazing, both of them.

We took it very easily for a couple of days. Then they suddenly seemed to come to life – so we set off down Adderley Street for a day's shopping. They couldn't get over the fact that there was no clothes rationing and Mummy and Trish bought five pairs of shoes each.

They were dying to see the children, of course, and as we arrived at Bulawayo station John was there with Jill and Richard. He popped

Rich through the window onto Trish's lap and I saw with a shock that his arm was encased in plaster of paris.

'Just a greenstick fracture,' John mouthed at me.

Rich didn't seem any the worse for wear and as we drove out to Mzingwane they were fascinated by everything, particularly Jill's very colonial-looking brown school hat! They kept commenting on how lovely it was to be warm and away from the deprivation of England, saying the year after the war had, in many ways, been worse than the war itself.

It was fascinating seeing Mzingwane through Mummy and Trish's eyes – and reassuring to them to see that we were living in relative civilisation, although they were intrigued by the lamps we had to pump up each evening as we had, as yet, no electricity. How distinctive those lamps were – the squeak, squeak, squeak, squeak as John pumped air into them under pressure when they grew dim, the constant hiss through the evening and the long moving shadows they threw on the walls.

I was amused to see how all the young bloods of the area found ever increasing excuses to pop in and casually take a look to see what this younger sister of mine looked like! About three days after they arrived, our senior agriculturalist, Roy Alvord, appeared at the door and seemed to find rather more excuses than the others in the following weeks. He just kept dropping round, usually to initiate some riveting discussion with John on culverts or pigs in labour!

Unfortunately, my mother and sister had arrived at the very hottest time of the year, with storms rumbling about but no rain as yet. I had to warn them about the thunderstorms. Because we were on an ironstone belt, right next to Isi'Koveni we had the most terrifying storms imaginable.

They would start with a little low grumble over the hills in the distance, with lightning playing along the ridge. Then they would start to move a little closer. We would sit and count the seconds between the lightning flash and the crash of thunder to gauge how far away it was. The house was struck frequently. In our first storm that year, a sow and four piglets were struck and killed a hundred yards away from our new agriculturalist, Rex Coleman, and a bunch of schoolboys. The children were intrigued to hear that when they did an autopsy on the pigs, they had blue lines right through their flesh.

251

Mummy and Trish thought it was all rather spectacular but I was secretly terrified of the noise and violence of it all.

We had all our friends and staff in to meet my family and Mummy's golfing prowess quickly became the talk of the village. She found herself involved almost immediately in ongoing tournaments with the local postmaster, Rex Wilmore. We had to warn her to beat a hasty retreat if there was the slightest sign of an electrical storm around as the golf course was notorious for being struck.

Trish continued to be a tremendous hit with all the unattached men in the district. We became a little suspicious when we heard the doleful sounds of "I'm a little on the lonely… a little on the lonely side" being played on a clarinet from the little green tin hut next door! We felt Roy Alvord was sending a musical serenade with a clear message.

It was nearing the end of the year and the building and carpentry projects were hurriedly being completed to a stage where they could be left for the long school holiday. It looked as though we were going to gain approval for a Beit Hall and this would make an enormous difference to the school. John's end-of-year report was positively buoyant:

> There has during this past year, been a more vigorous spirit in the school: boys and staff have worked well and there has been less of the unsettled atmosphere, which pervaded the school last year. The departure from the African staff of one who was a disturbing influence, but who was clever enough to allow nothing tangible to be held against him; and the stimulation of interest in intellectual matters which Mr Mills has given; plus the excellent discipline maintained by the housemasters, have all helped to raise a sense of community.

> The head boy this year has in all things set an excellent example.
>   Hitherto I have often been critical of African staff that they have allowed too close a relationship between themselves and the boys. I now realise that it will always be extremely difficult to establish any other relationship so long as some of the staff are of much the same age as the boys they have to teach. Prefects too, find it extremely difficult imposing discipline on men. I see it as an essential that the children be subjected to discipline by others of their kind. An 18-year-old prefect can instil a discipline into a 16-year-old boy much more easily than a 24-year-old prefect can discipline a 22-year-old pupil.

The policy of putting responsibility onto the African staff has been continued and is showing its value and they are beginning to appreciate and understand that responsibility. Two who have held responsible posts confided to me that the African is not yet ready for high responsibilities. Such humility is most refreshing, and underlines the fact that the practice is often more difficult than the theory.

'Interestingly, Nan, they are doing pretty well, but in almost every case those from chiefs or headmen families are the natural leaders. Young Kayisa Ndiweni and Jason Zipapamoyo are showing enormous promise and both are likely to end up as chiefs. But I have to keep encouraging and urging the others on to accept responsibility and leadership. They still tend to be all too quick to abuse their status, or to pass that responsibility back again.'

John had started up the regular days of discussions, which he had always held in the Gwaai area, with the local chiefs and headmen. This Mzingwane/Esigodini area was much bigger so it was a great pleasure to see that on almost every occasion, everyone whom the chief had invited had taken the trouble to come. John would take Roy Alvord or Rex Coleman with him on occasions, as well Teachers Bulle, Moyo and Malusalila. They discussed every possible aspect of the school – the reason this type of curriculum was offered, the potential for the boys in the future, the desirability of staying at school longer and the contribution the boys could make to local building or agricultural projects, if they would like them to do so.

John had always insisted on tough discipline and in the accepted manner of the time would use the cane when necessary to reinforce a much-needed lesson. But he was well aware that times were changing and was always interested to know what the chiefs themselves felt about discipline and how it should be meted out.

'You white people are much, much too soft,' one of the old headmen said. 'Why only yesterday a cheeky boy in my village was boasting how he had been able to make maningi (lots of) trouble at the school. He was saying that the teachers were only laughing at him. But this was not good trouble and this is a bad boy. I know him.'

'If you let these boys think they can do what they like,' said another, 'we cannot teach them their place when they come back. They think they are now too smart and they think they have more brains than we have. They are wrong. They must learn how to live in the village before they can learn to live in the town.'

'You must beat the boys,' said the Chief. 'There is too much change now for them and they can be very hard for us.'

John brought up the question of leadership and how difficult it was to get those boys who were not from the families of chiefs and headmen to take responsibility.

'Ah! But you cannot,' was the general consensus of the group.

'The new Rhodesia will want many, many men of leadership – there are not enough from the traditional families.'

'Ah, but you cannot,' was all he could draw from them, as they slowly shook their heads.

'No, you cannot.'

It did not give John much comfort.

There had been concern for some time that the lethargy displayed by some of the boys might have its roots in bilharzia, the enervating disease so prevalent in the waters throughout Central Africa. The health department was asked to come out and test the whole school. It was pretty shattering when 90% showed a positive reaction to the skin test. All of them were treated. Following the treatment the Health Department gave a talk on bilharzia and this caused a lot of interest from the boys who thought lethargy was just something you lived with.

In that year, for the first time, almost the entire African staff was Rhodesian... Mothobi was the only exception but tribally, he was closely affiliated to the Makalanga tribe from around the Plumtree district. John had been delighted to welcome Herbert Ramushu back, having completed his studies in South Africa. In addition, he was, at last, going to be gaining his promised two new staff members from Britain, Gresham and Carrigan would be taking over the Academic and the restructured Construction departments respectively.

Roy Alvord left us at the beginning of 1947 to join the African Agriculture Department in Salisbury. We were even more suspicious when Trish suddenly announced that she had decided she would like to stay on in Rhodesia and would probably go up to Salisbury to see if she could find a job.

The war had meant she was trained for little more than radar plotting and other associated skills, none of them of any use whatever in Rhodesia. But within a few weeks she'd found a job with a vet.

Murton would now be stepping up to take Alvord's place and the young South African Rex Coleman who had been with us in an acting capacity, had applied to take Murton's place. So for the first time in 1947, John was going to have a full complement of staff, European and African, and best of all, most of the African staff had now been with him for many years. Their loyalty through the move and their under-standing and commitment to what they were all trying to do had never been greater.

When the new staff arrived, John found it very stimulating having the new blood and their new ideas. Herbert Ramushu had gained enormous stature in his time away and he and the two new Englishmen in particular, saw things more objectively and from an outside perspective. It was a great opportunity to review everything they had ever done and to have to argue for its validity or otherwise.

The new hospital at the school was completed and was under the care of Sister Weir, who spent some of her time at the Essexvale Clinic. A new orderly was appointed to help her, Nason Madeya. He was an excellent fellow and deeply religious. While Lalan went on well-deserved long leave he carried on the work at the school. We were very fond of gentle, unassuming Nason and the kids would find any excuse to go up and see him.

'We are fortunate to have a man with such a high sense of duty and of such sympathy for his patients,' John told Head Office.

Despite the increasing number of high points, the unsuitable curriculum and the resultant high failure rate were still causing prob-lems:

> The proportion of failures in Standard VI was the highest we have experi-enced during the past eleven years. This large number was accounted for primarily by the English language paper, which was absurdly difficult. It is interesting to note that six boys who were taking Standard VI for a second time averaged 15% less this time round.
>
> We have come to look upon the Standard VI examination as something of a farce. I do hope that something will be devised to bring its conduct up to the normal standard, which should be expected of a public examination.

Eric Gresham was turning out to be an interesting man. I was delighted to find that he had been involved in a great deal of choral work in England. He was delighted to hear of my musical background and my piano playing.

He approached me one day saying that he was interested in trying to teach the boys Handel's oratorio, *The Messiah*. I was intrigued with the idea. How on earth would he do it? It seemed to be an extremely ambitious venture, but Gresham felt sure they would respond. Would I be interested in accompanying them? Well of course I would!

For several weeks, I heard him teaching groups of boys by tonic solfa. It was an incredible job and all done in his – and their – spare time. Then came the day when we needed to start rehearsals with the piano. Fortunately, we had a large front verandah on our house and the choir of 100 boys crowded onto the verandah to sing. After a few hilarious false starts, when they were as startled by what I was doing, as I was by their volume of sound, I was astounded at what he had already achieved with them.

It was powerful, exciting music and the boys were thrilled with it. They sang in full, four-part harmony as written by Handel, but they sang with the rich, strong and unmistakable voices, the nuances and the vibrancy of Africa.

'This is excellent, Gresham,' John said one evening as he sat listening in the garden. 'We must perform it at the Heany Hall in Essexvale.'

We hired the Heany Hall and gave a concert comprising several excerpts from *The Messiah*, with John doing the narration and a well-known singer from Bulawayo, Marjorie Cooke, singing the soprano solos. The hall was filled with crusty old Afrikaner farmers, English members of the Police force, a few Rhodesian-born families from the Native Departments and Greeks from the stores and bottle shops. It was received with acclamation.

The following week Miss Cooke contacted us to say she thought it was so outstanding that she would like to arrange for four of the country's best singers to perform the solo parts with the choral work done by the school choir in the City Hall in Bulawayo. And she wanted them to do the entire work.

It was an exciting time. I was filled with enthusiasm again and my life seemed as though it was at last going to start providing me with everything I loved and had been trained for – music and, now as an added bonus, drama as well. Gresham was keen to persuade John to take the plunge and do a play. For the first time, he felt the school was running well enough to allow him the time to do it.

There was plenty of talent in the village and our first success was with two one-act plays, *Little Glass Houses* with a cast of six WI women and *Dark Brown* – a very exciting thriller in which John turned out to be a hangman. The WI asked if we would take the plays round to several other WIs in the Matabeleland area. Again, for the first time, John felt able to do so and that it was good for school staff to be seen actively contributing to community ventures.

The plays went down so well that it made me realise a lot of women in the farming districts in particular were starved of things of interest to do. Through the WI, I started to put together a library of plays that could easily be produced by women in remote areas.

The following year I produced and acted in *The Paragon* by Roland Pertwee. His brother Guy used to do our drama coaching at Hillcote in Eastbourne. This was a strong, dramatic piece of writing and the performance was such a success that again we were asked to take it to Bulawayo.

By this time a little school had opened up in the Heany Hall run by a local woman, Connie James. Jill was one of the founder members and had taken to it like a duck to water. She loved it. There were only six pupils there that first year but as well as a little tentative tennis coaching, we were able to find people in the district who taught ballet and riding and I added to it, by offering to teach piano.

None of us charged for the lessons, but it did mean that our children were going to be able to take part in activities which might otherwise be denied them.

This was a very happy time for us – me with music and plays, which had been so much part of my life before I came to Rhodesia – and for John the school seemed now, to be going from strength to strength… to such an extent that John started coming home saying, 'another politics-free day!'

Then Trish and Roy announced their engagement. This was wonderful news and selfishly I was delighted to think that my sister would be living in Rhodesia as well. They were married in our garden with Jill and Jenny as bridesmaids in pale blue sprigged muslin and Richard as a demure little pageboy in blue linen trousers and a blue shirt. They behaved impeccably and loved every moment of it. Trish and Roy were going to be living in Salisbury. Mummy had decided that she'd like to come back and live in Rhodesia as well, but she needed a couple of years to sort everything out at home. As we saw her off back to England, we promised to go home and see her before then.

Trish's wedding had come at the end of a long drought. In fact, the last eight months had been hard going and with real concerns that the school would run out of water. After a huge hue and cry, a pipeline needed to be constructed to draw water from the Ncema Dam–Bulawayo main in order to keep the school going.

To ensure that this would not occur again, the school decided to build a small dam with an earthen wall. The building of the dam was not only of great importance to ensuring the school's future self-sufficiency, but was also being used as a training exercise and the boys found the engineering feat very useful.

Easter 1948 was the time for our first parents' weekend. John had been looking forward to this for years. All the wives of the European and Native staff chipped in and did the catering on a massive scale. It was planned like a military operation and every school house was cutting up and preparing food for weeks.

Then came the great day.

Parents and families started arriving from all directions by foot, by bus and by car. They came tentatively, nervously, shyly.

Every bed in every dormitory was immaculately made, every locker meticulously cleaned out. Small bunches of flowers were put in jam jars to welcome them. Every bed in every dormitory was taken up by the visitors – mums and sisters sharing in some, dads and brothers in others.

The boys all had to find their own places to sleep around the grounds or in the bush, but strict guidelines had to be followed. Everyone met out under the trees for breakfast and other meals, served by the staff. They loved it! The Sports day took place and house prizes were competed for with deadly seriousness and much enthusiasm. They left on foot, by bus and by car and they left feeling confident and happy about what their children were achieving at Mzingwane.

Johnnie came to bed at the end of the weekend holding his arm and saying, 'Now I know how royalty must feel! Almost every parent came to shake my hand and say how much he or she had enjoyed the weekend. It was worth that hard work just to see their faces.'

The boys went home with their parents for the holidays and a wonderful atmosphere of unity and high spirits was in evidence right round the school.

We were so pleased that Harrie had been persuaded to come and spend time with us for the first Mzingwane Sports weekend. It had brought many happy memories of similar Plumtree weekends.

'Bring the right staff in, keep the boys busy and disciplined and it all begins to fall into place.' John said as the last schoolboy left. What a relief it was to see the sheer delight in John's eyes after all the upsets over the Plumtree business.

At that moment, Richard came rushing in with a scarlet face, pouring water all over the floor from his tiny little watering can...

'Fire, Dad, fire – Skoveni's on fire!'

We rushed to the back of the house and there was Jill, also scarlet in the face, trying to put the fire out with a hosepipe – with Richard running to and fro with his little watering can.

John had to call all the staff out to help fight the fire which, after all the months of drought, was away and up the hill in minutes. He was not happy. Particularly when closer examination showed that it looked suspiciously as though it had started very close to the edge of our garden. It took hours to bring it under control. Normally the school-boys would have been here to help. This time we had to ask the Native Department and police to help bring it under control.

'What happened Jill?' John asked.

The story came out – playing with matches and stamping out the grass as it burned. Lighting another, bigger bit and of course letting it burn a bit more... when all of a sudden a gust of wind had taken it out of their grasp. We were very angry with them.

Dinner was eaten that evening in a stony silence. Richard kept trying to break the ice.

'I do love baked beans,' he said to our stony looks.

It was so silent that dear Harrie could bear it no longer. She turned to me and pleaded, 'Please speak to them!'

Matches did not need to be put on the "don't touch" list for either of them!

The time had now come to gear up for the performance of *The Paragon* in Bulawayo while the school was on holiday. It was an excellent play and John was to play the part of a blind man. I took the part of his wife, as well as producing the play. We co-opted Merle Coleman, by now John's administrative assistant, to play the spiritualist, Jessica. Trevor Booth was his "paragon", who turned out to be his ne'er-do-well son and James Inskipp, the District Commissioner and his wife Audrey played the parts of the local Laird and his lady.

John and I undertook the stage management and denuded our house of furniture for props, as well as handling the publicity. We'd been offered Bulawayo's premier venue, the City Hall, for the perform-ance and had decided to put it on for three nights.

We were really nervous as to whether or not anyone would come to see it. But the first performance was sold out and bookings for the other two looked very promising as the curtain rose on the first night. We opened the curtains with confidence.

I quickly learned one very valuable lesson!

It was one of the most tense establishing moments of the whole play, when John had just hurled a priceless camera across the stage, roaring, 'a Leica Camera – for a blind man?!' The place almost held its breath as James Inskipp had to respond.

I heard the faintest titter in the audience... then another... and another. I looked over towards him – and oh no! his moustache had become detached on one side and he was valiantly trying to turn his back on the audience and stick it on again. It would not stick and every time he spoke it flew up and down with a life of its own. This was our debut in the City Hall.

Suddenly from the depths of the City Hall, I heard a voice I recognised.

It was that dratted Maurice Mills. 'Take it off Jimmy!' he roared.

Fearful of destroying the moment completely, I urged him to pull it off, which eventually he did. After a final burst of laughter, the audience settled down again and we rebuilt the moment. He did not wear his moustache again!

The next day, the critics were kind:

"GRIPPING DRAMA WELL PERFORMED"

John Hammond played the part excellently, capturing the accent, the hardness and the characteristics of the blind man who would not have his wishes frustrated. The standard he set was matched by the rest of the cast, for from beginning to end they never faltered. Nancy Hammond, in the difficult role of the magnate's second wife held the role centre stage – and produced it as well.

The play was presented for the first time in Southern Rhodesia to a full house. The run is to be extended for a further three days.

It really was a triumph for a tiny wee place like Essexvale – full houses for a week.

We began to feel more confident about the potential for the eventual staging of *The Messiah*, but had decided not to rush it, but take our time over production and rehearsals, as learning the entire work was a huge task.

John's report for 1948 is interesting in that with the influence of new staff members, new stimulants and new achievements, he was developing new philosophies and thoughts about education for the Africans. He felt that it would be of enormous benefit to have a girls' school within close proximity to Mzingwane as there were many lessons to be learned in the interaction between boys and girls. He was conscious of the second–class citizen role still being played by most women in the country and felt the time was right for change. His suggestions to Government, however, fell on fallow ground.

The report, however, reflected the general buoyancy of the school:

At long last there does now seem to be a greater sense of unity amongst the staff. More and more do I feel that the European and African staff are at one in the task of training pupils. Whereas for many years past I have felt that the African staff saw their position as one in which they had to stand with the pupils against the European staff when conflict seemed likely, there now seems to be a more solid feeling of the staff working as one.

We are beginning to get more grey hairs on the heads of our senior teachers and they serve to add weight to their influence over younger members of the staff who might tend to have a disturbing influence among the boys. The policy of lowering the school age is also bringing results and removing the familiarity between boys and staff, which undermines discipline.

The next step to be taken is in the training of prefects up to a full sense of their responsibility within the school. It must be a gradual growth. There is still some confusion in the minds of the staff regarding the precise function of the prefects. On the one hand some are inclined to allot duties to prefects and to expect them to assume responsibilities which should be undertaken by the staff themselves; on the other there are those who resent the comparative immunity from punishment, which has been made the privileged position of a prefect and who would expect them to be subject to the same minute supervision by the staff as are the other boys.

I have attempted to make plain that prefects are also under instruction in leadership and they need guidance in these lessons every bit as much as they do elsewhere but that, at the same time, they are given certain responsibilities which must be counterbalanced by equivalent privileges.

The success of the first parents' weekend had also produced reflections on the best way of encouraging the African pupils to reach their potential and to accept the mantle of leadership when it was offered.

'I find it very interesting, Nan,' he said as we sat down to the background hiss of our evening lamps, 'that we are still having real difficulty encouraging the senior boys to accept responsibility.'

'It's surely, inevitable isn't it? It'll probably take generations to change it,' I offered.

'Sadly, I don't believe we have generations. Political pressures are mounting. We have to find some other method of speeding it up or they'll be forced into leadership without altruism and it will become autocratic and power-based. I have been very concerned at how quickly those boys who are not used to taking responsibility abuse the benefits they are offered. We have to turn that round as the traditional leadership families may not be the ones whom the country chooses politically in years to come.

'I think the success of those house prizes at the sports weekend were a clue. They were fought for so hard and their achievement was regarded so highly. Perhaps we have to appeal to man's base instincts first before we can tap the heights.'

He developed this further in his report to Head Office, re-thinking some of his earlier strategies in the process:

Where I once felt that the best way to develop the African was to build upon the communal ideas which were traditional in Native society, I am now coming more to the opinion that he will first have to go through a period of competition which will raise up distinctions of leaders and the led. While this seems a reactionary step, there appears to be no other way by which the necessary incentive to progress can be provided.

It is unfortunate that resort has had to be made to a call to lower nature, to the greed for wealth and power, but there seems no alternative other than the assumption of completely dictatorial powers, which would give the required results with sufficient speed. Amongst most races it is necessary to make a similar appeal to greed if progress is to be maintained...

From this argument it is concluded that the policy hitherto followed in this school of giving no awards and prizes to boys should be changed and that more use should be made of the granting of colours and the competition for prizes in order to induce greater effort. Attempts will be made to build up the prefects and the school teams into a leadership team which it is hoped will play a large part in the training of future generations of school-boys.

Gresham, the new Academic head had thought the school should be concentrating more fully on the academic and that "industrial subjects are an unwelcome intrusion into 'education'". John felt this was an understandable and likely viewpoint from an Englishman coming from a set of English circumstances, but was pleased to see that the more Gresham worked at the school, the more he agreed with the need for a more all-encompassing education.

John had applauded the start, that year of the first purely academic school at Goromonzi in Mashonaland but he was still quite sure this should not yet be at the expense of the industrial schools:

We have to keep before us the need for training in academic subjects, in practical work, in physical development, in cleanliness, in discipline in all its forms, in team spirit, in music and the arts, in punctuality and in behaviour, in honesty and all the other virtues. Argument centres not so much around the actual content of what we try to teach but on the relative importance of each.

No final conclusion can be reached and no one man can claim the monopoly in being right... It is only by trial and error and by continual adjustment that we can hope to achieve the end, which we have set for ourselves.

We have had one peculiar attitude emerge this year... a feeling amongst some of the boys that they should not have to contribute to the School's welfare for fear they contribute too much... some have almost given the impression that they consider they should be paid for the work done during their lessons! There are contributory causes... but they have served to disturb the smooth running of the school.

In conclusion, the year has given me cause for satisfaction in many ways... not least the comments from employers on the quality of boys we are producing. The final judge of the success or failure of the work done in a school is the employer. It is satisfactory to feel that, in general, the boys from Mzingwane are bringing credit to the system, which we are endeavouring to follow.

With the seeming abundance of staff at the school and a new and cohesive spirit, I found myself longing to see England again. John had so much leave due to him by this stage, that we decided to go over for six months the following year before Mummy came out to live in Rhodesia. We could put the children into school over there, which we felt would broaden their horizons quite considerably.

But first of all, we were in the final rehearsal stage for *The Messiah* in Bulawayo. There had been some interesting developments in our attempts to find a venue.

The City Hall would not permit us to perform there. They had nothing scheduled at the time we wanted to perform, but they would simply not allow Africans to perform in the City Hall. We felt defeated and very disappointed. In fact, we were incredulous, but there seemed little point in making a performance about it and it was vital not to upset the pupils who were by now, so excited at the prospect.

What on earth could be done? John and Gresham were insistent that it should also be performed to an African audience, but where on earth could that take place?

Then one of the Bulawayo City councillors approached us and suggested that the Jewish Guild Hall might be willing to have us perform there and he would be happy to make the approach on our behalf.

We went and had a look at it and although not quite as grand or as large as the City Hall, it would do. But what about the other perform-ance because even the Jewish Guild Hall would not be allowed to have a totally African audience at that stage?

After quite some scouting around, we eventually decided upon the Municipal Beer Hall. It was a pretty shabby old place with acoustics like a barn, but it would hold 2,000 and it had an area where a stage could be erected quite effectively. We would have to hire in a piano for the occasion, but otherwise, it was certainly workable. The question was whether the patrons would be sober enough to enjoy the perform-ance. It was worth a try and everyone we spoke to there was most enthusiastic about it.

The performance at the Jewish Guild Hall was absolutely excep-tional.

The hall was full and that in itself was a miracle. To have 800 whites come and listen to a black choir was quite something at that time in the country's history. To see them all rise involuntarily to their feet at the end and applaud and applaud and applaud was quite something else! We were immediately asked if we would come back and do another performance in two weeks' time. The logistics were a bit complicated, as this was the first Saturday of the school holidays. The choir was asked how they felt about it. Every single one elected to stay on and sing.

We were delighted. But first, we had a performance to give at the Municipal Beer Hall the following night.

Saturday nights in an African township at the time were like a lively, if chaotic great party. Everyone was out and about, and busy going places.

Just making our way to the Beer Hall, through the crowds of people wandering down the roads, with lorries full of singers was hard enough. Installing the piano and erecting the stage had been a story in itself, with progress constantly hampered by the intense curiosity of hundreds of people milling around watching what was going on and roaring with good humoured laughter at what we were up to. They were fascinated to know what on earth we were going to do. It was a little hard to explain!

As we approached the Beer Hall that night, we realised that the milling throngs we were trying to hoot out of our way, were all heading in one direction – to the Beer Hall! There were thousands of people everywhere. We eventually made it through to the hall ten minutes later than we had planned to start! The four European soloists were looking a little uneasy at the mass of humanity surrounding them but the mood was friendly and open – if a little inebriated.

The choir was dressed immaculately. Smartly ironed khaki shorts and shirts with ties and polished and shining faces. They had been drilled not to look at the audience, not to smile but to have a pleasant and relaxed look on their faces – and to watch the conductor! In these conditions, that was a huge task. But they were magnificent.

The noise was incredible. Great shouts and roars of laughter would erupt all over the place. The air was thick with a fog of cigarette smoke. I didn't think we would ever make ourselves heard – or seen.

Gresham took up his position and looked over at me hoping this would drop the noise level. Not a chance. He did it again. Nothing. This was going to be chaos.

A third time he took up his stance. I found to my horror that my sustaining pedal was not working. I signalled frantically to him to wait. It was pitch dark and I couldn't see anything at all. There must be something wedged under the pedal. I reached down to see if I could dislodge it and found a drunken patron sleeping peacefully with his head in such a position that the pedal would not depress at all.

I tried shaking him to wake him. No reaction.

A fourth time, Gresham stood ready to go. We had to do something, as we couldn't expect the boys to maintain their composure for much longer.

I struck up as loudly as I could without my pedal and played the whole of that stirring introduction … without anyone hearing a single note.

I looked at Gresham.

He took no notice and raised his arms for the first chorus.

The deep-throated roar of a hundred virile young voices burst across the room.

There was a startled reaction. Everyone stopped talking and turned to look at the stage. The only sound for the next few minutes was the rustling and scraping of a massive crowd of people finding a place to sit and ending up with rows six deep standing at the back and down the sides and central aisle.

You could have heard a pin drop.

There was not a sound through that first half, not a cough, not even for one moment. It was as though they were holding their breath… until we got to the Hallelujah chorus. Suddenly the audience could not contain itself – we were in Africa after all! As one, they rose to their feet clapping and laughing and joining in the hallelujahs. It was the most magnificent experience. It was as much as I could do to keep playing. Gresham's eyes were so full of tears he could hardly see what he was doing.

'Hallelujah,' they shouted. 'Hallelujah, Hallelujah, Hal – le – lu – jah!'

The choir was superb and sang brilliantly through it all.

At the end of the chorus, Gresham waited with his arms outstretched until the huge crowd was silent once again. John's authoritative voice cut through the silence with his narration. The performance continued – in absolute silence.

We reached the Amen chorus. Again, the audience rose, but more subdued this time. As it drew to an obvious conclusion, again the audience joined in the singing, again they clapped and stamped and roared to the most stunning climax of sound and emotion. As the final notes died away and a tumult of applause and shouting took over, the grins started. One by one the boys allowed themselves to enjoy it – the soloists, John, Gresham and I all laughed and turned to applaud the choir.

They had excelled themselves and what was more important they had loved every moment of it.

I thought the acclamation would never stop. But at last the choir filed off the stage.

The lights came on and I bent to gather up my score. My friend was still lying under the pedals – with the most beatific and peaceful smile on his face.

Chapter 12

The halcyon days

February 1949 saw us all heading for the sea again, this time on our way to England. My beautiful Cape was dry and burnt after a long hot summer and we boarded the *Stirling Castle* in temperatures well over 100 degrees. Poor Jill was terribly sick for most the trip, but otherwise we thoroughly enjoyed the journey and found we were on board with England's famous MCC. Richard was in his element watching the Bedser twins, Denis Compton and Len Hutton with their daily practice in cricket nets set up on deck.

We became great friends with George Cox, a Sussex cricketer and master at Winchester, who had been coaching at a leading South African school. Eventually the only way we could keep Jill's mind off being seasick was when we were sitting up on deck in the roughest weather with dear George, playing word games.

I disgraced myself when having reached the finals of the tenniquoit, I found I suddenly couldn't let go of the tenniquoit ring when I served. Everyone was watching and cheering us on – a huge crowd – including the members of the MCC! Time and again I tried and time and again the ring disappeared up into lifeboats or over the rails as it swept into the sea. It was excruciatingly embarrassing and I spent hours afterwards in the cabin weeping inconsolably.

We arrived in England in the third week of March and it was absolutely freezing. The children couldn't believe it and kept looking at me with accusing eyes.

'You told us England was wonderful Mum, but it's very cold,' said Rich.

I wrote to Trish:

I've been trying to find time to write to you for days and so far haven't been able to do it until now! Gosh, life here goes about 100 times quicker and I have to stir up my old stumps to try to keep pace! And the cold! The first weekend we were here there was fog for two days, seeping damp cold and dark all day and then it changed to gales and gale warnings and snow in parts of England. Well, really – I'd quite forgotten what it could be like and had on two woollen vests, two woollen brooks and one silk pair, two jerseys and a dress indoors, then had to wear a coat and scarf on top when I went out! Could hardly move I was so cold!

I brought about 300 lbs. of food and six dozen eggs and three ball jars of butter and with all our ration books there seems to be tons. (I really don't know what all the people grumble about so much in the food line – I know it's better now, but they seem to have got in the habit of it – everyone I've met seems to live far better than we do!)

I went on to describe an old girls' reunion we had held, giving a vivid descriptions of all the people we had been at school with – including Bert Brown, our old headmistress. It was good to see her again.

We went to the theatre, we went to concerts, we played golf and we stayed with friends all over the country. I had to battle with huge swells of wishing we still lived over there. Yet I realised I was no longer part of it – my heart was well and truly buried in Africa and my two children were most certainly not English! They stuck out like sore thumbs – tanned and scrawny and much more independent and mature than others of their age.

Mummy's house in Exmouth was lovely. Apart from the new sitting room suite which we had bought especially for *The Paragon*, most of our furniture was still old cut-down paraffin boxes and I found it hard to reconcile our poor offerings with all the superb antiques she owned. I'd been away a very long time.

The children went to off to Welbeck School each day. It was a short walk down the road from Mummy and they'd set off cheerfully each morning – a great novelty after dusty trips in the old green truck. Jill at last started to show some interest in music but riding up on Woodbury Common was her real joy. They both grew to love England after the initial shock of the cold and seemingly constant grey days. They would spend hours packing up their lunch boxes – another great novelty, as there was no afternoon school in Rhodesia. They did find the afternoon school with no sport a bit testing, but

all these differences were good for them in challenging their precon-
ceptions about life.

I felt fit, well and quite at home of course, but despite that my final
note to Trish says:

*I think England is simply wonderful and everything in it, but somehow
think I shall be more satisfied with Rhodesia, which I quite miss.*

I also wrote a glowing letter to Harrie:

*Jill has been busy all the time with swimming and riding and various "ploys"
and she is quite fearless in the sea and on a horse – swims quite well and
stays in the water for hours, never wants to come out. She is always playing
the piano too, generally "Dear little Buttercup" as Mummy taught them a
lot of the Gondoliers songs and then took them to it. They loved it and you
will enjoy hearing R sing "Dance a Cachuca" with great spirit, rolling out
"manzanillo" etc. "I stole the Prince" is his favourite. Then of course he has
had terrific successes everywhere he's been; his charm has quite overwhelmed
everyone. I quake to think how they will settle down again after all their
exploits here.*

The children had been so happy in their little school that both John
and I agreed that it would be good for them to have another term
there. This meant he would have to go home before us and we would
follow two months later. It all seemed fine – until he left.

I wrote:

*At last this hideous day is over and I am now, 10 p.m. in bed very tired after
our early waking this morn. I can picture you out on the foggy sea in a hard
little bunk and oh how I wish I were there with you. It's now 16 hours
since you went and the worst part must surely be over. Poor Jill cried bitterly
after you left and didn't want anything but you...*

*Could we start tuning in to each other again as we used to... I will on
Sunday evenings starting with the Sunday you are back at Essexvale i.e.
Sun 15ᵗʰ Sept – 7'30 p.m. for you and 9'30 for me for 15 minutes – OK?*

*Goodnight my darling wonderful Johnnie – what a fool I was not to go
back with you...*

John's letters were full of the progress of the Church buildings and the problems of departmental heads. Lalan had bought a plot of land for her retirement and the Heany Hall was developing a bowling green and swimming pool. It was going to be the very height of civilisation! At the school he was coping with another serious bout of typhoid and thankfully, was completely lost and longing for us to return:

Gosh, it seems an age since I saw you all… being in the house only makes you seem further away, as I have to remind myself continually that you will not come into the sitting room from the passage… it will be a joy to have you all back again and to hear the kids running about.

The Essexvale Church was growing towards completion and it looked as though the consecration would take place just after we got back. Gresham had been asked to train up the choir for the occasion and all the boys involved in building the church were to be present to see the Bishop knock three times on the big wooden doors. The carpentry boys under Roger Malusalila were in the process of designing and carving those doors and they looked as though they would be appropriately magnificent.

The whole exercise had been invaluable in integrating the school into the community. Since *The Messiah*, opposition to what we were doing at the school had virtually disappeared – or at least, John was hearing nothing untoward directly or through others. The school had taken on almost celebrity status in Matabeleland.

For me, that extra three months in England seemed never-ending – the only plus was in seeing how well the children were enjoying their work. They were quicker, more lively and ten times more interested in the world around them than they had been when we arrived. On 17th October, we left on the *Warwick Castle* for the trip home:

I feel extremely sad at leaving England, I can't tell you how much and it all looked so perfectly beautiful when I came up with Dick in his car this morning – I've fitted back into it so easily that I feel all wrong leaving it again. This does not mean that I'm not just aching to come to you as I am, and that is far more important. It was awfully stupid of me to waste my time being so wretched that first month without you, but you mean more to me than anything else and I feel so much nearer to you already now that I'm on the boat. I can't write anymore as the kids are very clingy and whiney – overexcited and overwhelmed with people – they'll soon settle.

Jill was now coming up for her tenth birthday and we felt it was time for her to go to a more formal school. She was not being stretched enough at Essexvale. We arranged that she would go to Coghlan in Bulawayo in January as we knew and respected the headmistress. Jill would be a year younger than most of her class, being a December baby, but we felt she would be well able to cope scholastically after her time in England.

With Jill's schooling sorted out, it was time to concentrate on the consecration of the new church. Maurice Lancaster was a monk and our local parish priest. He was wonderfully far-sighted in his understanding of the importance of clearly showing the role the school had played in the building of the new church. All the boys and staff were to be there in VIP positions.

The church looked gracious and cool with its lofty roof. It was built using an attractive reddish local stone and became another vital project for the boys, as many of them came from areas where there was a lot of good building stone. Their skills had been honed in this process and the stonework was good. The doors were also suitably impressive and fitted together perfectly.

The whole school turned out as a sort of guard of honour, handing out leaflets and welcoming the guests. Rex Coleman and Trevor Booth would be opening the doors in response to the Bishop's knock. I was playing the piano for the grand entry and the subsequent hymns and had dressed up in my best finery – flouncy hat and all.

The church was filled to capacity. Three loud knocks echoed around the stone building. There was hushed expectation as Rex and Trevor moved forward to sweep their respective doors open with a flourish. Nothing happened.

The way they were made meant that one had to be opened just slightly ahead of the other for either to open. Three times they tried. Nothing happened. Slight panic and a few speculative looks… another three knocks… then Rex pulled his door a fraction before Trevor and thank God, they swung open.

The Bishop and his suitably impressive retinue walked in with solemn pomp and unruffled ceremony. The doors now let in a shaft of sunlight so bright that I couldn't see my music! Someone rushed over with a sunshade and shaded the pages for me, but was so busy watching what else was going on that the spines caught up in my hat.

I hung suspended by my hat for the rest of the hymn before my assistant realised what had happened. The rest of the occasion passed without any further commotion!

We were very pleased at the level of recognition given to the school, 'a living memorial to these boys…' the Bishop intoned.

Christmas came and went in our beautiful new church and suddenly it was time for Jill to go to boarding shool. I wept bitterly at seeing her go – our intact little family was suddenly disrupted… but at least I had Richard for several more years. He was a dear, willing little boy and he trotted off to Mrs. James' quite happily on his own. Knowing that Pat Pattison was now headmaster, we had put his name down for REPS and hoped to get him a place there when he was nine or ten. It was a lovely school about 25 miles from Bulawayo, in the Matopos, and the main building was an original and very gracious Dutch-gabled home.

A call from Pat in July shattered my hopes. 'I have long waiting lists for the next six years – but I could take Richard next term. After that I cannot guarantee him a place.'

'No, not yet!' I cried to John. 'Both the kids gone in the same year. I don't think I can cope with that.'

What agony it was. John and I sat late into the night discussing whether or not he should go. He would be only seven. It seemed so young. But it didn't look as though we had any alternative. Richard was so far ahead at Mrs. James' school that it wasn't doing him any good. Before long, I was treading the same path I had taken only six months before with Jill, this time buying royal–purple blazers and grey shorts and trying to put on a brave face so that Rich wouldn't be upset.

Jill came home for the mid–term weekend. She hated Coghlan. She was pale and wan. We knew there was something wrong as she was so desperately unhappy. I would go in to check her at 11 o'clock at night and she would still be awake. The weeping when we took her back made us feel that perhaps we shouldn't bring her out at weekends and that by letting her stay at school she might settle better. But this only made it worse.

One weekend it all came out – there was a lot of very nasty bullying and some disgusting "initiation ceremonies" going on and Jill, with what must have seemed to be her rather English ways, was being picked on by a group of pretty tough girls. "Want a fist fight?" was the immediate suggestion if anyone looked at them or crossed them in any way. Fist fights out by the rainwater tank at the back of the hostel

The Hammond family in 1914, outside their home, the original Plumtree
school huts. L to R: Ian (Skinny), Bob jr, Harrie carrying Patrick, Bob
Hammond, John and Jean (Jinny)

'The Yeoman of the Guard',
Plumtree 1927. John as Fairfax,
Patrick as Elsie, unknown as Point

Robert Woodward Hammond
Headmaster of Plumtree School
1906–1936

Harriet Hammond, the plucky, indomitable, wee Scot

John Hammond, aged 19, wearing his first suit and tie, just prior to leaving for Cambridge University, 1929

Jean Swire-Thompson (Jinny), c. 1935

Peterhouse 1st XV, 1932. L to R: K.E. Bond, J.M. Hammond (having just been awarded his Cambridge 'Blue') and J.F. Burford

John back with the family again in Rhodesia, 1935. L to R: Medeline Alston (Harrie's sister), Rose Alston, Harrie, John and Bob

North Street in Southminster at the time of Nancy's childhood. Oakleigh is the house in the background on the left. Madame Angeloff's school is the first house on the right

The Manor House, where Nancy was born, shown here decorated for the coronation of King George V

Nancy at her happiest on Bobby, with Fred French in attendance

Kitty Sugden with her children, from the left, Trish, Dick and Nancy

Nancy in 1914

Portrait of Nancy

Oakleigh today. Now a B&B and renamed Saxegate

Nancy at the piano

John's first house at
Tjolotjo, 1936

John outside the new
Headmaster's house, 1936

John wearing his old Plumtree blazer
outside the Tjolotjo guest huts, 1936

John shows off his banana crop

The Tjolotjo choir welcomes Nancy, December 1937

Local chiefs and headmen arrive to inspect the new bride. Note John's new car in the background

Nancy pensively watches the Gwaii River in flood

John and Nancy's wedding, 11th December 1937. Here they pose in the Gibbs' garden after the ceremony at St. John's Cathedral, Bulawayo

Nancy peers anxiously from the truck as the waters of the Gwaii River rise above the mudguards

A span of oxen pulls the truck from the floodwaters in the nick of time

Delivering the post – the Gwaii in flood, 1938

John, Sister Weir (Lalan) and Nancy pose on the rickety suspension bridge a few feet above the Gwaii. Made from beaten-out paraffin tins, the bridge was washed away two days after this photo was taken

Nancy and Aaron display the boom-slang that came through the sink and was dispatched by Aaron. Nancy holds the snake's severed head and top 10" in her right hand

Back to England to visit Nancy's father. John and Nancy on deck, 1939

Tjolotjo staff party

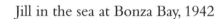

Jill in the sea at Bonza Bay, 1942

A formal government 'Indaba' with local chiefs and headmen

Bath time with Lalan

'The Tin House', John and Nancy's first home in Mzingwane, 1944

Richard, aged 3, and Jill, aged 6, on the front steps of the Mzingwane house

Jill and Richard in fancy dress, c. 1953

The Paragon, performed at the Bulawayo City Hall, 1952. John, playing the blind man, is seated, with Nancy, as his wife, standing next to him. Nancy also produced the play. Merle Coleman (on the right) played Jessica, the spiritualist

The Chidikamwedzi huts on Ian's (Skinny) Umvukwes farm. The scene of many happy Christmas and family gatherings

Goromonzi Sports Day. Staff and pupils enjoy an inter-house field event. *Photo courtesy of Noel Estcourt*

The Goromonzi Beit hall, taken on the school's 50th anniversary in 1995

The Girl's Hostel at Goromonzi – typical utilitarian design so prevalent in all Rhodesian schools. John tried desperately to improve its character and appearance

Goromonzi Prefects c. 1959

Back Row, L to R: Costin Dhlamini, David Dhliwayo (?), Nehemiah Munyoro, Hosea Mapondera, Edmund Garwe, Nathaniel Mathanda, David Murangari, unknown, Caxton Kadungere, Basil Muzorewa, Raymond Chieza
Front Row, L to R: Unknown, C. Chirwa, Herbert Matondo, Liberty Mhlanga, Cornelius Sanyanga, John Hammond, Christopher Mutambirwa, Maxwell Pswarayi, Aaron Mabaye, Buzwani Donald Mthothobi, George Mungwira

Gormonzi 1ˢᵗ Football XI 1959

Back Row, L to R: Unknown, Unknown, Unknown, Rangarirai Mumemo, Unknown, John Hammond
Front Row L to R: Murambiwa Harinangoni, Unknown, Aeneas Chigwedere, Unknown, Stanslaus Madyiwa. Goalkeeper: George Nhare

Portrait of the Headmaster. Taken for Goromonzi School in 1960

The proud father. John with Jill shortly before her wedding

Jill in her television days, 1972

The family together at Bishop's Mount in Salisbury, for Jill's wedding 24th August 1962

John outside the FAO building in Rome – a lonely figure ostracised from the assembly because of sanctions. Nevertheless, he was able to convey what was being done for the "Freedom from Hunger" campaign in Rhodesia, which created much interest

The Headmaster's house at Domboshowa. A very beautiful, happy home

John is awarded the Order of the Legion of Merit by President Clifford du Pont

Still inseparable, John and Nancy on holiday in Tasmania, 1994

John in 1975, as guest speaker at one of many public engagements

John and Nancy celebrate their Golden Wedding anniversary with Jill and Richard. Borrowdale House, Harare, 11th December 1987

Betty Sugden, Dick's wife, outside
the Beit Hall at Goromonzi after
the memorial service for John.
She is flanked by Bishop Crispin
Mazobere (left) and Headmaster
David Mutambara

Flowers on the font at
Christchurch, Borrowdale, Harare.
"Fambai zvakanaka Shamwari"
(Go well Friend). After John's
death in October 1996

Nancy in the garden of her home at Glenelg, South Australia 1997

were an everyday occurrence and Jill was certainly never going to be a natural fist fighter.

It was serious enough for John to want to have a word with the Headmistress, Miss FitzSimons. But we agonised over the fact that doing so might mean it would be taken out on Jill. Her desperate unhappiness, however, led him to talk to her. Miss FitzSimons was sensitive to the whole affair and she handled it very well. Things seemed to improve from that day, without Jill being implicated. But, sadly for her as well as for us, she was never happy at that school.

All this turmoil did not help us in sending Rich off. The ghastly day came after a wonderful three weeks' holiday together in the August holidays. Jill's music was coming along well and she would be taking Grade IV piano exams in a month's time. We dropped her off and then set off to REPS. Richard looked so smart in his new, oversized uniform with, what still seemed very odd to me, a trilby hat perched on the top of his head. We had agreed to drop him off and leave as soon as we could – to minimise the agony for everyone. We did... but the agony did not leave me for many months – particularly in the evenings... there was no one to tuck up in bed any more. I missed his cheerful little presence around the house, his Jabula pedal car careering up and down the verandah and his constant demands to know what things were. After a couple of weeks, I could no longer stay away and we arranged to go and visit him.

I thought I'd never recognise him amongst the sea of little boys in purple. But there he was, coming out of Chapel. He caught my eye and flushed scarlet! He wouldn't come over to us and ran on with the others. We went and fetched him, but it took a while for my kissy, lovey boy to come back.

The main thing was, he loved it at REPS.

With both children at school, I had to find something to keep me occupied. I had been asked if I would stand for the national committee of the WI and Johnnie encouraged me to do so even though it would mean quite a bit of travelling around the country. I was duly elected onto the committee and given the national portfolio of Convenor of Cultural Arts. This was perfect as it would take my mind off the ache of not having the children around and I could indulge my love of music and theatre.

I decided to set up a library of easily-performed plays which women all over the country could tackle and then inaugurated a national WI drama festival. This soon gathered momentum and every year at least 12 branches would put on plays and enter the festival. Over the following weeks and months I travelled a great deal giving talks around the country, making acquaintances in Salisbury and Umtali, giving advice and adjudicating the plays.

But I never found it easy being away from John – my life really wasn't enhanced by his not being there and wherever possible he would arrange a visit to Head Office to coincide with my trips.

The school was, by this stage, producing some outstanding youngsters and after many years of effort, the seniors were starting to understand the leadership/responsibility scenario. Boys leaving Mzingwane were snapped up almost before they left us, into increasingly good jobs – with constant reports coming back to the school telling us how very good they were – in fact, how much better they were than anyone had anticipated.

It was very satisfying.

'There you are Nannie – white attitudes will start to change wherever these boys leave a mark. It gives me more pleasure than anything when a European gives us these wonderfully positive reports on our boys.'

Once the boys had been within the influence of the school for six or seven years, they responded admirably to what they were being taught. In other schools however, it seemed as though the emphasis was on the teaching of academic subjects only. It was a feature that made John fearful for the future of the country:

Concern is felt for the future of industrial training in our present educational system. In many schools the importance, which was attached to practical training in the primary schools seems to be lessening… in many the standard of achievement in industrial work is appallingly low.

I would not like it to be thought that I express this opinion with only the future of this school in mind; it is prompted by the serious concern, which is felt for the whole future of race relations in this country. No one will deny the keen desire of the African people for training in a trade when this school is able to accept less than ten per cent of those boys who want to come here.

It is not without certain self-criticism that I emphasise my anxiety… I feel that had we built less elaborately at this school, the cost of providing other schools of this type would have appeared less formidable. Had I to do a similar job again I would wish to make a very different approach. The expensive type of building which we have erected here will, no doubt, provide good propaganda value in support of our intentions for the development of the African, but it means that the real work of development must be retarded by the wish to avoid high expenditure.

The need to move the school without undue delay did make it necessary to employ paid labour excessively. Had that not been the case I would have liked to see the School grow by its own efforts and this should be the aim with the building of new schools. Buildings should be simple and local materials should be used wherever possible. The pupils in training should themselves do the major part of the work and paid labour should be used as sparingly as possible. Only in this way do I see hope for being able to provide, within reasonable time, more schools of this type to meet the growing demand.

I am convinced that the way to encourage political strife and uneasy industrial relations is to concentrate only on the academic side of our curriculum, to the detriment of practical training at this stage. The African is no different in his expectation that education will increase his labour value.

The European employer is not averse to paying adequate wages to those Africans who can give an adequate return in work.

The present stage of development of this country requires practical workers who can help in its physical growth. There is, as yet, little room for the African who can do nothing except read or write.

Yet we are turning them out of our schools in thousands every year; they are of little value because they have to be taught their jobs or they have to have constant and expensive supervision. The boys themselves think that a pass in Standard VI should qualify them for a better job where their academic attainments can be used, but find that no one is prepared to offer them an adequate wage unless they can do some practical work.

Frustration grows and the national consequence of this is that, unable to earn an adequate wage, they resort to the use of political pressure in order to gain their ends. Their behaviour is no more than is to be expected. The blame cannot be put on their shoulders unless we, who are responsible for their training, do something to meet the present requirements of the country, which, coincides by a happy chance, with the desires of many of the African people themselves.

How prophetic John's words would be as events unfolded in the next few decades in Rhodesia… his fears were all too real. He went on to say:

277

My plea is for balance… academic subjects provide that wide vision which leads to ambition and provides the incentive to work. But in the economic life of this country today, these same academic subjects do not provide the means of satisfying those ambitions. We provide the vision but not the means of attaining it and we build frustration and strife. I am afraid of the immediate results of this divergence of policy.

The decreasing importance which I believe is being placed on practical training in our primary schools is, in my view, tragic because I can see it as leading to nothing but a considerable worsening in race relations throughout the country.

'I know those sentiments should not be included in an Annual Report,' John muttered to me, 'but I have been up to see them, I have talked to the wisest African and European heads I know and I believe we are simply creating a major problem for ourselves. Perhaps by formalising it in a report, Government might take some notice.

'I am still having a battle with those four boys in Standard VI but I think we might have found the answer for Ignatius at least.'

Ignatius had been one of a group of real "tsotsis" (rogues). They found academic work difficult and had battled to find a place for themselves in the school where they could shine. Sadly, they didn't seem to make it on the sports field either.

Then they discovered music – or more accurately, Ignatius discovered *The Messiah*. We, in turn, discovered that he had a most beautiful baritone voice. As he began to blossom, he encouraged his mates along with him and by the time they came to leave school they were useful and contributing citizens. In advising Head Office, John wrote:

No doubt they were attempting to gain influence and cheap popularity amongst the other boys by resorting to misbehaviour because they lacked the ability to make an impression in any other way. I always look upon it as a failure on the School's part merely to take the easy way out and refuse to re-admit these boys.

It can generally be found that there is something in their make-up, which, if discovered and cultivated, will lead them away from their anti-social attitude to the general benefit of all their work.

It must be the school's task to find this particular crack in the hard crust, which these boys like to build around themselves. The task assumes enormous proportions in a large school – particularly where European staff have to watch their social relations with the African staff.

It can only come through the African staff and prefects assuming more responsibility for discipline, for moral standards and for that teacher-pupil relationship on which any good school must be built. It is only when looked upon in this light that the true significance of our primary and secondary schools in the future of the African race can be evaluated.

There was now going to be no suitable school at all for the teachers' children even in Essexvale as it was closing down. Protracted negotiations were taking place to get the London Missionary Society's school at Matshetshe to move closer to Mzingwane. The closure of Essexvale School would have an adverse impact on attracting the calibre of teacher Mzingwane needed.

Then an extraordinary suggestion came down from Head Office. The boys were to be taught a "foreign" language and the recommendation was that this should be Swahili.

Why Swahili? If a foreign language must be taught what is wrong with what we are already doing with English? This will be the very much more suitable lingua franca in the future. IsiNdebele does have its limitations as a literary language, but even if the time devoted to its teaching were a complete waste of time I would press for its retention on the timetable. One has only to look at our Southern neighbour to realise how large a part language can be made to play in nationalistic politics. African nationalism may be but a newborn babe, but to stop the teaching of the local native language is to disadvantage a people. Ultimately, English must be the language of both black and white.

The rains came with a vengeance and John came home filthy dirty one day.

'We have a real problem. The new dam wall has not been consolidated and the last storm brought the water right over the wall. I've just had the whole school and staff out trying to fix it, and hopefully we can hold it. But another storm like that will finish it.'

Fortunately the dam did hold and they were able to "consolidate" it sufficiently to provide the alternative water supply the school needed in drought years. Soon after this we learned that at last, electricity was to be installed at the school. What excitement there was as men started installing mysterious wires and lampshades with bulbs in them, drilling out power points for the carpentry shop and kitchens and lacing great wires through the sky.

"Turn on" day came and that night it was spectacular looking down on the little school "village" twinkling below us. Lots of the boys climbed Skoveni to see it better.

I confess that I was terrified of it! We'd had some early electric light at Hillcote but I had never used irons or cooked with it. I liked the comfort of my hot old black coal stove with its kettle constantly bubbling on top. When John arrived with a new electric stove I was completely daunted by it.

'Will it make scones?' I remember asking and, 'What happens with all this electricity flying about in the air – does it harm us?'

I was assured that it didn't and within a few months had grown to appreciate how much cooler the kitchen was without the hot old monster. But storms took on quite a new dimension.

We seemed to be struck by lightning more often now that we had electricity and when that happened the plugs would spit out great yards of explosive flame. John and the kids had driven into Bulawayo one day during the holidays and when they returned they found me in bed (on my rubber mattress) wearing my (rubber) tennis shoes and clutching a (rubber) tenniquoit ring. I had been told that rubber would give me some protection! It must have been an odd sight and with peals of laughter the family teased me for years afterwards.

Mzingwane was a happy time for us and we formed great friendships. We played lots of golf and tennis and we'd go over to friends' houses for dinner. One of the most popular activities was ballroom dancing in the Heany Hall and once a stage was built to accommodate our plays, we could also have live bands along. This was high excitement! The kids would have their beds in the back of the green truck and they'd all play about in the dark with their friends for a while before we put them down to sleep.

For the kids, apart from tennis and riding, climbing *kopjes* or camping, we seemed to go to an endless round of fancy dress parties. Why they were so popular I don't know, but I always had to dress them up as something or other – absent-minded professors, Charlie Chaplin and Snow White seemed to be the favourites.

While we were in England we had ordered a very smart new Morris Oxford. We drove it around while we were on holiday and then the car was shipped out to Rhodesia. It was the envy of the neighbourhood and a pleasure to drive. Dear Mummy, having seen our rather poor furniture on her previous visit, sent us one of her antique clocks at the same time that Auntie Craig sent me her Broadwood piano – a boudoir grand. Our household suddenly took on an altogether more exotic appearance.

I found I had to tread carefully with old Mrs. van Blerk. I never knew if she was going to misinterpret some action or word I had said. I spoke glowingly about our trip to England, and she suddenly said, 'Why did you have to come out here and spoil it for all of us?'

I recoiled. She really seemed to dislike English people – apparently viewing us as a group of pinko liberals and having this new car was really too much for her altogether. I was muttering about her to Johnnie one morning.

'The Afrikaner people,' he replied, 'are as different from the English as the Spanish are from the Swedes, Nan… they are tougher than we are. She doesn't mean any harm by it but it illustrates why we feel as we do whenever we go down to South Africa.

'There is an almost tangible hatred between the races down there and the repression of the blacks is disgraceful. But they don't seem to see it like that. The Rhodesians, black and white, are thankful to cross the border at Beitbridge and put it behind them. But as Stella has said, they do seem to have some answers and despite everything, there seems to be quite an understanding between the races down there, particularly in the country areas. I just cannot believe it will last.

'The saddest thing for us is that we are being tarred with the same violent, repressive brush as the Afrikaner in South Africa… and if we don't move fast enough, the outlook here is gloomy. I sometimes feel there is just no chance we can move fast enough…'

I tried to be a bit more charitable to Mrs. van Blerk but it was hard. A few days later, the phone rang to say that Mr. van Blerk had been killed by lightning. I felt awful. John and I both felt we should go to his funeral and we were just getting ready to set off when another phone call told us he had come to life again!

It was extraordinary – apparently the lightning had left him totally paralysed and unable to speak, move his eyes or communicate. The horror that he might have been buried alive was very real – but stuck out on their farm, they had not thought for a moment to call out a doctor to verify his death – so the coffin was ordered and the funeral arranged!

Johnnie's health was giving me increasing cause for concern. Soon after we returned from England, he'd been hit very hard on the shin by a cricket ball when playing a game against the school. Then he was hit in the same spot again. It caused phlebitis in his leg and for almost seven months I had to dress it constantly with anti-phlogistine to reduce the inflammation and of course he had to keep it raised whenever he sat down. It meant he had to cut down his bike riding and he chafed at the lack of exercise.

Mummy arrived for another trip in 1952 and John and I, Trish and Roy drove down to the Mozambican port of Beira to meet her. She looked wonderful and was quite back into her stride again after the war. She was aiming to immigrate to Rhodesia in about 1956. She was going to be with us for about four months which meant the kids could get to know her again and she could decide, finally, if coming to live in Rhodesia permanently was really what she wanted.

Before trotting off to Kenya to spend some time with Bob and Mo, Harrie decided to come down and catch up with Mummy too, so we had a great time with both the grandmothers. Being able to travel around calling on all her precious children was a great joy to Harrie and she would spend a couple of months with each, helping out and re-establishing contact.

Anne, Skinny and Morrie's daughter, was about to be married to Charles Fisher, son of the Archbishop of Canterbury, Geoffrey Fisher. It was to be a wonderful wedding in Canterbury Cathedral and Harrie had hoped to be able to over there in time. But at over 80, she had to admit, reluctantly, that it was a bit too much for her.

I was driving her in to Essexvale on her way up to Kenya when suddenly the car seemed to fly off the road and we landed in a ditch.

'Och, what are ye up to?', Harrie cried in her typically Scottish way.

I felt awful and thought I must have lost control, but in fact the tie-rod had snapped and I'd lost all steering. Fortunately, we were both unhurt by the experience. Johnnie, who was meeting us in Essexvale, came back to fetch us. So we were at least able to see her off to Kenya in great style, if not quite as much comfort... in the faithful old green truck.

Mummy had a wonderful four months playing golf and catching up with friends – half of it spent with us and the other half with Trish and Roy in their log cabin in Salisbury. As we prepared for her departure we decided to time the trip down to see her off at Durban, having a holiday with the children in Natal. I was always keen to take the kids to the sea whenever I could and this trip might give us a chance to clear up John's persistent phlebitis.

The phone rang. It was Bob from Kenya. Harrie had died quietly that morning. Just before she went, she told Bob and Mo how she had been to Anne's wedding and in minute detail, described how beautiful it all was. This gave Bob real comfort. Anne and Charles were actually married the following day... but we always felt quite sure that Harrie had been there after all. A great presence had gone out of our lives. We were going to miss that indomitable little soul so much. On hearing the news Johnnie became very quiet, but I was pleased that it gave us another good reason to be away together.

Jean and John Swire-Thompson had been transferred to a job in Johannesburg so it was good to catch up with them on our way down to the coast. Anthony, with his voice showing signs of breaking, was almost as tall as his father. How time flew! We had a wonderful few weeks at the Goodwill Hotel in Amanzimtoti before seeing Mummy off on the *Cape Town Castle*.

At about this time, there was a lot of trouble at the country's first entirely academic school, Goromonzi. Pupils were reported as having gone on the rampage and the local white community was up in arms and demanding its closure and removal from the area.

The headmaster was a dear and an old friend of the Hammond family, George Miller, the same man who had composed the poem on Bob Hammond's death. He was a gentleman, a scholar and a poet and kindness personified. Unfortunately, more than a gentle poet was obviously needed at Goromonzi.

Miller was running arguably the most important African school in the country, and it appeared that the pupils had spotted this academic gentility and were taking every advantage. His Deputy, a man called Hoffmann, seemed to be doing as good a job as was possible in difficult circumstances. But the local white community lobby was strong and they were very antagonistic toward the school. The situation did not look at all promising, which was a great concern to Government, as the development of the school had been an important step in the growth of African education.

Johnnie was now being called upon almost continuously to give talks to important visitors about what was being done in African education. At one briefing given to a visiting group of influential

British parliamentarians, he developed a theme I was to hear often:

'Education of the native peoples of this country can be split into three periods.

'The first was before the arrival of the Pioneer Column, when the London Missionary Society started a school at Inyati, in 1859. Their primary objective was to convert people to Christianity with some education along the way. Forty years later they had converted 12. During the Matabele Rebellion, 10 returned to fight with their Impi and the two who remained faithful were killed by those Impi, on the steps of the Mission chapel.

'The second was the period between settlement of the country in 1896 and the start of the Second World War. Government and the Missions now joined forces in trying to persuade parents to send their children to school. While Government schools were still based on Christian teaching there was greater attention to those skills which would be of immediate relevance to their local communities, or in the gaining of employment.

'But, it was a very difficult time for the old people. They didn't like this "education" as their children would come home filled with new knowledge and quickly lost their appreciation for the family, their respect for the elderly and for the traditions of the past. During this time we had infinitely more capacity than we had students.

'The third period was from 1940 to the present. And now the rush began. The African felt that the European had unending power. At first they thought that you only became employed if you had a white skin. Then they began to see that there was more to it than that. Perhaps it was because he spoke English... so, speaking English became the great demand.

'At Tjolotjo, at the start of this third period, we were at the top level of African education of that day, taking them up to eight years of schooling. But I had the problem of having to use teachers who them-selves had no more than that same education, in order to cope with the influx. Most of my senior teachers were still imported from South Africa.

'By 1950, only ten years later, the demand was so great that Mzing-wane could take less than a tenth of the applications it received. It was the same story around the country. Frankly, we couldn't cope. Inevitably, quality came down – frustrations grew.

'Demand increased further... to the point where critical decisions had to be made – did we educate everyone partially and to what sort of future... did we educate a few really well so that they in turn could educate their fellows.

'In the last couple of years, the Colonial Office has differed in its understanding of the needs of our people, by comparison with what we feel on the ground out here. They want us to follow the Lugard formulation, of educating the whole population academically to Standard VI... yet they are not prepared to give us any additional funding to do this.

'We'd be educating the masses all right – but in country areas in particular, educating them to what? There would be no jobs or satisfaction for them at that low level. Any education with no way of satisfying the incentive it creates, can be a dangerous thing. It is the spur to ambition that arises out of stimulation of the imagination... creating expectations which cannot possibly be fulfilled.

'This is less of a problem for those in cities, as there are more opportunities in industrial or commercial concerns where those with an academic training only can be taught their jobs. For them, it may be adequate... but in rural areas where by far the greater numbers still live, a markedly different approach is necessary.

'We have argued that with the birth rate as high as it is and no support whatsoever from Britain, it is the taxes of a small and predominantly white workforce that can support this increased demand for black education. We cannot tread on their goodwill too heavily.

'Our approach has been, therefore, that it is more important to build a wider base and balance, even though by so doing we may not give as many the foundations to enable them to reach the top as might be desirable. We can only promise a primary education to the vast majority of Africans who enter schools at the moment, so the more practical and industrial this training, the greater the likelihood that they will be able to obtain jobs or be at the forefront of sound community growth.

We have to be aware that amongst all this, we are also training for the future good leadership and stewardship of the country.

'Sadly, we are still only talking about the education of boys. Many attempts have been made to open schools up to girls, but there is no demand and we cannot yet fill even one class of girls. The day the girls start demanding education is the day that I shall start to feel that the country is maturing.'

John had their attention completely by now as he concluded his speech.

'We believe our greatest job right now is to teach enough teachers to teach. To do so we have moved our Primary Teachers Lower Certificate Training on to post-Standard VI, giving them a ten-year course. This will enable them to teach well up to Standard IV.

'We are negotiating urgently with Government to run a concurrent academic stream giving an expanded four years post-Standard VI. So far we are not having much joy.

'We are also negotiating with Government to ensure that these young teachers get a wage comparable to that which they can receive in the private sector. At the moment it is less than 50% of that figure and, as such, it is no great incentive to stay teaching. Again, we are not having much joy.'

John's speeches always stirred the pot and this one did result in some substantial further monetary commitment from Britain towards the cost of African education. It also resulted in a major Government commission to examine the effectiveness of current African education policies.

In the meantime, back at Mzingwane, Gresham wanted to do another oratorio and he had been rehearsing *Judas Maccabeus* for months. The Jewish Guild Hall was keen to have us back again and our four soloists were equally keen to be involved. This time, the *Bulawayo Chronicle* deemed it sufficient an occasion to send a critic along:

FINE PERFORMANCE BY NATIVE CHOIR

An appreciative audience filled the Jewish Guild Hall, Bulawayo on Saturday to hear a rendering of Handel's oratorio "Judas Maccabeus" by the Mzingwane African School.

The choir conveyed an appreciation of the dignity and grandeur of the theme quite remarkable in so young a group of choristers. It was at its best in the chorus "Tune your Harps to Songs of Praise" and the "Hallelujah, Amen" showing throughout a sensitive understanding of tone values.

Excellent as the Guild Hall is for the ordinary run of entertainment, surely a better one can be found for such performances as that presented by the outstanding performers who entertained us last Saturday.

We couldn't have agreed more... but we still weren't allowed to perform at the City Hall.

Richard was very happy at REPS under Pat Pattison's firm but fair discipline and we had managed to get him in to Plumtree from the first term of 1956. Jill would be starting at Townsend the following year and was looking forward to getting away from Coghlan. I loved my Cultural Arts activities… and best of all Mzingwane was going from strength to strength.

Then Head Office told John that they wanted him to join the Inspectorate.

'I'm a schoolmaster Nan. The thought of sitting in an office all day simply appalls me. I know it's promotion and I know that the time is probably coming when I should consider something else. Whatever it is, has got to be worthwhile.'

'Are you interested in Maurice Lancaster's concept of St. Stephens at Balla Balla?' I asked somewhat nervously. I still found the heat at Essexvale pretty oppressive and Balla Balla was considerably worse.

'No, I've thought about it, but I don't think I would have the freedom there to produce the sort of boys I can achieve here.'

In October 1952, John received a call from the Chief Native Commissioner, Powys-Jones – a man for whom he had great respect.

'John, I need you for the most difficult job in the country,' he said, but would say no more. John was asked to travel up to Salisbury for further discussions.

'Are you a disciplinarian?' he was asked. 'Because only a man who is tough of mind and body can possibly cope with this job.'

The job in question was Goromonzi. We had feared it might be. The place now seemed to be absolutely out of control. Miller had resigned and the Department needed the right man to try and pull it together again. The school was full of the country's best and brightest boys – their potential for good was absolutely enormous. Their potential for influential and substantially destructive bad … was absolute.

Powys-Jones took John out to look the place over. He met, and liked what he saw of, Hoffmann. He did not like what he saw of the scruffy, surly boys who lounged indolently round the classrooms with their hands in their pockets, and who were rude enough not even to stand up when they were addressed. This was the minimum of acceptable behaviour from all civilised people at the time. The whole scene was an anathema to John.

'Are you beginning to understand the depth of the problem?'

287

Powys-Jones asked. 'We believe it is very nearly unmanageable and I am telling you this so that you are under no misapprehension about what you would be taking on.'

John came home very reflective. 'It is ghastly, Nannie. I have never felt such open hostility in my life. What on earth have they been up to over there?'

I was aghast. 'Do you really want to take on something as awful as that?'

He took my hands and answered very slowly. 'I feel I must consider it. The Department is desperate. These are the brightest boys this country has – someone has to steer them in the right direction or we have absolutely no hope at all in Rhodesia and we might as well pack up and leave right now.'

In practical terms, it would mean that both Jill and Rich would have to come down to Bulawayo by train each term and that, agonisingly, we would be that much farther away from them and unable to see them even at weekends. I didn't think I could bear it. My heart felt as heavy as lead. But the children seemed happy to try it. So I had to stop being stupid and just accept it. We felt we might consider moving Jill to the Girls High School in 1955 as we had no particular allegiance to Townsend, but Plumtree was far too important to us all to consider moving dear Richard.

After many, many days of "swithering" about it, John agreed to take the position.

The ultimate irony for me after the hideous Plumtree debacle, was that in order for John to qualify sufficiently to take the job at Goromonzi, his own position at Mzingwane would have to be upgraded to "Head of Secondary School Junior High". It was amazing how, when they wanted something done, the powers-that-be would and could move mountains.

The upgrade was dated 1st January 1953 and his appointment as Principal, Goromonzi Secondary School took place 19 days later.

The Mzingwane staff were horrified – particularly the Africans. Dear excitable old Dembi Bulle came almost running up the drive.

'Mr. Hammond, I am very nearly crying myself. Now you are leaving me at this place, is this school going to stand without Mr. Hammond? Everyone thinks the school will close the next day because, Mr. Hammond, you have done such good works for the school. You cannot leave us, it is not true that you are leaving us for that Goromonzi School?'

John sat him down and started talking through the implications of the move, only to look up and see old man Mothobi, Herbert Ramushu, Dennis Moyo and Roger Malusalila walking up the drive as though they were going to a funeral. As they arrived, Nason Madeya walked down from the hospital. Then various schoolboys started to walk up the hill as well, disbelief on their faces. It was like a wake.

'You are our father. You are a great teacher and loved by all Africans.'

'What is to happen to all the industrial work at this school? Most of the boys who are doing good industrial work around the country have gone through Mr. Hammond's hands.'

Nason Madeya came over and stood by my side... it seemed almost as if he was speaking to himself. 'Mr. Hammond is a wonderful head-master who is a very able, big figure. His motto is "deeds not words, fully with purpose and unity". He is a wonderful man, full of kindness and love to all.'

Then the Orderly turned to me too and held out his hand. 'Thank you for your kindness to me. You are a true, faithful and beloved mother.'

Roger Malusalila shook my hand. 'I will never forget that the Principal of this school, Mr. Hammond, would come to camp with the Boy Scouts. He taught us to love one another – and even to love our enemies.'

Once they had left, the wives came, mainly to talk to me. Dorothy Moyo came up bringing the most beautifully embroidered tablecloth and mats with her as a farewell present. Her note said:

Dear Mrs. Hammond,
Will you accept this little gift from our family? This being a token of love and appreciation of our long stay together. May God bless your new home and find life pleasant as it has been the case here.

Our last Christmas at Mzingwane was tinged with sadness – and a huge dose of apprehension. John had never really known what the African staff and boys felt about him, he was a very firm disciplinarian and he'd always believed in maintaining the distance between them required of his position. This outpouring of emotion was something we were not used to.

The Roelkes had left the staff by now, Maurice Mills and Roy Alvord were in Head Office and the few Europeans left on the staff were relative newcomers. They understood that the school would, of course, carry on under a new head. We were particularly pleased when John's cousin, Hugh Watson (Aunt Eila's second son) was appointed in his place. We knew Mzingwane would be in safe hands.

The village gave us a series of the most heart-warming send-offs and dear old Rex and Merle Coleman were quite devastated that we were leaving. Rex came up at one of these parties and in his open, honest and wonderfully warm way, said, 'Mr. Hammond, if ever I have the chance to work with you again, believe me, I'll be there… trouble is there is not much place for an Agriculturist at Goromonzi.'

It was very sad to be leaving after being such pioneers of this school, and I found I was looking at it and trying to absorb and remember every single nook and cranny of the place as we set about preparing to go.

We did wonder where on earth we were going to when John received a letter from Powys-Jones just after Christmas, which said:

Dear Hammond,

Formal approval of my recommendation that you be promoted to the Head-ship of Goromonzi has just reached me and I hasten to congratulate you and to wish you and your wife well in the new post.

As I told you, when I saw you here the other day, I look on this post as a most important and responsible one and, as I told you, a far from easy one.

That you will make a success of it I have no doubt, but you will doubt-less need the well wishes of your friends!

And so may the New Year not only bring you good health and happiness, but also the strength and wise counsel that you will need.

Chapter 13

The great heartbreak begins

John agreed to start at Goromonzi by the end of February 1953, having handed over the running of Mzingwane to Hugh Watson. We packed up the furniture and then enjoyed another heart-warming round of genuinely sorrowful farewells. I decided to stay with Hugh and Phyllis for a few weeks then follow on, bringing Jill and Rich up at the end of the first term. After our worries with Jill at Coghlan, I was keen to see her well settled at Townsend.

I was excited about moving up to Salisbury – the climate was much cooler in Mashonaland and Goromonzi was only half an hour or so from a city which had always appealed to me. I also liked the thought that there were about 40 girls at the school and co-education was being encouraged. I felt sure there must be some role I could play by which I could give tangible support – possibly helping with Girl Guides or something similar.

We had become increasingly apprehensive over what we'd been hearing about the school in those last few weeks before we went up. There seemed to be nothing but a constant succession of terrible tales of schoolboys running riot and causing serious problems in the area. There was a massive job to be done.

John was going to stay with the Hoffmanns until the furniture arrived, which would be an enormous help, and give him the chance to get to know his deputy and learn more about the school. A huge old Glens truck arrived to load up our furniture. It seemed to fit in quite easily, but I was worried about the driver who was loud and over-friendly.

'He's been drinking,' I said to John with my tendency to look on the dark side.

'No, no, I don't think he has,' John reassured me. 'He'll be fine.'

291

Unfortunately, I was right. Two hours down the road, the pantechnicon went over a cliff. My beautiful new grand piano and the precious antique grandfather clock Mummy had sent me the previous year were left broken and lying in the veld for two days before we even heard about it. The driver was unhurt and fortunately the company was prepared to take full responsibility and would have everything fully repaired. But it wasn't that easy to repair an antique clock in Southern Rhodesia at that time. This whole episode delayed our departure even further.

Hoffmann had been acting Principal for the few months since Miller retired. He organised a meeting of the School Council to welcome John on 24th February, starting with lunch. The main agenda item was the opening of the new Beit Hall a month later on 28th March.

During that first week at Goromonzi and as their chats over sundowners in the evenings became less formal, Hoffmann confided to John that he had hoped he would get the job of Principal. He admitted he had been most disappointed at not having been appointed, but he felt sure they could still work together.

John wished he had known this in advance, but assured Hoffmann that he would very much like to work closely with him as he was impressed with what he had seen and believed he had been doing a good job. John told me that he enjoyed these evening discussions as they covered a multitude of topics and he respected Hoffmann's lively intelligence, dedication and concern for people.

One evening, John broached the subject of why the discipline had fallen off so badly and why the school was in such disrepute.

'Oh, do you think it is bad?' Hoffmann asked. 'Well of course, I don't really believe in enforcing too much discipline – taking time to talk and reason with them until they see your point of view is usually far better. The African is not here to be disciplined. He is here just to cram in as much learning as he can for the future. I know of many European schools where the discipline is no better than it is here.'

'I cannot believe we should even contemplate doing any adverse comparisons with European schools,' John ventured. 'I'd like to see this school conform to becoming the best possible learning environment for the young African. I'm most certainly not interested in taking the worst of any European schools and making that the standard for Goromonzi. This place must set the pace and the standard as the best school it can possibly be.'

John realised Hoffmann wasn't listening. 'And as for these local farmers and landowners, they're all so filthy rich, ex-British Army and diplomatic corps – don't take any notice of them, they just don't like the thought of having an African school on their doorstep.'

John hadn't yet met the neighbours but he recognised that his own attitude to education of the African was still not the popular view, so he conceded that Hoffmann might well be right on this last point.

But his head started to spin regarding Hoffmann's comments on discipline. John had seen enough of him already to see that he was obviously a good teacher, but this approach to discipline was diametrically opposed to John's thinking.

'Of course my philosophy is basically communistic,' Hoffman went on. 'We must spread the message of revolution and rights to these people, after all they are the cream of the crop and will lead the new Rhodesia.'

'I think you are wrong. They are most certainly the brightest and the best, but they are here to be fully educated, to find their own personal strengths and develop those to the best of their ability. They must be trained to lead the country wisely and to understand the enormous responsibilities, which come with those rights and privileges,' John protested.

This was going to be more difficult than he had realised. John found out that it was the Chairman of the School Council who had promised Hoffmann the job – the Government apparently, did not want him there. It became more and more obvious that John's appointment was in fact a terrible blow to Hoffmann, as he had hankered for the job for some time. So there was a platform for immediate antagonism and John now found that he was "basically communistic" – believing that the best way to achieve objectives was by causing dissatisfaction with what they had.

'It would be irresponsible for us to spread the message of revolution,' John said. 'The African has only had just 60 years of exposure to the European way of doing things, and during that time the country has been designed to run as a sophisticated western economy, which is complex in the extreme. It would be grossly unfair to expect them to be able to cope yet or to even create an expectation that they might be able to do so.'

'They will run it in their own African way of doing things,' Hoffmann replied.

'But they have been so keen to embrace everything European that their own African way of doing things is fast disappearing. In that vacuum where the traditional leaders no longer hold the sway they once did, it will be the power hungry, the loudest talkers and the most persuasive who take power... particularly if we have not had enough time to lay a sound educational base. Surely we have learned the lesson of what has happened in other parts of Africa?'

'But the move is unstoppable. African Nationalism is starting to call the tune in South Africa,' Hoffmann argued.

'I agree, but South Africa has had 250 years of white influence and it also has a much more repressive and racialist white regime. I can well understand it in their situation. Here we really do have a chance to do things differently... unlike white South Africans who regard the country as their land, the European in this colony is moving pretty constructively towards an understanding that the Africans will eventually run the country. There is a growing reservoir of good will.

'We surely have to give them every encouragement to feel that when the African takes over, he will be capable enough to do it well... or there will be a real backlash.'

They would keep on with their discussions until late into the night. John was interested in Hoffmann's point of view, but could not believe that it was right and he found himself becoming more and more anxious at the idea of running the school with Hoffmann as his deputy. He had spent so much time with the African people and knew what a disciplined society they had once been and what disruption there was now that those traditions were disappearing. Living in the same house as the Hoffmanns, he couldn't confide in me either when I phoned.

On the night before the children and I were due to arrive, one of the staff came running up to say there was a riot in the dining room. John and Hoffmann went down to find utter and absolute chaos. Food had been thrown all over the place, chairs were overturned and broken, boys were fighting each other. John strode through like a colossus.

'This is disgraceful!' he boomed, in the enormous and very commanding voice he could muster when occasion demanded.

He grabbed two senior boys by the scruffs of their necks. 'If you value your place in this school, have the boys clean up and put the chairs back under the tables NOW! Any that are broken can be put into that corner.'

Absolute silence descended. Shocked faces turned, mouths hung open. Nobody had ever spoken to them like this before. John strode out of the room. After a few moments of confusion, the dining room was apparently returned to order in complete silence, the broken chairs were stacked in the corner and the boys retreated to their dormitories.

At assembly the following morning, John quietly but sternly talked of 'unacceptable behaviour… I don't expect that of the future leaders of our country… uncontrolled idiocy… not the way to deal with this type of issue.'

He looked over to the Head Boy and said, 'Ushewokunze! I want to see you in my office immediately assembly is over. For the rest of you boys – Mr. Gorton you will please supervise – ten times round the soccer field and don't think any of you can slack off, because you have to be back for your first lesson in 20 minutes time. Anyone who refuses or is not back in time, can expect to do 20 times round the soccer field tonight – and I will be watching you. Girls, you may take a 20-minute break until the boys have finished.'

He noted that they filed out of the room for the first time in an orderly and quiet manner.

'Right, Ushewokunze – what is at the bottom of this?' John had watched the Head Boy on a number of occasions and felt he had seen a slight look of distaste on his face at some of the behaviour of the boys.

'Sir, Mr. Mahpahlo is giving us very small portions and the boys are hungry.'

'Do you think that is the case, or are the boys making it up?'

'I think it is the case'

'Well, how would you deal with it?'

Ushewokunze looked at John in surprise. 'I will do whatever you tell me.'

'You are the Head Boy of this school, Ushewokunze… I expect you to be making those kinds of decisions. In future, I will expect you to come up with the solutions. Today, let us both go down and speak to Mr. Mahpahlo and find out what the problem is.'

As they strode down to the dining hall, John asked the boy, 'Do you approve of what happened this morning?'

'No sir, I do not,' he said.

'Do you mean that, or are you telling me what you think I want to hear?'

Ushewokunze looked at John with a curious look in his eyes and just the smallest hint of a smile. 'But Mr. Hammond, I think you know us very well.'

'I do,' John said. 'I was brought up almost as one of you. Never think that with me, you can get away with anything that you can not get away with from your own chief.'

'Sir,' Ushewokunze said, 'if that is your way of thinking, I understand you. I think we can make it work.'

John knew there was still a long way to go, but he'd been watching the boy with interest and there was a depth of integrity there, which could be helpful.

'Mahpahlo, what is the size of the helping you are giving to the boys?' John asked.

Mahpahlo measured out a generous plateful.

'Now what is the size you are really giving the boys?'

'Ah, but that is it'

'I don't believe it, because if that was it we would not have had a riot last night.'

Ushewokunze came in carrying a plate. 'Here sir, I have found a plate which has been prepared for lunch.' It was a considerably smaller helping.

John told Mahpahlo that he would be doing spot checks on the portions being given out and that if he found this happening again, he would be fired. The school was ordering plenty of food, so if he was dishing out such a small amount, what was he doing with the rest of it? Any suggestion he might be stealing it, would mean big trouble.

The kids and I arrived that evening and although John had had what might be termed an element of success through this incident, I could see at once that he was deeply disturbed. We left the kids unpacking and greeting the animals again.

'Let's get out of this place,' John said as he directed me to the car.

He didn't speak as we drove out to the Jamaica Inn, but his knuckles were white as he gripped the steering wheel. It was only when we were sitting beside the Melfort Lake with a drink in front of us that he let it all out.

'I am near despair,' he said. 'You have no idea how bad it is. I am not at all surprised that the locals are so furious. Boys in uniform have been seen lying drunk by the side of the road. They're insolent, rude, and bloody-minded. But the worst thing of all is that at least half the staff here thinks along the same lines as Hoffmann. "Oh this is Africa, they're so hard done by, just let them do just what they want." Hard done by, my foot!

'We must be sensitive to present social backgrounds. Even here at Goromonzi with the country's cream of the crop, we know we'll have to teach basics like use of a latrine. But otherwise, they're normal, healthy teenagers like any other, white or black, who require a firm hand if they are ever going to reach their potential, or make their way through life's difficulties. It's unbelievably patronising to think otherwise.'

'You can't hold back my duck,' I said. 'You know you're right.'

'I suppose so, but you begin to doubt it – and yourself – very quickly. Mzingwane seems such heaven by comparison. I have to make a speech for the opening of the Beit Hall in two days' time and I haven't the heart even to start.' He took my hand.

'Thank God you are here Nan. It has been absolutely awful without you. Two nights ago I was invited to attend the monthly debate. I don't think I'll ever forget it. The subject was extreme and I did wonder if it had been set on purpose knowing I would be there. It was to the effect that the African would have made more rapid progress had he been left to himself. I was interested to see how both halves of the debate would handle the issue.

'Well – this was no reasoned or objective debate. I was shocked beyond belief. The behaviour was downright rude and insulting towards the European staff present. I felt sorry for the boys who were opposing the case. Every point they made which favoured the white man was greeted with sneers and snarls, which had an almost animal ferocity.

'What I saw was not the African pupil I have known for the last 17 years. This was ugly, destructive, menacing, and I still do believe, completely out of character. It was unlike anything I have ever seen or felt before. It felt downright evil. It was as though they had lost their senses completely – the baying of a frenzied mob.'

He sighed. 'So much for the privileged cream of the crop who think they are so ruddy marvellous. Give me my Mzingwane boys any day.'

John was very despondent after only three weeks in the place. What on earth was going to happen? He told me about the incident in the dining hall and what had transpired with the Head Boy.

'He does give me a bit of hope. If he's been subject to the nonsense Hoffmann's been feeding him for the last six years, yet he still glimpses the truths of what I am saying, we might be able to turn it around. Obviously I can't just give in, but believe me, we have one heck of a fight on our hands to move this school to anywhere near where it should be.'

Mr. and Mrs. Hoffmann came round to meet me the next day. I was on my guard with him immediately and could only see his overly charming manner as obsequious and underhand. But I was almost surprised to find that I liked her a great deal. She was a hard working, honest and delightful woman with a couple of very nicely behaved children.

'Isn't it extraordinary? They discipline their own children beautifully...'

The local farmers and residents had been invited to the opening of the Beit Hall. None turned up, except those in an official capacity. This was a clear sign to John of just how bad local feeling was about the school... and the reality that it might jeopardise its continuation. The Beit Hall was magnificent, generously spacious with equipment for any stage show or presentation which might be needed. The Library next door was beautifully designed and the Beit Trust had given a generous donation for the purchase of additional books.

John knew this first speech he would be giving at the opening of the Beit Hall, was vitally important and that the boys were keener than they might ordinarily have been to know what he was going to say:

In the first three years that pupils from this School took the Cambridge School Certificate, only three out of 83 were unsuccessful. It is a remarkable achievement.

However, it is too early yet for us to judge with certainty how the former pupils of this School will react when faced with the greater freedom and the larger responsibilities of the outside world. We have the evidence, as far as examinations can test it, that they have the mental capacity to do well.

We wait now for those reports which trickle in from time to time, telling of success and failure in the world for which we are attempting to train them. Should any of you come in contact with those who have been trained here, I hope you will spare a moment to tell us how you find them. Please do not attempt to spare our feelings – we are keen to know of our failures as well as our successes.

We want to know if they have the right attitude to their work, if they are well mannered and if they accept responsibility. We want to know whether our attempts to train their characters are producing results.

Examinations are satisfactory things for schoolmasters. They assess objectively the success, or otherwise, of one's work. Unfortunately they do this so successfully that there is sometimes a danger that we may come to the point where we feel that the work of the classroom is all that matters. I am asking that as many of you as can do so shall act, as the opportunities occur, as examiners of our efforts to make these boys and girls into useful citizens.

It is imperative that we should succeed in this task because we are now training those who will be foundation members of a new class in African society, who will have to assume responsibility, not only in their own professions, but in the social growth of the African people of this part of the world. On them will rest the responsibility for maintaining and building up standards of morality and integrity and behaviour, which will act as a pattern for those lower down the social scale.

When we try to assess the educational task before us we have cause to wonder whether our efforts can ever produce results quickly enough. Schooling cannot be hastened. We still need to take a sixth of man's allotted span to bring him to the stage where he can begin to be fully educated and nothing can contribute very much towards hastening the process.

The Beit Hall was designed to seat 600 people and the report in the local newspaper, the *Rhodesia Herald*, the following day, called it one of the finest Beit Halls and libraries in any Southern Rhodesian school:

The Hall is 118 feet by 50 feet and the library 85 feet by 38 feet. The connecting buildings, which link up the two main buildings, provide a librarian's room, a newsroom, a committee room and a kitchen. It is equipped with a cinema projection room and a stage 53 feet wide and 27 feet deep.

While the hall was being built, members of the London Old Vic Company visited Goromonzi and one leading member of the company remarked that this was the only stage in Rhodesia he had seen which was really suitable for Shakespearean productions.

The Guides and Scouts had been detailed to take people round the school so that they could see what happened where, and after morning tea, the school put on a play in the new hall. It went down very well despite John's apprehension. More remarkably, the students behaved well and were smartly turned out.

Hoffmann came up straight away and congratulated John on an excellent speech. It came across to me as hollow and I realised I was going to have to be careful not to predudge him because of the affect he had already had on John. Two or three other staff members came up and said 'thank you, thank you, thank you' most sincerely, intimating that the turnaround in attitudes in only four weeks had already been remarkable.

John asked me to take time to get to know the wives of the local community as he regarded the imminent threat of closure of the school as the biggest problem he faced. Fortunately I still held the portfolio of Convenor of Cultural Arts in the national body, so there was no barrier to my joining the Bromley-Melfort branch of the WI straight away.

For the first couple of meetings, I could have cut the atmosphere with a knife. Nobody bothered to talk to me. It was only when the area of Cultural Arts came up that I could command any attention. We held our meetings at the prestigious Ruwa Club, which was frankly pretty daunting in the circumstances and was the one club I knew we could never afford to join. I did catch myself gazing wistfully out at the beautifully laid-out golf course, so attractively complemented by the deep thatch and steep pitch of the club buildings.

The wealth in that area was considerable and initially I felt pretty intimidated by it all, thinking longingly back to my down-to-earth old friends in Essexvale. The children hadn't had any success in meeting others of their own age and they were feeling, probably for the first time ever, resentment at what they represented. There were not many children among the staff at the time and I remember being concerned that with them both at school in Matabeleland, they might find it difficult to make friends. I saw them off on the train at the end of the holiday with a leaden heart.

By the third meeting of the WI I began to feel a lessening of the antagonism towards us and realised that the area must be beginning to notice some differences in the school.

Apart from the new Beit Hall, the school buildings were patently unsuitable for the job. They had been designed by engineers who hadn't the foggiest idea what the inside of a boarding school looked like. The dormitories were ghastly barrack rooms with 30 boys in each and a couple of small rooms for prefects. There was no resident staff member anywhere near them, so the boys ran riot. The bullying and intimidation was fearful.

The school was about to build two new staff houses, so John changed the plans straight away putting them adjacent to the hostels. The staff didn't like it at all and said so. John insisted, discussing with them the enormity of the intimidation problems and how he felt sure this measure would reduce them. They agreed... but very reluctantly.

To make matters worse, half the school and all the playing and sports fields were across the other side of the busy main access road from Salisbury and Ruwa to the farming area of Goromonzi.

John came back one evening saying wearily, 'I know it's probably improving a bit, but if you asked me to rank the situation between total chaos or a well-run school, I'd have to say it was still anarchy.'

One of the most senior teachers was Majuru. He was rather aged, but he was a man of stature, he had been at the school for a long time and his wife was doing a very competent job running the community school for the younger children of teachers.

Hoffmann seemed to put great store by Majuru and John went over to talk to him about the inauguration of a house and housemaster's system. He said to Majuru that he would like to appoint him as one of four housemasters.

'Ah no, Mr. Hammond, I would not be comfortable with European staff as assistants to me in the house. I don't think Africans are yet ready for this.'

John pondered over this. They had certainly been quite ready at Mzingwane, but perhaps it would take more time yet to gain trust. He decided to appoint four Europeans to the positions, one of which would of, course, be Hoffmann.

The next day, Hoffmann was at his office door saying that Majuru was very unhappy that he had been overlooked and that he, Hoffmann, did not think it was right.

John looked at him. 'Didn't Majuru tell you that I had asked him to be a housemaster? He told me he didn't want to take it on.'

'That's by the bye,' Hoffmann retorted sharply. 'He was a house-master before, so he should be again.'

'When I went round asking about the house system, nobody mentioned to me that there had ever been one in place.'

'Well, there was. It didn't function very effectively,' he conceded, 'and two of the housemaster positions fell vacant several years ago.'

'Well, since my arrival, Hoffmann, there's been no evidence what-soever of any member of staff functioning as a housemaster and I had gathered that this had been the position for a number of years.'

No sooner had Hoffmann left, than Majuru was at the door.

'I will not work with Mr. Lawton,' he declared.

'Majuru, you are not being fair with me,' John said. 'You know I spoke to you only two days ago and you told me you could not work with a European as your assistant. So what do you want me to do? I must have some system of housemasters in position because this school is in trouble and I have to make it work properly.'

'Well, I should have been a housemaster,' he insisted.

'It's too late now. The people have been approached and the announcements made.' John looked up at him. 'Will you try the system out for the balance of this term before you pass judgement? Mr. Lawton is a fair man and I will speak to him about it and ask him to make sure you get the seniority you deserve.'

Majuru left, taking a cloud of discontent with him. John couldn't believe it. After a few moments, he decided he needed to put himself in a position where he could act quickly if necessary and he wrote to Steve Davis, his new head of Department:

Majuru probably has more influence with the boys of this school than any other member of staff. My conversation with him yesterday gave me the feeling that he is strongly biased against most of the European staff and for this bias he may have been given some justification. He is, I have heard, given to spreading political ideas amongst pupils.

Serious trouble in African schools usually originates from some member of the staff. Should Majuru choose to provoke trouble in this school he undoubtedly has the influence with the boys, which could make them follow any lead he might give.

Should he persist in his attitude of non-co-operation with his housemaster that, in itself, will have the worst possible effect on the boys. I would prefer to anticipate trouble and to remove its cause before it happens and am asking if you could bear in mind some transfer or interchange of staff which could be carried out at short notice should the need arise.

As John looked out of his office window a couple of weeks later, he saw Hoffmann and Majuru standing under a tree with their heads together. Hoffmann gestured towards John's office. They were obviously discussing him. He turned back to his latest report:

Every member of the teaching staff is now attached to one of the Houses and Housemasters have undertaken the direction of all extra-mural activities and House competitions. Housemasters have taken charge of House pocket money and have been able already to get a fairly intimate knowledge of the pupils in their Houses. This has been of immense value in the determination of character and integrity.

John was still plagued by the fact that there was nobody on the staff who had ever worked in a boarding school before. They had no understanding of the huge extra responsibility, the complexities or sensitivities involved. What's more, in the past three years the school had gained four academic teachers straight out from England.

Not only had they never worked in a boarding school environment, but also they had absolutely no idea how to interact with Africans.

'I find it extraordinary Nan.' he said, 'that we don't seem to be able to get the message through to these English immigrants – as we have always found, when they first come out think the Africans can do no wrong. They invite them into their houses, exchanging confidences and generally going right over the top. But almost to the day, about two years later, they turn into the most radical racists you could imagine and treat them like dirt, hurling abuse and belittling them.

'Why do they get so hung up about people with a different coloured skin? It's appalling for the pupils; they don't know where they stand. It's no wonder they have precious little respect.'

'Well, I remember when I first came out, I really didn't know how to relate to them at all,' I said quietly. 'They are exotic and different looking to us you know, Johnnie.'

'I know duckie, I must remember that, but the sooner I can bring some Rhodesian-born teachers onto this staff the better. Then we'll gain balance back into the picture.'

Poor Johnnie, he really had problems now. The staff was deeply divided and moving into two camps – those who liked what he was doing – and those who didn't.

On my side of things, I was enjoying meeting the local people of Ruwa and Goromonzi who, despite all I had heard, were turning out to be well-educated and more realistic than I had been led to believe. They quite quickly recognised that there was a different hand on the tiller, saw what we were trying to do and largely took the pressure off.

A couple of months after I had arrived, I was helping out one day by collecting the school's milk from a neighbouring farm. The farmer's wife, Mollie Hughes, one of my WI compatriots, asked me to pop in for a cup of tea.

At that moment, her husband, Jack popped his head round the door and said, 'I would like to recommend you and John for honorary membership of the Ruwa Club in light of the wonderful changes you have brought to Goromonzi School.'

I was flabbergasted! Perhaps things were starting to get better after all and we were just so involved in it all that we didn't recognise it.

It had been the practice to hold Sports and Speech days on alternate years at Goromonzi. At the beginning of November, the first Sports day was upon us. It was only one day and had none of the presence and participation of the wonderful parents' weekends, which had become such a positive feature of Mzingwane and Tjolotjo.

As I walked down to the field on that first Sports Day, to help with timekeeping, I could hardly make my way through the crowd of people thronging through the gate. I caught sight of John's face with sheer disbelief written across it. The 220-yard race had just started and there were more of the contestants' supporters running on the track with them than there were outside watching! It was absolutely impossible to judge the winner.

Piccanins from the local reserve were running all over the place completely out of control, barging into the guests of honour and creating havoc. I thought back to the days we had so enjoyed at Mzingwane – the inter-school sports days with Tegwane and the excitement of each race. They did not have to put up with any of the rabble we were now facing at Goromonzi.

John called Hoffmann. 'Is it always like this?' he asked.

'Yes, isn't it wonderful?' He beamed. 'The chaos of Africa!'

John couldn't believe his ears. The staff seemed to be full of impractical academics that should have been in universities, not schools… they had simply no idea of what constituted a good sports event. What's more, it appeared that they would rather put up with an out-of-control situation, than having to face it and keep order.

He turned away despondently.

'This must change next year, sir.' It was Ushewokunze. 'My chief would not let this happen in the village.'

'I'm interested that you feel that…'

'I am a very fast runner, but nobody knows who has won the race – because everybody wants to run.'

'Well everybody can't run, Ushewokunze. Will you help me to make this work like a proper sports meeting next time?'

The Head Boy nodded his agreement.

Towards the end of term there was another fracas as the result of this chaotic sports day. Two staff members, Dr. Finlayson and Mr. Deans were in charge of ensuring that all chairs and tables were returned to the school. Forms 1 and 2 were detailed to help.

When the chaos of the sports had finished, there wasn't a boy in sight. The two men went down to the hostels to send them back again to finish up and fetch the chairs. All the boys returned except two. One of them, who refused to give his name when asked, walked defiantly away in the opposite direction.

Mr. Deans caught him by the collar. The boy swung round and hit Deans on the head with his fist. Deans retaliated and kicked the boy. There were many witnesses and the others in the dormitory all said the boy had made an unprovoked attack on Deans. But the boy, of course, said the first assault came from Mr. Deans and that 'he had even not hit Mr. Deans at any time.'

John called everyone concerned in to the office to try to get to the bottom of what had happened. It was very plain that the boy had been at fault. John told him that unless he apologised, he would be expelled. He did not apologise.

John called Hoffmann in to tell him what had happened and say he would be expelling the boy concerned. Hoffmann was furious and disinclined to believe that any pupil would make an unprovoked attack on a master. John asked him to please go away and find out for himself. He returned in due course.

'Well, apparently this lad is a bit of a hot-head,' Hoffmann conceded. 'I have just found out that it was this same boy who made a serious assault on another schoolboy last year. His record of behaviour while in this school has not been good.'

The boy was expelled.

As the end of the first year approached, John sat down to write his annual report with considerable relief that the school would be empty for the next six weeks:

The most urgent task during the year has been the tightening up on the standards of discipline. These had become very lax and frequently took the form of mass indiscipline by the boys. There have been cases of hissing at members of Staff, catcalling and riotous shouting when lights go out in the prep room, a disinclination to obey orders and bad behaviour during athletic meetings.

The general tone of the school has been bad and it will take several years before the more evil influences can be eradicated. This will only be achieved by united action from the staff. The main point of division has been between those who hold that kindliness and softly spoken persuasion are the only ways to attain obedience and those who believe that in this world there is still a need on occasions to be firm.

It is doubtful if the two outlooks can ever be reconciled, and my endeavours so far have been directed mainly at trying to ensure that these differences are not further complicated by the introduction of personal animosities into the dispute.

Racial issues complicate the matter since disciplinary measures, which would be unquestioned in a European school, are considered by the racially conscious to be no more than a venting of racial hatred on the unfortunate pupils.

I have ventured criticism of the layout and planning of this school, but I feel compelled to take this point further. Much of the criticism levelled at this school has, I am sure, been due to its having been built on a main road. All that happens is open to the public gaze. If the public who view what goes on were all sympathetic towards this kind of work, there would be less to worry about, but many of them look with eyes which only want to condemn. Eyes that could find much to ruin in any school. To place a school of this kind astride a public highway was, to say the least of it, very lacking in tact.

Much of the criticism which we now suffer is nothing to do with Goromonzi School but should be directed against the youth of the local Reserve who are frequently mistaken for pupils by those who pass by.

One of the people I had come to know through the WI and liked enormously was a talented musician and writer, Betty Scott. One day I heard a knock at the door and there was Betty, popping in for a cup of tea. Now, this was a breakthrough! Something that would have been quite normal for all my friends in England, was a triumph at Goromonzi. None of the other women I had been mixing with was yet prepared to come into the school itself – they seemed almost afraid to take that step. I was inordinately pleased and Betty began to pop in more and more regularly. With Betty having had the courage to "cross the threshold", so eventually, did the others.

Soon I found myself involved in requests to put on a play. The Ruwa Players was formed and I persuaded John that a repeat of *The Paragon* would not involve him in too much work as he knew the part so well, and it would help to take his mind off the school. The rest of the cast was not too hard to find although nothing of this nature had ever been performed in the area before. The Ruwa Club provided the perfect setting and again, the play was so good that we had to extend our run for a whole week.

Gradually, this wealthy community, which might well rather have kept the African in his place, was beginning to understand the importance of what was happening at Goromonzi. John's greater visibility at a place like the Ruwa Club, meant he had a chance within a more social environment to talk to them and to pass on his vision for African education.

They asked him to speak at a farmers' meeting and then at the WI. They began to notice an improvement in the behaviour of the pupils – instead of the slouching, shoulders drooping and hands-in-pocket youths the community had suffered for so long they now watched the same students striding freely with heads up and seemingly with a renewed enthusiasm and confidence. They saw caps raised in greeting and an obliging, cheerful attitude.

What was more important was that no more complaints went in to the Education Department. Finally, at the end of that first year the most uplifting thing of all was that, on the last Sunday evening service of the year, I looked round to see gruff old Willie White, a farmer who had sworn he would never put a foot in the place, sitting quite comfortably in the back row of the hall.

There was still a lot to do, but the school was on the way up.

At the beginning of 1954, Mrs. Hoffmann asked me if I would take over the Guides. She had been valiantly coping with them for the last five years and felt the time had come to hand it over. I was happy to do so, but the numbers were so great that I felt I also needed a bit of help. Kay Boast, wife of the District Commissioner at Goromonzi, who was later to become a very good friend, offered to come and give me a hand.

307

I asked her to read out the excuse notes, something which had been the practice for those who were unable to make it. If they were sick we would pray for them or make something for them and the Guides would then deliver it. Kay was reading away, when I heard her stop. I turned round and she was trying desperately to stifle her giggles. One of my best Guides, Emily, had written to ask me to excuse her "because she had a boiler between her legs".

Fortunately the girls howled with laughter too and they ended up knitting her a little "boiler" in memory of the event. It was wonderful laughter and for the first time I felt as I had done at Mzingwane, that we had crossed that barrier and were now in a normal, healthy pupil/teacher relationship, not a black/white or any other uncomfortable situation. I mentioned it to John. He also found it a very good sign.

John had again accumulated lots of leave and he had to take it. I was keen to see Mummy again and help her with the planned move to Rhodesia. John needed to take his mind off the day-to-day problems of the school. We planned to take the last term of the year off, which would mean less disruption for the children. Fortunately, both of them were well ahead in their classes and could afford a term away at this point.

The middle term of the year would therefore be Jill's last term at Townsend, as we had decided to move her to Girls High in Salisbury at the beginning of 1955. As we were making our plans in January that year, John's sister Jean and her John were transferred back to Barclays Bank in Salisbury. This was going to be wonderful for us all, as we'd been such very close friends in the early days. But in March, he was suddenly taken ill. I went in to the bank and was shocked by how ill and thin he looked.

It was cancer. Following an operation, he was told there was nothing anyone could do.

It was horrifying in its suddenness and the fact that it was larger than life, happy-go-lucky John who was affected. The older Swire-Thompsons arranged for a second opinion in Johannesburg, which simply resulted in a second operation – all to the same end. Jinny and John were going to need a lot of support.

We both agreed that I would take the children over by boat first, thereby giving John a couple more weeks with them both in Bulawayo, and that he would fly over in early September. Someone had suggested we try the Holland Afrika line as apparently the cabins were large and airy and the food was very good. We were booked to sail from Duncan Docks in Cape Town on the *M. V. Orangefontein* on the 14th August.

John was apprehensive about leaving the school in the hands of Hoffmann again as it was starting to come on so well, but we had little option – and after nearly two years, he needed to gain perspective on what had been achieved and what still needed to be done.

Three weeks before we were due to leave, we were visiting Jean and John in their new home, when I fell down the stairs. I couldn't get up and was in immediate pain. I found myself at the end of that evening up to my right knee in plaster of Paris, with a broken bone in my foot.

Just my luck! This is going to make the trip fun, I thought. Thank goodness the kids were older and able to look after themselves.

Well, I had no idea what was in store for us! The plaster was removed the day we left as the doctor thought it would probably have mended, and it would be much easier for me to walk round the decks and corridors. But by the time we arrived in Cape Town, I was in agony and my toes had gone black. I had to find another doctor who re-plastered it and concocted a rather gimcrack rubber heel, telling me not to walk on it for two days.

Well we were leaving that night and it was impossible to hop up the gangway – or should I say down the gangway. The children were horrified when they saw the ship.

'Mum, it's a tug!' said Richard. It was minute – only 8,000 tons. Instead of looking up three or four storeys to the decks of the Union – Castle liners they were used to, we were looking down from the wharf onto a rusted old iron deck, which proved to be just outside our cabin. I tried hopping down the gangway on Jill's shoulders, but eventually had to put pressure on the new, still wet plaster.

When we boarded the boat we found Rich was in a cabin with two other men and Jill and I were sharing with two women. I begged and pleaded to have him with us, as one of my main concerns was that he would be in a different lifeboat if anything should happen in this little cockleshell. To no avail. I hated the thought of Rich being in a cabin with strange men I didn't know, and was glad to find that both were similarly separated husbands with their families on board. Both were just as worried about that separation. They promised to look after Rich for us.

From the moment the ship started, Jill and Rich were sick. It was such a small ship that even with a slight swell it rolled horribly. Jill was sick for the entire voyage, hardly eating a thing from Cape Town to Southampton. She was pale, wan, listless and absolutely miserable.

Within a day, the new heel on my plaster had broken and I had to ask the ship's doctor if he had a pair of crutches I could use. Well, I should never have asked! Before I knew where I was, I was kneeling like a horse while the doctor and the ship's carpenter hammered blocks of wood onto my plaster.

This didn't work and ended up with my having to go to the doctor almost every day either to have it taken off, or have a new one put on.

'Och'n'tochter – the ship's doctor,' other passengers would cry as he came into sight. He then took rather a fancy to me and was always finding one excuse or other to come round. The children were very distressed to find me crying in the cabin one morning, trying desperately to relieve the pressure on my ankle with a small pair of nail scissors. My toes were black again, and as tight and fat as sausages with the pressure of the plaster. No tenniquoit this trip!

On the night of the traditional fancy dress party I managed to persuade Jill to leave her sick bed and go dressed as St. Trinians. She was vomiting as I dressed her up, poor child. The colour of her face was so deathly white that she looked almost green – pretty much in character with the role she was playing. She won a prize, which was something, but unfortunately the ship's purser was very drunk and started making passes at Jill, inviting her back to his cabin. He told her to come back and kiss him the next day but not to tell me! When last seen, he was throwing £5 notes out of the porthole with gay abandon.

The next day, the seas were mountainous and crashing over the iron deck. We had all the doors and portholes battened down. The cabins on Richard's floor, which was one down from ours, were awash even though the portholes had been closed. Rich had been delighted to find a flying fish on his bed! I was just glad he didn't realise the implications of a whole deck of flooded cabins.

It was terribly worrying without John there. Jill spent most of the trip lying on the bunk or on deck just praying for the end of the trip. I was in terror nearly all the time as the boat seemed so tiny on this great ocean.

I found it impossible to sleep, particularly when it was rough, as you literally had to cling onto the side of the bed so you didn't fall out while objects crashed down off the shelves. We were all awake and scared out of our wits one night when it was particularly bad and to comfort ourselves put the lights on and talked for hours. We eventually dropped off and awoke to hear Jill saying in a very tense little voice, 'The engines have stopped.' Well, she was up and out on the deck in a second to see what had happened.

There was no crew anywhere in sight, nothing. She sobbed as she ran through all the lounges and dining rooms – nobody. Then she looked out across the iron deck to see a huge pall of black smoke pouring from the engine room. She was absolutely panic-stricken. By this time, other passengers had started peering out of their cabins. It felt as though the crew had abandoned ship and left us to it.

We eventually discovered that one engine had burnt out altogether and the crew was down in the engine room, having trouble putting the core of the fire out. We had to crawl along with the most awful smell of burning for the next few days, leaving a great thick cloud of very dense black smoke behind us.

We were just recovering from that, when one of the men in Richard's cabin came to find me and said Rich had an awful pain. I found him with his knees drawn up to his stomach, screaming with pain. The ghastly doctor came and said he thought it was his appendix and he wanted him in the hospital to keep an eye on him. I begged to keep him as I didn't know what he'd do to him over there in 1st class, but he insisted. We would have to cross the iron deck in a terrible gale with waves crashing across it and I couldn't possibly go with my foot all plastered up. Fortunately two stalwart young men took him over.

Next day, the seas calmed and I was able to get across the deck to see him. He seemed much better, but I had to dissuade the doctor from ordering a helicopter to fly him to some obscure place in North Africa! I was horrified to see his room mate in the little hospital ward. Something had fallen on his head seven days beforehand, and he had been quite dotty ever since. Rich said the nurse had thought he would be all right, but told him to ring the bell if the man attacked him in the night!

To see the grey outline of wonderful England appear was the most indescribable feeling. We couldn't wait to get off the boat and onto dry land, we fell into the arms of my brother Dick and his wife Betty, weeping with relief.

A week later both Jill and Rich contracted a type of scurvy from the lack of fresh fruit and vegetables during our three weeks at sea. Their gums swelled up, they felt ghastly and couldn't eat. It was a nightmare – and still no John with me.

A doleful comment in my letter caught the agony of the moment:

Oh dear, I do hate being away from you – I feel as tho' I'm not married at all and never will be again. I do hope you will catch that plane on the 8th. Do remember that planes do leave on time!

It was wonderful to see him again and he did arrive on time. We'd promised ourselves a few days in Paris so we left the children with Mummy and went off with light hearts to enjoy the Louvre and anything and everything else which might be of interest.

It was the best holiday we had enjoyed together for a long time – so far from the problems of Goro'. We were thoroughly pampered by Terry Wills, Betty's brother, and were shown the very best France had to offer in our short few days with him.

Ten days later we received a telegram from Jean with the sad news that John Swire-Thompson had died. John had been my husband's closest friend for many years, so this was a terrible blow to him. I was very glad we had the distractions of the holiday to take his mind off this major loss.

The children loved England this time and it was amazing to me how much they could remember from previous trips. We visited friends and family in many different parts of the country and ended up staying for ten days, just before Christmas, at a hotel just behind Marble Arch. London at Christmas was something neither of our little colonial children had ever imagined could exist. We wandered down Oxford Street, looking at an animated toy-bear band in a Selfridge's window, nearly lost Richard when he jumped on a bus too early on the way to see the Queen at the Palladium, and then spent a blissfully happy Christmas Day with all my family around us in Exmouth.

We had left Goromonzi far behind, until a letter arrived from Marjorie Chapman, John's administrative assistant:

…things have been getting slowly worse for some weeks and I have seen several sides of all the various doings. Deans collapsed at School last Friday and is now on sick leave. I feel that the whole thing has a nasty taste about it.

Deans (as I told him) did stick his neck out but the chopper was waiting and Deans didn't stand a chance. I think he broke down under organised mental strain.

He had applied for two days' leave and the reply from the Department was that occasional leave was not granted to teachers, but he could apply for two days from his accumulated leave. Hoffman just sat on it. Not being used to underhanded work, I said "yes" when Deans asked if we had had a letter.

Finally Deans went in to see Hoffmann and asked Denys to be a witness to the conversation. I cannot help feeling that there has been dirty work at the crossroads but of course have no proof. Mugwhela volunteered that he was very sorry they would not have Deans for English.

My life in the office is best left to the imagination! If it were only that I wouldn't mind, it's just the general atmosphere of double-dealing, which worries me.

I hope you wont mind me telling you all the foregoing but I feel forewarned is forearmed and I look forward to the time when you will be back and take up the reins again. If only I had something concrete I would contact the Department, but it would only look like "tale-telling" at present.

John was fairly philosophical about it all. 'Well, at least it's not entirely my imagination – and you can't believe what a relief that is.' Her next letter, however, was more serious:

Alf Morris and Hoffmann have come to blows – something very fishy happened over Zachariah whom Hoffmann summarily dismissed. Three days after he had left we had a call from the Police saying they had a boy there who said he had been dismissed without notice or money in lieu of. Hoffmann went to the camp and the next thing we know is that Morris has to go and finds that Zachariah is being charged with rank disobedience at work! The result, Zachariah gets 21 days. I do not profess to know the whys and the wherefores, but I feel Zachariah definitely was let down somewhere.

I have also had great trouble with the books and decided the only way to keep my books in order was for Hoffmann to draw out £200 and then for me to balance the House accounts and get each Housemaster to sign out the money. It sounds simple enough but I have nearly become a nervous wreck in the doing of it.

It would have been better had I had complete charge of the safe, but Hoffmann's suggestion that I had the keys in the morning and returned them to

him at night was far from satisfactory to my way of thinking, so I said no –
all or nothing at all.

I think really the trouble is, knowing that there is no straightforward
backing behind one, and the knowledge that anything one says is agreed
with to one's face while the very thing one has said is a subject of laughter
in another place. Now for far more interesting news... the dam is filling up
and only needs 1" to the top of the spillway...

Alf Morris was a sensible and delightful man who John had taken
on to oversee the kitchens and the improvement of the school grounds.
He came from the mission field and did not have a degree. Unfortunately certain academic staff members treated him as lower than the
low as a result. Hoffmann in particular.

Interestingly enough Hoffmann's end-of-year report, which he had
written in John's absence, was supportive of many initiatives John had
started, such as the housemaster system which was, according to him:

...working excellently and the reports of housemasters should provide a valu-
able assessment for reference when pupils have left the school.

Prefects have been more effective, possibly due in part to increased privi-
lege and aloofness. The early morning PT has undoubtedly been of excellent
effect on the school in the matter of health and discipline and has certainly
given the prefects, who usually take it by Houses, valuable training beyond
the actual operation itself.

I would like to pay tribute to the administration of the Headmaster who
is always most willing to listen to suggestions from members of staff and
gives great encouragement to experiments in development put forward, as
well as being a great source of inspiration himself in this direction.

'If only I could believe him Nan. If only I could. I'm now so suspicious of his every move that I am going to have to try to overcome it
or it will overwhelm me... and that will help nobody. The sad thing
is that essentially we would make an excellent team – if only we
worked to the same agenda. The trouble is that most of the time I
genuinely don't know what his agenda is. Take this as an example –
why is he writing so positively about my initiatives? I cannot imagine,
because he has opposed every single one of them.'

John was delighted with his intake of Form Ones in 1955 – at last
they were coming in at the right sort of age and their eagerness to be

314

part of Goromonzi was touching. It was now a tremendous privilege to gain a place at the school and the great majority of new boy and girl entrants certainly recognised that.

But wow! the school had slipped back in the three months we had been away. It was remarkable − as we arrived back we saw that the same slouch of the shoulders, the same rude insolence was back. The same inability to look you in the eye. John was fed up.

'Look at me boy, when I talk to you,' I heard him say one morning. 'You look at your friends when you talk to them, why don't you look at me?'

I worried about him terribly, because he was not good at dealing with this sort of insubordination − this and the "hidden agendas" bothered him so much. He was too straightforward for it and felt that playing politics was simply wasting time particularly when there was no time to waste.

Then one day, soon after we returned, two of his old Mzingwane boys came to see him and they delighted us both with their tales of what they had been doing since they left school. They had excellent jobs and were doing very well, receiving glowing comments from their employers; both were so open and pleasant and so patently grateful to John for what he had achieved on their behalf. When they left, John was inspired again to "get this Goro' lot moving".

But he was to be pre-empted by a formal complaint from Hoffmann, directly aimed at Alf Morris, because ostensibly Morris's kitchen staff were so poor that they didn't bring enough saucers to go with the morning tea cups! John was astonished at the banality of it all, but he took the time to answer:

Wilson, the boy who brings the tea, has 20 each of cups and saucers for staff tea. He it is who has been bringing only half a dozen and I gather that his reason for not bringing them all is that most of them are never used. This would seem to be a sensible enough reason to me. However, he has been asked to bring the full quota in future whether they are used or not.

You will, I hope, see that your complaint regarding the shortage of saucers was wrongly directed at Morris. What worries me is that you should have used such a small matter and one so easy of solution, as substantiation of your assertion that Morris is constantly giving pinpricks to his staff.

Regarding the shortage of salt in the Dining Hall on Sunday evening, Yafele tells me that he did not see you on Sunday evening, so I assume that your mentioning of the matter arose from a report from Simpson who had seen Yafele. I find the matter even more problematical when Yafele tells me that on Monday morning after breakfast there was still some salt left in each of the tins on the tables.

'Can you believe the waste of time of all this Nan?' John raged. 'He didn't even bother to ask Wilson directly. What is the man up to?... I feel as though there is a time bomb round every corner. Shortage of saucers and salt – really – we have much more important things to be bothered about.'

To prepare Head Office, John wrote:

I am of the opinion that there is a certain "brewing up" at the school. It may develop into something unpleasant. There is no doubt that we have lost ground and this is particularly annoying after a very good term last term.

I have been in these schools long enough now to sense the atmosphere and whether trouble breaks out or not, I do feel that the tone of the school is now right for such trouble.

I am sending you three things to look at... firstly a list of things put in to me by Hoffmann. He claims that whatever he wrote was no more than an attempt at helpful advice. Perhaps it was, but I can't help the suspicion that the hysterical language used is merely there to whip up feeling. There is little doubt that Hoffmann is working up feeling against Morris, while Majuru works on the boys. When I asked him whether he had questioned the boy regarding the saucers, he came over all pious and said he did not wish to interfere. You will dismiss this as pure pettiness and so it is, but it is typical of the way in which a man can campaign against another with not more than petty jabs.

It is possible that I am inclined to exaggerate the importance of this place to the country. Most of the criticism from outside has stopped. That, however, is a very negative basis on which to judge the place. I cannot take it to the stage where there will be positive praise of what we are doing so long as we have a divided staff. I do not think this can ever be achieved while Hoffmann and his chief lieutenant Majuru are here.

You have seen the pleasant, jovial, earnest and enthusiastic characteristics, which he displays and you have seen the charming side of his nature. For the first term I was here, I was impressed by that also, it is only as I have worked with him that the petty, spiteful and dishonest aspects of his nature surface.

If you think I am wrong and too severe on the man, I would suggest that you make further enquiries from those who know him well. If you still feel I am wrong, please tell me and I shall take myself elsewhere. If however, you accept the honesty of my purpose and the accuracy of my judgement, then please do something about it as quickly as possible.

'I don't know that I'll get any reaction from Finkle (the new man in Head Office),' John told me, 'but Nan, I am not prepared to work here any more if every decent thing we try to do is denigrated and undermined. If this goes on much longer, the place will be in turmoil.'

It did go on – and on – and on. The political climate was hotting up, and for people such as Hoffmann, it was absolutely heaven sent. Fort Hare, the leading black university in South Africa, had been much in the news for some student insubordination, which resulted in some difficult outcomes for all involved. In October, John called the entire staff together:

There are several things about the school which are causing me worry and about which I wish to do some straight talking.

What I have to say is designed primarily to try and heal the present rift, which divides the Staff. The rift appears to me to be so deep and so wide that it cannot be much worse and I hope that it may open the way towards bringing the two sides together.

He went on to paint a picture of the school as it was when he had first seen it, for the benefit of several newer members of staff who might have been bewildered by his comments.

If you have read the Fort Hare report, you may say to yourselves "It can't happen here". I am trying to make it plain that it has happened here and it will happen here again unless we are of one mind about what we are doing and the methods we must adopt to maintain what progress may have been made since then.

In my experience, though others will very likely disagree, race relations never suffer from the enforcement of high standards of discipline. Only at Goromonzi have I been criticised for being too strict. I can recollect several occasions where they have been critical of leniency. The normal boy prefers a school where the discipline is strict. It was the request of the Head of the School that I introduced the marching up to Sunday services. Two other cases this term

317

have also shown how the boys like discipline in order to protect themselves from their own weaknesses or from the persuasion of their fellow pupils.

Boys will, of course, make the most of it and there is no ear that they would rather grouse into than that of any member of staff who may appear to show sympathy and this, I regret to say, is where much of the serious trouble in African schools starts.

In my opinion, and this has been confirmed by an African teacher, trouble in school is almost always brought about by a member of Staff or a very old pupil who should not be in school. In every case the pattern was the same, a clever jibe here, an insinuation there, a half-truth planted where he knew it would do most damage.

The troublemaker stays in the background planting the seeds then leaving others to cultivate and water. Always over-friendly with the boys, but when I was about, putting on a show of maintaining discipline. The boys were played upon until petty complaints assumed in their own minds an importance beyond what they merited.

I have told you this so that you may recognise the type and be on your guard. I have the authority to close the school down completely if trouble materialises and I hope you realise from that that it will be the pupils who will suffer if anyone attempts to use the school as a tool to achieve his end.

I expect loyalty to your colleagues. Criticism, whether direct, implied or suggested of one member by another should never be made in the hearing of pupils. This should be axiomatic and I regret the necessity for even having to state it.

I expect loyalty to the Head and please make sure that you understand me, I do not mean sycophancy. Heaven forbid. Everyone who has any self-respect will insist upon his right to criticise and I would be the last to discourage this. But the criticism must be offered in the right place. If you have criticisms, bring them to me. What I despise and condemn is the one who, having criticisms to make, prefers to keep them as Staff room gossip.

It is this kind of thing which leads to stories coming back to me, from as far away as Umtali that some in that area feel that they must commiserate with all at Goromonzi because of the terrible things that I do.

Good race relations depend upon mutual respect; respect must be earned, it cannot be granted by any political action. It is our duty to help the boys and girls of this school to earn such respect; not only on the examination mark sheet, but in good manners, polite and considerate behaviour, honesty and reliability – the virtues which any good school tries to inculcate into its charges.

I will end with this appeal to you all.

1. *that you try to reconcile your squabbles.*
2. *that you accept with considerable reservation any criticisms of me or any other member of Staff until you have heard both sides of the story.*
3. *that you accept no statement attributed to me unless you hear it from me.*
4. *that you support the policy, which Government wants, followed, and which it has appointed me to interpret and put into effect.*

Please remember — neither right nor wrong is ever wholly on one side.

Things improved marginally for the last couple of months of the year and by the time Speech Day came round the school was in a more positive and buoyant state of mind. One of the problems still faced was that the average entry age was much too high:

One thing, which still makes the work of our schools difficult, is the age of the pupils who are in them. In any European school covering the range of education, which we offer here, even a 19-year-old is considered a misfit. He is no longer a boy, but a man, he should be either at an institution catering for a University standard of work or he should be out in the world. At Goromonzi we have an age range of 13 to 26.

Consider the loss of productive capacity resulting from all the 16-, 17- and 18-year-olds who are still in the primary schools. Even the more advanced countries of the world cannot afford to keep youths of this age in school... can we, with our very limited resources, do what even a Welfare State cannot attempt?

Think also of the extent to which many of the African children aged 10, 11 or 12 who are excluded from schools because their places are occupied.

That we have been able to get along with such a wide age range is remarkable and an indication of the great keenness to learn that nearly every pupil has. They are attentive and anxious to learn and present few disciplinary problems there. But in many respects we miss the liveliness of the very young, we find that the mischievousness, which often leads on to many useful lessons in living, is overshadowed by the almost extreme seriousness of the present approach to work.

Good exam results come from hard slogging, rather than through that intelligence which learns despite every effort to sidetrack a teacher off his path, and every temptation to think of things other than the job in hand!

But we have boys and girls in this school who are young and I for one look forward to the day when the school is full of them. We need prefects of

17 and 18 who are near enough to the mischief-making age to know how best to deal with it.

We are constantly being told we are providing less education for the African population than we are doing. Some comparisons are interesting. 1932 was the year in England and Wales when the full impact of the post-war population bulge was being felt in their schools. If we do a comparison of that year with what we are doing, in 1932 in England and Wales, the total number of children undergoing full-time schooling at public expense was roughly 150 for every 1,000 of the population. This includes nursery schools, elementary schools and secondary schools, which were wholly or partly supported from public funds. 150 for every 1,000 population. Southern Rhodesia today is providing schooling for 180 out of every 1,000 of our African population.

How quick people were to criticise. Facts like these started to put some of the more blatant misrepresentations into proportion but they took so much time to research. However, John felt it was vital to carry out that work, so that he had the hard evidence ready when there was a campaign of mischief making going on, to counter the fact that the boys were being filled with erroneous facts and subversive and unhelpful thoughts.

Jill would be writing her Cambridge School Certificate at the end of 1956, so it was a serious year for her. She was rather set on a career in medicine, which made my heart quail – we would never be able to afford six years at medical school – but she decided to take Latin, Maths and Science in order to attain the marks she would need to gain entry.

The joy of her life at the moment, was Bonny. She had longed for a horse ever since Mrs. Booth's riding lessons at Essexvale and we had heard of some people at Marandellas who had an old horse we could have for nothing. One night, just before midnight, we met Bonny off the train at Melfort siding. Jill rode the long 12 miles home, with us following behind her in the car, lighting the way. Bonny was no show pony but Jill loved him dearly and the school holidays were now filled with donkey derbies. Richard, Ian and David Chapman on donkeys called Sadza and Mputu, and Jill rather grandly parading about on Bonny.

It was Richard's first year at Plumtree. He had been put into John's old house, Milner, and we were both looking forward to resuming our acquaintance with the school. It was many years since John had visited his old home because we had fought a little shy of it after the Plumtree "incident". But now, Pat Pattison had returned as Headmaster so it was all very satisfactory for us – and for Richard.

Probably most exciting of all for me – Mummy was on her way to live in Southern Rhodesia – with the promise of an almost immediate visit from Dick and Betty as well.

1956 started well. John was pleased with an even better intake than the year before, both in terms of the reduction in age and the promising calibre of youngsters coming in.

'They are so refreshing Nan. You can't believe the difference.'

Hoffmann still lurked like an unpleasant shadow behind everything. There was a cave down by the dam where I used to walk the dogs and I would frequently see him in there, head to head with a couple of prefects. He would always jump up and be perfectly charming if he saw me, but I could see from the body language just what was going on.

April meant that it was time for Richard's first Plumtree sports weekend. We saw so little of him with only 12 weeks of school holidays per year that we jumped at the chance of spending the four days of Easter at his school and of being part again of the Plumtree scene, but this time as parents. The only complication was that Hoffmann was not going to be able to stand in for John as he was in hospital and would only be returning the day after Easter.

My heart was heavy as John told me that although the festivities started on Thursday night, he didn't think he could leave until Friday as the school would be in rather less experienced hands. We would also have to come back first thing on Monday instead of waiting for the prizegiving that afternoon. It was a long trip. We would end up spending more time travelling than we would at Plumtree. But it was worth the slog.

'This blasted school,' I muttered. 'Sometimes we have to come first Johnnie.'

'We will duckie, we will. Just give it a bit more time yet.'

We revelled in the two days we had at Plumtree. It was apparent that Richard was growing in stature with the independent and free nature of the place – an inheritance that still persisted strongly from his grandfather's day. We caught up with many friends and it was, without question, the most delightful weekend we had enjoyed for many years. All too reluctantly we left at 4 a.m. on Monday to be back for the resumption of school the next day.

A week later John received a letter signed by five members of staff, lodging a protest about the fact he had put Denys Chapman in charge while he was away. Denys was, by far, the longest serving housemaster and therefore the most senior, but John was also clear he was, in any event, the most responsible. The complaint arose because Chapman taught a practical subject and they felt he should not be in charge of an academic school – even though many of the students had gone home for the long weekend and there were no lessons taking place!

Hoffmann's name was at the top of the list. John wrote to the Department:

When I put Mr. Chapman in charge for a weekend, I considered it to be a purely internal arrangement since my absence from the School could not absolve me from responsibility for anything, which might have gone wrong. Had I been on leave the responsibility would then have fallen on another, but, on this occasion, I considered that my responsibility for the School was in no way diminished by my absence. Since the responsibility remained mine, I left in charge the one whom I considered would be best able to ensure that nothing would go wrong.

'How can I possibly do a decent job of work when I am constantly distracted by the stupidities of something like this?' he said that evening, the benefits of the Plumtree trip now completely obliterated.

'I have asked Finkle to come out tomorrow to look at what is happening out here. I have decided to hand him my resignation unless Hoffmann goes.'

'My love, I feel you should resign anyway – this job will kill you.'

'Well, let's just see what happens.'

The letter was posted and when John came home that evening, he told me he had also put in an application for the position of Provincial Head of the Inspectorate. John had at last realised that he had really had enough. I was absolutely delighted.

Next day Finkle came down and spent all morning at the school talking to boys and staff. I had them both home for lunch, but felt that the conversation was rather stilted and awkward with me around. I left the men to it, to chat about the future.

But I couldn't keep away. For three hours they talked. For three hours I listened at the door and prayed that John would have the determination to stick to his plan. The provincial inspectorate job would be challenging but less wearing and I was not prepared to lose the most precious thing in my life to the strains and stresses of this place. There still seemed to be precious little appreciation of what he was doing, under the most trying circumstances – and he was still receiving very little support from Head Office.

Finkle was doing his hardest to persuade John to stay. I groaned inwardly as I heard him wearing John down.

'Just give it another two years, John. That'll turn it around.'

'Another two years here will just about finish me,' I heard him say. ' But, OK, I'll give you that, but please be sure you can mount a rescue operation if I fall down on the job.'

When he came out his face told the story, I rushed over to hug him and we clung to each other hoping and praying that he would have the strength to be able to continue educating and turning out the leaders the country needed within the difficult environment of Goromonzi. The one positive aspect of this decision to stay was that Hoffmann would be leaving the following week.

Chapter 14

Golden times –
but the heartbreak returns

We started noticing the differences in unrelated little ways. The girls I had come to know so well through Guides were laughing more easily again and what was more important, laughing with rather than against us. Mr. Majuru volunteered to take on extra duties saying almost mysteriously, 'I have some time to make up.' The boys sang better in assembly, they looked smarter at morning inspections, there was a sudden and dramatic fall off in all that bullying and intimidation in the hostels.

By the end of the year, John's own step seemed firmer and more self-assured and the rifts in the staff had all but disappeared. It was sheer joy for me to pop down at morning break and hear the peals of healthy laughter floating through the corridors and staff room.

In September, we were due to move into another house across the main road and I was busy sorting out the painting and starting up a garden from the bush. I looked forward to moving farther away from the school, so that we could sit out on the verandah in the evenings and escape the trials of the day without having them right on our doorstep. The house had been designed with a folding door between the sitting and dining rooms so that we could cater more effectively for the ever-increasing flow of VIPs.

Staff movements were still a problem and disruptive for everyone concerned. As John completed his fourth year at Goromonzi, he realised that from a complement of 22 staff, only four had been there when he started. The school had been such an unhappy place for so many that some movement was understandable, but he was concerned at the ease with which the Department would summarily move people around. His report at the end of 1956 remarked on the changes in his four years and said:

There have been 23 permanent departures from the staff at Goromonzi in this time. Reasonable standards of teaching and behaviour have been maintained but these constant changes must have a bad effect on the development of the children. No two teachers approach any lesson in exactly the same way, nor do they have the same methods of handling pupils nor the same manner nor the same accents. Each change requires adjustment by the pupils and must involve the loss of much effective teaching time. Where any man wishes to remain in a school he should be allowed to do so without any loss of seniority for future promotion.

The school now had three full-sized football fields and a permanent running track, four tennis courts, two hockey fields and two netball pitches. Next on the agenda was a cricket pitch.

For the first time, Goromonzi won the inter-schools athletic contest held at Kutama – in fact, it was the first time in the history of the competition that it had been won by a school other than Domboshawa or Waddilove. The excitement was intense. John's satisfaction was that the event had been superbly run, and the athletes excelled themselves, and so did about 60 pupils who had asked if they could go along to cheer them on. There was a feeling of community developing at the school.

There was also an increased amount of extra-mural activity taking place… dramatics emerged strongly, as the pupils were natural and unaffected actors, but among them were a number of budding playwrights whose plays were very successfully enacted in Shona and Ndebele. Singing was always a highlight, and there were tense and exciting inter-house drama and singing competitions of real quality. The Young Farmers Club, the Photographic and Cultural Societies were moving forward in leaps and bounds… and games like chess were being played keenly in the evenings.

In addition to the Scouts and Guides, the pupils had asked if they could start up a Wolf Cub pack as the age of entry into Form 1 started to drop. The seniors were now running this very effectively and it was a good way of encouraging new pupils to become involved in school activities. The Student Christian Association held regular weekly meetings on Sunday evenings and had a consistently strong following. Some of the senior boys and girls asked if they could set up a Sunday School class for the young piccanins in the reserve. These initiatives were all solid signs of a healthy school.

Every Saturday, there would be some sort of entertainment arranged – if it wasn't a cinema it would be concerts, games evenings or talks, all arranged by a Committee of pupils themselves. Current Affairs university lecturers, leading Africans and Europeans in a variety of fields would come out and give their time in talks, workshops or seminars. Choirs and orchestras would arrive from Salisbury and the Salvation Army band was a highlight of the calendar. Sometimes the school would negotiate an event of international interest, such as a concert by the famous singer, Mr. William Warfield, which was organised through the US Consul General; or a much appreciated demonstration by US athlete Bob Matthias.

I was touched when one of the Committee members asked if I would give some concerts on Saturday nights. I wasn't sure that the school would be greatly interested in classical music, so I put together a very light programme, playing popular songs of the First World War and light classics of that era. These went down well, and I was asked to do more. So I practised hard, and tried to theme the evenings so that the audience gained a little understanding of how this type of music had developed, highlighting the differences in the backgrounds of, say, Chopin and Mozart.

Some of the students really seemed to enjoy the concerts and one of my favourite letters said:

Your last Saturday evening's performance, Madam, is to my mind the type of entertainment we should be encouraged not only to appreciate but also to take away with us when we leave this place

Perhaps my view of this is not very popular here, but let me assure you, Madam, that those with whom I have come into contact since that day wish such evenings were given much more often. They, like me, are convinced we can learn more from such than from our day-to-day Kwela or some such daily music we hear around us.

I have a faint liking for symphony music and I think cultivating or being helped to cultivate a liking for the Classical Music would put me and those of like mind on the rails perhaps forever.

If many do not appreciate Classical Music, would you Madam, mind playing to those liking few? We should be grateful.
Your student, David Makamure

I was interested by how much encouragement I got from one boy who had appreciated one concert and written to tell me so. I began to realise how remorseless it must feel to John when he was giving of his very best all the time, to be constantly misinterpreted and undermined... and why he gained such pleasure from unsolicited moments of appreciation.

At around this time, and right out of the blue, came a suggestion from the Headmaster of Prince Edward, a well-considered European government school in Salisbury. He said he would like to bring the boys of his Scientific Club out to give some presentations and try to set up a similar club at Goromonzi. He expressed an interest in an ongoing, close association between the two. This close association was formed and persisted happily for many years. Then the Headmaster of Peterhouse, a leading private school near Marandellas, invited 12 pupils to attend a concert given by the Rhodes University Choir.

John was so pleased. The more the schools interacted the more African and European pupils would understand and accept each other. He was very keen to capitalise on these overtures and in turn arranged for cricket matches to be played between Goromonzi and other European schools. The barriers that had once been there were falling fast.

In addition, there had developed over the years a better relationship and understanding with Mission schools and Training Colleges. John could phone Heyi Malaba at Waddilove or Mac Partridge at Luveve and have immediate empathy with them in terms of what they were all trying to achieve. He was always very happy to send his boys on for further training under Mac Partridge's skilled eye, and knew he would get the highest calibre of students from Heyi. Whenever he talked to Heyi, John would remember back to the dedication of the Malaba parents at Tjolotjo and how that devotion had paid off in that they now had one son a minister in the Church and another son running an institution like Waddilove. If Waddilove had good students above the Goromonzi allocation they were allowed, John would, on Heyi's recommendation, always do his best to accommodate them.

These were good, positive times and his report for the year ended:

The standards of discipline throughout the year have been satisfactory. There have been few cases of serious breach of discipline though much still remains

328

to be done to improve standards of honesty among pupils. The Prefects are doing a lot to eliminate this and every attempt is being made to build up opinion against this kind of thing.

Some pleasing reports have come back to the School regarding the behaviour of pupils when meeting people outside the school. Such reports are very gratifying…

Demand for places continues at a high level and a noticeable feature is the increasing demand for secondary education for girls. For the first time it would have been easily possible to find 40 or 50 suitable girls for admission to Form 1 in 1957 – the first time I would have been able to fill a whole class of girls. In my opinion the opening of a girls' secondary school is now one of the most pressing needs of the educational system.

John still used the cane as the ultimate punishment. It would only be administered, and only ever by him, once a certain number of impositions had been gained by any one pupil. He believed most sincerely that a few quick strokes of the cane was a great incentive to good behaviour, but, what was more important, it was over and finished with, without the lingering resentment of a longer and more arduous punishment. During this key period, John felt one of the greatest signs of improvement was that he was now using the cane so rarely that it lay gathering dust on top of his cupboard.

The day still started with PT and inspection for the boys – not the girls. They would stand by quietly watching the proceedings.

One day as he was striding down the lines of perfectly turned out boys, his gown blowing in the wind; he felt a frisson of anticipation or excitement running through the ranks of the more senior boys towards the back. He knew something was up.

By this stage John was very bald on top and he had a fringe of hair running round the sides of his head that only just met at the back.

As he strode down the line he spotted a youngster in Form IV, Edmund Garwe. He was hard put not to laugh. The boy had shaved his head to match John's bald pate.

'Garwe, I think you and I have something to talk about,' he said without a smile.

When Garwe showed up at his office later in the day, John invited him in sternly and made him wait while he finished a paper he was working on.

Without looking up, he said, 'What you did today took a great deal of courage. You might well expect to be caned or perhaps even suspended for such a deed.'

'Yes, sir,' said the almost bald youngster.

John sat back. 'I regard what you have done as the sign of a healthy teenager and I like your spirit. However, we cannot have the whole school doing the same thing or thinking that it is in order to do this type of thing, can we?'

'No, sir'

'What do you think I should do about it?'

'Maybe a small caning... a very small caning?'

'...And you will shave off the rest of the hair on your head?'

A very, very small caning it was... with the solicitous enquiry as to whether he had a sharp razor available to shave the rest of his head.

When John related the story to me, he said he had been so pleased to see genuine naughtiness taking place rather than insolence.

'The boy's eyes were like saucers, Nan – he was terrified – but he still had the guts to do it. I like him – he's potential Head Boy material in a couple of years time.'

Next day at inspection, as John strode down the lines and without checking his step as he passed the shining, hairless pate, he said quietly, 'Nice haircut, Garwe!'

The school was going much, much better... but it would have been naïve to think that trouble was behind us.

It had been the rule, even before John took over, to read out the mid-year examination results in assembly. As he stood up to do so in the mid-term of 1957, there was a murmuring amongst the pupils. John looked over to the Head Boy, who hung his head. He started to read again – and again the murmuring took place. There appeared to be only a small number involved by the sound of it, but it would have to be dealt with. John stopped the assembly and said he would be talking to the Head Boy and that a decision would be taken on what had arisen, to be announced at assembly the next day.

When the Head Boy came in to his office, he handed John two small pieces of paper. The first was an anonymous note he had received, headed "Cops and Captain":

What have you done about our petition? What are you our head for? If you ignore our wishes. Sadza and impositions???

We want you to negotiate with the Principal and if you don't...??? Now Two Days more and if nothing is done before Tuesday...!!!

'This is very nasty... what have you done about it?'

'Well sir, I did not know what to do for a while. Then I decided to write back and reason with them. The other note is a copy of what I first wrote when I was planning a letter to send back to them. The letter was going back signed by myself and the prefects and you can see what I was planning from those rough notes...

We just can't understand your fears — the Principal is always ready to nego- tiate with us provided we ask in a good way. I am of the opinion that the Prin- cipal thinks that the school lists are good for us, since we never requested him as father to stop the system.

'What has the reaction been to this?'

'Today was the reaction, sir.'

'Right. How are we going to tackle this?'

Headmaster and Head Boy sat for the next hour talking through the pros and cons of the affair.

'Do you know who is involved?' John asked.

'Yes sir, I do, but I ask you to believe me that it is too hard for me to tell you.'

John was happy to respect this, but not to let them feel they had got away with it.

'They don't like the reading of the lists in assembly, sir,' he was told. 'Those boys who are lazy or who don't get high marks are cross when their names are read out. They feel that their school reports will tell them whether they have to do more work.'

'The school reports can too easily be ignored, particularly when parents can't read them. This is something that is common practice in many schools. It is designed to say "well done" to those who have gained good marks. I also use it to encourage the boys and girls who have improved even if they are at the bottom of the list. My experi- ence shows me that this is one of the best ways of encouraging those at the bottom to improve.'

'I know that, sir'

'How widespread is this feeling?'

'Most of the boys are cross because the school has been very happy

331

but these ones who are causing problems are bad intimidators, especially for the new boys.'

'It is important that I know who they are because I cannot fix the problem otherwise. If you can find a way to tell me, that will be fine. In the meantime, I think your letter has given me an idea. I will tell them in assembly tomorrow, that I have had long negotiations with you, but that the lists will continue to be read because the request to stop reading them was not done in the right way. I will always listen when I am asked to do something... but I will not do anything unless I am asked in the right way.'

At assembly the next morning John said that he was very angry to see the threatening letter which had been written to the Head Boy but that he did not know who had written it. Because the murmuring had been the coward's way of doing things and the boy or boys concerned had chosen this way of airing a problem, the whole school would have to spend an hour weeding the new cricket pitch that afternoon. He extended an invitation to those boys who had wanted him to stop reading the lists to come and discuss the matter with him at any time. He was not surprised when nobody came forward.

A few days later, John found a note under his door – *"the boys you want are N and P"* it said. John was just considering what he was to do with the information, when he received a letter from his old teacher and friend at Mzingwane, Roger Malusalila:

> *I was on my way to Marandellas on the train last week when one of your Goromonzi boys was seated next to me. We started to talk about you and I said I had worked with you at Mzingwane. He asked if I would give Mr. Hammond a message without telling him who told you. I said I would. He then went on to tell me about some trouble you had had at Goromonzi and said that most of the boys regretted that it had happened. He said the names you needed were N and P.*
>
> *I hope I have not mixed up names as it is now some days since I spoke to the boy.*
>
> *I am now a farm boy, I milk, herd, feed pigs and what not, I have done this for two weeks now. Some life for a change!*

John smiled with fond memories of the man and was pleased that he was taking the chance to spend time away from Mzingwane and be back home for the holidays.

Now that he had corroboration of those names he'd be able to act without incriminating the Head Boy or any of the prefects. Both boys involved were expelled. It was interesting that the girls very seldom seemed to become involved in these disruptions. John wondered if they would when numbers increased, but somehow he felt it was unlikely. The girls would be naughty in a different way, but they tended to respect the bigger decisions and the reasons why.

What was surprising – and gratifying – was how many letters came in from his pupils during the following school holidays. Most of them saying that they were sad about what had happened. One letter came in from a boy he regarded very highly and it gave him great encouragement. He was pleased to be able to pass on these sentiments and expressions of hope to the staff which were, almost without exception, right behind what the school was doing.

You will be glad to know that I have been with a publishing company for the whole holiday. I have enjoyed every minute of my work and I am glad to be experiencing what office work is like.

I herein enclose £7 for my school fees, which is part of my pay. I hope it's something that will make me work harder as I am clearer now how hard it is to earn money!

I was very sorry sir for the happening of last term, well it's something that has to be fought out by the application of a fatherly solution and I can well remember a few lashings from my father when I was young because I had done what was not right. I have a belief that it's only at school where each one of us has a chance of learning how to think straight and I believe we have not realised how short some of us have got to be still at school.

It's my conviction that each day is an important verse in our life and we can learn much that can be of use to us in the near future. Life outside is too fast to give one a chance to train him the right way. I also believe that if any of us are going to be good leaders, we must learn to be good followers of what is right. I hope sir, you will continue to lead us as your flock and I am sure one day your training will be a guiding factor in each one of us.

I hope and pray that the new term will start with a new spirit among the students and I think many regret the happening as I have done.
My parents send their best wishes to you and Mai Hammond.
Your pupil,
Hosea Mapondera.

Thank God, John thought – if boys of the calibre of young Mapondera are prepared to speak out against this kind of thing, then the future leaders of the country would have a chance of achieving something sound and good.

John had written to the father of both boys who had been the cause of the trouble and was a little surprised to receive a response from one of them:

Thank you for your letter of the 5th instant informing me that my son will not be readmitted into school this term.

I am deeply sorrowful and I cannot do otherwise but to let you know that I am sending him to you at the re-opening of the school term. You are the father and whatever he does you have to severely punish him.

I am a member of the Police force and my son is expected by right to set a very high standard of good behaviour. If he does not, then the Principal of the College must take drastic measures and I will support the Principal.

Sir, see what you can do with him, I was able to pay all the fees this year. Punish him severely.

John was in a bit of a predicament. The father was obviously very distressed at his son's behaviour. John had already expelled the boy and was not sure whether taking him back, even if it was to "punish him severely", would be the right thing to do – yet he had great sympathy for his father, who would have had such high hopes for the lad.

At that moment there was a knock at the door.

'Mr. Hammond, may I see you?' It was Majuru. 'I have this boy you expelled back here.'

John called him in and told him about the letter he had just received from the boy's father.   Then he looked at Majuru.

'Majuru, I am only just beginning to feel I can trust you again. I felt you had been filled up with some of the words one of our previous staff would use to cause problems. I want to ask you outright. Was this boy one of those who would listen to those words?'

'He was, sir,' Majuru replied. 'But I would like to try and help because I know this boy and I know the father. The boy told me about his father's letter before I came to see you. I am asking if you will take this boy back, give him a strong caning, then give him to me for six weeks to talk to and to show him that he is wrong.'

John agreed to do this. It was risky because he still wasn't quite sure where Majuru stood – but it was a way of resolving the problem and John was a firm believer in Africans disciplining their own people. If it did not work, he would definitely be expelled for good.

The climate was now ripe to introduce a parents' weekend at Goromonzi. This had never been attempted at the school before, the only interaction with parents taking place was during the alternating one-day Sports or Speech Days. John always liked to spend time listening to parents so that he could gain an understanding of what their problems were. He wanted them to feel part of the place and in turn, to be able to speak to them in greater depth about what the school was doing.

It took two months to organise a full parents' weekend, combining Sports and Speech Days, similar to those at Plumtree and Mzingwane. As the date approached several of the boys suddenly put up a protest at having to find a place to sleep in the bush. They seemed to think they were much too grand for this kind of arrangement.

When this was revealed, the boys really received the sharp end of John's tongue as he told them of his own experiences at Plumtree, the fact that the same arrangements were still in place and of what a success the weekends had been when introduced at Mzingwane.

'The trouble is Nan, some of these boys are too grand by half. It doesn't seem to infect the girls as much. But the boys really need to be pulled down a peg or two to gain some understanding of how lucky they are. They seem to feel that because they've gained entrance into Goromonzi the world is their oyster and everyone will now owe them a living. Unfortunately, the sad reality is, that when most of them go home, they are probably treated like the demi-gods they believe they are…'

The staff wives rallied round to do the catering and with 150 people expected it took quite a bit of organising. The domestic science girls did the cooking and found it great fun to be working hand in glove with staff wives. John took the opportunity to ask each class to put on an exhibition of work done that term, with each extra-mural activity demonstrating what they did. The choirs would sing and a play be performed. It was to be a very full weekend.

The parents arrived in their droves and were allocated to "boys" and "girls" dormitories. It was good to see that the dormitories were, despite the protests, as neat as a new pin. The girls had been given the job of making them look pretty and there were great bunches of

BELOVED AFRICAN

flowers in the centre and little cakes on each bedside locker. They tied ribbons round the bed heads denoting which was the "red", "green", or "yellow" dorm'.

The standard of the sports was very good indeed. Some of these boys could go on to become great athletes. They had always been very good at running, particularly long distance, but competitors in events like high jump were now putting in a challenge to the national records. John was especially pleased to see that the boy who won the high jump was the one who had sent the threatening letter to the Head Boy. Majuru had done a fine job.

John's speech to the parents was very well received:

The aim of all of us is to turn out young men and women who will be useful, hardworking, reliable and responsible citizens of this young and vigorous country.

If the school tries to insist upon certain standards of work and responsibility, but the parents care little for those things, it will be the child who will suffer. In the same way, if the parents set a high standard of behaviour and discipline and the school does not demand a similar high standard, again the child will suffer and the parents will be disappointed. In all things we must try to work together.

I always welcome reports from parents upon how they find their children when they are at home.

The Staff will do all they can to make life pleasant and successful for the pupils at Goromonzi, and the pupils for their part have a responsibility to make Goromonzi a pleasant place for the Staff to work in.

We are undertaking a vastly important piece of work. Work which calls for the very greatest contribution each of us can make because the price of failure would be very high indeed.

As he left the podium, a ramrod-straight and distinguished looking father put out his hand. John didn't recognise him, but saw that his eyes were moist.

'Thank you *baba* (father). You have made this police father very happy.'

At this stage there were major moves taking place on the political front in the country. Southern Rhodesia was now part of a Central African Federation of three countries, including Northern Rhodesia and Nyasaland. It had been felt that Southern Rhodesia, which had

336

achieved the most in terms of infrastructure, economy, education and health systems, and Northern Rhodesia, which had the wealth of the copper mines behind it, brought together with the smaller, agriculturally based Nyasaland... could become a future force to be reckoned with in Africa, working together as a federation. Bureaucratically however, it brought fair overload catering for a federal government on top of national governments.

There had been many doubts as to how effective it would be — particularly from Southern Rhodesia's perspective, as there was a feeling of having to "caretake" the other two countries. But each had been promised that should Federation not work, they would be granted their independence from Britain. It seemed, as a result, to be a reasonable deal.

The political stage at the time was dominated by a powerful, but genial presence in the rotund shape of a Jewish former railway engine driver and a man of earthy and practical wisdom, Roy Welensky — a man who was to become a considerable statesman.

Jill had gained a good Cambridge School Certificate with Matriculation Exemption, which was sufficient for entry into a South African university. When she realised that medicine was going to be too costly, she rather grandly announced she would be a vet. Edinburgh had the best veterinary course of any university but that was out of the question, not just because it would be far too expensive for her to regularly travel there from Southern Rhodesia, but also because it was difficult to gain entry from the colonies. So we looked at Ondestepoort in South Africa. This would mean she would have to learn Afrikaans and there seemed little point in that.

So we examined the possibility of physiotherapy, but the country's Chief Medical Officer, Jimmy Robertson, told us quite categorically that there were very few opportunities for girls in positions of that nature in the country at that time. Occupational therapy, on the other hand, might be a possibility. But Jill wasn't the slightest bit interested in occupational therapy.

Most of her school friends would be going to Cape Town University while most of my friends' daughters were going overseas to be "finished". I had always liked the thought of her going to England after school. We had looked at finishing schools, but she wasn't keen on that idea. Although she was very musical and had the qualifications, she wasn't interested in music as a career either.

So eventually we agreed she would do Form V anyway, as this would give her a year post-Matric before going down to South Africa and she could study biology in that time. She felt this might be an option to pursue at university. She might also stay on for Form VI, being a year younger than her class.

John and I agonised over what to do. She was very bright but there were few scholarships or bursaries for girls in those days.

We were not well off and had to conserve our income carefully. We had Richard to think about as well – and at that time, it was still considered that girls would get married and be supported by their husbands, while boys would have to be the regular income earners.

We had looked at a number of lovely finishing schools, like the one at Ashridge in Kent, all of which Jill turned down rather contemptuously. She was still set on going to university with her friends. We eventually agreed to her doing a year's secretarial course in England ... thinking this would do her no harm in the meantime and hoping that we could see how things turned out after that.

As she reached the end of Form V reality dawned that she would not be going to a South African university. She rebelled completely about staying on at school another year. She told us she hated the other few girls who would be carrying on into Form VI and she asked us why should she do it anyway if she was only doing a secretarial course? In her book at the time, this was the lowest of the low. It was not an easy time.

In the last week of January 1958, Jill and I went to see her school friends off on the train to Cape Town University. My heart was in my mouth as I saw the longing on her face. I wept inwardly at the difficulties we had had in being unable to send her to university – especially when John's pupils seemed to gain all the scholarships they needed. It wasn't fair.

I arranged to take her to England as soon as I possibly could after she left school. It would be a good chance for Mummy to go back and see friends and I would spend three months with Jill settling her down. She was only just 17 and it felt so young for her to be leaving home. We managed to get her a place at St Godric's college in Hampstead. She was very upset to be leaving and being the only one of her friends going to England. Dear Rich saved up his money to buy her a radio so that she could keep listening to the World Service to hear how we all were at home.

After a trip that lasted three days, flying only during daylight hours, as was normal at that time, and landing at Ndola, Entebbe, Benghazi and Rome, we arrived to the dankest, darkest, greyest Britain I could remember. I left Jill at her new residence which seemed just as dank, dark, grey and dirty. it was a great disappointment and I felt wretched at the awfulness of it all. I wrote to John:

> *I must confess I was disappointed in the S. Godric's buildings – very old and rather drab in and out, creaking floors and it didn't look over clean. I would say they were adequate, but that's about all. Jill thought it all a bit shabby but once she gets to know the girls and starts doing something I don't think that will matter. We left Jill just going into supper with a lot of girls – all new and one from Bulgaria. She was looking scared stiff and didn't feel like supper…*
>
> *I wasn't overjoyed with the place and kept wondering in my usual infuriating manner whether we shouldn't have sent her to Ashridge or Cape Town, but Ann reassured me strongly that she would reap far more benefit through being near London and all that it offers.*
>
> *Jill was very depressed, but I think it was the darkness, strangeness and sharp, rude familiarity of the Cockneys that depressed her. I can understand it perfectly! She's quite enjoying the work but said the teachers were going too slow for her.*
>
> *Life is too short for me to be away from you for so long. How nice it would be if your letter tomorrow said you were coming over to that conference at Cambridge in June… but I am thinking of you with much pleasure this eve. having a good old chat with Davis at Gwelo, and tomorrow you'll be seeing our dear old Rich – simply lovely.*

My close childhood friend from Southminster days, Jill Castle, rescued us from the dumps, arranging for Jill and me to spend a memorable weekend with her family of four on their farm near Epping. They were warm, welcoming and wonderful to her and invited her to come out any time she wanted.

She was so determined to get out of the secretarial course as soon as possible that she ended up completing the 12-month course in six. Eventually she did settle and grew to simply love her time in London and we had a dreadful job getting her home again! In the meantime, she made her own decision to study piano at the Guildhall School of Music and Drama while working with a firm of stockbrokers in the City.

Richard in the meantime was taking a leading role in the annual Gilbert and Sullivan musicals and in school activities in general. He had dropped into Plumtree life very easily. My constant and continuing anguish was how little we saw of him being so far away. It looked as though he was going to be as tall as John and the race was on to keep his clothes fitting and to recognize him again after each three month gap.

1958 and 1959 were almost unremarkable in that the school was simply doing increasingly well. There were the niggles of any school of course, but none were like the problems of the past and certainly none of them reflected the "sick school" syndrome we had known in our early days at Goromonzi.

The staff had been settled for a while when one of the housemasters, Edward Mazaiwana, was offered the chance to study in the United States. John advised him to grab the opportunity. Edward completed his graduate course in education and wrote to John in August 1959:

Early this year, you had visitors from the United States at Goromonzi School. They were brought out there by Bishop Dodge of the American Methodist Church. They arrived back in the States before I left, and came to our College to see me and to speak to the students about their visit to Africa. One of the things that impressed them most of all was Goromonzi School. They said that they had had a wonderful reception and that the Principal had taken much pains to take them round the school and show them the work that was being done there.

I was so happy to hear these people speak so well of our school and its people. I also attended the first concert given by the Ambassador Quartet from S. Rhodesia in New Jersey. After the concert, I was told by the boys that they had been to Goromonzi School to sing before they came out. They were very appreciative of the comments and suggestions which Mrs. Hammond had made to help them improve their performances. I thought Mrs. Hammond might be glad to hear that. I am sure she probably did not realise how much she had done for these boys.

I spoke to a Lions Club in North Stockton some time this year and after I had spoken they decided that they would try to raise enough money to provide two or three scholarships each year at Goromonzi. I mention this to you because I think that it is important you know something about it before the money is sent to your school. Will you advise me as to how you would like to receive this money? You will be under no obligation as to how these people will want their money used.

The next significant event in the school's life was that for the first time, John had a Rhodesian-born European teacher, Noel Estcourt, appointed to the staff. Noel had been educated at Plumtree and had just returned from teaching at a school in England. He was a younger version of John and completely at ease with the pupils.

'This must be one of the most difficult jobs anywhere in the world,' Noel remarked to John one evening shortly after he arrived. 'You're managing not only an "all-boarding school" of the highest achieving and brightest boys and girls in the country, but the times are charged with politics, not only here, but right across Africa. If the political temperature rises in the country, it must do so here as well.'

'Oh, it does, it does,' John laughed, 'and the pretexts under which the pupils will protest are quite extraordinary — mythical worms in the *sadza* (maize meal) for instance.' He became more serious. 'The worst thing is that it is so time-consuming and distracting... and it takes you away from the really important issues.

'All I can do is thank God the school is so much better than it was when I first came here.'

Noel's initial impressions were the excellence of the open, yet friendly and courteous behaviour of the boys and girls, and their complete dedication to learning when in the classroom. But he was pretty shocked at the poor standard of staff housing which was provided, by comparison with what he had been used to in England!

He was interested in the way that John dealt with potentially tricky situations with the pupils when they arose. He was chatting to me one morning.

'John has such dignity and presence,' he said. 'He always manages to be courteous but speaks firmly in that beautifully modulated voice of his that carries such authority.'

I couldn't have agreed more!

'I'm impressed,' he continued, 'with the strength of his Christian convictions and principles and the expectations he has of his own personal duty and responsibility — which, of course, he expects of us as well. He makes me feel this is the most important job in the country, yet he trusts us to continue our work without prying surveillance. He's a great guy, that husband of yours!'

"Oh Noel, and so are you", I thought. I knew how much John was relishing having someone else on staff who was not only completely familiar with boarding schools but also understood the Africans so well.

'Never forget Noel,' John said one evening, 'we are working for two or three generations hence. This country will benefit increasingly from a foundation of generation upon generation of well-educated citizens.'

The number of girls at the school were by now assuming significance of their own – among them. Sarah Chavunduka, our first Head Girl in 1956. She became the first African girl to be admitted to university.

Her sister Agnes was one of my favourite Girl Guides. She was so promising that when Guide Headquarters contacted me to say that they would like to send an African Guide over to a major Jamboree in London, Agnes Chavunduka was the name I put forward. We rallied round to make sure she had everything she wanted and excitement was intense when we heard Agnes had been presented to the Queen.

She came back sparkling with excitement. One of her duties on her return was to give a talk to the Girl Guides' Association in Salisbury about everything that had happened. I escorted her into the room. She was a little taken aback to see there were about 200 people there. But she was very brave and I was enormously proud of her and the excellent speech she gave to them. It was full of colour, light, laughter and the observations she had made about England were full of insight. From all I heard afterwards it was clear that the whole audience thought she was exceptional.

John asked her to give the same talk to the school. She was quite happy to do so. But the Agnes who took centre stage at the school was a very different person from the one I had seen the day before. She hung her head, shifted from foot to foot and said things were "quite nice". Eventually John had to step in and thank her. She rushed off the stage with relief.

I was furious that she had let herself down to badly. I asked John.

'What on earth is wrong with her? I cannot believe she was so different. You should have seen her yesterday, she was magnificent.'

John looked at me. 'Today Nannie, she was a second-class citizen and as such she had to show her place in front of the boys. I should have realised that earlier. But it is so wrong. That girl will go far if she can just overcome this dreadful barrier.'

Following this, John wrote to Head Office and demanded some

good women teachers for the girls. For once, they responded promptly with the offer of two young women who had just come out from England. Janet Prosser and Janet Pearson brought a breath of fresh air to the school and to the girls in particular. The female students seemed to hold their heads just that little bit higher, take their responsibilities that little more seriously as the girls began to feel that they were not destined merely to be down-trodden wives and mothers, with no voice.

Since John had first come to Goromonzi he had had only one assistant in the office. Marjorie Chapman had been valiantly trying to fulfil the role of secretary and bursar but it meant that a lot of the administration kept falling back on John's shoulders. He was furious when a second "Goromonzi" was started at Fletcher in Gwelo and the Headmaster there was allocated a bursar, secretary and shorthand typist immediately! John's nagging and letter writing seemed to have no effect whatsoever. To change the pre-set allocation for Goromonzi seemed to be far too difficult!

All of this was beginning to tell on John's health. He was always a bit delicate and now he had a succession of blood clots in his legs, which were causing me enormous anxiety. All of them a result of that blasted cricket ball on the shin at Mzingwane. We had to be very careful of him when these clots started up, he had to go to bed with his leg up and take blood thinners to try and disperse it. So the school would be run temporarily from the bedroom – this curtailed his activities and frustrated him terribly, making him uncharacteristically tetchy.

One of the outcomes of his sojourn in bed, however, was the start of a Goromonzi newsletter, which went out to all parents, past and present students. The newsletter in April 1960 reflects just what was going on at the school:

*Head of school is **David Zamchiya** with **Aeneas Chigwedere** as deputy, **Tsitsi Makoni** as Head Girl with **Marion Musa** as deputy and the school prefects are **Samson Mahati**, **Stanislaus Madyiwa**, **Solomon Nengubo** and **Abraham Harid**.*

The report went on to list those who had attained their Higher School Certificate the year before, those who qualified for university entrance, the Cambridge School certificate results and the prizewinners for the last year. Then the old boys news – pages and pages of it, all making for fascinating reading:

Payne Masuku (to whom the editor is indebted for much of this information about former students) teaches the post-Standard VI building course at Tegwane.

Wilton Munjoma is headmaster of Chakadini School.

Sarah Chavunduka graduated from the University College of Rhodesia and Nyasaland.

Enos Mbofana is the editor of "Fact" and did a very good job on the Federal Pavilion at the Bulawayo Trade Fair.

Liberty Mhlanga left for the United States on 26th November to study at Clark University of Massachusetts. He is at the moment in Boston watching the snow fall.

Hosea Mapondera is on the staff of the Rhodes National Gallery after a year in America on a Ford Foundation grant. He studied African cultures and gallery organisation.

Edward Moyo is head of the African Service, Federal Broadcasting Corporation in Bulawayo.

Edmund Garwe, **Cornelius Sanyanga**, **Buzwani Mothobi**, **Mutumba Mainga** and **Gertrude Kazunga** have all passed their first year exams at the University College.

Buzwani Mothobi writes from the University: "The Goromonzi colony now numbers about 20 souls out of a total black population of about 49. Three ex-Goromonzi boys have made the athletics team this year, **Costin Dlamini**, **Eubert Mashaire** and myself and three others have made the soccer team, **Cornelius Sanyanga**, **Samuel Gozo** and myself. Cornelius has been outstanding and everywhere we have played, all have thought highly of him. All three of us took part in the first multi-racial match ever to take place in Lusaka; for those of us who had never played before a real crowd, the roar was something to remember." Buzwani adds that he is the first African to play in the Mashonaland cricket league.

Distinguished visitors to the school last term included **Dr. Fisher, Archbishop of Canterbury**, who made a surprise visit. This term visitors have been an almost weekly event – Americans, Indians, West Indians, some with scholarships and grants at their disposal, others to see African secondary education for themselves first hand.

344

Marriages
Esrome Kuruneri to Bertha Makuto
Ephraim Chamba to Servic Kuruneri
We wish you all well

Other news
A number of old students are now overseas. **Hagar Mapondera** *has completed a third year at Gloucester Royal Infirmary.* **Jean Zulu** *is at Charing Cross Hospital,* **Tryphena Ndlovu** *and* **Jane Choza** *are at the Deaconess Hospital in Edinburgh and* **Annabella Kuruneri** *has started nursing at Canterbury Hospital.* **Aidan Chidarikire** *is at Woolwich Technical College,* **David Phiri** *and* **James Kaminjolo** *at Bristol University and* **Nehemiah Munyoro**, **Don Mvuti** *and* **Etherton Mpisaunga** *in India.* **Christopher Mutambirwa** *has gone to Rome.*

One last word. The editor has to rely greatly on second-hand news of many of you and is not in a position to check upon everything. If we have mis-reported your doings, described you as doing the wrong course or mis-spelt your names, please write and correct us.

With all good wishes to you wherever you may be.
J. M. Hammond

One of the greatest pleasures John had at Goromonzi, was being able to admit the sons of his past teachers to the school. Buzwani Mothobi was one of these, as were Samuel Malusalila and Jill's first playmate, Ernest Bulle.

A recent letter from Roger Malusalila however, had bothered him a little. He had been having some problems with Samuel, and Roger had written a couple of years beforehand, asking John to take him after an unsuccessful stint at Tegwane. This time, Roger wrote:

Delinquency might be inherited but I have begun to realise now, rightly or wrongly, that some headmasters, teachers and parents alike are responsible for its existence.

My Samuel could have been anything. At Goromonzi Samuel was not allowed to sit back. He was made to keep on his toes. I am sure he cannot have reason to regret that for those who took his place at Tegwane sat back and, well, did not get through. I hope my son will be sensible enough to work very hard so that by the end of the year he obtains his GCE and that my claim will come true that some clay might be bad, but some moulder can make a reasonable shape with it.

Samuel has mentioned something about the Chibero School... I learn that the fees are about £150 a year, if that is so, I am sorry I just cannot venture. I have been thinking of giving him a year at the Fletcher School next year, that is if he does get his certificate of course, but he seems very much interested in this Chibero. Please sort it out for me and see what you can do for me.

I must say thank you Mr. Hammond, even if Samuel may be anything else tomorrow, for all that you and your staff have done for him. I may find myself in Salisbury during the coming school holidays, but I cannot promise to see Goromonzi due to lack of time. I do send my best wishes.

John was concerned because Samuel was a boy with such potential but they had battled to keep him focused and moving forward. John would not have liked to see him attend Fletcher, as that school was now going through very much the same sort of trouble as Goromonzi had seen seven years before. He resolved to keep an eye on him and see if he could help him gain entry to Chibero.

While John was in bed, still quite ill and depressed by the confines of the bedroom, he received two letters, which heartened him enormously and kept him in touch with his old boys and how they were getting on. It was his greatest delight to hear how they were doing... and I was always so pleased that so many of them thought fit to keep writing year after year, to let him know of their progress.

Liberty Mhlanga wrote:

I was very sorry to hear that you are sick. I thank you very sincerely indeed for the recommendation that you made to the Rhodes Livingstone Institute to take me up as a Local Research Assistant. I am very excited at getting such a job.

You have done a wonderful job for me, Mr. Hammond, and your actions towards me have been those of a father for the seven years I have known you. This Institute is doing research work in labour turnover in Rhodesian Industry. This entails the interviewing of labour and recording the information accurately. There are four factories on which we are working, one in Ndola, one in Lusaka, one in Bulawayo, the makers of Philips Radio, and the other is here, Springmaster.

From the core of my heart, I wish you a speedy recovery Sir and thank you very much indeed for all that you did and that which you are doing for me and the country at large.

'There you are my Johnnie — it is worth it isn't it?'

'Oh yes, of course it is. Liberty is an outstanding young man. He'll do very well.'

The other letter was from Vic Vusumuzi who was now at the university in Salisbury, thanking him for sending on some testimonials and adding:

Mr. Hammond, as a father I think you will allow me as a son to speak to you frankly. First, I am not a Nationalist; secondly I am not aggressive, nor rash. In me there is something of curiosity, which may be a quality of all youths entering the adult stage or perhaps the usual expressions of 'varsity loudspeakers.

You do not know what value talks between you and me bring to me. Rather than a Nationalist, regard me as a son you can bear to be questioned by. Discussions between you and I always regard as family talks. They set me lines of development. I speak to very few people on the other side of the colour line except where I notice provocation and social slighting is intended against me as an individual. I speak to you as a father, not a white man.

Vusumuzi went on at some length to argue a good case for the future of the country, concluding:

I hate nobody. I hate power and mutual hatred. The latter is the only thing around which my talks centre, but if I am not understood well I can be mistaken as a "racialist". But certainly, extremist is not what I am, or intend to be. I am not offended by anything you say to me.
I promise to measure up to your testimonial next year.

Goodbye for now,
Vic Vusumuzi

John had written to me within weeks of his return to Rhodesia in 1935 about the awesome responsibility he felt being a teacher in Native development and wondering whether he could measure up to it. That feeling of responsibility and inadequacy, never left him. Now that social change was taking place so fast, he'd ponder almost daily over whether he was taking the right path or not. Somehow just keeping open these vital lines of communication with his old boys was very important for his wellbeing.

At the end of the year, he had another excellent letter from David Zamchiya, the Head Boy at the time. He was writing to tell John about a meeting of the National Affairs Association which he had been invited to attend. But first he outlined his time at Goromonzi:

When I first came to Goromonzi in 1955 I was both small and young and virtually friendless. You brought me up so well that I became a boy of reasonably good behaviour. After staying at the school for six years I managed to go away without being punished by a prefect or a member of staff... and I managed to avoid your cane for the whole period I was there!

When I was appointed a prefect in 1959 my first reaction was that I was now freer than most of the boys because I thought to be a prefect meant plenty of privileges and rights to be enjoyed and no duties and responsibilities. After a while, however, I realised that the position was one of trust and responsibility and I devoted my energies towards living up to a high standard of efficiency and duty-consciousness. A big surprise was when you told me that I would be Head of School for 1960. I never thought such a high honour could be conferred on me and when I compared my age with those of my contemporaries and the people I would have to control, my only consolation was that you had taken everything into account before you appointed me.

The year was not altogether easy particularly because of what was happening inside the whole of Africa and I was happy when, in spite of its ups and downs, the year ended without a serious crisis. I do thank you for this wonderful opportunity. The amount of experience I gained in this one year exceeded that which I got in the other five years.

Would you please extend my gratitude to Mrs. Hammond who helped us very much over the piano and made our music much more pleasant to listen to. Her ready willingness to train the Girl Guides made the girls better people and Tsitsi and I were helped greatly by her influence over the girls.

David went on to describe the meeting of the National Affairs Association. As a thumbnail sketch and description of what was happening in the country at the time, it is both insightful and graphic:

The meeting was very interesting and the amount of agreement between the different races surprised me. Those who spoke told us how discrimination affected their society and the participants of the conference all agreed that immediate repeal of legislation, which promotes racial strife through discrimination, was necessary. The problem that faced us all was what to do about the situation and how to make other citizens of Southern Rhodesia feel as we do.

Dr. Rodgers gave a correct review of the conditions in this country. While he said that Southern Rhodesia was not unique in its racial policy, he clearly stated that the whites in this country should stop assuming a feeling of superiority and start respecting the individual. There should be freedom from state interference, freedom of speech, movement, assembly and worship. He concluded by saying both blacks and whites had a duty — the latter to implement their beliefs in democracy and the former to protect the ideals.

Dr. Palley categorically stated that the statute law of the country is not fair in that it looked at different societies differently. He said it was to the benefit of the Europeans that they should not only change their social and political attitude but that the government should take the lead in legislating against discrimination. Basing his talk on discrimination in shops, hotels, cinemas, restaurants and social and sporting centres, he said that discrimination should end and, while he had the belief that most people recognised the necessity of changing the laws, what he did not understand and what he required a psychiatrist to explain to him was, "Why we people do not do it!"

Mr. Wright, a Euro-African, spoke on behalf of the coloured community and complained that the European always tells other races to get civilised first without setting the standard. He compared the struggle to a football match on a field without goal posts and in which it was up to the referee to say who had scored.

Unfortunately, Mr. Takawira, who was at that time threatened with arrest, did not come.

Mrs. Rosin said that the change should come, but it should be evolutionary not revolutionary. Legislation for discrimination, she said, should be removed, but there should be no legislation for integration. Multiracial schools should be voluntary and there was need for the educational emancipation of the African woman.

Mr. Murishi said that the Land Apportionment Act was an experiment which failed, but instead of providing more land for the Africans, the government made a mistake by introducing a sister act, the Land Husbandry Act. He advocated more contact between races for the purpose of discussion and

349

said that courtesy was required in shops and other places so that such abusive terms as "nanny" and "boy" could disappear. Let's be like pianists and play both black and white notes in order to produce harmonious music.

An Indian who spoke, Mr. Patel, astounded us by revealing the amount of discrimination from which the Indians suffer. A leading industrialist, Mr. Hughes, said there should be facilities for training Africans in more practical skills.

Finally Mrs. Mhlanga, a nurse and journalist, moved the audience almost to tears by outlining how the law of the country, by not providing enough facilities, was making it impossible for the African to reach acceptable standards.

Mr. Margolis who chaired the meeting, gave a summary and said that change was necessary and quickly, but the situation should be that in which the rule of law obtains.

The meeting was on the whole very successful and a great experience to me. I now know more about discrimination in this country and how some Europeans and Africans differ in the way in which they think about our problems.

I am now at home anxiously awaiting my results so I cannot tell you anything yet about my plans. I should be able to let you know more soon after the results.

I am sorry if I have been too long to maintain your interest in my letter, but I could not cut it shorter as I wanted to say what I learned and did in six years and also wished to summarise many speeches in a few minutes. Thank you very much for everything.

Yours sincerely,
David Zamchiya

Within a few days, another letter arrived from another David – this time David Phiri who was studying Social Anthropology at Oxford University:

In my last letter I wrote that I was leaving Bristol University for Oxford. I put aside the rivalry between Oxford and Cambridge! I used to be a Light Blue supporter due to your influence and enthusiasm, but my affiliations have now changed and I am a great supporter of the Dark Blues!

Never did I dream that I would one day be a member of this well-celebrated University. Fortune has really come my way and I consider myself

350

lucky. My proudest moment was to see in the national papers here – D.A.R. Phiri (Goromonzi, S. Rhodesia and St. Catherine's). I am so proud to have gone through Goromonzi and I estimate Goromonzi to be one of the best secondary schools in Africa.

Mr. Hammond, if you have any photographs of Goromonzi I would love to have a few copies please. I have none in my possession and I talk so much of Goromonzi to my friends and I think I would make it easier for myself if I had a few photos. My photo album would be enriched! We are all so proud to hear about Sarah.

My best wishes to the staff, pupils and Mrs. Hammond.

We were all delighted to hear shortly after this, that David had won a Blue for golf. John sent off a telegram immediately, congratulating him and signing it "Concord".

He received an excited letter back from David, saying it was the first congratulatory telegram he had ever received and asking how he knew that the boys had nicknamed him "Concord". He went on to say he had been equally staggered on leaving Goromonzi that John had said how much the school would miss him – he was then Sports Captain and Deputy Head Boy – and then went on to reminisce about all the wicked things Phiri had done. David had thought he had got away with it all!

'Isn't it a delight to see how well he has done Nan? He was a clever boy, perhaps a little on the lazy side, but he's obviously overcome that. Do you remember that time when we were coming back from Jack and Molly Hughes and we were flagged down by that group of boys who had obviously been up to no good? As we approached I saw young Phiri dive into a ditch head first when he realised it was me! It was a wonderful sight! There had been a beer drink up at the Hughes' compound and those boys had sneaked out. I never had to punish him for it because he always looked so uncomfortable whenever I mentioned the words "beer drinking" in his company – which I did frequently!'

When John first started in African education he was concerned that the social situation of the time would never permit the close relationships his father had enjoyed with the schoolboys at Plumtree. In my view, his greatest achievement at his schools was to see how he and his team of staff had managed to cross that barrier. Many of his ex-pupils were now mutually respected friends and they continued that relationship through letters and calls for many years.

The country was in a delicate political situation. The Federation looked unlikely to survive and Northern Rhodesia and Nyasaland were in the process of gaining their independence as Zambia and Malawi respectively. Southern Rhodesia had been peremptorily dismissed from this process and told it could not automatically have its independence ...so much for the promises of the British Government. I felt almost personally responsible.

The country's Prime Minister at the time was a shortsighted academic, Sir Edgar Whitehead. He was not charismatic nor a good public speaker, but we believed he was a good man and he was in the process of drawing up a constitution, which would see a hand-over of power to the African within 25 years. It was pretty radical thinking for most of the country's white population and it was obvious that a referendum was going to have to be held soon. By the beginning of 1961, the NDP (National Democratic Party) led by Joshua Nkomo and Ndabaningi Sithole, was taking part in some constructive negotiation. But there were many who thought 25 years was too long to wait.

There were a number of whites who also felt this and were busy stirring the pot for revolution rather than evolution. One of these was teaching at the university and he had been invited to address the school's Cultural Society. He responded in the affirmative saying he could talk on "the true history of Zimbabwe-Monomatapa, African and Western values or the nature of nationalism: an historical survey".

The government had been watching him carefully and although John did not know the man personally, he was informed that beneath these harmless titles would be an evening designed to cause havoc and unrest in the school. He talked it over with the Head Boy and the Secretary of the Cultural Society. They agreed the invitation be withdrawn.

Following a furious letter back from him, John replied:

I was aware of your alternative suggestions for a topic for your talk to our Cultural Society. Despite this, I regretfully had to reach the decision I did. The time may come when you have to shoulder similar responsibilities and I think you will find them no less distasteful than I do.

I was surprised at your assumption that it was "trouble" that I feared. While schools have suffered recently in this way and, who knows, it may be our turn next, I do have sufficient confidence in my senior boys to feel that they would not allow a matter of this kind to disturb them.

Only the fool in the Africa of today would claim that he has the true and complete answer to our problems. Many decisions that are made will undoubtedly prove to be very wrong; on the other hand, many that are severely criticised today may bring the best solutions. Happy is the man who need make no such decision but merely stand on the sidelines and criticise.

Jill was due home for Christmas 1960 and we were longing to see her again. She came out by boat and was going to take the train up to Salisbury. A phone call from Cape Town told us that she would actually be driving up with someone she had met on the boat and that this someone was male. My imagination ran riot. I realised this was a very different Jill from the timid soul I had left behind. She arrived looking slim and attractive and, to be frank, I was rather glad when it became clear that she and the chap were only friends and that there was no other relationship between them.

Jill was staggered when she saw Richard, who had been an average-sized 13-year-old when she left for England, and was now a 6 foot 4 inch voice-broken 16-year-old.

It was good to have her back, though it took her some time to settle and make friends as most of her school friends were still completing their third year at university. But she no longer seemed to regret not having gone with them and had obviously had a whale of a time in England. One of her proudest moments during that first few weeks at home, was going down with us to her first ever Plumtree weekend and seeing Richard perform as Captain of the Pinafore in another Gilbert and Sullivan. It was especially heart-warming, as he was Head Boy that year.

At the beginning of that first term of 1961 the leading science teacher at Goromonzi fell ill. This was a real problem as good science teachers were not easy to find and there were sizeable science classes taking both Cambridge and Higher School Certificates at the end of the year. John sent an urgent letter through to the Department and they promised some action by the start of the term.

On the first day, John was just signing in the new pupils and announcing the names of Head Boy and prefects, when Hoffmann turned up.

'Good morning Mr. Hoffmann. What can I do for you?' John asked.

353

'I'm coming back to help you with your science classes,' Hoffmann said.

John could not believe it. After all they had been through. Since his time at Goromonzi, Hoffmann had caused endless problems at other schools to which he had been appointed. Surely the Government knew how explosive this situation could be.

'I'll stay in town, so you don't have to provide housing and I'll come out three days a week,' Hoffmann said.

'Well if he's not on the premises, it might be all right.' John told me that evening. 'But really, of all people – to send Hoffmann here again! I think the people in the Department sometimes have no brains at all. Particularly when the country itself is so delicately poised politically. It's sheer stupidity.'

To be fair, Hoffmann seemed to behave pretty well during that first term and John began to relax and hope that he had learned the wisdom of his ways.

The school's main sports event was looming over the first weekend of April and Lord Malvern, the elder statesman of the country and the architect of plans for African Education in the mid-1930s, was the guest of honour. He had opened Goromonzi 15 years before. In his speech before Lord Malvern and all the pupils and their parents, John's said:

On behalf of the School I would like to say how very much pleasure it gives us to see you all here today. This weekend has provided a record turnout of parents and there are some 240 parents and relatives who are expected to sit down to lunch today. I am very pleased that this occasion, which we offer to parents to see the school and visit the place where your children spend so much of their time, seems to be appreciated.

In a school of this kind, there is no other way in which Staff can get to know the parents. I know from my own experience as the parent of a boy at a school of similar type, that one of the more pleasing features of a weekend of this kind is the opportunity provided to get to know other parents. It is probable that friendships will grow between parents just as friendships will grow up between those who learn here.

My Lord, you were the consulting engineer for the foundations of the large structure, which African Education has grown to be. The laying of foundations is unspectacular work, it lies buried under the soil and never catches the eye... yet the edifice is only as strong as the foundations will permit it to be. Many of the parents here today are the stone and cement and steel which provided the concrete of these foundations and you will be able to form an opinion regarding the strength of that base from the sons and daughters which have grown from those foundation members.

When you opened this school, there were some 50 boys. Today we have over 250 boys and nearly 100 girls. The average age of the 50 who made up the first Form 1 was nearly 18 years. Today the average of our first form is well under 14.

At the opening of the school, My Lord, you expressed the hope that those who went out from this school would go back to their Reserves and help to bring advancement there. There are many that have done that as teachers in Mission primary schools and through valuable work for their communities in other spheres. In many cases, however, the lure of the lights has been strong and the majority of our old boys and girls have found their way into the cities. Many have gone farther afield in search of educational opportunities they could not find here. Your own profession has attracted a useful number – two old boys are qualified medical practitioners working in this country, there are four or five others going through medical training at Natal and two more receiving prizes today, leave in September for Britain to pursue their medical studies there.

Two old boys have followed a similar line in the veterinary field, both in Britain. Another is doing dentistry in London and another, also in London, is being trained as a pharmacist.

Many girls have taken to nursing, firstly in Natal and in more recent years in our local hospitals. There has been a steady trickle of girls to the United Kingdom in search of both nursing training and adventure. One old boy is a qualified lawyer, another is in London reading for the bar and a third will be leaving on the same errand shortly.

There is a fairly large group of old boys at Roma University, some dozen or so in India, one or two at Makerere and the invasion of the USA is getting steadily under way.

One old boy is studying to be a librarian in America and another is doing Agriculture there. A third will leave shortly with the aim of entering the church. If only a fraction of those whose applications for American Scholarships I have had to fill in recently are successful, it is probable that our largest contingent overseas will be in the States.

I have left details of our own university until last. There are now 22 old boys and girls of Goromonzi at the University College in Salisbury. Many, in fact most, of that contingent are with us today and we are delighted to see them.

I am particularly pleased that we now have one old boy and one old girl on our staff, while at Fletcher, most of the Science staff are old Goromonzi boys. There are many others scattered about doing useful jobs in industry and commerce. They are scattered in all corners of the country, keeping books in the sugar estates in the Zambezi Valley, manufacturing tyres in Bulawayo, one as a pilot cadet with Central African Airways and several in the Civil Service.

This sounds rather like a catalogue from a department store, but I hope it will give you a picture of the kind of thing that those who have been through this school are now doing.

I am particularly pleased with the way the boys and girls here are taking on an increasing measure of responsibility for the organisation of their lives. We have now reached the stage where those entering Sixth form are aware of the exacting nature of the academic exploration that lies ahead. In our games and athletics we are getting to the stage where the spirit in which the game is played is of greater importance than the result.

Time alone will tell whether this school will ever deserve to be called "great". I think, however, that the babe you christened 15 years ago is making rapid progress through infancy with no serious childish complaints to impair its steady growth towards boyhood.

We work on the well-tried system, that senior boys and girls must both serve and control those who are more junior. We aim at high academic attainment and I confess, quite unashamedly, that we use intensive competition to that end. Athleticism plays a large, but not a disproportionately large part in our training. We try to provide many avenues through which the boys and girls may find some place where each can shine in no matter how humble a way.

After a superb weekend that was attended for the first time by large numbers of the local residents of Ruwa and Goromonzi, both black and white, the parents and old boys said their good-byes and the last bus full of pupils rolled out of the gate. Hoffmann went home for the holidays.

Four days later, trouble was brewing at Luveve, the Teachers' Training College near Bulawayo. John was sad to find that it had involved two of his old boys and that they were expelled as a result. Two days later he received letters from both boys asking him to intervene on their behalf. This he did, sending copies of their letters to the Principal, Mac Partridge, a genial Australian whom he had come to know well and respected highly.

Mac sent back an in depth account of what had happened concluding:

I am conscious of increasing influence, political in origin, external to this College, which is designed to prevent this place in particular, and African education in general, from achieving any success which might go to the credit of the present Government. African nationalism might have much to gain from spoiling tactics. These lads of ours are but tools, yet only too willing.

John had both boys in to see him and he spent about four hours with them trying to understand the root of the problem. There was no doubt that the boys had both behaved very badly but John was keen to know what was behind it all. He felt that this sort of carry-on was essentially out of character for either of them.

Eventually, and after much discussion, they painted a disturbing picture of the level of intimidation being meted out to anyone who was deemed to be in a privileged position. They were reluctant to say exactly who was doing it, but merely said "nationalists". They understood what they had done and more particularly what they might have thrown away. John wrote to Mac suggesting that after a cooling-off period, and provided they re-applied properly, with due remorse for what they had done, perhaps he would consider re-admitting them. He added:

One gets to the stage where nothing they do can disappoint one any more and one cannot help but be rather doubtful about the value of it all. They can be so easily duped by all that is going on and it is one of the more difficult things to make them see where their real interests lie.

I think we are fairly fortunate in having a good bunch at the top of this school, who realise that they have more important things to deal with for the present. Their influence is quite marked and one can but hope that the present attitude will persist. Yours will be a more difficult bunch to handle. It might be worthwhile insisting that all who go to you should have had a year in employment first. That might serve to make them realise that life can be hard.

The country was now gearing up for the referendum on Sir Edgar Whitehead's 1961 Constitution. The NDP and Britain had agreed to its terms and conditions and now it was up to the white electorate to vote for or against it. They would, in essence, be voting away their present position and power and there were some emotive things being said. In the heated lead up to it all, John noticed his prefects becoming more edgy.

'What is it?' he asked them.

'There are people telling us things,' was the only reply he could elicit.

I went out walking with the dogs again. Sure enough, there was Hoffmann in his cave with bunches of boys talking head-to-head. I reported back to John, who called him in and instructed him not to go round putting subversive ideas into the pupils' heads. Hoffmann walked out of the office.

Feeling the rumble of discontent around the country, Sir Edgar decided to call up several thousand Europeans as a police reserve to help the regular forces maintain law and order and if possible, reduce intimidation over the period of the referendum.

In the heightened political climate, it seemed as though some of the African Nationalists feared that there might be a positive outcome to the referendum. It almost seemed as though they were going round stirring up trouble in an attempt to make the European electorate nervous enough to vote against it.

Two of the Goromonzi staff were called up. Noel Estcourt was one of them. This was going to provide a bit of a hiccup, but the remaining staff were able to cover all classes affected, which was the main thing. It was likely that the call-up would be for the best part of a week.

On the Tuesday morning assembly John announced the hymn and I struck up the introduction as usual. Then a cacophony seemed to swell out of the body of the people in the hall. It was a mix of throat-clearing and coughing. I kept on playing as loudly as I could and some started singing.

By the third verse, they were mostly all singing, but it was pretty poor stuff with none of the vibrancy of a normal assembly. The hymn finally finished. John stood on the stage and said nothing. There was absolute silence. He quietly looked down the rows of boys as if trying to memorise the expressions on their faces. Some dropped their heads, others started shuffling their feet.

Very slowly and quietly he said, 'If any of you have anything to complain about, you know the right way to do it. You know this is the coward's way. You know this is the way I despise and I will act very harshly if it continues. You may go now, but you boys will do an extra 30 minutes of prep this afternoon. Mr. Hoffmann I would like to see you please.'

The boys filed out looking mutinous — the girls, frightened and uncertain.

'What's at the bottom of this Hoffmann?'

'Why do you ask me Mr. Hammond?'

'Because I know you well enough to know that if there is any trouble at this school it will have something to do with you,' John said as he strode towards his office.

'You shouldn't allow the teachers to be called up for police reserve,' Hoffmann blustered.

John stopped dead in his tracks and turned to face him, well aware that there were many ears listening.

'Hoffmann, I don't have any say over whether teachers are called up or not. My job, and yours, is to equip the boys and girls of the school to be able to make their way in this country as it is now.

'This is a decisive moment in the history of this country and our Prime Minister has decided it is necessary to call people up in order to maintain law and order during the referendum.

'It is quite beyond my jurisdiction to change anything of that nature, outside this school. At this moment it is also beyond the jurisdiction of the boys and girls to change anything outside this school.

'In time, I have no doubt that will change. At that stage, I hope that pupils from this school will be at the forefront of that change and that it will be made with wisdom and integrity, helped by what they have learned during their formative years here.

'If it is within your ability to prevent this happening again, I would advise you to urgently do so. May I remind you that I have the authority to close this school down completely should it be deemed necessary. I will not hesitate to use it.'

Reports were coming back all day of rumblings within the school. John spent most of the day walking slowly up and down the corridors and into classrooms trying to determine the mood of the various classes and groups within the school.

He called the Head Boy and prefects in.

'What are we looking at here?' They were nervous and reluctant to reply.

'Did you know anything about what happened this morning?'

'No sir, we did not,' replied the Head Boy. 'I was shocked like your-self at what happened at assembly – we all were.'

'There have been people visiting the school.'

'Some of the staff have been talking to some of the ones in the school who are troublemakers. There are always some ready to listen.'

'Don't they understand what they will be throwing away?' John asked. 'Don't they understand that we can do nothing about it anyway?' There were no answers.

When John came home that evening, he said,

'I'm at my wits end Nannie. I was so sure that they would be strong enough to stand up against it. They have been so outstanding. What's got into them? If they can't stand up against this, then everything I have been trying to do has been worthless.'

I was almost paralysed with the horror of it. My brain didn't seem to be functioning. John had been here for four further years since Finkle had persuaded him not to take the inspectorate job and give Goromonzi another two years. He had certainly done that. The school had improved so much, that he had felt encouraged to stay on a little longer. He had done much more than his fair share and he had done it with no more support in the office – after nine years at this place.

My resentment came bubbling up. His health had been affected. Our lives as a family had been affected. It was grossly unfair. Then I realised John was talking.

'I have made some plans for tomorrow. This is what I want you to do.'

John was up before dawn the next day praying and pacing along the verandah. There was no problem at early morning drill, or at inspec-tion. They filed in for assembly.

I struck up the introduction. Hesitantly at first but gaining in strength, the noise started again. The boys all dropped their heads so we could not see who was doing it. It was a malevolent, angry sound. Clearing of throats and coughing with a growling level of voice under-tone. I kept on playing. The noise grew louder.

John signalled me to stop. When everyone had quietened down, he signalled me to start again. I played the introduction. The noise grew. He asked me to stop.

As soon as they were quiet, he said, 'You will all go to your dormi-tories and sit there in silence until ten o'clock. Then you will come back and we will try it again.'

The staff and prefects had been instructed to stay in the dormitories with them.

In the midst of this horror, it did give John some small satisfaction to see that Hoffmann was the only one who did not obey the instruction.

At ten o'clock, everyone filed back into the Beit Hall. I remember thinking what a beautiful day it was, winter had lifted a little and it was the first really warm day for a couple of months.

I started to play the introduction. The cacophony started again. It was horrible. The ferocity and antagonism were very frightening.

John signalled for me to go outside.

As I left the hall, I signalled Alf Morris as we had arranged. I then went behind the stage so that I could hear what was going on.

'This is the third time we have tried to conduct assembly and each time you have chosen the coward's way. You know very well that I can do nothing about things that do not concern the school, yet you choose to display hatred to the people in this room who have only your well-being in mind.'

John talked quietly but very firmly for ten minutes.

'I have no alternative but to expel you all.'

There was a shocked intake of breath. Nobody had thought in their wildest imaginings that he would expel the whole school!

'Your parents will be receiving a letter from me, detailing exactly what has happened and what course of action I intend to take. Prefects, Head Boy and girls, you will stay behind. Form VI, file out to your dormitories and pack your things.'

The boys filed out with triumph on their faces until they saw the Beit Hall ringed with members of the Police Reserve. They suddenly crumpled into the uncertain youngsters they were. When they reached the hostel, a bus was waiting for them.

'Form V, file out to your dormitories and pack your things.'

'Form IV, file out to your dormitories and pack your things.'

By midday they had all gone – some singing defiantly as they left. Most looking shattered.

To those left in the Assembly Hall, John said, 'The school is ringed by Police Reservists for your protection and will continue to be so until the end of term in three weeks' time. I understand that you are under considerable pressure and I have ordered two buses to stand by for anyone else who wishes to leave. For those who stay, normal lessons will resume tomorrow morning.'

Nobody else left.

But my darling husband looked as though his heart was broken.

His stricken eyes acknowledged his thanks to me as he left to head for the office. Eventually at 7 p.m. when he still wasn't home, I went to find him. He was sitting writing a letter to the parents of those boys who had been expelled. It was the most wonderful letter.

All I remember is that he concluded it with, "…these… were your sons".

The school swung back into action the next day, with John bombarded by press, parents, boys, the Department and politicians. He talked to nobody until he had sent those letters off to the parents.

'Nannie, I have got to get away at the end of this term. I have told Finkle I will be taking a term's leave. I have invited the parents to re-apply for a place at the school if they wish their sons to come back but I will only take back the ones I believe are worthwhile. It means the next three weeks will be hell on earth, but will you make all the arrangements? I want to leave here as soon as I can.'

I arranged with Rich that he would come down with us for the school holidays, and rang Jill to tell her what had happened. They were both aghast as the papers had been full of it. I told them not to worry, as John seemed to be well in control.

Only two parents did not re-apply. 52 boys were not re-admitted, 30 of whom were due to write their School Certificate examination at the end of the year. Many of the parents expressed their horror at what had happened:

…we African parents are not happy about what our children are doing because it shows that if these sons take over, there will be no law, no pity and they will not care for the poor and there will be no religion and they don't have any schools and hospital. They do not know the need of their country.

One of the parents wrote to *The Herald* complaining about the fact that his son had been expelled. There is no copy of it, but we were very touched when one of the local white farmers who had initially been so antagonistic to having the school at Goromonzi, replied:

Mr. K should get his facts right before blaming the principal and teachers of Goromonzi Secondary School, all of whom are doing a first-class job of work in the service they give to the African scholars.

Only two teachers were away on duty as Police Reservists during the Referendum days in July and helping to maintain law and order can hardly be called "introducing politics in school". There was more to it than this, as the students themselves very well know. They were more than mischievous; they were downright rude and insulting to their principal during morning assembly for prayers, day after day, and they were punished, and quite rightly so.

The principal also took the trouble of sending a letter to every parent explaining what had happened and stating the reason for the action he had taken. As a parent Mr. K. should have received one of those letters so he should have been aware of the true facts in spite of any stories which his son has given him concerning expulsions. If he were still in doubt, an interview with the principal of the school would soon have convinced him.

L. J. Anderson

So many letters flooded in that John was hard put to answer them all.

Richard now had his driver's licence and we were going to share the driving down to South Africa. We had hoped to leave at lunchtime, but at 6 p.m. John was still hard at it.

Eventually, we went in and insisted on him leaving, saying that he could finish his letter when we were on holiday. We could see that he was absolutely beaten physically and emotionally and we were extremely worried about him as we drove away from the school and up the hill as fast as we could.

The letter he had been writing was to an African Federal politician, Jasper Savanhu, who had written a very supportive and encouraging letter saying how shocked he had been by the incident. It was only ten weeks later that John had the heart to finish the letter:

Dear Mr. Savanhu,
Your letter has followed me to the Transkei where we have been spending a part of our leave. I have not been at Goromonzi this term and have tried to put the events of last term out of my mind. Your letter brings them back again and I must thank you for your expressions of understanding of the problems involved. I hope it may be possible after I resume duty in January, to discuss the matter with you fully.

Like you, I am most concerned by the lack of integrity on the part of those, who were probably in the majority, who would not stand out against

363

those who were quite prepared to create such an unpleasant state of affairs. This is particularly worrying at a time when these youngsters are being recruited in the Civil Service.

We shall stand little chance of building up a stable Civil Service or one which can be relied upon, if we cannot find boys and girls with the courage to stand out for what they know to be right. Academic standards alone will not suffice.

It was largely to drive this lesson home that I took the steps that I did. I believe that if 350 young people can learn to be loyal and obedient, no matter what the pressures upon them may be, it will have a far greater long-term benefit than the passing of the School Certificate by some 30 boys.

I see my job as one of laying foundations for two generations hence and if these 350 can pass the lesson on to the 1,000-odd children they will produce some progress will have been made. The effective lessons in moral conduct can only be implanted by the parents of small children. When we get them in the schools it is too late for us to have any real impact unless the right seeds have been sown. Hence the need for those of us involved in African Education to take the long view.

I must disagree with your statement that the participation of secondary school pupils in civil disturbances is a "world-wide phenomenon". University undergraduates do partake in this kind of demonstration but, as far as my knowledge of it goes, secondary schools outside Africa are seldom involved. That it does happen in Africa is probably due to the fact that secondary school pupils in this continent do occupy the same intellectual status within their own society, as university undergraduates do in other countries.

What eats into the souls of those of us who teach in schools like Goromonzi is that, whereas in other countries where students demonstrate, the expressions of their feelings is directed against those who formulate the policies, which they consider to be objectionable. They do not, as a rule, vent their spleen upon those whose sole purpose is to assist and guide them.

One can try to be patient and philosophical about these matters but it is very hard. One can try to make excuses for the boys but I find it very difficult after what I had to put up with last term. At present I am inclined to feel that it is just not worthwhile. I think that what probably hurt me more than anything was that not one of my three Hostel Superintendents, who should have been in closer touch with the boys than any other members of the staff, reported anything to me before the trouble broke out… nor did they contribute anything towards finding a solution.

I am trying to heal the wounds, but I do not think that I shall ever feel quite the same again towards Goromonzi. It is possible that when I get back again I may feel differently, but the hurt has gone very deep, because I could find less excuse for this bit of trouble than for any I have met before and because of the very horrible expressions which I saw on the faces of the boys.

I hope we shall be able to talk this over when I get back. You may be able to assist in removing some of the despondency, which I now feel and which 2½ months of leave has not dissipated.

John was never able to keep his appointment. Jasper Savanhu was killed a few months later in a mysterious collision with a train ... on an open and empty road with the railway line clearly visible for miles on each side.

Chapter 15

... and so it ends

The alarm shrilled out its appointed time. I woke with a start – and the awful feeling that I shouldn't have been sleeping so late. It was still dark, but I knew there was some reason I should have been up and ready early this morning.

I reached over to touch John. The bed was empty.

Then I remembered. Damn! Today of all days, I should have been up before him – making a cup of tea and sitting with him as dawn broke, distracting him from the reality of what lay ahead. I went outside in the half-light and found John sitting out under the big tree in the garden with his Bible.

He looked up with his usual smile of greeting but with what seemed to me to be infinite weariness. I ran out across the lawn to kiss him good morning.

'Oh darling, I'm sorry I slept – I meant to bring you your tea...' I was stumbling over my words.

'I'm fine Nannie – don't worry. We're as ready as we can be and they'll all be arriving soon. We've plenty of time to go down and greet them. I have some good old friends to catch up with today. So you go and have a bath first while I just finish this.'

Thank God that through it all, our love for each other was still the core of our lives. We were completely interdependent – me on John for his wisdom, his kindliness, his vision – he on me for my ability to make him laugh and keep him sane in what seemed for us both, to be an increasingly insane world. The country we knew and loved was now fighting for its life and we had grave fears for the future, as Britain seemed hell-bent on forcing us into a decision, which could and should have been avoided.

As I ran the bath water, I thought back over what had happened in the last few years, and the paths that had led to us being part of this critical event today – in particular in the months since we had left Goromonzi.

John had been almost destroyed by the political manoeuvring's at Goromonzi. He still could not come to terms with the fact that the pupils he'd helped bring to such a high standard of achievement had been unable to resist being sucked into the political unrest of the time. Those great boys and girls who were showing such promise, who were keen and bright-eyed about the role they were going to play in the future... had just given in.

'If I can't teach them to stand up for what is right, even if it's not a popular stance to take, I can't teach them anything. I thought there was a chance... I really thought there was...'

I thought back to our decision to get right away at the end of that ghastly term in 1961 Richard drove us down to the Cape and spent a couple of weeks with us. The first stop had been the Zimbabwe Ruins – always a special place for us. Richard and I had supper alone that first night. John lay down on the bed as soon as we arrived and was fast asleep in an instant. Emotionally and physically finished.

In fact, it had been a very long time before he was able to pull back from the despair that gripped him. He seemed unable to make even small decisions, like whether to go to a film, or walk along the beach. He was unable to be light-hearted or to smile – with any real pleasure or joy. I'd catch him sitting with a book on his lap, staring into space – for hours.

I could only sit quietly beside him, trying to anticipate his needs and praying he'd come back to normal. I could only pray that Hoffmann's influence would be moved sufficiently far from Goromonzi to allow us to return and get things back to normal.

Jill was working on the creative side of an advertising agency, mainly in radio and television production and loving it... and to our absolute joy, Richard had been a very good Head Boy at Plumtree. It had been a tonic to be with him for that invaluable three weeks sharing his wonderful sense of fun.

Almost imperceptibly, John started to come back from the brink and take pleasure in the achievements of the kids and in his over-riding love for the family.

Slowly, slowly, he did come to life again. Slowly, we were able to talk at a deeper level. Slowly, he was able to speak about Goromonzi...

I just let him talk, pouring out the sadness, the let-down, the disbelief, the anger, the hopes and finally, understanding the failure of those hopes.

He had begun to question everything he had done, every decision made, every action taken... and for the first time since the early days at Tjolotjo I felt his self-esteem slipping as harsh blow after harsh blow made him almost physically reel.

'I'm an old style of schoolmaster Nan. I believe firm and benevolent discipline is the answer for schools like this... but perhaps those days have gone... perhaps it has been a waste of everybody's time after all...'

Two weeks before we were due to go back, he was almost his old self again. My heart burst with happiness. Things *were* going to be different – John had turned the whole school around once and nobody could yet quite believe what had been achieved. Even the hostile local white community had responded when they saw the changes – and the pupils had done so well. It had slipped back. Of course. It had slipped back badly... but it was going to be all right. John was so sure now, that I began to believe it too.

We drove home, full of optimism. We'd arranged to meet Alf Morris on our way through.

But as soon as John saw his face, he knew there was something wrong.

'What is it Alf?'

'It's Hoffmann,' Alf said, his voice shaking with emotion. 'He's been coming back to the school twice a week while you've been away, and he's up to his old tricks. The place is in turmoil.'

John nearly fainted. Both Alf and I had to catch him and steady him, before sitting him down in a restaurant for a cup of coffee. He turned to me, and I saw absolute despair in his eyes.

'I can't go back Nan. I'm sorry, I just can't go back.'

He sank his head in his hands.

I pleaded. 'Alf, take us to Jean's please. John needs more time.'

In fact, he needed no more time. He had made up his mind – if we were to survive, he had to take action immediately.

He went straight in to see the Department the next morning and told them that nobody could possibly run the place with the complete lack of support that had been displayed by the African Education Department. He put in his resignation on the spot, to take effect immediately, but agreed to go back and finish that one last term.

There was uproar. While I was arranging to pack things up at Goromonzi, Finkle was trying to persuade John to go back. But this time he was adamant. He was not going back while there was even the slightest chance of Hoffmann being around.

Things move slowly in Government. Hoffmann would be taken out of the picture – but it would take time. After hours and hours of discussion over the next term, we were sure the decision was right. We had unwittingly been in the forefront of political change now sweeping the country – and we had been under that pressure far too long.

Throughout that turbulent last term, John tried to keep on doing what he did best – keeping his staff together, keeping them focused, reminding them of their first priority.

After the event, so many people had written to us, black and white. So many were quite extraordinarily and touchingly, supportive... so many were desperately concerned for John's welfare. But they could not possibly understand. The tale was too complex to tell – the explanation of it so simple, yet so overwhelming in its implication. Few could ever really appreciate or know what we had been through.

Only those on the staff at the time would remember some of the nightmare it had been. Most were too shattered, themselves, to do anything much more than just keep phoning to see how he was. Janet Pearson had written to us and her letter gave us some strange comfort in what she said:

You were a great influence on me, I admire you and I agonise with you in your difficulties. I remember when I first met you just before Christmas in 1956. I remember how big you were, how strongly built. You beamed down at me, and asked me to wait while you fetched your bicycle.

You then preceded me through the area of the staff houses and I followed in the car. I remember being impressed by your starched khaki shorts, long socks and highly polished black shoes! I had my work cut out to drive sufficiently slowly to stay behind you and yet not stall the car.

Every time we crossed a sleeping policeman in the path, you turned in your saddle and pointed it out to me. I thought this was the height of courtesy... I later realised, it was just typical of you.

I was very much in awe of you, although my diary in February 1957 said, "Saw Hammond in a new light when he read and commented on

370

School Certificate results. He had the kids hanging on his every word, made them roar with laughter. His timing was perfect."

I find it hard to comment on what you have been through – it has been my first experience of seeing a man in an impossible situation. You have had to run as a school, what was really a highly politicised sub-university. The fact that I cannot comment is due to the fact that I have lots of brash 30-year-old solutions to most things, but I can see no solution to this situation.

Janet had hit the nail on the head. There were no solutions for my dear Mr. Chips of a husband, so dedicated to providing boys and girls with the educational foundations to enable them to become leaders with good standards and values, but whose world had been turned upside down by insidious political interference.

Perhaps most painful of all, was what John saw as the duplicity of some of his white staff who had fostered a rush to independence at almost any cost. They deliberately fomented grievances and any slight sense of injustice to satisfy agendas John could not comprehend.

'They really cannot understand the African people. These kids are not stupid – they will have seen right through them I feel quite sure. They may be useful now, and the unscrupulous will use them to the hilt, but I suspect they will be sidelined when it comes to the crunch in the future.'

There was an edge of bitterness in John's voice. I wondered at which point I had lost that idealistic young Cambridge graduate.

'I'm scared by what I see for the future if the political leaders that Britain is listening to at the moment achieve power,' he had confided to me. 'I'm scared by their lack of leadership experience... bothered about their real motives behind this rushed grab for political power... and frankly, I am now terrified of what the future holds for those who have been educated and are taking leadership roles – and I am talking black here, not white.'

'How do you think the Nationalists will relate to them?' I asked. 'Will they see them as threatening – or will they use their talents and skills as they should?'

'My head tells me of course, that they must use them to the benefit of the country... my heart says they may dispose of anyone who knows more than they do, or who points a finger at abuses of power... particularly anyone who has chosen that political arena.

'We're being squeezed into a time frame which may condemn this

371

wonderful country to a future as bleak as some other countries in Africa. We need another two generations of education at least... but the way things are going, we're just not going to get it.'

Due to their educational qualifications, his pupils would already be entitled to have a full vote immediately under the qualified franchise introduced by the 1961 Constitution. The Nationalists saw them as productive and well off and feared that they just might feel the gradual power-sharing concept proposed under that constitution was the better option.

If they were a threat they would immediately become a target, particularly those boys and girls who had decided to go into public or political office. Those who were in business or the professions were slightly less affected.

Now we watched with trepidation and anxiety as ex-pupils from both Goromonzi and Mzingwane were targeted for violence, torture and in a couple of cases, suspected murder.

It was truly heartbreaking.

John had been appointed straight away to Head Office, but found it stifling and longed to be back in a school. I felt him disappearing more and more in that environment. Somehow it seemed to emphasise all the struggles he and other heads of African schools had had.

They had fought for greater education allocations – but they had had to accept the fact that the country was still so pitifully undeveloped that it had to marshal and allocate resources very carefully. The tax-paying public in Rhodesia was so small... and still heavily dominated by Europeans. Attitudes towards African education had changed dramatically since the 1940s, but it was hard to stretch the altruism of the white taxpayer too greatly.

The debate still raged; whether to educate everyone to the highest standard possible, which, because of the sheer numbers involved, could never be more than a basic six years of schooling or to give everyone at least primary school education and then take as many as humanly possible through to Higher School Certificate level and for a few, tertiary entrance.

John's concern had been that the first option would see vast numbers of half-educated people, all with increased expectations that jobs and wealth were within their grasp. All becoming frustrated and bewildered to find there was nothing for them as full employment would prove quite impossible, due to sheer weight of numbers, while the country had the highest population growth in the world. Having raised expectations, it would be cruel to expect anyone to return happily to herding cattle.

The risk had always been that those not fortunate enough to be schooled to higher education would be susceptible to anyone who came along preaching a new or more seductive scenario full of potential "opportunities". This had already started happening with the interest shown by the Russians at Mzingwane in the '50's and now by the Chinese.

John believed that the answer was to educate as fast as it was possible – properly and well, so that the country would at least have that core of educated people with the ability and understanding of the requirements, to take on leadership and responsibility.

The "Winds of Change" speech by British Prime Minister, Harold Macmillan, had signified not only an increased demand for black independence, but also and more significantly, Britain's own agenda – in particular, her loss of will to govern her colonies any longer.

'The Brits can't wait to be rid of us,' he'd start – then remember that I was English. 'Sorry, my duck, but it's true. They have their own agenda – and part of it must be that they want to be seen by their trading partners in the rest of Africa and Asia as being squeaky clean and cracking down on racialists.

'White racialists – that's what we have been labelled... can you believe it? It is too idealistic to say we should not have come here in the first place – if we hadn't, it would have been the Germans or the Portuguese. It has happened. My firm belief is that Britain had learned a great deal about colonization of countries with existing indigenous populations, which is why our constitution, as the last of the new British colonies, entrenches so much concern for the African people's welfare.

'Mostly I believe we have tried hard to advance the lot of the African people. We have heaps of unthinking idiots, I know that, but those of us born here understand and respect each other's strengths and weaknesses and live with each other pretty well.

'...those blooming Brits will cast us off without another thought. They really couldn't give a damn whether the Africans are ready or not – as long as they are seen to be doing what they perceive the world would regard as being the right thing.

'Nan, like it or not, the black people of this country are living in a

373

still developing, but now very sophisticated western economy. The opportunities are enormous *provided* the economy remains buoyant. I know I'm beginning to sound like a stuck record, but how on earth can anyone in all honesty expect them to take over and run it well when they have, in the vast majority of cases, not even one educated parent behind them – it is unrealistic.'

I was never very interested in politics, but I had, at least, gathered that implementation of the 1961 Constitution would have removed any remaining powers "at present vested in the Government of the United Kingdom". It would also ensure that Africans were steadily brought into governance by easy stages until our Parliament was a wholly non-racial institution.

The British Government, with the endorsement of Joshua Nkomo, one of John's old boys, and leader of the National Democratic Party, had agreed to confer independence to the country, upon acceptance of the Constitution by the electorate. The British Government had been instrumental in putting the terms of the new Constitution together. They would retain only the titular headship applicable to any one-time British Colony. Nkomo, also a party to drawing up the Constitution, agreed fully with the terms and announced he would cooperate in making them work.

Unfortunately, intimidation of black voters became worse and worse in the weeks leading up to the vote. Ultimately, few of them felt a trip to a polling booth was worthwhile. If only they had done so, things might have been different.

65% of the Rhodesian electorate, by now almost entirely white voters as a result of the intimidation, agreed to accept the terms of the referendum held in July of that year – effectively voting themselves out of office.

We can only presume that neither Joshua Nkomo nor the British Government expected that result, for in the most remarkable about-face and only weeks after the outcome of the referendum was known, the British Government reneged on the agreed white papers by ensuring that it would still remain in control of major decisions.

Nkomo returned from London, having rejected the terms outright and was allegedly responsible for instigating a reign of terror in the townships and rural areas. Those in the firing line were helpless, defenceless civilians who had dared to think differently. They were the African elite – the educated, the well-to-do – they were the schools, the rural councils and chiefs, the trading stores.

To that point, John had watched Nkomo with interest and was pleased to see him emerge as one of the true leaders of the country. He'd always been an exceptional and John had employed him in several capacities in order to ensure he could complete his School Certificate. Joshua was someone he could trust with the future of the country. But seeing what his former pupil was doing almost drove him to despair – his "sensitiveness of spirit" made him feel almost responsible for what Nkomo was doing.

'Who got to him Nan?' he shook his head in despair. 'There was a better way to go. The old Joshua would have shown the world what Africa, under good disciplined leadership, could do. The new one has sold his soul to someone.'

'It must have been difficult for him...' I ventured tentatively.

'Oh, I'm sure it was – but nothing in public life is ever easy. I had such high hopes for him. Now he seems to be the direct cause of all this murder and mayhem. At one time, his eyes shone with love for his people and the vision of what he could do for them. He was, to me, the epitome of the strong, fine Matabele leadership of the past – of Mzilikazi and of Lobengula... he could have taken this country into the 21st century with honour and stability, in partnership with the Europeans. I'm afraid for what lies ahead now...'

With the change of heart by Britain and the Nationalists the country was in crisis... trying to understand and to sort out which direction to take in circumstances which seemed to change almost on a daily basis.

I found myself thinking back to our early days at Dombo' in 1935. I remembered John's concerns about discrepancies in the standards of white and black housing and about white staff having free access to school farm produce like meat, milk, cream and butter. I remembered his frustration with the social mores of the time which dictated that he would never be able to know his teachers and pupils as real friends, as his father had done, with such mutual benefit, at Plumtree.

Yet, after those initial misgivings he had grown to know, to trust and to love many of the wonderful teachers and pupils who had worked with him over the years. It was still my greatest joy to see an African face light up with recognition: 'Ah, Mr Hammond...'

He'd suffered the distaste of many Europeans over many years – people who felt he must be a radical left-winger to be teaching black pupils. But ultimately his dignity, his refusal to compromise on matters of discipline and morality, his total commitment to the production of future leaders with integrity and ability had won wide respect both sides of the colour line.

Then came a new job offer – a new challenge. This time, it was the establishment of a Community Development Centre at Domboshawa. This time, he'd be training adults at grass roots level.

Yes, this was a challenge – which might be worthwhile. And again it took him out of the office and back into a learning environment, in a place we had always loved.

It looked as though there would be some excellent staff with him. He was delighted when Noel Estcourt was appointed as Deputy Head. Noel had proved invaluable to John and had acted as Head at Goromonzi when he had left so peremptorily. His Rhodesian upbringing, with the natural affinity with the African people that this seemed to bring, had been integral in the decisions made together, which helped turn the school into one gaining respect as not only equal to but better than most European schools at the time.

He'd also heard good reports about the man who'd be playing a key role in the fulfilment of the new policy, Chad Chapunza… and dear dependable old Rex Coleman would at last be working with him again, as he had been appointed from Mzingwane to manage the farm at Domboshawa. With luck he might even have Rex's lovely and competent wife, Merle, as his secretary again.

Although the new position appeared to be another potential political minefield, John felt that with the increasing pressures for instant change, development of rural communities at the grass-roots level was absolutely vital.

It offered him the opportunity to be back doing what he loved and believed in most – down-to-earth, practical training and preparation for those who needed it, but who'd had the least access to academic schooling. He'd be working with people based in the country, people caught between the timeless pleasantries of a relatively stable and unchanged rural way of life and the threatening restlessness of their young returning from the inquietude of the cities.

John was appointed on 3rd October 1963. It had felt as though we were starting all over again. We were going back to the place where our love, our hopes and our determination to do something worthwhile with our lives had taken root and flowered. This was where we'd spent those idyllic three months getting to know each other after 15 months of letter writing. This was where I had hoped we'd start our married life. This was where we might heal the hurt and betrayal of Goromonzi.

Domboshawa had always been a wonderful place. It had large, graciously built homes with easy access to fresh farm produce and outstanding school buildings and facilities. It was a little village in itself, a real show place, but best of all, it was only 18 miles from Salisbury and therefore, with direct access to those in positions of influence.

As we approached Domboshawa, sunk in our own thoughts I knew that while I remembered the betrayals of trust and the shock to me with my gentle English background, of the early years in Tjolotjo John was, as always, agonising over whether he'd be able to make enough of a difference. Most important, whether there was still enough time left to be able to do so.

I found myself continuously anxious about John nowadays. He no longer seemed to have the physical resilience that was once such a characteristic of this well-built husband of mine. Worried about the cynicism, the discouragement, the dejection, the loss of faith in the future that had built up over the last few years. Worried that the inevitable hardening of that sensitive spirit was steadily destroying a man without a manipulative or political bone in his body ... a man bewildered by artifice or deception of any kind who had been forced to learn some bitter lessons. He seemed suddenly to be very fragile.

Community Development was one of the more attractive planks on which the Rhodesian Front, under Winston Field, was voted into power in December 1962. John didn't agree with the harder line of the Rhodesian Front and was disappointed when the United Federal Party, under Sir Edgar Whitehead, lost office.

After 15 months of terror following the referendum on the '61 constitution, Whitehead had been forced to clamp down and ban the NDP. The Rhodesian electorate felt it had been conned and lost faith in Whitehead's ability to lead the country any further.

As a result, Winston Field was elected as head of the new government when the recently formed Rhodesian Front swept the board in December 1962. He was an open, honest farmer who won the hearts of the electorate as a down-to-earth man of the soil who, they felt, could be trusted to negotiate better with the British than the earnest and academic Sir Edgar.

John liked Field, but was concerned that many of the RF's political platforms were hard-edged and uncompromising. However, he did agree with their Community Development philosophy.

This was designed to encourage everyone throughout the country to come under the influence of a local government authority – not just those in urban centres. Government saw this as a way of devolving some responsibility for primary school education into local communities. The population growth was so great that the stated aim of giving every child an education at primary level was becoming impossible to manage.

But Government had still not spelled out how it would put this new structure into effect. It hadn't yet told its own officials, let alone anyone else – and John found he would now be responsible to five separate Government ministries! To carry out all they envisaged, there was going to be a huge training job to be done. But how were the staff to construct the courses or identify participants in this communications vacuum? How was it all to be managed thereafter?

As we arrived to take up the new position, there was still this extraordinary lack of clarity. An article in the *Rhodesia Herald* the week before, by noted political commentator Phillippa Berlyn was headlined: "The community development idea has become muddled…"

This was going to increase the pressure on staff and advisers at Dombo'. In addition, there remained in some quarters, considerable uncertainty as to the future of Domboshawa itself, with a large number of people, black and white, keen to see it return to its original use as an industrial school.

Finally, and, probably because of this lack of clarity on the whole issue, Community Development was being seen as a form of apartheid and the propagation of this idea had quickly been adopted by many who 'should have known better.'

It was against this confused background of promised projects, which had increased demand to a point where it was very difficult to manage, that we drove up to what had been the Mylne's old house – the headmaster's house at Domboshawa.

The sense of déjà vu was overpowering. In one of John's very first letters to me in 1935, when he was describing Domboshawa, he talked of this lovely old home and speculated over whether we would ever live in that house ourselves. It had been the scene of many happy parties and events on my first trip to Rhodesia, the year before we were married. I was thrilled to think we'd be living there and determined to play my part in supporting, encouraging or whatever was needed. I settled happily into the house and spent a couple of days going round to meet the new staff and ensure that they were all right.

It was a happy time – but after my early experience of outside PKs, I was amazed to find that this huge great house still had no inside toilet – in 1963! This would have to change – immediately! I made it my personal crusade – and won! My lightness of spirit is reflected in a poem which I penned in an irreverent moment – and sent to the Department. (With apologies to Gilbert and Sullivan!)

> **Ode in gratitude**
> *Oh joy, oh rapture unforeseen, behold this vision glorious*
> *So light, so bright, so shining white, at last my plea's victorious*
> *My health – oh how it has improved and that too of my spouse*
> *As well as being beautiful – It just completes the house*
>
> *No longer do I have to flee in terror from each bat*
> *And after all – it did seem odd at night to don a hat*
> *To save myself from Dracula who languished in his lair*
> *And every time that I appeared flew straight into my hair*
>
> *Ten steps only now we take – instead of thirty-nine*
> *Oh thank you, thank you very much… it really is just FINE*

As soon as we got there, John was involved inevitably, in much more serious matters. At first it seemed to be a round of endless meetings, of which one of the most productive was with Roger Howman, a leading member of the Government. He was an old Prunitian, for whom John had a lot of respect, and the architect of the Community Development policy. Roger's letter to John had been one of the reasons he took the position:

> *The establishment of African Local Government is the natural evolution of Community Development. But we have some concerns from the Missions who are reluctant to relinquish their control of Primary Education.*
> *However, the Judges Commission has an unanswerable case for placing primary education under Local Government auspices. So the training of able administrators, council secretaries, officers and councillors themselves, as well*

as a variety of District Officers and Community advisers is of paramount importance in the scheme of things.

It had been a meeting of like minds – they both felt it was vital that communities preserved their own disciplines and cultures. This could be a way of doing it. Hand in glove however, was the need to equip those communities enough to be able to provide good primary education in situ before their best students went elsewhere for secondary education.

John found it most enjoyable working with adults for a change and of course, he knew so many of the friends and relations of all the men and women who attended the courses. In fact, he seemed to be enjoying every moment of it.

Once again, part of the business of setting it all up was to travel around the country talking to the chiefs and headmen, to local government advisers and to the people, on what these changes might mean. John was always at his happiest talking to these wonderful old men – many of whom were now trusted friends. In fact, I have seldom seen him happier than when he was in that first year at Dombo.

He respected the profound and complicated process of discussion, tribal law and custom, ceremonial rites and spiritual approvals which lay behind the choice of a hereditary chief. He admired the way they would consult with the whole community sometimes for days on end, to achieve consensus. Once that consensus was achieved, the people would have complete faith in their chief to represent their views accurately and in their best interests.

Government policy was to put into place relevant courses to train the greatest number of people in the most effective way, in the shortest possible time. Generally, it appeared that the Chiefs and their people liked the idea and felt it would give more of their community the chance of at least some education. They were concerned, however, about how it would be funded and maintained.

The new Government was finding its feet but seemed unable to communicate what it was trying to achieve nearly effectively enough. Training within the institution was soon going from strength to strength, but those being trained were not finding things easy once they'd left Domboshawa to put their techniques into practice. This was because District Commissioners still didn't seem to understand the function of the new Community Advisers. John began to doubt if the training methods they had been asked to put into place could ever be effective under these conditions.

When approached about the position, while glad to be out of Head Office, John had reservations. One of his earliest reports to Government after taking up the position, he said:

> *My greatest anxiety is the feeling that we are to be the main agency in the initiation of a policy which few senior officials have taken the trouble to understand fully.*
>
> *Village workers are being trained to initiate a new pattern of thought in tribal areas; a pattern of thought, which it will be almost impossible to change, once it has taken on. At Domboshawa we are going to be instrumental in bringing about these changes. We all believe they are highly desirable, but there are many that disapprove of the training we offer and the methods we advocate. Much of this disapproval arises from ignorance...*

Despite this, in that first year, all 240 Community Advisers had been to Domboshawa for training, and 1,026 other administrators, council secretaries and clerks, and councillors had been there to attend seminars and other short courses.

The Chiefs suggested it would be useful if they were also briefed fully. So a series of courses was organised for Chiefs and Headmen, initially run by the Department of Conservation and Extension and then by Local Government and Community Development.

This first hurdle of gaining approval by the Africans themselves had been achieved to a great extent by the end of the first year.

Noel Estcourt started by accompanying John on these trips then started to go off on his own. He came to love the trips as much as John did and after one particularly long trip, he popped in to tell me about it.

'Nancy, I still find it intriguing that John knows and is known to such a huge number of Africans right across Rhodesia. When I travelled around the country it was amazing to find people in far-flung places who, in our casual conversation, would find out about my ties to Goromonzi and Domboshawa and they'd all say the same thing, "Ah... then you would know Mr Hammond."

'I am always impressed by his memory for names of people and their extended family relationships. He is just ideal in this position and I love working with him because as always, he trusts the professional integrity of his staff, and out of that trust comes cohesion and a happy, effective community.'

But storm clouds were gathering and Rhodesia was heading for its most serious political crisis yet.

Britain was determined to rush through a form of independence on the British basis of "one man, one vote" and with no understanding of how naïve the majority of the still rurally-based population was about what on earth a vote really meant. Britain was aided and abetted by a now more militant Joshua Nkomo and his right-hand man Ndabaningi Sithole.

'If we are going to hand over power Nan, the Chiefs must be in the mix somewhere. They are the traditional rulers. They can explain the changes to people far better than we can. They've have been brought up to lead since they were very young.

'They're fine people, full of wisdom and concern for their communities and although it's changing fast, about 90% of the Africans in this country are still closely affiliated with the tribal system and regard it as the core of their society.

'Even today, the Africans' social, spiritual and economic life is shared by the extended family of neighbours and community... the fabric of their kinship is intricately woven and is something I admire immensely.

'I don't believe that Nkomo and Sithole have yet shown that they have the experience to lead a Western-style government... they seem too easily swayed by manipulators. We cannot have people who've never held a position of leadership of this kind run a country on their own. There will always be plenty of do-gooders who'll argue the idealistic point in favour of an immediate hand-over.

'But *none* of them have real understanding of the African consensus decision-making process or the huge amount of learning needed for an African leader to adapt to the individual decision making needs of a Westminster style of government. Neither of these two could manage the complexities of this Government, matching international dictates with the expectations of the people – yet. They need time.'

'What is Britain thinking of?' I wondered bleakly.

John went on 'Surely they understand that these inexperienced nationalist leaders seem so easily to turn things to the benefit of their own personal agenda rather than the best interests of the country? My heart breaks for us all, if we're to be ruled by these chaps. A government such as we have now, requires firm but altruistic leadership, they will be completely at sea with that at the moment and might eventually have to resort to rule through some sort of dictatorship. This would lead on to the entrenching of their own power at the expense of their people.

'We either need another 20 years, or sufficient time to educate another generation... or somehow the Chiefs must be in the seats of Government from the beginning.'

This was an area where John found himself in total agreement with the Rhodesian Front but Winston Field had fallen on the sword of his own transparent honesty in the machinations that occurred during the dismemberment of the Central African Federation. He appeared to have been thoroughly out-manoeuvred and used by Britain's wily Minister of State, R. A. Butler. The suspicious and uncompromising Ian Smith had filled the vacuum and the push for independence was now gaining momentum. Smith was felt to be the right man at the right time.

The main concern was that Smith was also quite tough enough to declare his own form of independence if pushed too far. However, he had said in a BBC television interview in September, that the British Government had told him that if he could prove he had the support of the majority, they would grant independence based on the 1961 Constitution.

It had always been Government policy to discuss matters of national importance with the Chiefs as the most effective mechanism of communicating with the whole population. Rhodes had done it first at a massive *indaba* (meeting) in Matabeleland in 1890, the Government had done so in 1923 when Southern Rhodesia became a colony of the Crown. Again, in 1939 when Rhodesia was dragged into the Second World War ... and again at the time of Federation in 1953. The Chiefs would be briefed and they would be consulted with their concerns taken into consideration in the final outcomes. Despite the reservations of the British Government as to its acceptability as a test of majority support, Smith wanted another *indaba* involving all the Chiefs and Headmen.

He wanted it to be held at Domboshawa.

We knew the Chiefs were being intimidated... that each day there were countless stonings, with villages being burnt and that the lives of the Chiefs were in danger. They had become the very deliberate targets of the Nationalists who knew all too clearly the Chiefs' ability to win the hearts and minds of the people, at their expense.

Smith believed an *indaba* had to be held quickly, before the Nationalists gained any more ground in either their intimidation or their discrediting of the Chiefs. John was asked to put the organisation in motion for an *indaba* to be held at Domboshawa only three weeks later, on 22nd October.

Unfortunately, Smith's timing was not good. The first time the British Prime Minister heard about these plans was apparently on the eve of a tightly contested British election. The Conservative Prime Minister, Sir Alec Douglas-Home, distracted by his own election issues, responded to say that the British Government could not support the idea of an *indaba* as any measure of majority opinion.

The next day, the Labour Party under Harold Wilson, was elected with a parliamentary majority of five. The damage was done. Home's last-minute rejection of the *indaba* meant Labour could renege on any earlier promises made about tests of acceptability.

So it was in this highly charged atmosphere, that the *indaba* was to proceed. It was hoped that most of the 190 Chiefs and 420 Headmen would be able to get there... but now there was going to be nobody from Britain to listen to them.

The organisation behind it all was enormous. John kept saying to everyone likely to be involved at Domboshawa, 'It has to be right – it has to be absolutely right... we cannot afford anything else to go wrong. The Chiefs have to have our protection, they have to be seen for the leaders they are...'

It was to be done with maximum security, with everyone accommodated either in the dormitories or in tents. Nobody was to be allowed off the premises during the course of the *indaba*. Classes had to be suspended and only those who were supposed to be on the property would be accredited and allowed entry into the area. Police with dogs would constantly parade the perimeter.

Now, everything was ready. As I set my alarm that night to make sure I was up at 5.30 in the morning, it seemed as though the last cogs had finally fallen into place.

And now I had not woken up in time.

Breakfast was hardly over when the Chiefs started to arrive. We both went down to the main reception area to greet them. My eyes filled with tears to see these dignified old men, dressed in their scarlet robes of office as they clasped hands with John – so pleased to see him there

384

with them at this critical point. Many of them told the most dreadful stories of what they had suffered in the last year. Torment, torture, death, the destruction of villages and crops. I found myself weeping – and knew John would be almost too choked up to speak.

And still they came – defying everything that could be thrown at them, to make sure they took part.

One of his old boys and a leading Ama'Ndebele Chief, Kayisa Ndiweni took him to one side, 'Nkosi, we know the British Government probably won't listen. But look – we have all come. Everyone. Every Chief – every Headman to the most junior of all… has come. Perhaps, Nkosi, when they see all of us here, they will listen. We have important words to say to them about our troublesome children who have no right to speak for the African people of this country.'

The *indaba* began with Chief after Chief taking his turn to say his piece. They said they deeply regretted the fact that the British Government had treated them with such disrespect. First they'd displayed lack of courtesy in not receiving the delegation of Chiefs who went to London to talk to them in July and now, they'd refused to send anyone to the *indaba*.

Chief after Chief, in their time-honoured way, sent the message of their people and gave their wholehearted approval to the 1961 Constitution as the basis for independence. Chief after Chief, Headman after Headman, repeated this approval to show their consensus and what was more important, the consensus of their people.

At lunch, John caught up with Chief Kayisa to ask him how he felt it was going.

'They are not here, nkosi. Their television people have brought their cameras, but the cameras are still. They hold them to their eyes, but they are not taking the right pictures – for I know the light on top of the camera must show red to take pictures. However much truth we speak, they will not be satisfied. Do we have to take them to the graves of those who have been killed? But then they will not believe the Nationalists have killed them. If we show them the damage done to the churches, the dip tanks, the schools – will they be satisfied? I don't think so.

'I believe they wish to hand us over to the Nationalists and there is nothing we can do to stop it. And look, we have, every one of us, come from the farthest places in the country. But there is nothing we can do to stop it.'

The old man took John's hand in his, and his eyes shone too brightly as he said, 'Nkosi, if they do not listen to us, this is the death of our society as we know it.'

He turned slowly, to move off to the next session. As he drew near the entrance into the main hall, John saw the old Chief pull his shoulders back, put his chin up and march in for another round of talking. They were not going to give up easily.

John felt overwhelmingly tired. He walked to the office. Merle Coleman looked up as he came in – saw him loosening his tie, saw the perspiration on his brow and the pallor of his face.

'I'm going to lie down Merle… it's all been a bit much.'

She offered to take him round in the car, but he refused. She watched his progress with concern as he walked away. A few moments later, still uneasy, she walked after him. He was sitting down on the kerbside, with his head in his hands.

She wrote to me later:

I tore off to find Mr. Estcourt and we both watched him. He would not have been charmed if we had followed him. One of us rang you. We were so relieved to see you run down the path and see Mr. Hammond put his arms round you as you walked very slowly into the house.

John was gasping for breath and making a deep grunting sound. He was in great pain.

'Where is it darling?' I cried.

He pointed to his chest. I helped him into bed and mopped his forehead as best I could… then rang Merle.

'Please find the doctor for me Merle – John's very ill.'

Twenty agonising minutes later, as John groaned, tossed and sweated on the bed, I heard a gentle knock and turned to see Merle at the door.

'I'm sorry Mrs. Hammond, I have pulled every string I can and so has Mr. Estcourt – but no doctor is going to be allowed through the security screen until they have been accredited. They can't do that before the morning. And I'm afraid they can't bring an ambulance through the cordon either.'

I shook my head in disbelief. I didn't know if John was sleeping or unconscious. What on earth was I going to do? Dear Noel came in and said he would immediately take over John's role and I should not worry about that. Oh thank God.

John seemed to be peaceful so I took the chance to ring the doctor myself, describe the symptoms and ask what on earth I should do until he came the next morning. He listened gravely. Then he confirmed that it was very probably a heart attack and that the next 24 hours were critical. He advised me to have John admitted into hospital as soon as we could the next morning. In the meantime, I had to keep him quiet and sit with him to give him all-important closeness and comfort. "No visitors", he said. "Absolutely *no* visitors".

I had been sitting beside John for a couple of hours when I looked up to see that it was already dark. The sweat was pouring off him. I kept mopping and mopping it up, he was hardly conscious. Just occasionally, rousing enough to recognise me.

I had to find something to eat, as I felt overcome and faint with the worry of it all. I opened the back door for a breath of fresh air.

I leaned against it and closed my eyes, thankful for the cool nights of high altitude in the middle of the hottest month of the year. I prayed and prayed and prayed. It seemed so cruel that after all he had been through.

As I opened my eyes to walk inside, I saw the glow of a cigarette in the dark.

'Who's there?' I asked.

'It is only me, inkosikaas.' Chief Kayisa moved into the light. 'How is Mr Hammond? Is he very sick?'

I nodded as a wave of emotion engulfed me.

He looked at me and said, 'I will wait here until he is better.'

My eyes filled and I could not speak. I grasped the old Chief's hands in silent gratitude for his presence and support as I turned to go back into the house.

I was awake all night. I had to keep on mopping his brow and giving him sips of water. All night, watching, wondering and fearing what might happen to the love of my life. I watched as the sky outside the window began to lighten.

'Hello Nannie.'

I looked over at the bed. He was back. Tired, but clear-eyed.

'I'd love a cup of tea.'

I was only too thrilled to get him one – I flew to the kitchen. Then I remembered… I opened the door. Sure enough, the cigarette was still glowing. I walked out over the lawn and the old man stood up. 'He speaks, Chief, and he wants a cup of tea.'

'My heart is glad.' He took my hand. 'He will get well again. Please, inkosikaas, please remember that to us Africans, Mr. Hammond is our father – he is the great teacher. He is loved by all Africans.'

I wept unashamedly as the proud old Chief took his leave and walked off for another day of trying to get the British Government to listen to him.

As I took the tea back to John, I could see he was bothered... he was tossing and turning in his agony.

But this time it was not a physical agony. It was absolute agony of mind.

'Oh Nannie – they're not going to listen – is everything we have worked for going to be in vain – have we been able to achieve anything at all?' He was so upset. On and on he cried out as I tried to calm him. I was frightened that this could provoke another attack.

As he settled a little, very quietly, I told him about Chief Kayisa. I told him that the old man had sat out in the garden for hours, because he hadn't been allowed to see him. I told him what he had said. John lay back and smiled. I felt him relax and he closed his eyes.

I saw the tiniest suggestion of a tear slide down his face and I knew that because of one glowing cigarette in the dark of a troubled night, my Beloved African would survive.

Epilogue

My father did recover from his heart attack. He was critically ill for some time and it meant he had to take early retirement at the age of 54.

He was named an Officer of the Order of the Legion of Merit in 1971. This was an honour instituted by the by now illegal Rhodesian Government, equivalent to, and in lieu of, the OBE. Britain no longer recognised the pariah colony or its subjects.

Despite this there was other, meaningful recognition. To his delight he received a letter from Mr. O. Mlilo, Headmaster of Mzingwane School in September 1976.

> *The School has received authority from Head Office, to name one of our new hostels after you, in recognition of your dedicated service to the school.*
> *I should be very glad if you consented to our naming one of the hostels "John Hammond House".*

It was not long before Dad became involved in the "Freedom from Hunger" campaign and was national Chairman for four years. During this period, and despite the sanctions imposed as a result of UDI, he was invited to the FAO Congress in Rome to present a paper. As Mum and Dad arrived, they discovered their invitation had been rescinded. All those with whom Dad had been having fruitful discussions now turned their backs on him. Only after lengthy negotiations with the convener was Dad allowed to attend the sessions. He was not permitted to present his paper. After much discussion, Mum and Dad both felt that the work being done in Rhodesia was so excellent and could be of such value to other parts of the world, that they decided to stay regardless, in the hope of being able to talk to some of the delegates.

It proved very difficult. They were completely ostracised by the

389

British and Commonwealth delegates in particular – receiving a note one evening from one of the leaders of the British delegation asking if they could meet "in secret" to discuss what Rhodesia was doing. Having spent many hours into the wee small hours every night, copying the speech he would have given; Mum would distribute it through the lobbies, toilets and any other places where it might be picked up, while sessions were in progress. As a result they soon began to attract a great deal of attention, particularly from the Asian countries – and many more meetings went on "in secret". The outcome of a number of these meetings made their decision to stay on, in the face of such antagonism, well worth while.

One of Dad's major contributions in his role as Chairman of Freedom From Hunger was the subsidised development, in conjunction with a commercial company, of a high-protein drink that was distributed widely to help combat kwashiorkor, a debilitating and potentially fatal condition arising from malnutrition. Dad insisted that a few pence be paid for every pint received in the knowledge that the product would have some value, would be appreciated and carefully used. The incidence of kwashiorkor during this time was significantly reduced.

During the mid-70s, Dad played the key role, on a voluntary basis, in running Co-Ord-A-Nation. This was an organisation designed to help bring communities, black and white, together – to help women who had husbands and sons fighting in the civil war. In many cases African families would have several sons who had volunteered to fight for the Rhodesian Army as well as sons who were outside the country fighting for either ZANLA or ZIPRA, the military wings of the two competing Nationalist parties operating from their bases in Zambia and Mozambique. The situation for the women in these families was appalling.

The white women also suffered as sons and husbands, up to the age of 60, were conscripted for long periods of call-up in the bush, leaving the womenfolk to run businesses and cope with children who did not know their fathers. By galvanising their communities Co-Ord-A-Nation became a pivot for *all* these women, helping thousands right around the country. It also opened a series of Forces' Canteens.

One of the greatest "hurts" of Dad's life took place after Independence in 1980 when Co-Ord-A-Nation held its final get-together before disbanding. Several hundred people were there, black and white, civilians and members of the forces. As a courtesy the country's new leaders had been invited, but it was thought unlikely they would come.

The party was in full swing when a hush descended and Dad turned to see the giant figure of one of his old boys, now a key member of the new government, Joshua Nkomo. A path opened up in front of him as he strode towards Dad.

Dad remembered the bright-eyed intelligent youngster whom he had encouraged and helped to further his education, the youngster he had admired and for whom he had held out so many hopes. He then remembered the man who had inexplicably reneged on the 1961 Constitution that, as a result created the circumstances which led to the Unilateral Declaration of Independence… and the bitter civil war with its unutterable cruelty to the civilian population that was to last for 15 years.

His heart froze.

Joshua strode down that long room. As he neared Dad, he opened his arms wide and said, 'My Principal,' enveloping Dad in a huge bear hug.

Dad was stricken but he could never be discourteous. He introduced Nkomo to several key people around the room. Time stood still as he did so … he was overwhelmed by his thoughts – thoughts of the responsibilities they had had as the teachers and leaders of these youngsters and of how terribly wrong it had all gone. His heart finally broke.

Mum couldn't face him at all and turned her back on him to walk away with tears streaming down her face.

A couple of years later, when he received the following letter, his sadness was all-encompassing. One of his best teachers at Mzingwane, a parent at Goromonzi and a close friend, Roger Malusalila, was dead:

Dear Mr. and Mrs. Hammond,
Roger had been in good health when one evening on the 10th October a gunman entered our bedroom ordered him out and said to me, 'Mdala uya buya mama' ('We will bring the old man back, mama'). I waited for him for two hours then I heard gun shots. I knew it was the end. In the morning I found him dead, hands folded as if praying. He was murdered with three others.

Friends and relatives visit us daily from different parts of the country to comfort us and pray for us. At present I am staying with Samuel – he has

four children – the first boy has just written his Form IV exams.
I hope you and Mrs. Hammond are in good health.
Yours sincerely,
S. Maluslila

When the opportunity arose for my father to leave Rhodesia and join his family in Australia, he decided to do so. I had always been concerned that Dad was so much a part of Africa that he could never survive away from it.

He said to me, 'Your darling mother has given me 50 years of her life in a country she was never really suited to. The least I can do is take her back to her beloved sea for the last years of our lives.'

Shortly before they left for Australia, they were taken to lunch at the Harare Club by Hosea Mapondera. It was a joyful occasion, full of happy reminiscence... until Hosea got serious and asked Dad, 'Why wasn't more done in African education?'

Dad replied that he would write to him about it. He spent some time doing so – but he never heard back and always wondered whether Hosea had received the letter.

John and Nancy settled well in Glenelg, South Australia and for nearly nine years he loved the new experiences of a new land, a new people and the easy access to world news and events. He was still intrigued by the state of the world, loved to hear qualified debate and was a lively and deep thinker to the end of his days. He enjoyed his last years in Australia – but he always kept in very close touch with Zimbabwe, with his friends and with everything that was happening there... and he continued to receive wonderful letters from his Old Boys.

Over a hundred people attended his funeral service in his new country, on the 18th October 1996 at St. Peter's Church, in Glenelg. Many hundred more attended a memorial service at Goromonzi School. And at their old church, Christchurch, in Borrowdale, Harare, some magnificent white and yellow flowers on the font held the simple epitaph:

"Fambai zvakanaka, shamwari"★

For Hosea, and anyone else who might ever have asked that question, I hope this book has provided some of the answers.

★ "Go well, friend"

Appendix 1

R. W. Hammond's
Farewell Sermon (1936)

Sunday, 12th April 1936

I face a difficult task tonight and I can only plead that the special circumstances of this occasion and the very special nature of this congregation afford me this privilege, which I believe to be far too great and important a one to be neglected or ignored. You will realise that such an opportunity cannot in the ordinary course of events come again to me and that the fact that in a very few days I leave this place, makes it possible for me to speak with a frankness and directness which would otherwise be difficult. I trust that nothing I say may, from its outspoken nature, give offence to or hurt anyone.

First, I want to speak as to the connection—as I see it—between religion and education and I would first briefly define these according to my ideas. By education I understand a process which begins on the day of a child's birth and the most vital part of which, influencing all the rest, is given in the first few years of a child's life by its parents, nurses and infant associates.

I believe further that this process of education never should and often never does cease while life lasts. I believe very firmly, as befits a schoolmaster, that during the years between infancy and the beginning of responsible manhood, education can best be given in a place, which has come to be known as a school. In some proportion of cases, diminishing with growing years, that education can best be given during that period partly in a school and partly in the child's home.

But I must first define a school, and to my mind the only place-which has the right to bear that honoured title, is one in which the

393

process of educating a child includes the education in body, in mind and in spirit and where education takes into account the whole of the art of living and not merely what should be the purely incidental art of making a living.

The Greek word from which school is derived meant "leisure" and any system which aims merely at training workers without regard to the non-working part of their lives must be intrinsically wrong—as utterly wrong as the attempts of rulers or governments to increase the population of the countries so as to ensure the possibility of large armies. And this precaution is especially necessary today when industry has to a great extent abolished the skilled craftsman, and substituted the machine minder, whose only hope of an interesting and worthwhile life must lie in his leisure hours. And so I cannot believe that the only essential part of a school is a collection of classrooms.

And now to return to the much more difficult task of defining religion. The experience of my life and a good deal of hard thinking, have led me to change and modify my views, but I have for some years back been content to define it to myself as consisting in the long run of only one real virtue, which seems to me to run like a thread through all religions, though smothered in many by fears and ignorance and superstition. That central thread or core I believe to be unselfishness— the willingness to sacrifice oneself for others.

I believe that the Christian religion contains a stronger core of this than others, and that the teachings of Christ Himself have it to a far greater extent that the doctrines of even any Christian Church. This spirit of unselfishness is present in almost all of Christ's teaching and on Good Friday we remember His final act of unselfishness and renunciation. I myself can see it too in the story of Easter and the Resurrection—that death is a negative state and that life alone can give this opportunity for exercising unselfishness, so that for Christ's work to continue and live there had to be a resurrection.

Now if this is considered as the central idea—the theme song—it can be found running through all Christian teaching and through many non-Christian religions. It may be overlaid so deeply with dogma and ceremony that it lies hidden, but I believe that it must be there in any religion which is to be a living one. We have all known this unselfishness lacking in many professedly religious people, and we have known it present to a high degree in some who might even be classed as heathen, and in others who neither know nor would discuss whether Christ was indeed God, or whether he was but a man living perfectly and teaching a perfect way of life to his fellow men and fellow sufferers.

And now, as to the relation between Religion and Education. Believing as I do that schools must care for the whole child, I maintain that there must be a religious influence at work in a school and that on this, the success or failure of a school's life and work will depend. And so I believe a Chapel to be as necessary a building as any other for a school. Unfortunately, it is generally the case that it is only in schools attached to some certain denomination that Chapels are found. Personally, I prefer that a school should be undenominational, just as I prefer a school drawn from a variety of sources, social and geographical—a school that is a cross-section of the country as a whole and not limited in any way.

I have reasons to be personally grateful to the Church of England; my home was in one of its parsonages, and my schools and university were closely attached to that Church. I have also reasons to be grateful to the Church for the work it did in founding this school and in helping it in its early years, and for its regular ministrations here, and for the lives of its clergy who have lived here as chaplains, and I am thankful for the kindly relations which have generally been possible here, and which have permitted of Padres of several denominations holding their services in the school.

But religion must not begin and end with the Chapel and with services—it may even exist independently of these—but it must enter into every side of school life. It must be a force finding expression in trouble and in rejoicing; it must see the good in everyone and help that good to come out and show itself; it must add interest and enthusiasm to work and to play; it must smooth out differences and difficulties and make any real enmity impossible. This religion will be shown far more in deeds than in words, and in the life taken as a whole of any that have it rather than by isolated acts.

It is not uncommon to find education systems, which regard schools as machines made to turn out certain standardised and exact products. I think this is wrong and that a school can be better compared to a forest or orchard—a collection of living, growing organisms sharing the same sun and air and soil in only slightly differing proportions, but bearing a great variety of different products to be put to different uses.

In such a school, masters can but guide and help their pupils to develop. This will need supervision and discipline both having to be exercised with much skill and care and tact which no machine-minding spirit will ever produce; and at the back of all their work there must be this religious influence running through the whole life and growth of each individual, and of the school as a whole.

And in such a school it should be possible to teach much to all which they can cherish through life. The love of truth and the love of the search for truth in so far as it can be found. The love of beauty in nature, in literature and in music – in all that is clean and sweet. The love of freedom—freedom with responsibility—in a world which in parts is steadily losing that freedom, or at least forgetting that it should be denied to none, and in others is almost accustomed to look on it as a crime.

It seems wrong in a British community to have to speak of being taught the love of freedom which our people have for centuries breathed in with the air of the lands which were theirs. But times change and tyranny can take many forms and even with us today there is real need to teach the love of freedom, and for many to learn that it is useless to teach that as a British virtue to subject races and then to deny it to them.

The love of skill in some worthwhile work of use or beauty. The love of fresh air, of birds and beasts and all God's creatures. The love of fine buildings and the noble things man has made to win his mastery over nature. The love of knowledge and the shame of wilful ignorance. The love of service for others—first for the individual, then for the small communities or family or school or town or nation, and finally, for all mankind, without which all lesser loves and royalties are empty and valueless. The love of manly strength and of fine, clean bodies.

I believe that the English Public School in the last half of the 19th century endeavoured to set the formation of character through such loves as these in the forefront of its ideas on the education of boys. I believe that in the last third of a century these ideas have spread to schools of many other types and I believe that our only hopes for the future lie in this direction. The world today presents the astounding paradox of man having complete control over nature and yet being willing to see the vast majority of mankind suffering from misery and want, from wars and famines and restrictions. This can only be due to fear, born of ignorance—ignorance leading to bad forms of government and giving opportunity for the exploitation of weaker nations and weaker social classes by the stronger. The great achievements of science and discovery and industry are being turned to ignoble ends or to those which are purely selfish.

And so, I would make my last words here a plea for education with a religious background, education conceived in no niggardly spirit nor one starved and stunted so that other interests may be protected, an education which will develop each and every individual whatever his conditions of birth or his colour so as to enable him to use his powers to the utmost of his ability and to the benefit of his fellow man. You have to carry on a school to know how few children get a real chance to do this nowadays.

The miserable economies made by the financial authorities controlling most State systems of education, the astonishing number of parents, even of the better-off class, who are unwilling to deny themselves enough to enable their own children to get a full education and those others who, while able and willing to give their own children of the best, are up in arms to prevent and thwart the State in its efforts to do so for less fortunate boys and girls.

We have been fortunate in this school in having many parents who were determined—at no matter what cost to themselves—to have their sons well equipped for life, but their spirit must become more general and in its own interests each State must be brought to see the falseness of the economy which denies to anyone of its citizens of the future full opportunity to develop to the full their powers of mind and body.

No schoolmaster can every be satisfied with his work in the way that a man turning out bricks or rails or machines can be, by feeling that he has made the best possible article out of the materials provided. A schoolmaster in laying down his work can only be conscious of his own weaknesses and his own defects and can only feel that considering these limitations he has with God's help done his best for his pupils; he can but hope that those pupils will grow up to be greater and better men than he is.

It is in this spirit that I commend to you this school. I believe that it contains the germs of greatness and that under Providence it can with the united work of staff and boys, old boys and parents, be made of great use and value to this country and to the world, of far greater use in the future than in the past.

R. W. Hammond
Headmaster, Plumtree School

Appendix 2

R. W. Hammond – Editorial (1936)

Tuesday, 14th April 1936

Sanderson of Oundle, Way of Grey, Hammond of Plumtree. How deeply a school principal may leave his mark on a school, a community, even a country has been emphasised at Plumtree over the Easter weekend.

With the close of the present school term and with such an interval as is necessary for the sweeping and garnishing that must necessarily be associated with the departure of one head and the installation of another, Mr. R. W. Hammond will cease to be Hammond of Plumtree in the peculiar sense in which he is Hammond of Plumtree today.

His faith in the future of the school he gave expression to in the course of his farewell address and he offered some observations on the reflections that crowd on the mind of a school principal who is laying aside his cap and gown. There does not come to the schoolmaster, he said, the same sense of satisfaction as to the man who has spent his time making things. There is not, of course the same possibility of a man reviewing his work and knowing it to be good and permanent; yet the material which the school principal has moulded... is material of a more permanent character than that which is worked by the craftsman; the influence, the example, the precept of the school principal may bear their fruit long after the best work of the most skilful craftsman has been forgotten.

Plumtree's remoteness gave it a homogeneity, which other, more centrally situated schools, necessarily lacked, and with that homogeneity came, inevitably, a greater measure of control and greater

398

opportunities to build up a valuable school tradition. And right well has Mr. Hammond laid the foundations and commenced the superstructure.

...Mr Hammond was urged by many to turn his talents to use in another sphere, the sphere of public life. He made no promise; he hinted, indeed, that the schoolmaster is not necessarily the best-equipped man to lead in public life... the not far distant future can decide Mr. Hammond's course of action.

In the meantime he may find satisfaction in watching the development of those to whom he has been mentor and in the fact that old boys of Plumtree School are playing a conspicuous part in the life of the Colony. It is essential that they should play such a part; it is essential that the old boys and old girls of all the Colony's schools should playa conspicuous part in the life of the country and in some measure the ultimate verdict of the success of otherwise of a school principal will be reckoned by the part which those who sat under him play in the country's affairs. Those who sat under Hammond of Plumtree have this to be said for them: that they start fortified by good precept and equally good example.

The Bulawayo Chronicle (abridged)

Appendix 3

John Hammond's Tjolotjo Sports' Day Speech (1938)

6th June 1938

It is customary on this day for a report on the year's work to be given. Before doing that, however, I want to thank you all for coming out here today.

That the journey is not a pleasure trip we all know; none better than those of us who live here. We have made an attempt this year to add a little comic relief to the monotony of the bumps. Our principal misgiving when editing the road map was that on first reading it through at Nyamandhlovu you would all turn round and go home again! I hope that what you have seen today has made you feel that the journey has been worthwhile.

By this time next year, I hope that the road map will be out of date. Next year a new and magnificent bridge is to be put across the Gwaai on another road. We owe this new bridge to the generosity of the Government, the Native Reserves Fund and the Beit Trustees. When this is completed the journey to Bulawayo will be less arduous than the one you have taken today, but even a new bridge cannot make an indifferent road perfect and there will still remain 15 miles of road on the new route which will be capable of doing damage to the springs of any car. But I sincerely hope that you will not let a mere 15 miles of bad road deter you from visiting us again.

Today, of course, the School is on show. Naturally things are looking a bit more spick and span than they usually do, but we have tried to give you some indication of what the School looks like on an ordinary working day. Naturally the boys work with greater enthusiasm when they have an audience to watch them; but you will have been able to get some idea of what we do here and how we do it. If any of you feel that you want to see more, I take this opportunity of extending to you an invitation to come out here when the School is in normal working order and to spend a day or two finding out more about the place.

This year, it was decided to limit the numbers of the School to 200. This was made necessary for two main reasons—water and accommodation. We have had anxious moments this year with our water supplies; in October last the second borehole gave signs of going in, one having done so the year before. Then in March this year, the third suddenly dropped just when it should have been at its best. A machine was rushed in to sink a new hole and has found an apparently excellent supply. This new borehole is not yet in use—the other two having picked up sufficiently to keep us going and our water problems are temporarily solved; I say "temporarily" because I would not dare to guarantee the life of any borehole in this area—only a very rash man would. When once an engine is put to pump on a hole it seldom seems to last more than three or four years and in spite of the thousand gallons an hour which our new hole gave on a test, I am still far from optimistic about the future.

The new dormitory, which was completed in January, has made it possible to house all the boys in good buildings. It would not have been possible to exceed our present numbers without having to go on using the old and very dilapidated buildings which have served as dormitories almost since the School started 18 years ago.

For the coming year, no funds have been given for the construction of permanent buildings... the dining hall in which you have just heard the boys singing, had to be left uncompleted through lack of funds. I regret that I am unable to say when work is likely to be resumed.

A few figures regarding the boys of the School may be of interest. They come from 26 different districts of Southern Rhodesia and from three neighbouring territories. There are 14 vernacular languages spoken in the School and 12 different religious denominations are represented; two boys claim no definite denomination; 86% of the boys are between the ages of 15 and 25, the average age being about 20. 23 of the 37 new boys who entered the School this year came from 15 different central or boarding schools—the other 14 came from Kraal schools.

401

Many of them travel long distances to come to school. Most of them come from Matobe, Gwanda, Mzingwane and this reserve, but some come from as far as Marandellas and Chipinga. One man arrived this year from Enkeldoorn. He was 36 and wanted to enter Standard 11. We hadn't the heart to turn him away, so he is here now struggling along, and hoping that his time here will help to improve his wage earning capacity and so make it possible for him to send his children to school.

The numbers following the different industries in the upper standards show the popularity of each... 20 take building, 17 carpentry, 7 farming and 15 tanning and leatherwork.

This year, Standards V and VI are allowed to specialise. Next year Standard VI and a post-Standard VI class will specialise and in the year after than specialising will only be allowed after boys have passed Standard VI. The lower standards do general industrial work, which includes elementary building, carpentry, agriculture and leatherwork. A course of metalwork will be started this year for Standard VI and I hope that in a year or two we shall be able to offer that as a further course in which boys may specialise.

The timetable is divided so that half the boys are on industrial work while the others are in the classroom. We try, as far as is possible, to relate the work of both sections. We are in fact, and have been for the past 20 years, giving the boys a grown-up form of what is being called modern education. Most of the boys have to earn their livings as soon as they have finished their schooling here. Their time at school is too short to allow them to learn by playing in the lower standards. That time will come, but meanwhile I sincerely hope that we shall not be asked to modernise to the extent of having free discipline.

Those of you who were here last year will have seen the progress that has been made since then. The new dormitory was built almost entirely by schoolboys and completed in eight months. The pupils get a certain amount of useful practice on these permanent buildings but most of their instruction is given on the teachers' cottages. Those cottages are of the type which we hope Natives will build in their Reserves. They are designed to show the Native that in the Reserves he has the material from which to build a good house. No very large cash outlay has to be made to purchase other materials such as glass, ant course etc.

The poles and grass are getting scarce in some areas; however, our boy's agricultural training should equip him to grow these things or at least to ensure that supplies are maintained in those areas where they do still exist. Personally, I am in doubt as to whether this is a right principle to follow. Should we endeavour to make the Native self-sufficient in his own Reserve, or should we encourage him to train for his wants? The greatest benefit to the country as a whole would undoubtedly come from this latter training. To make this trade possible however, he must have the wherewithal to buy his goods. Only two ways lie open to him to make money; firstly by selling his labour and secondly by selling produce and stock. In both of these his scope is limited by the very people who want his trade. And so the vicious circle continues and we, who are endeavouring to raise the standard of the Native population, see our own way out in making the Native self-sufficient, while at the same time we see the drawbacks of that practice.

At this end of the country, it is through stock that the Native will benefit most. If agriculture can be raised even to the level where famines need no longer occur, a great advance will have been made. We averaged seven bags of maize to the acre on the School plots this year. Only 15 inches of rain fell on those crops before they were reaped. That shows that even in this area, famines need not occur if sound methods of agriculture are followed. Even if only a few Natives, having learnt, then carry out the methods by which they get fair crops in bad areas, our time will not have been wasted.

But for anything over and above the bare necessities, the Native here must look to their stock and it is on animal husbandry that we wish to lay most emphasis. We are slowly improving the plant which we have for the teaching of this. New pigsties have been built this year and a new stone kraal. Both of these add considerably to the appearance of the cattle sheds. This year we hope to put up new milking sheds and sheep pens. Without them the instruction we give loses much of its value. Mere theory is insufficient; concrete results push home lessons much more quickly. I hope that when the time comes for us to ask for the necessary funds for this work that we shall be able to obtain the backing of the Honourable Minister of Agriculture, who is here today.

The tannery continues to do very good work. A Native Teacher is in entire charge of that section of the work. The results he obtains are splendid. Educationally it is an excellent industrial subject, particularly for boys who are too small to handle bricks or planes. Its value econom-ically in a cattle country is too obvious for me to have to mention it.

The exhibit of carpentry is not a very large one. There has been a great deal of building construction to be done this year and carpenters have consequently not had a great deal of time in the workshop. But you will have been able to see the type of thing we teach them to make and you will have had a chance to study the quality of their work.

Of the future, two things will always have to be contended; water and malaria. This year, an average of six boys were absent each day during April on account of malaria. Last year for the same period the number was 12. This may have been due to the short rains. We like to think that the improvement has been mainly brought about by the methods of control of mosquitoes which we have introduced, as well as to the extra clearing and drainage. Of one thing I am certain, this improved situation would not have been but for the presence here of Miss Weir. She has probably the hardest job on the place, yet never have I known it to be too much trouble to turn out at any time of the day or night to give assistance to those who need it. We are extremely fortunate as a district, to have her at Tjolotjo.

We might be able to reduce the incidence of malaria, but increasing our water supply is a different matter. No one, as I have said before, should dare to guarantee the continued supply of water in an area such as this. There are very few possibilities of damming; and overstocking in the neighbouring Reserve leaves the veld bare of all grass. As a result most of the rain which falls runs off instead of sinking into the ground. Before we can hope for adequate water supplies, the problem of over-stocking and soil erosion will have to be overcome. On the continu-ance of this adequate water supply rests the fate of this School. It is my belief that a definite decision will have to be made within five years.

Before I stop I must take this opportunity of expressing my grati-tude to the members of the staff for their loyal co-operation. In a School such as this where there are several branches of technical work, it is impossible to carry on if the is any lack of co-operation among the staff. For the past year, there has certainly been no such lack, and it is principally to this that I attribute the excellent progress which the School has made. I must also extend the thanks of us all to the ladies who have given so much of their time and trouble in the preparation of this lunch. At this distance from town, catering is not easy, especially when one has to deal with the unreliability of certain Bulawayo firms.

Lastly, I would like to emphasise once again the pleasure it has given us to entertain you here today, and to express the hope that we shall have further opportunities to show you a small part of what is being done towards the raising of the standard of a vast number of Natives in this country.

John Hammond

Appendix 4

Editorial on the death of R. W. Hammond (1943)

17th May 1943

A GREAT HEADMASTER

All manner of men are needed in building up a new country. The pioneers and early settlers blaze the trail and bring about settled conditions and then, when progressive development starts, men of other types are needed.

Rhodesia was fortunate in that when her educational system was in its infancy it attracted to its service Robert Woodward Hammond who was destined to serve the youth of the country for 30 years and to watch his first and only Rhodesian school grow from a tiny establishment into one of the biggest and finest in the Colony.

Hammond and Plumtree became inseparably associated and he established a tradition for the school, which has been carried throughout the Rhodesias and still further afield, to make its name honoured and respected. But his work went even further than that for his systems, administration and teachings were all of a quality that won them a place in the educational system of the Colony that was then in the making.

He found Rhodesia and the first generations of young Rhodesians in the formulative stages and it is to his credit that he moulded and shaped the destinies of those who came under his hand so that they became worthy sons of the country. His name and fame will live when other more scintillating personages have been forgotten, for he did a great work in a splendid manner.

The Rhodesia Herald

17th May 1943

DEATH OF MR. R. W. HAMMOND – 30 YEARS HEAD OF PLUMTREE

The death occurred at Shabani on Saturday of Mr. R. W. Hammond who will always hold a unique place in the annals of education in the Colony for his 30 years' work as Headmaster of Plumtree School. Mr. Hammond had been ill for two months.

When he was appointed headmaster of Plumtree in 1906, the school had a mere handful of children. The new head's outstanding personality transformed this position and he soon built up a school with a reputation which extended far beyond the borders of Rhodesia. From the earliest stages he envisaged clearly the ultimate development which he considered essential and when he retired in 1936 practically all that he had striven for had been achieved. He was awarded the OBE upon retirement.

After his retirement in 1936 he as appointed a commissioner to report on the system of education in Sarawak. On his return to Rhodesia he stood for Parliament as a candidate for the Bulawayo South constituency in 1939, but was not successful. Education remained his main interest, and in 1940 he accepted an invitation to become superintendent of the education and social welfare of the native employees at the Shabani Mine. This post he held up until the time of his death.

Freedom for Boys

Perhaps the outstanding feature of Mr. Hammond's work in the creation and guidance of Plumtree School was his consistent belief in freedom for boys—his faith that "Freedom always justifies itself". Liberty of thought in particular received every encouragement. He held it to be better that boys who are the citizens of the future should take a keen—even if possibly a one-sided view of a major issue of the day, than that they should be muzzled, or indifferent. His stimulation of their thought on such issues was an invaluable training for their future citizenship. And the personal example he set, of interest in every aspect of education, in suggesting new lines of thought, in willingness to listen to new ideas and to change when he was convinced that a rule or custom had outgrown its usefulness— that example was perhaps the most valuable of all his contributions to the development of the character of the youth of the Colony.

The inspiration of his personality and the success of his methods are alike tributed by the respect and deep affection of the many hundreds of old boys of the school who are today playing a worthy part in the life of the Colony.

The Rhodesia Herald (abridged)

Appendix 5

Opening of the Beit Hall – Goromonzi (1953)

28th March 1953

This is a big day in the history of this School and we are grateful to all of you for coming here this afternoon to share it with us.

The generosity of the Beit Trust is well known in the Rhodesias and we at this School have received much from them. During the past eight years, 180 pupils of this School have had their fees paid for them by the Beit Trust, while generous grants have also been made for the purchase of library books. Today, we are here to express our thanks for this magnificent Hall and Library. No School could every hope for better.

This Hall, designed on such generous lines, is equipped for any stage or cinematograph show which we may wish to put on. It will become the hub of the social life of the School and as it matures, it will record the School's history and carry the names of those who have served it well.

The Library, where we shall shortly have tea, is a beautiful room, admirably suited for its purpose. There the pupils will come to appreciate the value of intellectual exploration, beauty and peace.

These contributions to the education of the boys and girls of this School cannot be measured. They become a part of each individual, which will awaken in them new ideas of what is good and worthwhile. We are grateful beyond our powers of expression, to the Beit Trust, who have given us this wonderful building, and we can assure them that no effort will be spared to make this a worthy memorial of the Centenary of the birth of the Founder of the Trust. We shall endeavour to ensure that the Memorial will be in better people as much as in bricks and mortar.

It is difficult on an occasion such as this to give you a very comprehensive picture of what we are attempting to do at this School. Much will have to be left to your imagination. Samples of the girls' needlework and of the boys' art are set out for you to see. You will also have the opportunity of testing the girls' cooking when we adjourn for tea, while after tea a short play will be put on for your entertainment. For the rest, we shall be pleased if those who are interested will attach themselves to one of the pupils who have been detailed to help you look round the buildings.

In doing so, you will be able to picture for yourselves the normal everyday life which goes on here. It does not differ much from the life to be found in any secondary school. The pupils do nearly all their own domestic chores, cleaning the hostels, and tidying and developing the grounds and playing fields themselves. In the classrooms the scenes are much the same as in any school, except perhaps that the Staff have to spend less energy in persuading the pupils to work hard! In the dining hall and hostels there is the normal amount of clatter and chatter found in any school.

We cover the full range of secondary work up to the standard of the Cambridge School Certificate and some pupils, who aim to go on for study at Universities, return for a further year of post-certificate work. Results in these public examinations, have on the whole, been most impressive. In the first three years that pupils from this School took the Cambridge School Certificate, only three out of 83 were unsuccessful.

It is too early yet for us to judge with certainty how the former pupils of this School will react when faced with the greater freedom and the larger responsibilities of the outside world. We have the evidence that, in so far as examinations can test it, these pupils have the capacity to do well. We wait now for those reports which trickle in from time to time, telling of success and failure in the world for which we are attempting to train them. Should any of you come in contact with those who have been trained here, I hope you will spare a moment to tell us how you find them. Please do not attempt to spare our feelings, we are keen to know of our failures as well as our successes.

APPENDIX 5

We want to know if they have the right attitude to their work, if they are well-mannered and if they accept responsibility. We want to know, in fact, whether our attempts to train their characters are producing results. Examinations are very satisfactory things for schoolmasters. They assess, objectively, the success or otherwise of one's work. They do this so successfully that there is sometimes a danger that we may come to the point where we feel that the work of the classroom is all that matters. I am asking that as many of you as can do so, shall act, as the opportunities occur, as examiners of our efforts to make these boys and girls into useful citizens.

It is imperative that we should succeed in this task, because we are now training those who will be foundation members of a new class in African society, a class that will have to assume responsibility, not only in their own professions, but in the social growth of the African people of this part of the world. On them will rest the responsibility for maintaining and building up standards of morality and integrity and behaviour, which will act as a pattern for others. They are pioneers, and we are most anxious that they should start out along the right track. We solicit your co-operation in our attempts to achieve this.

When we look outside the confines of our daily jobs, where we are concerned primarily with the development of individual boys and girls... and when we try to assess the educational task before us in this continent, we have cause to wonder whether our efforts can ever produce results quickly enough. The speed at which results can be achieved in this 20th century has increased enormously in almost everything except schooling. The medical profession has devised rapid, easy and relatively inexpensive ways of controlling most epidemic diseases. The politicians have, at their service, all the modern means of telecommunication for the dissemination of ideas. Industry and Agriculture and Commerce all have mechanical aids to speed along production and turnover provided the labour to work their various devices is available.

But schooling cannot be hastened. We still need to take a sixth of man's allotted span to bring him to the stage where he can begin to be fully educated and no machine, and no vaccine, can contribute very much towards hastening the process.

In Africa the problem is made even more acute by reason of the enormous backlog which has to be made up. Added to this, we lack, in the main, the educated parents, who, in most other countries can lay

411

a foundation on which the schools can more easily build. On the other side of school life there have been, ever since this continent was settled by Europeans, more jobs than people to fill them and this has led to a lighter discipline and a more indulgent attitude from employers than has been the case elsewhere.

The schools, therefore are forced to carry not only their own responsibilities for the dissipation of ignorance and the inculcation of habits of discipline, but they have also, in part at least, had to take on some of the responsibilities normally assumed by parents. At the same time, they must try to turn out people whose standards of discipline and behaviour will persist into their lives after school because, in this country the thought of losing a job does not have the same disciplinary effect as it does in most other parts of the world.

This is our problem as I, a schoolmaster, see it. I am amazed that, taken by and large, our success in tackling it has been as great as it has, and that our failures have not been very much more obvious. We must, however, ask ourselves if the traditional methods of school education will ever, by themselves, be able to outstrip ignorance before it, ravishing our soils and wasting our resources, leads us inevitably to shortage of foods and goods and all the calamities that would follow in the wake of such shortages.

The "white man's burden" hitherto has been an administrative burden; today it is an educational one and is no longer solely the "white man's burden"—it is the "educated man's burden". If we are to overcome ignorance within the space of time allowed us, we cannot expect success if the schools system alone has to bear the main burden. Even assuming that all necessary finance were to be provided, the shortage of men and women to teach in schools, would still limit the rate of progress to a dangerous slowness.

I can see but one answer and that lies in the rapid increase of well-educated people, who, in their everyday lives, may assume some part of the responsibility. We cannot do it on our own. Therefore, every housewife who insists upon habits of cleanliness in her kitchen, and on hard work in her garden… every farmer who demands a straight furrow in place of a wandering one… every industrialist who insists on punctuality and high production, and every business man who insists on accuracy of work and honesty in dealing with other people, is contributing his or her portion to the solution of this problem. And if this problem is to be solved we must have more people more conscious of the immense task, which lies before us all.

To Africa's educated minority I appeal for a more conscious effort to assist in dissipating ignorance; to Africa's uneducated and semi-educated youth I would suggest that learning can be obtained elsewhere than in schools if you are but prepared to be taught; from Africa's parents, I request a firmer discipline of the children and insistence on good behaviour in the home, and a search for other avenues for the instruction of your children if you cannot provide it yourselves and if the schools cannot take them.

You will, I hope, forgive me for having thrust these rather pedagogic ideas upon you. I know that your interest in our efforts here is considerable and I have therefore taken the liberty of trying to put before you my idea of what our aims must be.

Ladies and Gentlemen, may I repeat our thanks for your attendance here this afternoon and once again express our very great thanks to the Beit Trustees and particularly Colonel Ponsonby for handing over this Hall and Library for our use.

I now have pleasure in inviting you to take tea in the Library, and to see our first production on this stage immediately afterwards.

John Hammond

Appendix 6

Goromonzi School Speech Day (1955–56)

It is with very real pleasure that I, on behalf of all in the School, welcome you here this afternoon. Speech days serve the double purpose of allowing us to indulge that very human desire to show ourselves off while at the same time calling upon us to give an account of our stewardship. Our debt to all of you here this afternoon is that you act both as an audience when we display a little exhibitionism and as judges of what we are trying to do. I hope that you have all taken the opportunity of seeing those aspects of the schoolwork which have been put out for exhibition.

I hope that you have judged its quality, assessed its value and tried to fit what you have seen into the picture of the country's growth and development.

It is my task now to try and fill in the background to the picture of the past year's work, because without it, what you have seen may appear to be no more than the highlights, lacking both perspective and proportion.

We have in this School at the present time a total of 327 pupils, of whom 73 are girls. They come from all corners of Southern Rhodesia and a few have slipped in from even further afield. They come from a variety of home backgrounds and have emerged from a great diversity of religious and educational institutions and they are selected to come here to be offered the chance of reaching the peak of the educational pyramid. Their ages vary from the correct age of 13 or thereabouts, for starting on a secondary academic training, to the very much over-age pupil, well into the middle twenties.

We offer them as good classroom teaching as most schools could hope to offer. We are generously staffed with highly qualified teachers and consequently we can offer a very good range of subjects. These subjects include those which must form the basic education for anyone going on to University, some of which are of particular value to those who will later become primary school teachers and others which develop practical skill, artistic ability and domestic training for girls. In addition to the more formal classroom instruction there is a considerable variety of activity, stimulated by the energies which members of Staff give to their jobs over and above the calls which duty makes on them. There are special classes in music and musical appreciation. Scouting and Guiding are flourishing and some of the senior Scouts are assisting with a Wolf Cub Pack. There is a keen photographic club. Those who like Art, but cannot fit it into their school instruction can continue with it in the Art Club. There are opportunities for the pupils to learn Chess and Draughts and other indoor games. There are the beginnings of a Young Farmers' Club and those who wish for more religious activity than the School programme provides, can join the Students' Christian Association or assist in the running of Sunday School classes. After tea you will see a small dramatic production into which the Drama Club has put much work. There is, of course, room for many more of such activities and we are nearly at the stage where a small printing press, a museum, a modelling club and perhaps carving and pottery could find a very useful place. Lack of time, and rooms to house these activities are problems, which must be met and, of course, we have to watch the funds available.

Games and PT cater for pupils' physical wellbeing. We are endeavouring to teach a variety of games rather than concentrating on football throughout the year. The boys have athletics and football as their main activities and cricket is making a good start. Softball is played with much enthusiasm and tenniquoits and table tennis are also available to them. There is considerable enthusiasm for tennis though the facilities are poor. We hope to devote more effort in the coming year to getting new tennis courts made. The girls play netball, take part in athletics and have rounders as their summer game. They have also shown enthusiasm for tenniquoits and a start has been made with hockey. The dam is providing very useful recreation for those who are keen on fishing and with all that water there, we hope to be able to get a swimming bath and to lay on water to the school grounds and the playing fields.

It will all take time, of course, and money and effort, but if we have patience we will get there. The School is just ten years old. Reasonably rapid progress has been made in that time, but we are still at the earth-moving stage and it will be some years yet before we can add the frills and the elaborations.

Further behind the scenes of the schoolwork, are the many chores, which every pupil has to do. While most of the school are doing a quarter of an hour's PT in the early morning, others are sweeping and polishing their dormitories, washing down their latrines and picking up the pieces of paper which, in any school of this size, always litter the grounds. In the afternoons, when prep is over, each House has its activity. One plays games, another is doing its laundry, another is doing manual labour to level more playing fields and the fourth devotes its time to the cleaning up and development of its particular area of the School grounds. The girls, meanwhile, have much the same kind of activities, except that they mend sheets for the whole school while the boys are levelling the playing fields.

I hope you will realise from this account of what goes on here, that there is plenty of variety of activity and plenty to occupy everyone. We try to bring out the full potentialities of those entrusted to our charge. Along with this, we endeavour to give them a realisation of the need for service to the community—and the good response to requests for blood donors is a measure of that success—we try to inculcate a sense of responsibility in the minds of those who are chosen as prefects and we try to encourage initiative where it wishes to branch out on any venture. It is this last thing that has given me much satisfaction during the year. In many small ways and in some big things I have seen pupils in the School taking the initiative and accepting the responsibilities, which follow upon the things, which they want to organise for themselves. The Students' Christian Association, which meets on Sunday nights, has been under the Chairmanship of the Head of the School this year. He has organised and conducted the meetings, arranged for Speakers and, where necessary, has invoked the aid of the staff. It has been very pleasing to watch the success, which has followed his efforts—as a culmination of those efforts this group will be putting on a Nativity Play tomorrow evening.

The Captains of games have also taken much responsibility in the training of their teams, taking them out for runs at both ends of the day and it was very gratifying that their enthusiasm helped us to achieve

416

one of the most successful football seasons in the School's history. We won the inter-school football competition after several very exciting games, and did not lose one match! The Young Farmers' Club is taking the initiative in several ways, and is growing vegetables and planting flowers. Tenniquoits was reintroduced largely through the enthusiasm of one of the boys, while another, maybe with an eye to earning some pocket money, started taking his camera to our various football matches and gaining the experience which, I assume, all Press photographers have to acquire.

These are some, among many others, which are indications of ways in which the boys and girls of this school are showing their initiative and accepting responsibilities. I very much hope that there will be increasing signs of this spirit as the years go by. There can be no doubt that these characteristics are what the young African must develop if he is to earn the respect of all and if he is to make that contribution to the Country's development for which we in this School aim to equip him.

And what, you may ask, are the dividends which the country as a whole reaps from this. From the classrooms we saw very good results in last year's School Certificate examination, 58 out of 59 passed and these results are a tribute both to the skill of the teaching staff and the industry of the pupils. Of those 58 who gained certificates, eight came back to work for their Higher Certificate, one or two went direct to universities and most of the others entered teacher training institutions, whence they will emerge in a year's time to help expand the work of the higher classes of primary schools. Others went into various occupations, mainly of a clerical nature and some of the girls are being trained as nurses in the Union.

This year, for the first time, ten pupils of this school are sitting for the Cambridge Higher Certificate examination. At least two of these we hope will be foundation students of the University College of Rhodesia and Nyasaland. I feel sure they will be a credit to the School. The others hope to go to the Union, some to Fort Hare to take degree courses leading to teaching jobs, three hope to take Medicine at Natal University, one would like to be a dentist and another a veterinary surgeon.

All of these will in time take their places in the ranks of the professions and we hope that our endeavours here will have given them the background to enable them to live up to the highest standards both professionally and ethically, which those professions so rightly demand.

There can be no doubt that opportunities in very many directions are beginning to open out for those young Africans who have had an education such as we offer. Government Service, Commerce and Industry are all making openings for those that have had a good secondary education. They are as yet, perhaps, doing little more than exploring the possibilities of offering interesting and worthwhile jobs to boys and girls of this School and others like it. They are, so to speak, throwing the ball to the young African to see what he will do with it. If he catches the ball neatly, knows what to do with it when he has caught it and plays it according to the rule of decent behaviour, many more such opportunities will be given to him. Whether this happens or not depends largely upon the young African concerned and upon what we can make of him when he is in school.

One thing, which still makes the work of our schools difficult, is the age of the pupils who are in them. In any European school covering the range of education, which we offer here, even a 19-year-old is considered a misfit. He is no longer a boy, but a man; he should be either at an institution catering for a University standard of work or he should be out in the world, making an independent living and contributing to the production of the country. We at Goromonzi have an age range of 13 to 26. I leave it to your imagination to picture the problems, which arise from this. I would like, however, to draw your attention to some of the wider implications in the country as a whole, of maintaining in schools the very many over age pupils which can be found in almost every African school.

Consider to begin with, the loss of productive capacity resulting from all the 16-, 17- and 18-year-olds who are still in the primary schools. Even the more advanced countries of the world cannot afford to keep youths of this age in school if they have not by then progressed well into the secondary stages of education. Can we, with our very limited resources, do what even a Welfare State cannot attempt?

Think also of the extent to which many of the African children aged 10 or 11 or 12 are excluded from schools because the places are occupied by those who should have been superannuated and who should be out working and producing.

We are also doing ourselves much harm in the eyes of the world by giving the impression that we are providing less education for the African population than we are doing.

1932 was the year in England and Wales when the full impact of the post-war population bulge was being felt in their schools. For that reason and also because the Butler Act and the fully fledged Welfare State had not at that time been introduced, I use figures of that year for a comparison with ours in Southern Rhodesia today. In 1932 in England and Wales, the total number of children undergoing full-time schooling at public expense was roughly 150 for every 1,000 of the population. This is the figure for nursery schools, elementary schools and secondary schools, which were wholly or partly supported from public funds. I repeat the figure. 150 for every 1,000 of the population. Southern Rhodesia today, is providing schooling for approximately 180 out of every 1,000 of our African population.

From this, it would certainly appear that with the places which we are today providing in African schools, there is room for every child to have six years of primary schooling. This is one year more than the Kerr Commission laid down as being the first objective at which we should aim. It would be an excellent thing for us if we could tell the world that we had reached the stage where every child received six years of education. Instead of that, however, we too often hear complaints that children of 9 or 10 or 11 are unable to get places in school and this, not unnaturally, gives the world the impression that we are further from offering adequate educational facilities than in fact we are.

Another point worth taking into account, is the fact that those whose education is behind schedule very often do not start their working lives until very much later than they should do. The education of a doctor, for instance, entails a considerable investment of money. Where the State provides that money they should demand on behalf of the community the fullest possible return. Yet a man who, because of the late age at which his education starts, only qualifies to practise as a doctor when he has reached an age of 30 or more, has fewer years of service to offer to the community than one who can start making his contribution when he is 24 or 25.

There is one further point I would make. By retaining in our schools large numbers of over-age pupils, we are not getting the best out of the facilities we offer. Six years of elementary schooling between the ages of 6 and 12 is of much more value to the child than the same instruction given between the ages of 10 and 16 or, as is often the case, between 12 and 18. In the same way, we in the Secondary schools can have a far greater impression upon, and can teach much more thoroughly, the child who is here between the ages of 13 and 18, than the young man or woman who gets here at 17 or 18 and struggles on to his middle twenties.

Hitherto, we have looked for a solution of the problems resulting from our limited resources to restrictions both on the opening of new schools or on increases in school enrolment. Surely the solution must be in thinking in terms of age rather than standards of attainment and turning away from the schools the older rather than the younger pupils. I know, only too well, how large a part sentiment plays in this. There is always the one that couldn't start going to school early because he had to herd the cattle or the goats; there is the one who had to leave school to work for a year or two to earn the money to take him on to the next stage; there is always the decent, hardworking, keen individual whom, one feels, should be given a chance. But every chance we offer to the 16-year-old in Standard IV is depriving some 12-year-old of his chance and, I submit that the 16-year-old is the one who should stand aside. There are growing alternatives for out-of-school education. Sentiment also takes a hand when it puts forward the plea that a 14-year-old is too young to start work. Few who say this ever stop to think that in Britain today, over 80% of the population start work at 15 and that before 1947, this same proportion started work at 14.

Hitherto, as I very well know, we had to have rather more mature pupils in schools. We wanted Demonstrators, and Medical Orderlies and Teachers who could start, immediately they left the primary school, doing responsible jobs. A 17-year-old Demonstrator would not have carried much weight with a grey-headed Chief and a Medical Orderly of the same age might well have done more harm than good. But those days are going. We now have grey-headed Demonstrators who can handle the more difficult old men in the Reserves and the 17- or 18-year-old youngster would come to no harm if he were made to mind his Ps and Qs when he first started working!

We must look at it today as an educational problem and try to see what methods we must adopt in order to get the best value for the money we are spending. It is a problem, which must be tackled by Government, by Schools and by parents. The parents must ensure that their children start going to school at the right age; they must learn that only some of the family will be able to go far with their education while others who do not show the aptitudes which secondary schools demand, must start work earlier and become independent of the father's income. They must also realise that pleas of poverty are not always very convincing when children who are quite old enough to fend for themselves are still being maintained in schools.

The schools will have to take a wider and more realistic view of things. They will have to remember that in being kind to an over-age child they are being crueler to the younger one. They will have to try to see the picture as it presents itself to the schools higher up on the educational ladder. Here, for instance, we watch with regularity, the 14-year-old in Form I, catch up with his 17-year-old classmate in Form II, overhaul him in Form III and race away from him the following year. There are, of course, exceptions—but this happens sufficiently frequently to be stated as a rule.

On Government, of course, rests the major responsibility. They will have to lay down the unpopular ruling, which will exclude from schools, those who will feel they have not had their chance. On them also will rest the responsibility for keeping up the flow of more and better trained teachers to ensure that those who do have six years in school get the best teaching which can be made available. They will have to plan ahead to the time when these six years of training can be made compulsory and that will involve school attendance officers, the compiling of statistical information and the registration of births. The provision, in fact, of all the background information, which any modern system of educational administration requires.

We have enough school places to take in every child—for six years of schooling—provided we are prepared to take the step of removing those who are overage. We have reached this stage despite the enormous backlog which has had to be made up over the past 20 years and we can, presumably, now hold our own against the large natural increase in school population which is coming.

If we have now reached this milestone, the next stage must be the improvement in the quality of the instruction we offer. This involves firstly, a higher educational background for the teachers, so that those who are untrained and inadequately educated may be replaced. Having provided a sound teaching staff for the six years of primary training, the next step will be the expansion of the six years to eight years as and when the country can afford it.

That boarding schools of this type have been able to get along as well as they have done with such a wide age range is really rather remarkable and is an indication of the great keenness to learn which nearly every pupil has. This great keenness carries even the older ones through the classroom work. They are attentive and anxious to learn and present few disciplinary problems there. But in many respects we miss the liveliness of the very young, we find that the mischievousness which often leads on to many useful lessons in living is overshadowed by the almost extreme seriousness of the approach to their work.

Good examination results from older pupils tend to come from sheer hard slogging rather than through that intelligence which learns despite every effort to sidetrack a teacher off his path and every temptation to think of things other than the job in hand! We need prefects of 17 and 18 who are near enough to the mischief-making age to know how best to deal with it, who will not tolerate obstreperousness in a junior but put him firmly and effectively in his place. But the 18-year-old has a difficult time when he has to discipline those older than he is, and prefects in consequence have to be chosen from amongst those who are old. Boys of 17 and 18 should be learning to take responsibility, they should be learning the fundamentals of leadership, but with our present age range they are denied these opportunities until they are too old to get the full benefit from them.

As a schoolmaster, I am very anxious to have schoolboys to deal with rather than undergraduates, and I feel sure that as taxpayers, you will want to see money spent to the best advantage, and not be devoted to those old enough to look after themselves and who should also be making a contribution to the country's prosperity.

A start has been made in tackling this problem. I believe that the facilities are available for a system of compulsory education, which would reflect great credit on this country, which is still so young and undeveloped. From the point of view of this school and the country as a whole, the sooner it happens the better.

It may seem that I have been critical of those older pupils who are now in this School. There are many of them who have made a very valuable contribution to the life of the School and I would be the last to decry their efforts. Most of them, I know, are impatient to get out on their own, to live their own independent lives and they realise, as much as anyone, that they would have got more out of their time here had they been able to come here at an earlier age.

Much of the credit for what success we have achieved here must go to them for the good example which they have set. But the major part of whatever success we achieve must also go to the Staff, and I am sure that the boys and girls would wish that I speak for them and add their thanks to my own for all the work the Staff has put in during the past year. We have had many changes in the Staff since the end of last year. More changes than any school should be expected to accept. That the work of the School has not suffered to a greater extent is a great tribute to all, Staff and girls and boys. I would like to thank them all very much for their outstanding efforts during this past year.

Finally I would like to thank His Excellency the Governor for coming here to speak to us this afternoon, and Lady William Powlett for consenting to present the prizes.

John Hammond

Appendix 7

John Hammond's Speech to Goromonzi School (1979)

13th October 1979

The story of education in this country is one of such dynamism and achievement, despair and hope that I hope it will one day be written. Not from the point of view of the professional academic that has already been done, but very much more in the shape of personal reminiscence.

My father came to Rhodesia in 1906 as headmaster of Plumtree School. For 20 years he and my mother lived in pole and dagga huts; I was born in one. Until I was 15, I and the other boys in the school seldom wore shoes except on Sundays. The main buildings for many years were old wood and iron structures, which had served as barracks for the army during the siege of Mafeking. Few of our teachers had professional educational qualifications, though most of them were university graduates. In the early days it was a church school until, owing to extreme financial difficulties, the government was asked to take it over.

A great friend of my father's was Mr. H. S. Keigwin, who was responsible for opening the first government schools for Africans; Domboshawa in 1920 and Tjolotjo a year later. These schools were originally started as local schools to serve the immediate areas in which the schools are situated. Very soon however, they became national schools drawing boys from all over the country. They were intended to assist people to improve their conditions by giving instruction in building, carpentry and agriculture at the same time as they undertook their academic studies.

I went to Domboshawa in 1935 and was given responsibility for the

424

direction of the academic work of the school. Colleagues of mine at that time were Cephas Hlabangana and Gideon Mhlanga who were the first two Africans in this country to be awarded university degrees. It is interesting to note that in that same year, we had, for the first time to refuse entry to the school to some applicants. In previous years, accommodation exceeded demand.

In 1937, I went to Tjolotjo and later that year, took over as principal. At that time, we still depended for teaching in our upper primary classes on men from South Africa. On my staff I had three amaXhosa, one Zulu and two Botswana. We had to rely on an ox wagon to bring most of our supplies from Nyamandhlovu, some 45 miles away. In one rainy season we were completely cut off, except by telephone, for two weeks, when the Gwaai River was in flood.

Some of the boys used to walk up to 100 miles to get to the school, they all slept on the floor in their dormitories and they played football in bare feet. Some of the pupils were older than I was and I recall cases where leave was granted at weekends for pupils to go home to visit their wives and children.

I would like to pay tribute to those who were being trained at the time—they were the grandfathers of boys and girls who now enjoy the facilities of schools like Goromonzi. For their secondary education they had to go to South Africa or work on their own through correspondence courses.

But of these, whom I knew as small boys, one is now a member of the Public Services Commission, another is a Regional Officer in the Ministry of Education; others are senior education officers, one is a Senator, several are Members of Parliament, others have made their way as businessmen and a variety of other occupations. Without them, much of the development undertaken in this country over the past 40 years would not have been possible. They were excellent people.

Meanwhile most of the primary school education and the training of teachers was being undertaken by missionaries. It must, however, be remembered that in the main, these men and women were preachers of the Christian gospel first and only undertook teaching because the need was great.

Malaria eventually drove us out of Tjolotjo. We had no DDT and relied on quinine as a cure. None of the modern drugs had been produced. At that time we were drawing boys from all over the country and many of them came to Tjolotjo from areas where malaria was not a problem. To give you some indication of what we were up against, I remember one term—we only had two terms a year in those days—when out of 230 boys in the school we had an average of 40 boys every day in hospital with malaria, throughout the term.

We moved the school to Essexvale and renamed it Mzingwane. It took us three years, because we had to keep Tjolotjo operating at the same time as we were building the new school at Mzingwane—much of the building was undertaken by the boys themselves, as part of their instruction.

At that stage, the department of African Education was concerned that too few girls were attending schools. We had passed the stage where parents believed that the herding of cattle and goats was more important than going to school, but there remained a strong prejudice against the educating of girls. When I came to Goromonzi in 1953, we were unable to find a sufficient number of suitably qualified girls to fill a single class in Form I, and we then ran a domestic science teacher training course to make up the numbers in the girls hostels.

Goromonzi School was opened in 1946 and was the first African school to prepare pupils for the Cambridge Overseas School Certificate. Before that time, what secondary schooling there was orientated towards the South African examination system.

Two points I would make about the opening of Goromonzi, Sir Godfrey Huggins, who opened the school, gave it as his opinion that Goromonzi would serve the country's needs for secondary education for Africans for as far ahead as he could then visualise. This surely must have been one of the few short-sighted observations he made. The second point is that the average age of Form I when the school first opened was 18-and-a-half years.

When I arrived, there were only two boys in Form V. Those who wanted university training had to go to South Africa. Girls who wanted training as nurses had to go to McCord Hospital in Durban, while those wanting to become doctors of medicine had to go to Natal University. There were few scholarships and bursaries for university training compared with the number available today.

I have tried to outline some of the highlights of African education during my involvement with it during the past 44 years. It is, I believe a story of which we can all be very proud. When I started at Domboshawa, the country was very poor. There were few industries, agriculture was, by today's standards, very unproductive and mining was still in its infancy. It is also worth recording that the population of the country was well under two million.

What I want to say to those of you who are now in this well-established school is that should you ever feel sorry for yourselves, should you ever think that the way ahead is very hard for you, and that there are not enough opportunities to give you full scope, think back for a moment to the conditions under which your grandfathers and grandmothers, your fathers and mothers, had to labour in order to get an education. Many of them achieved it and have made their way into the world with distinction.

You have many more opportunities and if you follow their example, you will not go very far wrong.

One of the major problems with which we had to contend in these earlier times was to try to marry the individualism of the school system under which most of the whites were educated with the co-operative outlook of traditional African society.

In our boarding schools the system introduced was based very largely upon the type of schooling offered in English boarding schools. This was the system which we knew and, rightly or wrongly, we passed this on to our African schools.

This system places much emphasis on the development of the individual; it is highly competitive and places great emphasis on individual responsibility. Some of you will shortly be receiving prizes for your individual efforts in the classroom. You have achieved this in competition with your classmates. This kind of competition ensures that everyone aspires to the top and is aimed at bringing out the best that each has to offer.

But there are dangers in individualism if it is carried to extremes. It can lead to arrogance, to selfishness, to the spirit which denies to others due recognition of their excellent qualities. If you have won a prize for Latin or mathematics, or any other subject, remember that the award is made for excellence in a very limited field. It says nothing about what kind of a person you are. It makes no comment on your ability in other directions. For these reasons it is important that countermeasures be taken within our schools to ensure that individualism, while being encouraged, is directed towards the overall benefit of the society in which you live.

To this end, it is important that the school should provide as much scope as possible through clubs, through individual projects, through games and through giving responsibilities to as many individuals as possible, so that each in his or her own way can make a contribution to the life of the school. Most of these opportunities will be provided by extra-mural activities. These are seldom provided by government and in making provision for them the school is heavily dependent upon parents and former pupils of the school, who by raising funds, by encouraging a variety of interests in their children while they are on holiday, will contribute so much to the life of the school, to the benefit of all the children who attend.

The aim must be to try to ensure that each boy or girl in the school has something to contribute. Through such contribution, no matter in how small a way, the individual will develop into a worthwhile member of the society of which he or she is a member.

In English schools much of this is achieved by a strong dedication to the Christian religion. The humility, which this demands, is a great counter to the pride, which can result in high individual achievement. If parents and former pupils wish to embark on a major project for Goromonzi School I can think of nothing better than the raising of funds for the building of a school chapel. A place where the boys and girls can worship, where they can seek peace to give thought to those higher values which are so important in this material world in which we live.

The second major requirement to counter excessive emphasis on individualism is the provision of opportunities for service. In this country there will be a great need for those who will render service to others in the days ahead. In rendering such service, individual expertise will be much in demand. But it must be offered in a spirit of unselfish concern for the welfare of others.

You will be faced with many temptations to amass great fortunes and there will be opportunities for this. In any individualistic society, there is no harm in this. But I hope that when the time comes you will not forget your responsibilities to lend assistance to the community of which you may be a part.

This responsibility, which is so strong a feature of African society, must not be allowed to diminish. It is a part of your heritage. I sincerely hope you will not allow it to die and that you will not allow selfish considerations make you disregard it. In this way our European attitude to individualism and your background of community responsibility can be brought together for the benefit of this country and for all the people who live here.

There I leave you with a thought that given a high standard of achievement which results from disciplined, individual effort, and marrying it to the high level of duty towards your communities, to which you are all heir, we shall build a society which will be the envy of many.

John Hammond

Author's Biog

This is Jill Baker's first book, although she has had numerous articles and critiques published in her life as a journalist in radio, television and travel journalism. She had never had any burning desire to write a book until after her father's death when she felt it was important to document his life, more for the family than anything else.

Jill's early life is mentioned in the book. Jill started her working life in broadcasting as a compiler of classical music in the record library of the R.B.C. She moved into a presentation role taking over *Music for the Morning* and other classical radio, and then television programmes. She became one of the anchor television news readers and presented many current affairs or culturally orientated television and radio programmes.

She managed the radio production section of Blackberry Productions before being asked to take over and develop the television and radio production arm of the then Z.R.B.C. and was the driving force behind the establishment at Independence of the Z.B.C's new Radio Three – presenting the morning shift for two years. She started to work increasingly in the tourism industry when she formed her own public relations company Jill Baker Associates.

When she went to Australia to commentate on the Brisbane Commonwealth Games in 1982 a move to Australia was on the cards and the family moved to Adelaide at the end of 1983.

In March 1984, Jill was appointed as Director of Radio 5UV, the first and one of the country's largest public radio stations, at the University of Adelaide. She was with the station for five years before starting her own company offering specialist management and marketing consultancy to the tourism industry.

Her parents, John and Nancy, moved to Adelaide in 1988 and they were followed a couple of years later by her brother Richard, his wife

Pam and their three children Tessa, Julie and David. John died in October 1996 and Nancy in February 2007.

Jill is very happily settled in this most beautiful part of Australia, but confesses that like anyone who has ever lived in Africa, she has those odd, inescapable, moments of yearning for the land of her birth.

Index

433